Fifteen Plates

"A one-pot meal: what is sophistication?
A meal of 15 little plates: what is the centre?"

from The Swallowers
by Rosa Vilaça Mesquita , p. 148

This is the ninth thesis reader of the TxT department. Traditionally, each reader's title was generated with etymological reference to the number of graduating students.*

This year's title, however, is not inspired by etymology, but is instead borrowed directly from one of the theses bundled in here. It made immediate sense.

The group of fifteen graduating students, who have been working both together and separately for the past three years, were suddenly forced to work 'in isolation' due to the global pandemic. The table of fifteen plates Rosa Vilaça Mesquita describes became something completely inaccessible, or even forbidden…

* Previous published readers: **TWICE FOUR** (2012), **ONCE FIVE** (2013), **SIX FOLD** (2014), TEAM TEN (2015), ONE LEFT (2016), ON ALL FOUR (2017), **EIGHTSOME** (2018) and **NINE DAYS** (2019) [titles in bold are available for purchase on lulu.com]

I0499887

Elena Braida

The Carrier Bag of Recipes

A RECIPE TO WRITE
A THESIS ABOUT RECIPES

**To find the answer
for the perfect recipe.**

Seek the right ingredients: herbs and spices, magic and health, disease and illness, yolks and pigments, good manners and behaviours, rituals and habits, bodies and objects. You might want to research the origins of a specific dish. Books and essays are great for finding inspirational guidance.

N.B.[1] You should adjust your recipe to circumstance and mood. It could be quick, fruity and refreshing, or it could become a stew, warm and comforting.

**Always listen to
your gut or stomach.**

Where should you look for your ingredients? Shop local walk around your neighbourhood. Always bring a tote bag with you. You might discover a Turkish shop or a local market, perhaps filled with not-so-pretty fruits and veggies. Observe the ingredients from a distance and let them whisper to you. "What's that?" Get closer, touch it and bring it to your nose to help you to understand if the idea has ripened enough to be used. Always smell the stalk. If you can recognise the sweet notes or the mild bitterness of its specific characteristics, take it! If you are not sure, ask the farmer, the bread lady or the librarian to help you. Avoid supermarkets or any places where things are unnecessarily wrapped with plastic. Those sparkling layers might trick you and throw you off in your research.

If certain ingredients are difficult to find, ask yourself where and how can they be replaced locally and seasonally?

**Let the ingredients
scatter over your workstation.**

This is the time to decide the tools you want to use: you might need a pot full of examples, a wooden spoon to help you stir your ideas, or a double-pan scale to compare the cases. A knife and a cutting board will help make it all come together. A colander and a grater are fundamental for making things sharp and ready to puzzle together.

Bring some water to boil.

Define the origins of each process, whether oral or written. Where does this recipe originally come from? Could you familiarise yourself with this food? Have a closer look at the structure. Ingredients, quantity, time, sequences... Can you follow the instruction? Are your hands already dirty? Footnotes and blank spaces are relevant too; allocate them a specific container.

Bubbl... bublbl... bbblublblbl... bubbbblblbl... as to move with a rippling flow, the way water bubbles down the side of a small garden waterfall. A stream burbles as it travels along its bed, bubbling over rocks and branches. The verb burble captures both the movement of the water and the sound it makes as it moves. You could also say that a brook or stream or river babbles or ripples or even trickles[2].

Containers are very important. Their wide opening waves at you, looking at you, and they are there for you. They are everywhere, they surround us, and yet we forget to fill them with references and meanings. Don't be shy, give each ingredient a specific receptacle. The glass jar is for the wet mixes, for those fluid notions, which might be hard to mix properly at first with the small dry particles of text. You need to observe and judge with your eyes if the substance contained in the clear glass is transforming into the elastic and soft dough you want. The aluminium bowl is for dry and synthetic references. Ceramic bowls are for herbs, which must be cut with the tips of your fingers. N.B. Do not use a knife to cut fresh herbs!! Contact with a metal surface will make the herb oxidase faster and lose

their freshness. After all, what's better than the smell of sweet basil stuck in that intimate aperture of your nails? They become brushes filled with smell, blending flavour and matter.

Leave the pots on the fire and let them simmer overnight. Remember to cover them with a lid; you don't want your sleep to be interrupted by unusual odours, and you definitely don't want to reduce the matter of your texts.

Bubbl... bublbl...bbblubblbl... bubbbbblblbl...

The place surrounding the fire is whispering to you. Uncover the pots, and with your hands, help the rich and flavourful vapours to reach your nose. To do so, place your fingers close to each other (like a cup), and position the hand behind the rising column of steam, with your palm facing your face. Bring it gently towards you. Enjoy as the cup wafts humid thoughts into your nose.

When ready, bring all the pots (still covered with the lid) to a table. The surface should be clear, big enough to allow you to have everything in front of you. Uncover them one by one and take your tool of choice maybe the soupspoon works better when the substance is a liquid and too fluid to catch, alternatively, the spaghetti spoon is useful when the dish consists of many linear and deep roots. You might find it easier to use a colander to help drain off some of the excessive theories.

Tasting is very important.

Using your fingers, take the minimum amount necessary for the maximum of flavour. N.B. Really do use your fingers. If you use a spoon or another utensil, you cannot tell the temperature of the matter, and you risk burning your mouth. Also, this way the body does not interfere with the temperature of the substance as much as a cold, dead, metal spoon would. You will immediately know if it's too hot to introduce into your mouth. And frankly, who hasn't licked their fingers to catch that last remaining bit of flavour.

If the substance is odd, you might need to stir it well. Occasionally, meaningless expression that lighter matter that floats above the rest can form a layer after being untouched for a very long time, much like a layer of dust that covers a long-untouched book in a silent library. Others pots might need some crumbs, or a sprinkle of powder definition. Listen to your mood, spice it up or make it bitter.

**When the flavours
are ready, it's time to mix.**

N.B. We are aiming to ensure that by the end of the text, the reader is left with a sense of fulfilment.

---

1 An abbreviation for the Latin phrase *nota bene*, meaning "note well." It is used to emphasise an important point.

2 Definition of to burble
   https://www.dictionary.com/browse/burble

WHAT IS A RECIPE?

"The recipe is a set of instructions to carry
out a process of transformation in general, which
through various alterations of one or more basic
substances (ingredients), both physical (produced
by actions) and chemical (produced through mixing
and changes in substances), gives as a result,
something different from the original elements,
usually of greater value or utility than the
ingredients themselves[3]".

The notion of recipe is not something extraneous to us. We deal with them in our everyday lives, consciously or not. Consider the instructions given by your grandmother on how to cure your sore throat, or the prescription you received from your doctor, which allows you to buy antibiotics for your inflamed throat at the pharmacy. "An apple a day keeps the doctor away!" a variant of the proverb, "Eat an apple on going to bed, and you'll keep the doctor from earning his bread", which was itself a popular 19th century expression in Wales. It is an example of how a proverb can also act as a recipe, in this case, a recipe for staying healthy[4].

The ancient meaning of recipe comes from the Latin *recepta*, a neutral participle plural past of *recipĕre* which literally means "things taken", since in medieval Latin the description of the processes usually began with the instruction to "take" the various ingredients[5]. Thus, the imperative "recipe" is an instruction "to take" the following elements. In English, "recipe" is nothing but the first word of each recipe, which functions as a command. Take the following ingredients (in order to) achieve something. A+B=C, that's the equation for a recipe. But what's in-between?

What makes the recipe a recipe?

Both the structure and the language of the recipe have undergone only modest transformations over the centuries. The only significant difference between ancient and modern recipes is that in the latter the doses are specified, times indicated, and the procedures described in more detail. This is explained by the fact that the ancient recipes were intended to circulate and be transmitted within a specific group of people (cook to cook, painter to his apprentice, mother to daughter). In the middle ages, for example, technical books (also called "book of secrets") had a very particular diffusion, and represented a precise literary genre. Every artisan workshop possessed a book in which technical passages and the annotations of experiments (the so-called "secrets of the craft") were handed down from generation to generation and gradually recorded. These books were therefore a mixed bag of useful information, written by experts in a certain field for other experts. Before the introduction of paper and books, bone, shells, wood, and clay were the most popular mediums for writing, and were used to record whoever and whatever was considered significant. Clay tablets are a perfect example of an enduring imprinted object, many of which have survived into modern times due to the durability of the medium.

THE MATERIAL FORM: THE CLAY TABLET

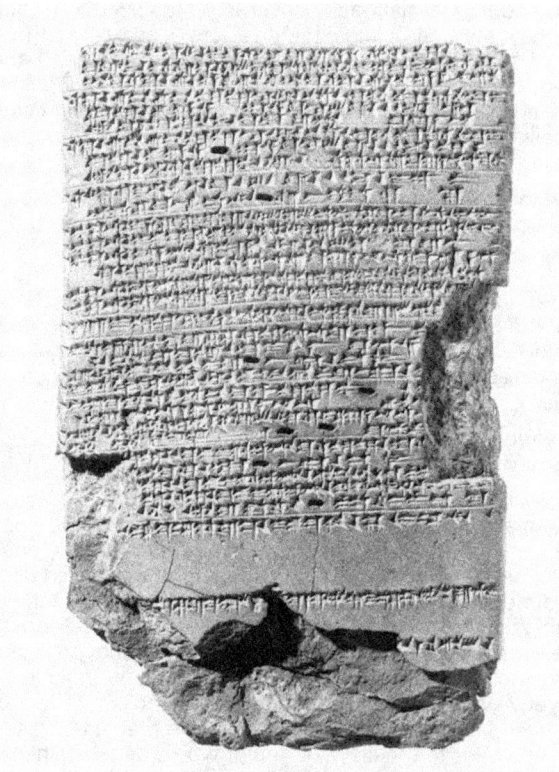

Fig. 1 – Tablet 26 on Epilepsy from the Babylonian 'Diagnostic Series'. Obverse of BM47753 in the British Museum, London. Period: Neo–Babylonian (ca. 626–539 BC).

BM 47753 is an important Neo-Babylonian manuscript of Tablet 26 of the Diagnostic Handbook, composed of 40 tablets arranged into six chapters. Tablet 26 is the first tablet of the chapter on epilepsy. The tablet is characterised by one of the earliest systems of writing called cuneiform. The word itself comes from the Latin term cuneus meaning "wedge", which is in reference to the "wedge-shaped" form made whenever the scribe would imprint the stylus into the damp clay[6].

So here is the first clue
But who did this?

The scribe was a professional copyist and a master ceramicist, whose job was to transcribe messages, myths, letters, poems, and eventually recipes. This particular tablet falls within the scientific category, or more precisely the medical one. N.B. The concept of science, which has been shaped in the context of modern industrial societies, does not reflect the realities of Antiquity. Here the word science includes areas of knowledge such as mathematics, astral science, medicine, divination, lexical text, school text, and practical texts of theoretical nature[7].

The tablet gives symptoms of epilepsy, assigns diseases with names, gives an analysis of causes, and describes the various ways that the symptoms present themselves. Text is arranged by subject according to body parts, and runs in a sequence from the head to the feet. As is typical in Mesopotamian scribal practice, each entry consists of two parts, a *protasis*[8]

---

3   Definition of recipe
    https://it.wikipedia.org/wiki/Ricetta

4   History of the proverb
    https://wordhistories.net/2019/05/24/apple-keeps-doctor-away/

5   Origin of the word recipe
    http://www.treccani.it/vocabolario/ricetta/

6   Cuneiform definition
    https://www.britannica.com/topic/cuneiform

7   Concept of science
    http://cdli.ox.ac.uk/wiki/doku.php?id=history_of_science

8   The clause expressing the condition in a conditional sentence
    (e.g. The "if you asked me" in, for example, the sentence "if
    you asked me, I would agree"). Origin: late 16th century via
    Latin from Greek protasis ("proposition"), from pro ("before")
    + teinein ("to stretch"). From https://www.merriam-webster.com/
    dictionary/protasis

and an *apodosis*[9]. The protasis states the nature of the case; with medical texts, this is usually the symptoms observed. The Apodosis states the treatment, much like a medical recipe. Modern translations uncovered words such as miqtu ("fall"), hayyatu ("fit"), and sibtu ("seizure"), as well as the names of several supernatural entities. On the one hand, the Mesopotamians made advances into the medical lexicon and disease terminology, but on the other hand, most of the causes were believed to originate in demons. That's when the magician comes in.

So here there are 4 figures: the scribe, who solemnly inscribes the physician's report of his objective experiences, and the magician, who obtains cures for the patient. Picture George Clooney, playing the part of Dr. Doug Ross in the 90s TV-series ER, entering your house arm-in-arm with Father Lankester Merrin, the priest depicted in multiples movie adaptations of the novel 'The Exorcist'. The tablet was such a porous object that it was able to bring together an extravagant and unusual care team.

How were the tablets handled back then?

The tablet measures 15cm by 10cm and is 3cm thick. Two dimensionally it fits on an A6 paper a birthday card, the postcard you receive from your parents whenever they leave the country on a trip, or the monthly envelope containing the phone bill. Three-dimensionally, it would resemble an English-Dutch pocket dictionary, or the book "Poems of Love" by Eugenio Montale. Maybe even a blue Tiffany's box concealing a fancy necklace. The clay makes the tablet light and comfortable to hold in your hand, yet it would become firm and durable object if fired. But in fact, the clay tablets weren't meant to be fired and preserved. By adding water to the clay, the tablet would once again become doughy and ready to hold a newer text. In the case of those tablets found fired and thus well-preserved, it is supposed that they were baked accidentally, perhaps by fire.

How did they circulate within this circle?

The physician reports the treatment to the scribe, who transcribes it on the clay tablet. The tablet was later handled by the physician and the magician.

Where was it kept?

In the fancy and well organised library of the physician? Or close to the herbal and fluid antidotes in the magician's home? Were they kept horizontally, or were they vertically standing between other tablets with no specific label on the spine?

The materiality holds upon these passages, carved by instructed fingers and organically shaped tools. It is a body itself, whether or not it's filled with the imprints of strokes and edges. Since it's a three-dimensional, a light-weight body, the recipe finds its principal carrier in people's hands so that the circulation between the figures is activated by the tactility of the object; therefore the functionality of the clay becomes the distinctive feature of the recipe. A recipe that deserves to pursue its goals in time and in the cycle (to understand entirely the circumstances of the patient in this case). Subsequently, it surrenders its materiality, the malleability that makes the tablet vulnerable to possible replacement by wet hands, which brings water to the surface. That is when it is made doughy and slimy and ready to host a new imprint.

Does the materiality of a recipe tie down its meaning and mobility?

The three-dimensional body of text can coexist alongside the objects that surround us, but what happens when we confide on a body of text written on a two-dimensional surface?

Where will its mobility lead us?

THE LITERARY FORM – LEONARDO DA VINCI'S NOTE

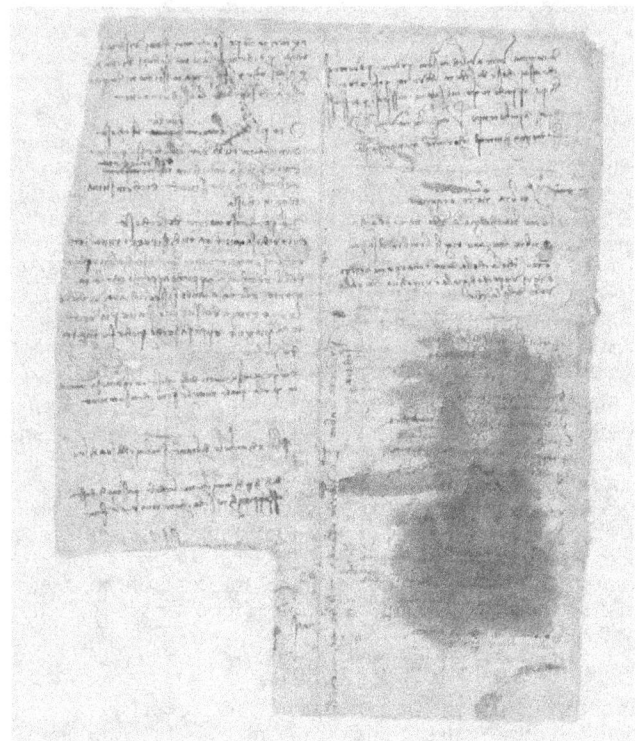

Fig. 2 – Paper, Pen and ink. Leonardo Da Vinci. 280mm-214 x 216-124 – Codex Atlanticus. Recto – Circa 1480.

Page 195 is part of the Codex Atlanticus, a twelve-volume, bound set of drawings and studies by Leonardo Da Vinci. The codex was compiled after the death of Leonardo in the late 16th century by the sculptor Pompeo Leoni, who personally attached the manuscripts page-by-page onto the large paper that was, at that time, typically used for atlases[10]. Codex Atlanticus deals with various subjects, ranging from architecture to botany, mechanics to hydraulics, studies and sketches for paintings to mathematics and astronomy, from philosophical meditations to fables, all the way to curious inventions such as parachutes, war machinery, and hydraulic pumps.

The specular writing system is what distinguishes Leonardo's taccuini[11]. The special character of this system is that it is formed by writing in the direction that is the reverse of the natural way for a given language, such that the result is the mirror image of normal writing: it appears normal when it is reflected in a mirror[12].

Leonardo was capable of writing from right to left. He was left-handed, and so writing from left to right would have been messy because the ink just put down would smear as his hand moved across it. This is one of possible reasons for the reverse inscription. Besides that, it's certainly possible that he just wanted to make things a bit more complicated for everyone. Perhaps the specular text was intended to disclose Leonardo's secrets. An open window to Leonardo's thoughts, but only for those able to crack the code.

Working at full capacity with both left and right sides of his brain, Leonardo's unquenchable curiosity and inventive imagination produced many contributions to society that were far ahead of their time. Leonardo was an observer: a person inclined to question everything around him, and make note of it in his taccuini.

---

9   The main clause of a conditional sentence (e.g. The "I would agree" in, for example, the sentence "if you asked me, I would agree"). Origin: Early 17th century via late Latin from Greek, from apodidonai ("give back"). From https://www.merriam-webster.com/dictionary/apodosis

10   Leonardo Da Vinci Codex Atlanticus https://codex-atlanticus.it/#/

11   Notebook, personal diaries.

12   Specular writing http://xoomer.virgilio.it/pwvbo/specular%20writing.htm

Page 195 is comprised of a left column where literature pieces are transcribed and a right column where is noted a technical recipe: a recipe on how to rehydrate dried oil colour. The two bodies of text reveal the alternation of unequal shapes in a harmonic context. It's a sign of the continuous creative production in accordance with intelligence, looking towards faithfulness to one's intuitions. The instincts and the emotional contents are melded so as to conduct this personality in a dynamic way. One by the other and each of them follow its own diagonal orientation, as it's suggested to encounter them as two separated entities which coexist on the paper. At this very moment the page is not mirrored (fig. 2).

The recipe states:

> "To rehydrate dry oil colours. If you want to rehydrate the dried oil colours, keep it soaking in the lye one night and with the finger mix the substance and pour into a glass and washed with water and in this way you will get the hydration of the colours that dry up.
>
> But let each colour to have its own glass, giving its own colour from time to time, and let it soak, and when you want to use it in tempera, wash it 5 or 6 times with reservoir water and let it rest. If the lye gets numb with some colour, make it pass through the felt. The lye raises the mass to peel and the too abundant niches, and it is better when it is left to soaked for three or four days in the warmth.
>
> And when you remove the leftover scraps, take them with a couple of clothespins and put them in fresh water and wash them with a sponge, if you don't want your nails to turn black. Having removed enough quantity from the lye, let it dry, like the tartar that forms in the wine barrel, and then turn it into oil. Beautifully yellow. Dissolve the arsenic sulphur. The mouth killed more than the knife[13]."

To do (something), if you want to (get a to a specific outcome), to keep (to hold on to), in this way (it leads to), when you want to (pursued something), make it (this way) to remove, to take, to dry, to soak. These verbs recall a familiarity with the Latin term recepta. While on one hand the conditional tenses are used to speculate about what will happen next, on the other hand the commands speaks to you, and you only. There is no other figure hidden in the text, neither a place where this process has taken place or where it should take place.

A lot of substances, no precise quantity and detailed movements that help you to follow the instruction.

Who was he addressing while noting down these instructions?

It might have been a fellow painter or his assistant Francesco Melzi, someone who felt the urgency of asking how the hell you re-use the dried out oil colours. The first space where this instruction acquires body is in Leonardo's head, where the question could have raised itself: "What can I do to… (Solve it)?" According with Leonardo's thought, truth is drawn from the direct experience of nature, from the observation of phenomena. "My things were born under the simple and mere experience, which is the true teacher"[14]. Phenomena are what it takes to acknowledge the proprieties of a certain manifestation. A+B=C, remember? By combining his knowledge of chemistry, oenology, painting, and most importantly, his intimacy with the ingredients, he did nothing more than heed the demands to experiment with matter and to find solutions under different circumstances.

Leonardo's internal references imprinted on his taccuini, which are still objects of study nowadays, are an example of how the evocative elements of recipes directly and indirectly addresses the recipient, here meant as a person open to receiving the knowledge and also able to contaminate it.

But what happens when the recipe intentionally speaks to external entities? When it addresses no one in particular, and in doing so it attracts the masses?

THE SOCIAL FORM: THE MANIFESTO OF FUTURISTIC COOKING

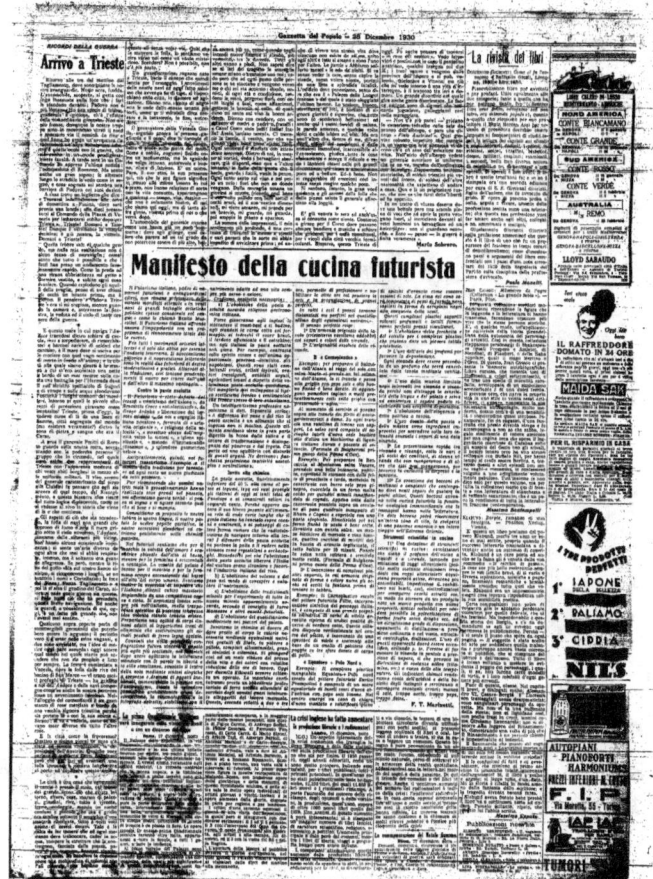

Fig. 3 – 'Manifesto della cucina futurista' in the Gazzetta del Popolo, 1930, Civic Library, Turin.

The Manifesto of Futurist Cooking was first published in 1930 by Filippo Tommaso Marinetti and Luigi Colombo, who was also known as Fillìa. The manifesto is comprised of recipes and dining suggestions which are somewhat unconventional, to say the least. On the 28th of December 1930, The Turin newspaper 'Gazzetta Del Popolo[15]' published 'THE MANIFESTO OF FUTURIST COOKING'. It reports:

> "We believe the following necessary first of all:
>
> A. The abolition of pasta, that absurd Italian gastronomic religion…
>
> B. The abolition of volumes and weight in the way nutrition is conceived and evaluated…
>
> C. The abolition of the traditional mixture in order to experiment with all the seemingly preposterous new mixtures …
>
> D. The abolition of the mediocre quotidian in the pleasures of the palate…"

The first paragraph of the article contains the term abolition four times. Abolition meant in the sense of 'to eliminate', 'remove from use', or 'renounce' (or induce others to renounce) something. It does not bring new flavours to the table, nor try to open up a discussion.

But who was this fearless man called Tommaso Marinetti?

He was born in Alexandria, Egypt on December 22nd, 1876, into a wealthy family. His father was a lawyer from Piedmont and his mother was a housewife who loved reading poetry to her sons. A passion for literature manifested itself during his adolescence.

---

13 Recipe https://www.leonardodavinci-italy.it/codice-atlantico
14 From Codex Antlanticus.

15 Gazzetta del Popolo was an Italian daily newspaper founded in Turin, in northern Italy, on 16 June 1848. It ceased publication on 31 December 1983 after 135 years of operation.

At the age of seventeen, he created his started literary magazine called the Papyrus, which mostly dealt with literary criticism. He was attacking and praising with the same energy, with a methodology, which eventually recurred in his manifestos. After graduating with a law degree in 1899, according with his father's wishes, he later pursued his literary career in Paris, where he would frequent the literary salons[16].

By the time he lost his parents and older brother, Marinetti was already working for a French journal in Milan. He was not only left with exceptional confidence but also with an unusual level of wealth which later allowed him to focus on drawing the foundations for what would become Futurism[17].

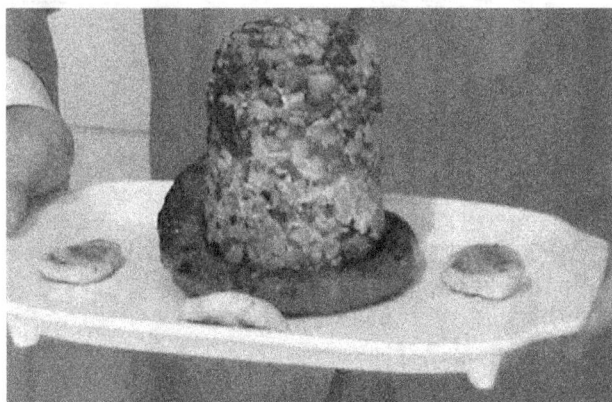

Fig. 4

The Futurists recognised that people "think, dream and act according to what they eat and drink", and so believed that the cooking and eating experience should be altered to better fit the changing landscape of the 20th century and, indeed, their own world view. Marinetti and Fillìa wanted to revolutionise the way everybody thought about food. And to do so, they wrote quite clearly in their Manifesto the passages later published in the journal. For example, some requirements for a perfect futuristic meal are: "Abolition of the fork and the knife for the plastic complexes, which can give prelabial tactile pleasure... A supply of scientific instruments in the kitchen: ozonizers... lamps for the emission of ultraviolet rays... electrolyzers,... colloidal grinders... vacuum stills, centrifugal autoclaves, dialyzers."

Now imagine that every Italian woke up, close to New Year's Eve of the year 1931 and right after the celebrations of Christmas, to read in a widespread journal that "all the defenders of pasta and the relentless enemies of Futurist cooking are people of gloomy temperament, content with melancholy and propagandists of melancholy... Only a Futuristic meal can cheer them up." Before digesting the text, which might have been chewed on as a big joke at first, Italians not only found themselves labelled as enemies of the Futurist movement (given their food habits), but even told that they ought to be cheered up during the festivities!

For example, one of the crowning achievements of the new Futurist cuisine was the Carneplastico, a meat sculpture (fig. 4). The formula was created by the aeropainter Fillìa. The Carneplastico is a synthetic interpretation of Italy's orchards, garden, and pastures an ode to the Italian landscape! It is "made up of a large cylindrical rissole of roast veal filled with eleven different cooked vegetables. This cylinder, placed vertically in the centre of the plate, is topped with a layer of honey and supported at the base by a ring of sausage, which rest on three golden spheres of chicken meat".

The recipes are structured in a way that together with the primary ingredients they described a whole new, totally different dining setting. From a detailed description of the consistency of the food such as "luminous sauce... cover with

threads... aeroplane shaped... pink plate tinted... form a large blob..." to the arrangement of the meal on the plate. During the dining experience, guests are asked to perform different tasks simultaneously while the waitress is spraying them with conprofumo and there is dismusica playing in the background. The verbs, as well as new Italianised terms used in the recipes, refer to a whole new choreography of senses driven by the urgency to adapt gastronomy to the concept of Futurism. Golden, cosmic, bombe, diabolical, aerodish, devil, immortal, the great, flash, freedom, ultra virile, sparkle, sky, intuitive, spicy, landing and awakener are a few of the adjectives used to name the dishes. However, they don't give much attention to the quantities as they even suggest "possible errors often suggest new dishes".

Little specification, no doses, no quantities, no cooking instructions, and a lot of attention on the outcome.

Speaking to a broad audience, from the upper classes down to the poor, how did the Futurists imagine Italians to react in their kitchens? Indeed, Futurists never really cared whether Italians were cooking balanced sculpture at home or avoiding pasta for lunch. If every Italian had embraced this new Futuristic regime in life, kitchen, and art, the movement itself would have lost its privilege as an elite group.

The anti-pasta crusade naturally drew howls of protest and received worldwide publicity, exactly the reactions desired by Marinetti. It allowed him to create an ambivalent ground where he was able to organise a real international promotional campaign to present Futurist dishes.

Despite the appearance of multiple places willing to embrace these new dining experiences, what was really happening under the dining tables was nothing other than propaganda.

What Marinetti did was to appropriate the universal and domestic structure of recipes and use them to fuel his idealistic program. In this way his proposition for a futuristic cooking was nationalistic and violent: "Spaghetti is not food for fighters!" he declared. It was not surprising that Marinetti became closely associated with Mussolini and therefore with fascism. In 1918, Marinetti played a leading role in the formation of the 'Futurist Political Party' (Fasci Politici Futuristi). This Party later merged with Mussolini's to form the Italian Fascist Party, and Marinetti went on to co-author its first manifesto[18]. The party, however, with both Mussolini and Marinetti included as one of its candidates, performed miserably in the 1919 Italian elections. Although Marinetti maintained close links with Fascism, he gradually began disengaging from its political side, preferring to concentrate on the less confrontationist issue of achieving the cultural pre-eminence of Futurism in the field of art.

In line with his urgency to set a solid ideological agenda, the Futurist Cookbook came out in 1932. A book where the script of the manifesto, the Doctor's opinion in favour, the testimony of the gastronomy experiences, and the 80 recipes framed within a narrative account of some successful futuristic dinners, combined together to prove that Marinetti was a great critic and writer, but not the ideal person to share a culinary recipe after all.

16 The Futurist Cookbook, 1991, by F. T. Marinetti (author), Lesley Chamberlain (editor), Suzanne Brill (translator), ISBN 9783956790034

17 Futurism was an artistic and social movement that originated in Italy in the early 20th century. It emphasised speed, technology, youth, violence, and objects such as the car, the airplane, and the industrial city.

18 Manifesti Futuristi, 2009, by G. Davico Bonino, ISBN 9788817028783

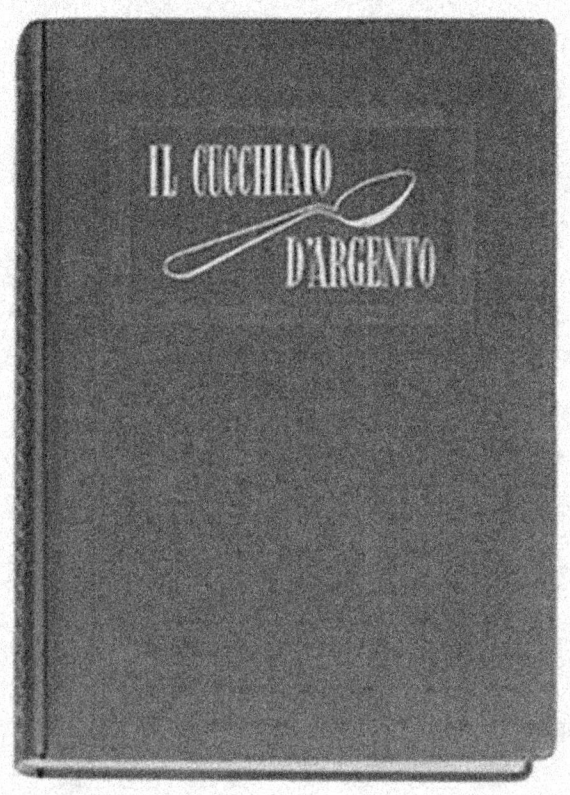

Fig. 5

All of the cases reported above have multiple aspects in common. Behind these bodies of text there is a maker and his urgency to convey his specific knowledge.

- The clay tablet on epilepsy is a set of instructions concerning medical help. A medical recipe, a health-care program implemented by a physician (and a magician) in the form of instruction that controls the care plan of an individual patient.

- The page of the notebook by Leonardo Da Vinci is a set of instructions in the form of transmittance. To impart to a successor, from master to apprentice. It doesn't state the recipients, but it defies it by using a detailed terminology which itself addresses those recipients who share the same field of interest.

- The journal in which the Manifesto was published is a set of political instruction, which addresses the audience and therefore speaks to the masses.

The recipe is most likely perceived as a frozen moment enhanced by the articulation of verbs of command, materials, quantity, and how these features are structured together. It is conventional to consider the recipe as a pre-moment before the act of committing yourself to the instruction and its procedure. The backstage before the climax of the final result. In the book 'The Craftsman', Richard Sennett states "Gastronomy is a narrative, with a beginning (raw ingredients), a middle (their combination and cooking), and an end (eating)." If we now apply this thought to all the recipes, culinary or not, they will be perceived as a stage where the narrative takes place rather than a passage itself; the reader will have to move through this narrative rather than focus on just one step, it is by imagining the whole process that you get outside yourself[19]. The recipe's realisation depends on the experience of the reader. A perpetual experience, because it belongs to the written and unwritten word, to the paratext, to the erased notes at the corner of the page, to the oral tradition, to the post-it left by my mother on the fridge, to the notebook filled with cut-outs from magazines and to the artists' practice. When the recipe is brought from an inner level to external (the social) it unfolds its characteristic as something sharable, available to everyone. And if something is made available to everyone it signifies that is open to interpretation.

The 1950 cookbook 'Il cucchiaio d'argento'[20] (fig. 5) showcases at the end of each chapter a space dedicated to personal recipes in watermarked writing paper interleaved within the text. It can be seen as a generous gesture from the publisher, who understood the mechanisms initiated by the recipes and therefore invites the executor to note down his own passages and suggestions.

"Expressive directions connect technical
craft to the imagination[21]"

Imagination can lead to contamination of a recipe. Indeed in the process of writing a recipe, the maker cannot take into consideration the background of every reader. He or she can write what they know by unpacking instructive meaning in . experiences he or she has lived through. Therefore it can be addressed by the title of the book, the ingredients, the tools used, and its terminology. But to really address the journey the recipe will undertake when and if published is unknown. Whether they are the culinary recipes bequeathed unto you by your ancestor or the list of precautions in the wood workshop, they all lead to a certain purpose: to make its contents sharable.

The maker, in these terms, allows the contents (meant as everything that is contained within something) of the recipe to over flow the written language and reach the reader. The contents is whatever is found between the lines by the reader: ingredients, metaphors, proverbs, tools, activations, verbs, rituals, the workstation and the emotional value and so on.

What if the recipe is perceived as a container itself?

The term receptacle comes from the Latin term *recipiens*, the present participle of the same verb that sees in the word recipe its origins: *recipĕre* (see page 7). 'Receiving, accepting' and therefore 'containing'[22]. As a consequence the term container acquired a dual definition: as being a recipient itself, something that holds together (knowledge) and at the same time the recipients who received this knowledge and take it as its own. To perceive the contents of the recipe to write a thesis as individual containers, some might hold verbs of motion, while others might look like jars holding the spices together.

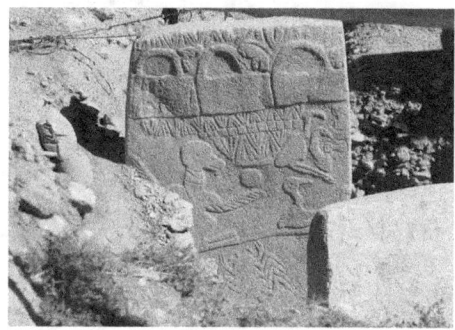

Fig. 6

This everyday object is caught within conflicting origin stories about the material history of human evolution. In her 1986 essay The Carrier Bag Theory of Fiction, Ursula K. Le Guin provides a counter-narrative to the anthropological theories that assert that the first tools created by humans were weapons an origin story that centres the hunter, the hero. The Carrier Bag Theory proposes instead that the first human device was not a weapon but in fact a container or basket used to gather and bring home food and other resources. Before the knife, the axe, the blade, or blunt objects of dominance and destructive force, was the carrier, the holder, the receptacle. This account offers a more inclusive narrative that centres the gatherer, the

---

19 The Craftsman, 2008, by Richard Sennett, ISBN 9780300119091

20 *Il Cucchiaio d'Argento* is a cookery book published in 1950 by the magazine of design and architecture Domus. It is one of the most famous and popular cookbooks in Italy, with over 2000 recipes.

21 From the chapter The Written Recipe, pg 193, last paragraph. The Craftsman, Richard Sennett.

22 Definition of receptacle
   http://www.treccani.it/vocabolario/recipiente/

nurturer, in place of the violent aggressor[23]. In fact the familiar shape of a container has been found on stone-carving and statues decorated by spirits and gods holding bags made by the Assyrian (c.a. 883–859 B.C.) in Iraq, in the ruins of ancient Göbekli Tepe (c.a. 9130–8800 B.C.) in Turkey (fig. 6), and in crafts made by the Olmecs (c.a. 1200–400 B.C.) of Central America. Experts believe that early religions worshiped the fundamental ingredients of life on earth that's why gods were represented holding sacred bags, a holy container, filled with sacred things[24].

Suppose we consider the recipe as the carrier bag of Ursula and the holy container of early civilisations. Would that perspective help us to see that the many characteristics of the recipe may be considered as necessary elements of a whole? Because isn't its purpose neither resolution nor stasis, but continuing process as well?

In this process, the recipe is read, re-interpreted, misread, re-arranged, underlined, understood, finally recapped, and maybe even erased. In this sense we could perhaps consider all forms of contamination an enrichment of the recipe. Thus the processes of contamination are part of the invitation that the recipe has in its meaning from the Latin term recipĕre, as 'things taken', and therefore it does embody all the information and ingredients everyone gathers in his own carrier bag.

REFERENCES

Fig. 1 Tablet 26 on Epilepsy. Web. https://www.researchgate.net/figure/Tablet-26-on-Epilepsy-from-the-Babylonian-collection-in-the-British-Museum-London_fig1_333658947

Fig. 2 Codex Atlanticus. From 16. Leonardo: favole e facezie. Disegni di Leonardo dal Codice Atlantico, con la collaborazione di Giuditta Cirnigliaro, Novara, De Agostini, 2013. (ISBN 978-88418-9724-9)

Fig. 3 Scan of "Manifesto della cucina futurista" in the Gazzetta del Popolo, 1930, from Civic Library, Turin.

Fig. 4 Picture of Carneplastico dish, from the youtube video "Carneplastico ricetta cucina futurista" by Elicrisio. Web. https://www.elicriso.it/it/cucina/cucina_futurista/

Fig. 5 Front cover art of the book "Il cucchiaio d'argento". Web. https://www.cucchiaio.it/gallery/articolo/tra-pochi-giorni-il-nuovo-cucchiaio-d-argento-e-in-libreria/

Fig. 6 Pillar 43, Göbekli Tepe, Turkey. Web. https://rgdn.info/en/gebkli_tepe._o_chem_govorit_lisa_perevod_doklada

BIBLIOGRAPHY

Life and works of Leonardo Da Vinci. Web. https://www.leonardodavinci-italy.it/

La filosofia in cucina. Piccola critica della ragion culinaria, Il Mulino 2012, Francesca Rigotti. ISBN978-8815234988

Dinner with Darwin: Food, Drink, and Evolution, University of Chicago Press 2017, Jonathan Silvertown. ISBN 978-0226245393

Italian Food, Penguin 1998, Elizabeth David. ISBN 978-0140273274

The Architecture of Taste, Sternberg Press 2015, Pierre Hermé. ISBN 978-3956791390

La Cucina Italiana. Storia di una Cultura, Laterza 2005, Alberto Capatti and Massimo Montanari. ISBN 978-8842076759

MOVIES

Big Night. 1996, directed by Campbell Scott and Stanley Tucci

La Grande Bouffe. 1973, directed by Marco Ferreri

The Cook, the Thief, his Wife & her Lover. 1989, directed by Peter Greenaway

Eat Drink Man Woman. 1994, directed by Ang Lee

Chef's Table. Vol. 1, Ep. 1: 'Massimo Bottura'. 2015, directed by David Gelb

23 Essay "The carrier bag theory of Fiction", by Ursula K. Le Guin, 1986

24 Handbag of the Gods. Web. http://lost-origins.com/perspectives-on-ancient-handbag-images/

Nina van Hartskamp

How to Breathe Together in a Changing Climate?

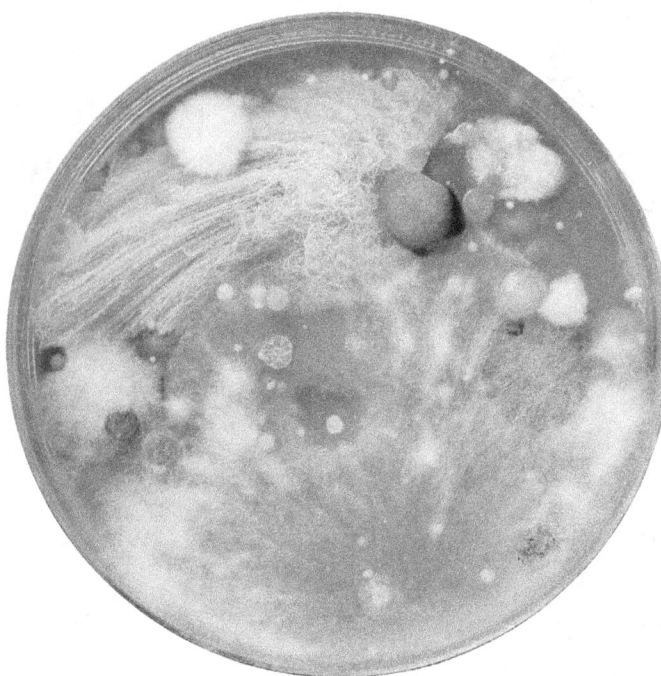

A cultivation of my bedroom air —
(seven days of growth)

'Ubuntu'[1]

My thoughts, my agency, my actions, my likes and dislikes, my love, my hatred, my preferences, my motivation, my ideologies, my dreams, my fears, my belief, and my stories are the result of the innumerable people, places, microbes, books, songs, ideas, artworks, and atoms that I have been in contact with. They are stored in my system, my body. They move in relation to each other. They transform; they grow, die, and are born again. They live within me. They affect my actions. They are me. Therefore, I am you.

If you are influencing me, I influence you. My hope is that our influence will be one that makes us grateful to be in relation to each other, because if we want to take care of our breath -that seems to be the first thing we need.

PREFACE – CONCRETE

Whenever I walk on a concrete road it makes me sad and I wonder: 'Humanity has sealed so much of the earth. Potential fertile ground, unable to breathe and thrive; how can this be changed?'

INTRODUCTION –
'I BREATHE' AS A METAPHOR FOR EXPERIENCING THE WORLD IN RELATION

'We are small organisms pulsating to the rhythm of the cosmos, and our activity is first of all inspiration.'

Bifo[2]

At the beginning of this year I asked myself: how do I visualize breathing? To me this is an exciting question, as it implies an all-encompassing visualization of life in its most basic active form. Life starts with an inhalation, as soon as we are out of the womb, and ends with an exhalation. In between, while breathing, life happens. It's a process composed of two opposites – full lungs and empty lungs – that rhythmically follow each other. Neither of these poles are good or bad. They belong to the same fluctuating process. Focus only on 'full' lungs and the process will stop.

Throughout this thesis I would like to examine the act of 'breathing' as a metaphor to support thinking about relational processes, as we are dependent on each other and our environment – from the smallest invisible life-forms to this whole earth floating in space – to breathe in some form. However, we can only focus on so many things at a time. If you take a photo and focus on one particular element, the rest gets blurry, but this doesn't mean that it doesn't exist. Life isn't a static image, it's movement. With every breath we can shift our focus; zooming in and out on ourselves in relation to our surroundings to deepen our experience and, inevitably, our narratives.

In '*A Philosophy of Emptiness*'[3], author Gay Watson argued that Western thinking, through the legacy of the Greeks, uses 'I perceive' as its primary metaphor for experiencing the world, whilst Chinese philosophies take 'I breathe' as a model to constitute reality. According to Watson, the metaphor 'I perceive' in Western thought has "*led to the priority of a conception of reality as an object of knowledge and to the division of subject and object, the first, or perhaps the second after the separation of presence and absence.*"[4] 'To perceive' derives from the Latin *percipere* meaning 'seize, understand'. If you take it apart it means: *per-* 'entirely' + *capere* 'take'.[5] In the light of this meaning it is possible to further develop the metaphor. Hence, it could be argued that a Western thinking subject 'perceives' the world as an object to entirely take in: breathe in. Meanwhile, the act of giving back – breathing out – is neglected. We obviously need both to live. Therefore, I would like to invite us to ponder on the question: What do our actions breathe out into the world?

Furthermore, if we separate and prioritize what's immediately present (visible) to us in opposition to what is absent (invisible), we risk overlooking the blurry spaces, which are necessary to investigate if we want to broaden our perspectives.

With rising awareness of global climate change, it would be a healthy choice to weave the metaphor 'I breathe' into the Western narrative that seems so focused on consuming, taking in. The carbon footprint of privileged Westerners, including myself, is much larger than that of those living in the Global South,[6] while these areas and their inhabitants are disproportionately more vulnerable to climate change. Much

1 A Nguni Bantu term that is often
   translated as '*I am because we are*'.

2 Interview with F. 'Bifo' Berardi by M. Azar,
   '*I can't breath*', La Deleuziana P226

3 G. Watson, *A Philosophy of Emptiness*. (2014

4 G. Watson, '*Around a Philosophy of Emptiness*', Essay from
   http://www.gaywatson.com/Around-a-Philosophy-of-Emptiness.html

5 Origin and Meaning of Perceive, from Online Etymology
   Dictionary https://www.etymonline.com/word/perceive

6 'The use of the phrase *Global South* marks a shift from a
   central focus on development or cultural difference toward an
   emphasis on geopolitical relations of power. The phrase *Global
   South* refers broadly to the regions of Latin America, Asia,
   Africa, and Oceania. It is one of a family of terms, including
   'Third World' and 'Periphery,' that denote regions outside
   Europe and North America, mostly (though not all) low-income
   and often politically or culturally marginalized.' Definition by
   N. Dados and R. Connell, *The Global South*. Volume 11, issue 1
   (2012). P12–13

of what the Global North consumes is mined and produced in the Global South. It could be argued that global neoliberal capitalism is building further upon the ruins of colonialism. The consequences include a loss of biodiversity, the rise of a sixth mass extinction, and damage to indigenous communities, our collective mental health and the health of our home.

While the narrative of a catastrophic future, "due to our actions,"[7] is spreading, it's easy to become anxious, paralyzed or overwhelmed by the hypocrisy of this situation, especially from a Western perspective. This has resulted in what the philosopher 'Bifo' describes as a collective contemporary condition of breathlessness. *"As there is physical and psychological breathlessness everywhere; in megacities choked by pollution, in the precarious condition of the majority of exploited workers, in the pervading fear of violence, war and aggression."*[8] Furthermore, I would like to add, due to a chaotic overflow of all this worldly information, a shortage of oxygen in our minds. The fear of breathlessness, metaphorically speaking can lead to hyperventilation, which then has the potential to endorse thoughtlessness.[9]

It is imperative to find ways to exit this state, as none of these feelings will contribute to a more thriving world. It is clear that our global economic system, with its multinational cooperation's and unethical politics, needs to change. However, the question remains: how can this change be facilitated? It's with this question in mind that I aspire to write and make.

Aspiration (noun)

1. A hope or ambition of achieving something
2. The action or process of drawing breath.[10]

I feel a response-ability[11] to care for the air, that connects all of us on earth, humans and non-humans alike, but within the capacity of my body. Does my capacity reach far enough to actually take care of the air that sustains our lives? What does care imply?[12] To date, my arts practice and actions have had a strong focus on collaborations with my direct surroundings, but here is a voice within me, which I call the activist, that keeps asking; 'Is a focus on your direct environment enough to bring change at a global level? Especially since the whole world is at stake?!'

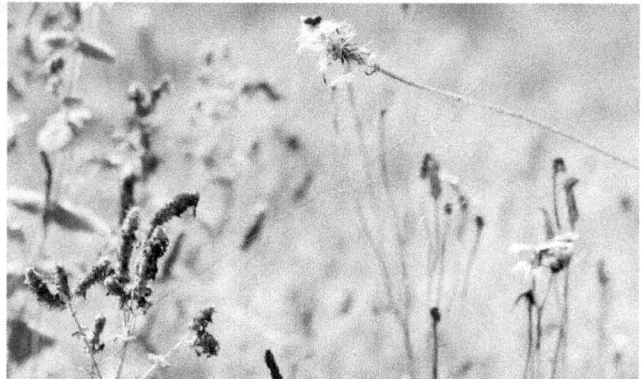

Co-web: A collaboration between a spider, two plants, a horse hair, and myself. (2017)

In response the maker says, 'I can only make with what's in reach, but hopefully these local actions will inspire some change.'

Even though the maker and activist in me seem to clash in their ideas of approaching this world, they both share the same dream. This is a utopian dream in which all of us together, to the best of our abilities within the framework of existing knowledge, take care of this earth; decolonize nature and co-create a world based on more symbiotic narratives with all humans and non-humans. However, whilst the global politics of the day focus on perpetual economic growth, exploiting the earth's resources, and keeping their hierarchical power structures intact, this might sound like a naïve 'Miss-Universe' world-peace dream. Nevertheless, we need dreams and we need to share them, because they form the inspiration for narrative shifts and actions for manifesting new realities.

It's definitely very ambitious to ask myself how to influence global politics through an arts practice, though it's a driving force behind my questions. One I won't be able to answer, at least not today. I do believe, though, that with every inhalation, we have a possibility to react to our ever-changing world in our own ways.

To overcome the 'condition of breathlessness,' Bifo suggests that we learn to *"breathe with chaos,"*[13] which according to him includes embracing the idea of human extinction. This might sound pessimistic, but I agree with him to the extent that death is part of life in which the will-to-live is entangled. If we want to care for life, it's just as important to acknowledge its endings, without being absorbed by fear or despair. However, this doesn't mean that we can't contribute our best effort to make the earth as liveable as possible for ourselves and for future generations. In the end we're still breathing and let's make that breath worthwhile. I believe this is what Bifo ultimately aims at, when he suggests that poetry (which I would like to extend to all art forms) can function as a tool for finding new respiration rhythms, because an art practice has a potential to *"receive rhythmic stimulations from the world and translates these rhythmic stimulations into the organism's breathing."*[14] Hopefully, in a shared experience, this will allow collective breaths to flow in more synchronic rhythms with what the earth gives and takes.

How do I breathe the 'global' world in, while breathing out an artwork, which can visualize our relational dependency and inspire more harmonious breathing rhythms?

I want to take care of the whole world.
Take it in.
Entirely?
Isn't that impossible?
I'm just a little pawn, a body amongst many
Floating in a complex, multi-layered space

While floating I dream,
a Miss Universe peace dream:
That all of us, all these little bodies,
take care of this earth, together.
But what does it mean to care?
Mother, what does it mean to care?

To care is to hold, to attach
To care is to create a possibility to heal
To care is to pay attention and listen
To care is to detach and let go
To care is to breathe, grow and die
To care is to support dreams,
to support life transform,
accordingly.

7   For further elaboration see chapter; 'Blue Marble and the Overview Effect; a Dangerous Perspective'

8   F. 'Bifo' Berardi, *Breathing: Chaos and Poetry.* P15

9   'Thoughtlessness', defined by Hannah Arendt in *Eichmann in Jerusalem: A Report on the Banality of Evil* (1963), as the inability to think beyond the commonplace.

10 Definition of Aspiration from Lexico.
    https://www.lexico.com/definition/aspiration

11 Various contemporary feminist science discourses (for e.g. by D.J. Haraway, *Staying with the Trouble*, 2016) have proposed the term 'response-ability'; cultivating a capacity for response.

    The feminist ethic of 'response-ability' focuses not on *being responsible* (implying an imparting duty or moral obligation), but on learning how to respond. What counts as 'response-ability' is not known in advance. Instead it emerges within a particular context and among sometimes unlikely partners, who learn how affect and to become affected by one another.

12 "Caring is not intrinsically 'nice', it always involves power relations. Processes of discipline, exclusion and harm can operate inside the matrix of care." From *Syllabus: Pirate Care* https://syllabus.pirate.care/

13 F. 'Bifo' Berardi, *Breathing: Chaos and Poetry*, (2019) P236

14 Interview with F. 'Bifo' Berardi by M. Azar, *"I can't breath"*, La Deleuziana, P236

INVISIBLE RELATIONS

"Art does not reproduce the visible,
it makes visible"

Paul Klee

I have always been fascinated by the invisible; from invisible life to invisible knowledge (that which I don't yet know), and from the 'invisible' body of the clitoris[15] to the metaphor of the invisible hand.[16]

Every research project starts in a field in which the invisible (unknown, not-yet registered or understood) is the agent of enquiry. Questions imply an invisibility, and carry the possibility to become visible in the future. One of the many roles of art and science, is to question the visible and tangible narratives in which we operate, and to provide space for the invisible to become tangible.

How do I approach the global world and visualize our connectedness through our breath, when most of the world is invisible to us? Our visual perception might reach far into the universe,[17] but our horizontal vision is limited by the simple facts that the earth is round and solid objects prevent us from seeing what's beyond. Furthermore, while the air itself appears invisible, it actually contains many worlds of microscopic life, visible once you zoom in.

Visibility is limited by the capacity of our eyes, and it immediately triggers the imagination of what could exist beyond, encouraging a potential exploration of 'invisible' worlds not yet discovered. The walls of my apartment, being solid, prevent me from knowing what my neighbours are doing, even if we live thirty centimetres apart. However, I can envision myself knocking on their door and asking them about their lives, their narrative worlds. Through all forms of communication (e.g. dialogue, reading, engaging with sounds, smells, art, etc.) new narratives and worlds can become visible. It can even be said that whenever something becomes visible to us, a new world comes into existence, as we are transformed. Art, therefore, is a worldmaking practice, with the potential to breathe out 'invisible' inner visions, to raise questions about our relationship with the world, and to provide space for other peoples' worlds to be transformed. What each of us make visible or tangible depends on the individual's focus, which in return is influenced by its relation to the worlds which it has been exposed to in the past.

In the next two chapters I will zoom in and out, to investigate when and where it's possible to breathe with the world and consider how this relational movement has the potential to transform us.

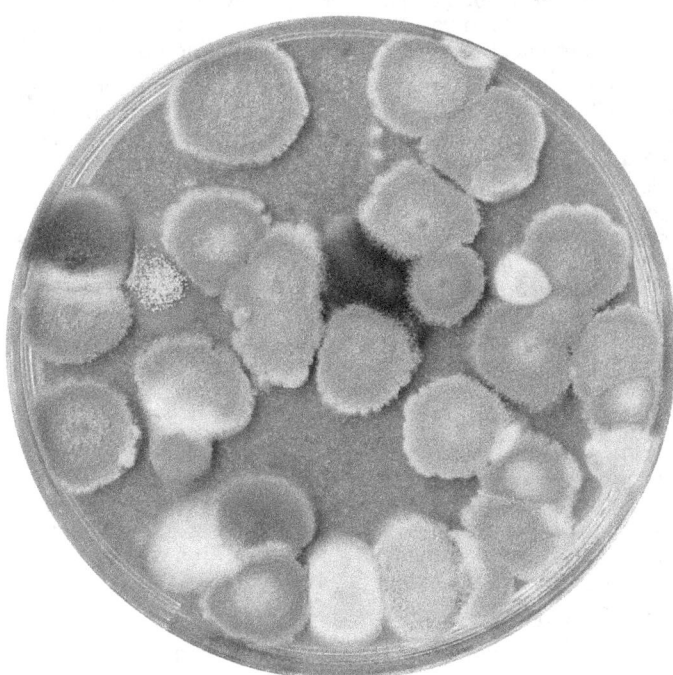

A cultivation of the bedroom air of my neighbour –
(seven days of growth)

15 The invisible history of the clitoris visualizes the patriarchal influence in our society. From 1948 till 1998 the full body of the clitoris was omitted from the Grey's anatomy book

16 The metaphor of the invisible hand was first introduced by Adam Smith in *The Theory of Moral Sentiments* in 1759 to describe how individuals' self-interested actions create an effective economic system in the interest of the public. Throughout history, this metaphor has been used to justify the laissez-faire economic philosophy that promotes a global free-market model without government interference. However, this reasoning has disregarded many other factors at play, like the environment and existing hierarchal power structures.

17 At the moment the estimation is around 13.8 billion light years away.

An Activist at Schiphol and a Maker at Home

3.00 PM, 14-12-2019, Schiphol Airport.

Extinction Rebellion and Greenpeace have organized a peaceful protest at Schiphol requesting a better plan of action to curb the pollution that the airport generates. This is motivated by the fact that the airport plans to add 40,000 extra flights next year. The protest demands a reduction of flights, an increase in the price of plane tickets, and more accessible train services as an alternative to short-distance flights.

On the floor of the entrance hall are about forty people lying on the ground in a chain, surrounded by at least twice as many police, mainly from the Marechausse (Dutch special forces). Other protesters, including myself, are standing on the side-line holding banners, cheering and singing songs. The police, all men, have formed a circle around the chain of people and look stoically ahead, arms crossed. Every ten minutes the Marechausse, in groups of six, physically force a protester to leave the chain and carry them outside to a white bus, surrounded by police on horseback. It's a strange spectacle.

There is one moment in particular when I get really angry, as they appear to be hurting one of the protesters. As I shout, I cross eyes with one of the policemen. They seem to say: ''So, what are you gonna do about it girl?'' The situation makes me think of Hannah Arendt's analysis of the Nazi war criminal Adolf Eichmann's inability to think, besides following the orders of his superiors. She argues that *the banality of evil*" lies in ordinary thoughtlessness.[18] These protesters are peacefully asking attention to be placed on safeguarding our future breaths. How can these policemen not understand that? It is their future, too. Perhaps it is hard to see beyond the requirements of your job that pays the bills, which seems to be the main focus under capitalism. How then, do we inspire others to think?

My mind races. I'm trying to think about what I can do, but I don't know. The boy who was slammed against the floor is now being carried away by six policemen. At that moment, I feel an intense urge to slip under the cord and join the chain, but I can't afford to get arrested, at least not this weekend. I have a thesis to finish.

When I get home, I look at my petri dishes full of microbial growth. I'm cultivating the air of spaces to visualize that we are constantly in a state of exchange with our surroundings through our breath. If we share a space, it is very well possible that the organisms that travel through my body might now be in yours. I wonder if I've shared some microbes with the police at Schiphol.

With a Microscope

'What can't I see?' may have been one of the fundamental questions leading to the invention of the microscope. Inventions never come into being through one person alone and it was contributions by the Greeks, Antonie van Leeuwenhoek, Galileo Galilei, and Hans Lippershy, among many more, that led to the co-creation of the microscope.

Through this quest to uncover invisible worlds, we now know that an adult person carries between two and three kilograms of microorganisms, necessary hitch-hikers in our bodies. They live on our skin, in our intestines, eyes, mouth, throat, nose, lungs and vagina. Without them we wouldn't be alive, as they help us digest our food and bolster our immune system. At the same time, they can make us ill to the point of death.

Without microbes, human bodies would not have been able to 'create' houses, cars, factories, atom bombs, plastic bottles, satellites, or the myriad other industrial products that have altered the earth so rapidly. Western narratives give the human species a lot of credit for creating, but in the greater scheme of things humans haven't really created anything solely by themselves.

Create: bring (something) into existence, late Middle English (in the sense 'form out of nothing,' used of a divine or supernatural being): from Latin *creat-* 'produced', from the verb *creare*.[19]

Everything we have produced already existed here on earth, just in another form of matter. In that sense, humans are more like experimental mixers or alchemists than they are creators (as we can't form something out of nothing), transforming earthly materials without really knowing where these transformations will take us.

I suggest that whenever we say, 'I'm creating,' we instead say 'I'm co-creating,' as that seems more appropriate, at least to my inner narrative.

Co-Creating with Non-Humans in Two-Fold

``If we are to learn to adapt in this world, we will need to do so with all the other creatures; seeing from their perspective is central to re-organizing our knowledge and perceptions.''

H. Davis & E. Turpin[20]

When I first saw Hubert Duprat's caddisfly larvae co-created jewellery[21] I was intrigued. It raises a question about what collaborating with non-humans actually implies, opening up a space for discussion. How do we work together if we don't speak a common language, share understanding, or feel each other's realities? How can I work with microbes without forcing my ideas upon them?

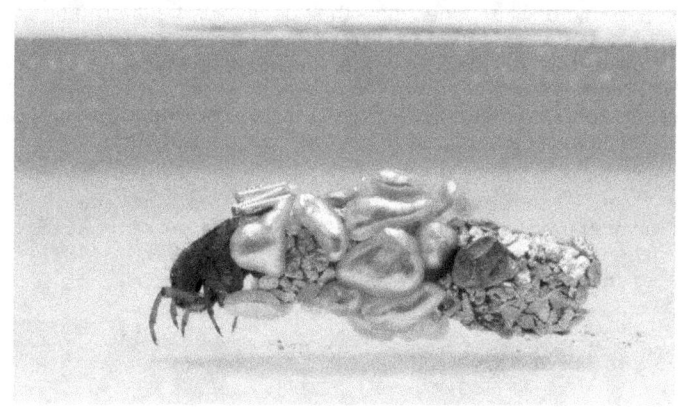

Aquatic caddis-fly larva with case (2006)

Some critics have described Duprat's practice as animal cruelty for forcing the larvae out of their natural habitat, to which Duprat responded, "*The work is a collaborative effort between me and them. I create the conditions necessary for the caddis to display their talents.*"[22] One could address this as animal cruelty, but it seems like a fairly non-invasive practice if you compare it to the process of co-creating a leather jacket with a cow. Ultimately, one chooses their own ethical boundaries within the narratives of their community. However, it's important to keep questioning these boundaries.

18 Hannah Arendt, *Eichmann in Jerusalem: A Report on the Banality of Evil*, (first published in 1963)

19 Definition and etymology of create from Lexico https://www.lexico.com/en/definition/create

20 Heather Davis and Etienne Turpin, *Art in the Anthropocene*, (2015) P13

21 Caddisflies are moth-like insects that live near streams, ponds, and rivers. Caddisfly larvae grow exclusively in water, where they protect their bodies by creating cases, or sheaths, spun from silk excreted by salivary glands near their mouth. For *Aquatic Caddisfly Larva with Case* (2006), French artist Duprat collected larvae from their natural environment, removed their cases and relocated them to a climate-controlled tank with tiny pieces of gold and precious stones in order for them to make new houses from these materials.

22 Interview with Hubert Duprat https://www.youtube.com/watch?v=0BlUUXx6akk 3.43-3.5min

As for my aspiring collaboration with microbes, I would like to draw on the methodology of Goethean Science,[23] which focusses on the relation between the object (natural phenomena) and the subject (the experimenter), and which is often regarded as pseudoscience in comparison to the Cartesian-Newtonian method that presupposes separation between the two.

> 'Goethe's work offers a scientific methodology that can help us to explore the universe we participate in. It can lead us to see beyond the perceptual blind spots of a strict adherence to a scientific epistemology based on the Cartesian dualism of self and world, and mind and matter, which has become culturally dominant in the last two hundred years.'
>
> D.C. Wahl[24]

In Goethe's philosophy all experiments are regarded as two-fold, a mutual and intimate interaction of the observer and the observed. Ideally, over time, as the experimenter's observed knowledge grows from their study with the natural phenomenon, so does their capacity for inner awareness, insight, imagination, intuition and inspiration.

In my opinion, if you want to investigate something thoroughly you need to spend time with it. You need to sleep together, eat together, and breathe together. With regard to microbes, we are already collaborating with them all the time, as they are in and around us. However, until now, I haven't given them much attention. By focusing on their existence - giving them space to grow in front of my eyes and reading about other human-microbial experiences – their behaviour, transformations, shapes, potential smells and colours will become part of my narrative. This will raise thoughts, questions and feelings with the potential to transform my inner world. Hopefully, through a visual representation, these discoveries and our interdependent relationship can contribute to new perspectives in other peoples' narratives.

> "Form is a moving, a becoming, a passing away. The study of form is the study of transformation. The study of metamorphosis is the key to all the signs of nature." – Goethe[25]

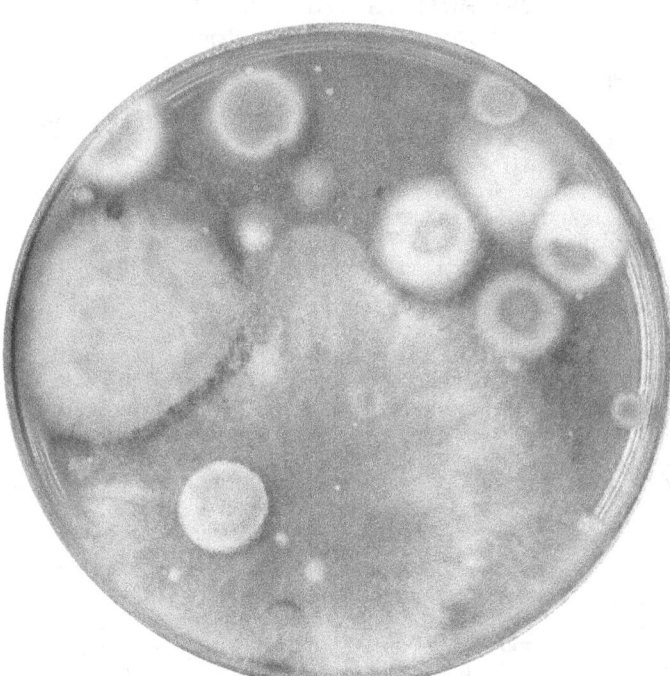

A cultivation of the bedroom air of a lover –
(seven days of growth)

ZOOMING OUT –
AN ATTEMPT TO READ THE GLOBE

'It matters what matters we use to think other matters with; it matters what stories we tell to tell other stories with; it matters what knots knot knots, what thoughts think thoughts, what descriptions describe descriptions, what ties tie ties. It matters what stories make worlds, what worlds make stories.'[26]

D.J. Haraway

A Global Web of Narratives

The narratives we live and weave throughout our lives are the foundation of each of our individual universes. The collective world is an assemblage of such universes, touching each other in actions and language. Narratives have and will determine how we live on earth together, although the world is big, and the stories told in other places may be very different to the ones you and I have been exposed to. Even our 'world-wide-web' browsers come up with different stories in different parts of the world.[27]

When we examine histories or imagine futures, we look at them through a lens shaped by our assembled narratives from which we assume and judge. There is no absolute collective truth, but rather a collection of agreements among a group of people. The merit of collective narratives is that they bring people together. The downside is that they exclude groups with different narratives to such an extent that collective narrative-clashes can co-create wars. Therefore, the stories we tell each other and pass on to new generations – in person, in writing, beyond language, in the digital world, or through art – are incredibly and dangerously powerful, especially when they impose themselves as absolute truths or when they present a one-sided perspective.

23　" In the essay, *The Experiment as Mediator between Subject and Object* (1792), Johann Wolfgang von Goethe developed his philosophy of science. *"The human being himself, to the extent he makes sound use of his senses, is the most exact physical apparatus that can exist."*

24　D. C. Wahl, *''Zarte Empirie'': Goethean Science as a Way of Knowing*, Janus Head (2005) P59

25　From *Die Schriften zur Naturwissenschaft, Zur Morphologie* (1806) by J.W. von Goethe. *''Die Gestalt ist ein bewegliches, ein vergehendes, Gestaltenlehre ist Verwandlungslehre. Die Lehre der Metamorphose ist der Schlüssel zu allen Zeichen der Natur.''*

26　D. J. Haraway, *Staying with the Trouble; Making Kin in the Chthulucene*, (2016) P12

27　As China and Russia are developing their own internet and countries like North Korea have a heavy censorship.

The Weight of the Globe

The following passage is written as a stream of consciousness in an attempt to illustrate the impossibility of grasping all the narratives of the world, to highlight the illusion that the world seems at hand through the world-wide-web, and to make tangible that breathing-in an overflow of information influences the rhythm of our breath. This can bring us into a 'condition of breathlessness,' the metaphor Bifo uses to describe the general sentiment of our times.

''I want to grasp the whole world: the globe. Understand it. Hold it in my hands. Save it. But what is there to save? My breath, I thought. Yours too.

You, who told me the world is on fire: Look at the Amazon! Look at Australia! So much injustice. So many wars. So much suffering. So much information.

All those voices. Floating through the air. I want to hold them all. Caress them. Care for them. Care for you. But all those stories; they spin. Spin over and over. Dreams without bodies won't materialise. Floating in space. On this beautiful big planet. How to breathe together?

I have to think of Atlas carrying all this weight on his shoulders.

What did Atlas actually carry?

I call ten people and ask them: ' What does Atlas carry on his shoulders?'

They all answer: 'The earth.'

How is that possible if the Greeks perceived the earth as flat?

I look it up. He didn't carry the earth, but the Celestial Spheres. The sky as an inverted dome. He stood at the ends of the earth in the extreme West, according to the Ancient Greek poet Hesiod. Which is now called the Atlas Mountains in North West Africa.

So, how come that we now -all eleven of us- think he carries the earth?

When did this narrative shift happen?

Again, I look it up, but now it becomes more difficult. Apparently, the Greeks, at least some, did know that the earth was round. One voice on the internet says that Eratosthenes of Alexandria (born 276bc) worked it out by measuring the shadows cast by the sun in two different cities and estimated the earth's diameter at 7850 miles. Another source states that it was Ptolemy who proved the world to be round. Yet another says that all educated Greeks knew the earth was round, and suggest that most educated people in the Middle Ages would probably have also known that the world was round, but kept quiet to avoid confusing the common people. However, Greek mythology did view the world as flat and so did everyone who took the Genesis literally throughout the Middle Ages. The association of Atlas and the earth began when the Flemish cartographer Gerardus Mercator (1512-1594) first coined the word 'atlas' with a collection of his maps, although he had a different Atlas in mind, as he was thinking of the mythical African king named Atlas, who was said to have invented the globe. Anyhow, nowadays Atlas is often depicted holding the earth on his shoulders.

[Here I go: I'm slightly out of breath.]

All this information, floating around in the world, in so many different minds, so many different stories. We can never be sure, but we can listen, read and weigh narratives against each other, and make up our own.

[Breathe, slowly!]

I thought that Atlas started to carry the weight of the world when the Western world began to perceive the earth as a globe in the 15th century, marking the beginning of colonialism. It seems that two things can happen when one perceives the world as a globe; either it fuels the wish to care for it or the wish rule it, to capture it all. However, talking about the globe, the wish to care and the wish to dominate don't seem so far apart. Because how can one care for something on the other side of the world? When you have never seen, listened to, or spent time with it? How can you care for something if you don't know what it needs? Isn't care something that happens in two-fold? In a mutual and intimate interaction? One person can't care for the whole world, but we can care for worlds within the world, because it seems that true care happens in action, in re-action to what we breathe in. Which only, truly comes into existence when we breathe together. Doesn't it?''

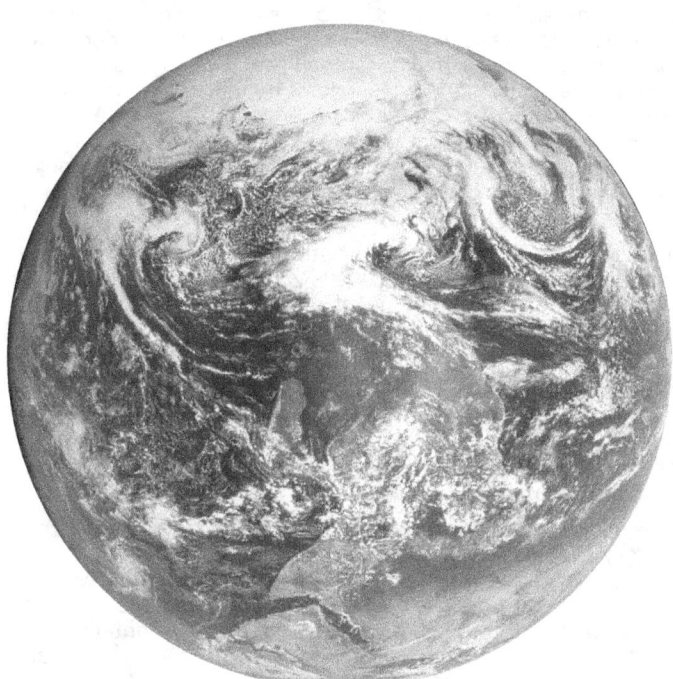

Blue Marble (1972)[28]

Blue Marble and the Overview Effect: a dangerous perspective

"When you're finally up at the moon looking back at the earth, all those differences and nationalistic traits are pretty well going to blend and you're going to get a concept that maybe this is really one world and why the hell can't we learn to live together like decent people?"

Astronaut Frank Borman, Apollo 8[29]

The iconic image, Blue Marble, is the first and only photograph in history of a whole, illuminated globe floating in space, taken by human hands. It is said to be one of the most reproduced pictures on earth. Printed on t-shirts, postage stamps, billboards, book covers, mouse pads, and almost any surface you can print on.

Today the globe as a representation, for the whole world, seems to have become a normality embedded in contemporary language and visuals. We are bombarded with terms such as 'globalization', 'global politics', 'global warming', and visuals

28 An interesting part of the Blue Marble story is that when the film got developed, the negative pictured the earth upside down, with the South above and the North underneath. To fit the dominant Western worldview the image was immediately rotated before it was depicted in the newspapers, but one only needs to flip it again to see how both strong and fragile collective narratives are. Another question we might want to ask ourselves is does this really represent the whole world? We only see one side, it being a flat image.

29 D. Cosgrove, *Apollo's Eye: A Cartographic Genealogy of the Earth in the Western Imagination* (2001), P258

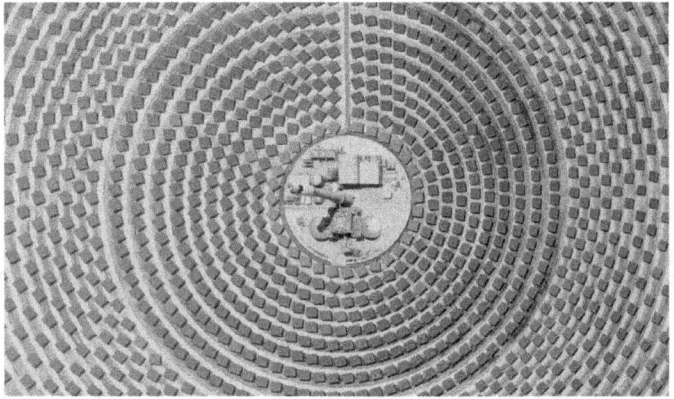

Gemasolar Thermosolar Plant. Seville, Spain. (2015) –
'Overview' Fig. 7

provided by satellites. This can be evidenced by scrolling through the online news or zooming out on Google Maps, giving the illusion that the whole world is within our reach. However, the globe is merely an image, a representation, a model, in the Western narrative to address the world, and is mainly seen on screens. To actually see the globe with one's own eyes, one needs to travel beyond the low earth orbit, which is twenty thousand miles away and from the 536 people who have been in space today, only 24 have travelled that far, and only three astronauts have seen it fully illuminated.[30]

The three astronauts who did, one of whom took the iconic Blue Marble shot, were E. Cernan, H. Schmitt and R. Evans, during the last manned Lunar mission, Apollo 17, which launched on December 7, 1972. *"They weren't supposed to be taking pictures. Photo sessions were scheduled events in a rigorous flight plan that detailed every step essential to success."*[31] However, against all the rules, one of them did take a photo, five hours into the flight, with nothing mentioned in the weeks that followed. Blue Marble came as a big surprise when the film was developed after they returned home. It became more valuable than the moon rocks they collected and the funny thing is that, until today, they all claim to be the one who took it.

When you read interviews with astronauts it becomes clear that seeing the earth from space is what makes the deepest impression, far more than the adventure itself or visiting the moon. It seems to evoke a cognitive shift in awareness of a fragile, interconnected 'one-world-ness', that was later defined by psychologists as 'the overview effect.'[32]

How beautiful would the world become if all humans could experience 'the overview effect', without having to go into space. Could that evoke a shift in environmental consciousness, perhaps even inspire world peace?

This question and its concurrence with an emerging Western Zeitgeist of the sixties, which was concerned about the environment and the state of the world,[33] may underpin why Blue Marble became such a widespread iconic image. Against that backdrop, Blue Marble was the perfect representation of our fragile home, floating in a dark vast space, that required all humans to unite: to care and work together.

Today, however, while we are exposed to many high-resolution commercial satellite images of our globe, it seems unlikely that these images will still provoke hopeful unifying-world-feelings. One could argue that satellite images and their 'god's-eye-view' perspective rather symbolize a glorification of human mastery of the planet through technology. Alternatively, some suggest that they can be used to raise awareness of the destructive results of human activity on earth as art historian B. Grant claims to do with his commercial satellite-image series, *Overview*.[34] However, the question of whether or not this is creating the desired effect is highly debatable.

The 'overview effect' or world-one-ness perspective might be seen as desirable for evoking renewed senses of environmental consciousness at first sight. However, there is another side to consider, because as art historian T.J. Demos stated, use of the globe as a universalization image *"denies the existing disagreements, pain, and conflicts happening on the ground, and the necessary dialogues and negotiation which are fundamental for democracies."*[35] From space, humans become invisible; you can't see guns going off, or mothers holding babies, or refugees in rubber boats, or polar bears, or lovers kissing, or families arguing around dinner tables – the world just becomes a peaceful ball. Anthropologist Tim Ingold has suggested that the image of the globe in the language of contemporary debate about the environment is problematic, because it turns the world into *"an object of contemplation detached from the domain of lived experience."*[36] We can't actually inhabit a global environment and even if an image of the globe would have the potential to provoke environmental consciousness it ultimately depends on what you do with that consciousness on the ground that makes a difference.

Moreover, when the idea of universalization, along with images of globes, becomes deeply integrated into our narratives, something dangerous can happen. It can enable the military-state-corporate apparatus[37] to disavow and obscure their responsibility for actions that impact our environment on a large scale and has the potential to make us believe that we are all evenly accountable for climate change. The implication that 'we', the whole of humanity, are the cause of the eco-catastrophe unfolding in front of our eyes (on screens) and that 'we' are doing it to ourselves needs to be questioned. Who is 'we,' really? All 7.8 billion of us? Most people on earth live modest lives and focus on their own worlds; taking care of their families, their community, and gardens (if they have one), doing their jobs. Some are fighting for their lives in warzones, and others try to save rainforests. 'We' are not all the same, 'we' all live with different narratives and breathe out different actions. The world carries a multiplicity of worlds, which can't be simplified into one image or model from far above.

The question becomes then: what kind of visuals or experiences have the potential to raise ecological awareness and demonstrate that we are all connected, without dismissing our differences?

30 To see the whole earth illuminated you need to pass a narrow
    point between the earth and the sun, for it not to have
    a cast shadow.

31 Al Reinert, *The Blue Marble Shot*, The Atlantic. (2011)

32 'The overview effect' was inspired by Frank White's *The
    Overview Effect – Space Exploration and Human Evolution* (1987).
    White was the first to conceptualize this shift in awareness.
    "*Some common aspects of it are feeling of awe for the planet,
    a profound understanding of the interconnection of all life,
    and a renewed sense of responsibility for taking care of
    the environment.*"

33 Due to the Cold War, American war in Vietnam, Apartheid
    struggle in South Africa, the tumultuous decolonization
    processes in Africa and Asia, and an emerging awareness
    of the problems of pollution, among others.

34 Benjamin Grant, *Overview: A New Perspective of Earth*,
    Amphoto Books (2016)

35 T.J. Demos, *Against the Anthropocene* (2017), P18

36 T. Ingold, *The Perception of the Environment* (2000) P210

37 T.J. Demos, *Against the Anthropocene* (2017), P17

BACK TO EARTH

It's time to travel back to the earth where we live and breathe, because it seems that if I want to support any change or care for this world then it needs to happen on the ground. It needs to be a movement in immediate response to the initial question from my activist, 'is a focus on your direct environment enough to bring change to a global level?'

'Yes. It's the only thing I can and should do, because I can't live on a global level and I don't believe that anyone (who cares for this earth) can.'

I've come to realize that my endeavour to understand the whole world, to grasp it all by vertically zooming out into space, is an ambiguous movement that seems to coincide with global corporate policy-makers spreading unifying narratives and imagery in order to control and prevent critical thinking. I would prefer my actions to speak for me in multi-folded, intimate dialogue with the earth. However, I'm intrigued by how images such as Blue Marble have the power to influence the narratives of so many minds. It seems that it's a two-way movement. Images seem to become iconic when they answer to a certain collective call, but how does one image (or multiple) actually influence collective narratives? Perhaps that is why I'm attracted to art making, as it seems to have the power to let local narratives reach further and inspire thoughts that in turn allow new dialogues to arise, with the potential to influence collective narratives. However, I do believe it's important to preserve a sense of locality, as we can only truly breathe and interact with the world from a local perspective. Maria Thereza Alves (who I recently discovered and greatly admire) is an artist whose practice embodies this idea.

Alves' research-based work develops from her interactions with the physical and social environments in which she moves. The work ranges from focalized and visualized indigenous histories with indigenous students in Brazil,[38] to an invitation for a forest walk with a focus on being-in-the-land.[39] Through dialogues she uncovers local needs and co-creates spaces of visibility for oppressed cultures and offers new perspectives. According to Alves, the relational practice of collaboration requires a constant movement across Western binaries, such as nature and culture, politics and art, and art and daily life. By refusing these binaries in her work, it becomes a political statement in itself and, to me, that is crucial in order for change to happen, because this has the potential to not only raise ecological awareness, but to embody an immediate manifestation of change.

Suddenly, I feel an irresistible urge to zoom in on the 'real' world again, the world of action, instead of zooming in and out on the world of thoughts. However, I would like to do something with the paralyzed – breathless – state of individuals; those of us who feel trapped because we don't know what to do against the systems in which we move, while facing climate change. How can I also involve other voices in my microbial research? Perhaps I could cultivate other peoples' spaces, ask them about their utopian dreams and co-create a local, microbial planetary universe full of breathing worlds.

Perhaps breathing harmoniously on the rhythm of extinction happens when we share poetry; the beauty that we breathe together within worlds, within a world that is in a constant state of transformation.

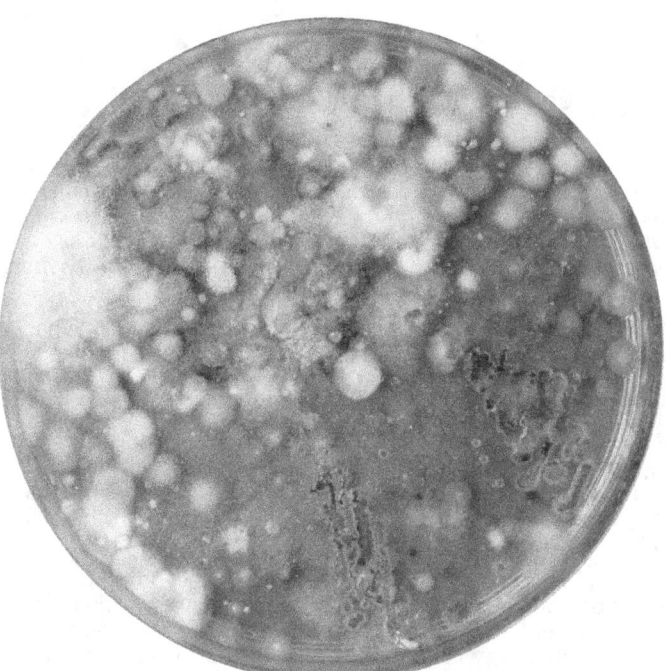

A cultivation of the bedroom air of a bird –
(seven days of growth) Fig. 8

38 Maria Thereza Alves – *Decolonizing Brazil /*
   Descolonizando o Brasil (2018)
39 Maria Thereza Alves, *Amatlan* (1993) Site specific installation

CONCLUDED MISSION,
OR SHOULD I CALL IT A DREAM?

A small intermezzo, saved from my notes: *Every time my mind goes into a 'game-over attitude,' one in which this planet can't be saved from human behaviour, capitalism, and inequality – I take a pause and focus on my breath: 'To return to the body where I was born' – last line from my favourite poem of all times: 'Song; the weight of the world is love,' by Allen Ginsberg and here I am again; alive, ready to twist things around.*

This thesis has been fuelled by an existential question: 'What is the role of art in a period of environmental destruction and potential for human extinction?'

By zooming in and out on stories, voices and lives within this world – including microbes, Bifo, Blue Marble, Caddis larvae, my invisible neighbours, T.J. Demos, Atlas, M. T. Alves, Goethe, and the Dutch special force – it has become clearer to me that the world carries multiplicities of worlds, many of which are and will remain invisible to us.

We (humans and non-humans) share the earth and air, but 'we' don't share the same perspectives and inner worlds that influence our behaviour and the state of this earth. I've come to realize that my wish to take care of the earth and understand it could actually become dangerous if an all-encompassing worldview denies or overlooks the existence of all of these different, inter-related worlds, as a unifying global discourse seems to do.

Rather than create a grand narrative, art can play a significant role, because it has the potential to visualise local, 'invisible,' worlds. Through sharing them with others they can influence our collective narratives. I still wish to influence global politics, but from a local, grounded perspective with others, because care happens in dialogue, in sharing, in a re-action to what we breathe in.

For change to manifest it needs to happen together, in actions. By exploring and visualizing the microbial world that is in and around us, I want to emphasise the 'invisibility' of worlds within the world and connect them to dreams of local 'invisible' people around me. This will be my on-the-ground personal-lunar-mission; co-creating an 'In-view Effect' that explores what and with whom we move on the ground in a bodily dialogue. A mission without a strict protocol, because the best shots are taken in between the lines, while we breathe.

BIBLIOGRAPHY

Franco 'Bifo' Berardi, *Breathing: Chaos and Poetry*, Semiotext(e) / Intervention series (26) (2019)

Interview with Franco 'Bifo' Berardi by Mitra Azar, *''I can't breath'' as a schizo-analysis; chaosmosis, poetry and cinema*, La Deleuziana – Journal of Philosophy, N.9 (2019)
http://www.ladeleuziana.org/wp-content/uploads/2019/08/Bifo_Mitra_I-can't-breath.pdf

Gay Watson, *A Philosophy of Emptiness*, Reaktion Books Ltd (2014)

Donna J. Haraway, *Staying with the Trouble: Making Kin in the Chthulucene*, Duke University Press (2016)

Suzi Gablik, *Conversations Before the End of Time*, Thames Hudson (1995)
http://www.conversationsintime.eu/beforetheend.html

Heather Davis & Etienne Turpin,
Art in the Anthropocene, Open Humanities Press (2015)
http://www.openhumanitiespress.org/books/titles/art-in-the-anthropocene/

Daniel Christian Wahl, *''Zarte Empirie'': Goethean Science as a Way of Knowing*, Janus Head, 8(1) P58-76 Trivium Publications, NY (2005)
https://pdfs.semanticscholar.org/6ea8/232dcc61b6c966b6fd6e177e93b7e7d7fcb5.pdf?_ga=2.46695908.27257235.1585166750-641605631.1572359934

J.W. von Goethe, *Johann Wolfgang von Goethe – Schriften zur Naturwissenschaft*, Reclame (1999)

Kelly Oliver, *Earth and World: Philosophy After the Apollo Missions.* Columbia University Press (2015)

Al Reinert, *The Blue Marble Shot: Our First Complete Photograph of Earth*, Article from The Atlantic (2011)
https://www.theatlantic.com/technology/archive/2011/04/the-blue-marble-shot-our-first-complete-photograph-of-earth/237167/

Denis Cosgrove, *Apollo's Eye: A Cartographic Genealogy of the Earth in the Western Imagination*, John Hopkins University Press (2001)

T.J. Demos, *Against the Anthropocene. Visual Culture and Environment Today*, Sternberg Press (2017)

T.J. Demos, *Decolonizing Nature. Contemporary Art and the Politics of Ecology*, Sternberg Press (2019)

Tim Ingold, *The Perception of the Environment: Essays on Livelihood, Dwelling and Skill*, Routledge (2000)

POSTFACE –
'CAREFUL' SOLUTIONS

Last notes, not to be confused with the conclusion.

I have written multiple introductions for this thesis. It's as if I got stuck in describing one entry point after another, in repetition, hanging above my topic, without going inside and finding a solution. People have warned me of this, friends and teachers alike. It's likely to happen when one addresses complex topics like climate change, when you try to offer a recipe to turn the tides. I am not the moon. I can't pull oceans towards myself. I am just a pawn, amongst seven billion and many other creatures, that is navigating through clouds of information.

However, solutions to take better care of this planet are out there. We are exposed to them every day. Within me there is an assemblage of entry points for practical solutions to stimulate care. A collection that has come into existence through encounters with texts, images, actions and people. Let's call them registered copies, selected from all I've been exposed to. However, these ideas are vital and alive, and they transform depending on the context. In my case they come up quite forceful and pungent these days. I recognize the same energetic urgency in ideologists and activists. I find it attractive, but I don't want to shovel my ideas in your face. I would rather seduce you with a friendly smile and create a space where we can softly assay the archives of information stored in our bodies, because that seems more beneficial if we want to come up with solutions together.

However, I have to admit that it's hard to keep a space soft when the archive of the other highly differs from my own. It's difficult to keep up a smile when I'm in conversation with a business man who travels three times a week by plane, because as we speak, I'm pushing some of my own ideologies under the surface to allow us to find a common space. The question is, should I? What would happen if I let the rat out of the cage? What would happen if I start preaching in the way my inner voice speaks to me, uncensored and one-sided? As this is my own safe space, I will take this idea to the test and write whatever comes to me when I think of living 'care-full'.

''Western society needs to go on a diet! Don't do too many drugs! Don't eat too much sugar! Think differently! Behave differently! Read Marx! Sit still for an hour a day and observe your thoughts, or your body, or count till ten and back, you choose! Spit on the Silicon Valley boys! Dive under! Go off Grid! Talk with each other! Leave the fossil fuels in the ground! Make love! Start a community! Have empathy! Change to a green bank! Listen! Listen to plants! Listen to the air! Read! Read to practice listening! Create safe spaces! More safe spaces for people to be themselves! Though, be aware that they are never truly safe! Overthrow capitalism! We need to come up with other value systems to measure human welfare than perpetual growth! Start a garden! Dream! Listen better! Embrace the queer community, even when your heterosexual-monogamous-love-wishes are not always welcome! Stay open! Investigate unknown roads! Take care of your body! Avoid plastic wrappings! Deconstruct your thoughts, but don't let them get lost to themselves! Enjoy, because without joy there is no point in saving your world! Beware; the world is your subjective world! Spit on Trump! Spit on climate change deniers! Well no, don't spit on them, just don't give them any more attention! Or listen to them and come up with counter arguments! If they don't want to hear them, barricade the streets! Go into politics if you dare and want to get unhappy for a good cause! Stop looking at your phone 80 times a day! Avoid planes! Travel the world on foot or by bike! Don't buy things you don't need! Share! Spend at least 20 days a year in a forest, otherwise you go crazy and you know it! Buy organic if you can! Don't be scared of death! Train your body! Brush your teeth! Relax once in a while! Have cold showers! Dissect your impulses, where do they come from?! Be nice to your friends, you will need them! Be grateful for life! You are not a god! Make people understand they are not gods! We seem to give ourselves way too much credit for life! Only buy second-hand! Beware of your position in society as a white woman! Don't spend all your day behind a computer! It will turn you into a talking head with typing fingers, that doesn't know it has a body! Be honest in your intentions, always, the only one who will truly suffer otherwise is yourself! Stop smoking! Think about your audience when you speak! Try to speak a common language! But don't forget what is important to you and express your opinions! Support those who are living good causes! If you need to be alone, be alone! Ask questions when you don't understand something! Again, be grateful! Learn a new language! Be brave! Never paint your face black again, as you did when you were 16 playing 'Zwarte Piet'! Remain aware that this is a white community, and others' experiences aren't the same as yours! Acknowledge your shortcomings! Don't get lost in anger! Cultivate what you love! Be vulnerable! Listen to people, when you have space for it! Practice empathy! And don't forget to smile when you look in the mirror! The first and last one you are responsible for is yourself, as long as you don't have kids!''

Bronwen Jones

Seeping Bodies

Introduction

How can words illustrate the longings and sentimentalities we have for space? It feels like a deeper yearning that can't be expressed through language. It is something bodily that quickens your heartbeat and brings a beaming grin to your face as you round the corner, approaching a familiar place you haven't been to in a while. These words I write, build up a boundary around me that I can't escape, that are supposed to explicitly represent the feelings I am feeling, but often these feelings can't be pushed through the construct of language. Sometimes instead they reside in the cosiness of a home, or the softness of an embrace with a loved one. Enclosed in a body.

What is built up in these interiors is something that can't be recorded, except in traces and stories and the objects that have experienced with us. It is a feeling inside, just as these words are contained inside this page, these feelings are contained within the body. It therefore isn't about this building, it is about the things that have been shared in and with this space, the moments of happiness and passion and longing and monotony that occur within the four walls.

It is the memories of events long passed and stories long told that bring a sort of mysticism to a building, one that keeps drawing one back to those walls. The same mysticism that brings fans trooping to the abandoned homes of celebrities, the idea that walls can contain a part of human bodies; the fingerprints of dirty fingers, the indent of an accident. We can be affected by buildings, just as we affect them, this reciprocity holds within it a mutual attraction.

A weave could also be a room, a pattern making up the form, or a knitted jumper, the lines of which you can follow and trace the impression of the maker, the threads containing the manipulations of their hands, the hesitations and confidences, similarly to the way you follow the voice of a poet, stanza by stanza. These things can fade and alter over time, words can fall out of circulation and find new meaning to different voices, yarns can become threadbare and be patched up by new hands.

These places are sights of habitation; a body, a room, a garment, a stanza. They are private places to dwell within, to think, to live; in solitude or as a place to invite a friend or lover into.

I write as a form of searching; to wander through the written word, to imagine different scales of bodies and play with our expectations of words, in addition to considering languages without words, in an attempt to un-define this space that is unnamable. So that you may read and define your own body through whichever form of language you choose.

The body of text

A body of text is a container. A combination of words fill up the space. Words are a translation of the original and derive from a language and history. The etymology of words and their usage throughout history connect them to certain ideas and stereotypes. These histories resonate differently through various bodies, yet they have the tendency to shift through the mouths that speak and the bodies that feel them. They are in flux, yet history sticks to them.

There is something inherent in the word *object* that makes us consider it as lower or less significant than the human body. To objectify is to –*degrade to the status of a mere object*–[1], this use of mere implies it is lower, and so to objectify a body is a hard act, the act of degrading another body below oneself. Enclosing words in a body of text make them vulnerable to being misread, misinterpreted and misrepresented, and the hard definitions of words tend to categorise and restrict human bodies.

I am not against hardness, hard can mean strong and solid, but it can also mean inert and rigid. I see softness as a strength, for to be soft does not make it the opposite of hard and thus weak (as we may have come to believe with its link to femininity).

Soft can mean –*easy to mould, cut, compress, or fold*– but does this need to have a negative connotation when it leads to –*sympathetic, lenient, or compassionate*– bodies? The need to be hard produces cracks in constructions and problems begin to seep out.

I wonder if a word can be soft or whether by definition it restricts the thing that it is describing. Take for instance the word normal, the adjective, defined as –*conforming to a standard*– categorises some bodies as typical and acceptable, whilst suggesting that whichever bodies lay outside of this definition must be abnormal. *Abnormal* meaning –*deviating from what is normal or usual, typically in a way that is undesirable or worrying*– is associated with the Latin word *abnormis* meaning –*monstrous*– giving the impression that if a body doesn't fit into the restricted borders implemented by this word then there is something wrong or undesirable with this body.

Is it then possible to break free of the confines of a language made up of words and instead seek other ways to communicate; perhaps the language of the body or of material?

The leaking body

The body is a contradiction. It is both soft and hard, leaking and contained, elastic and rigid, sticky and dry, melting and solid. It fits into and defies the expectations of words. It is somewhat predictable, yet incalculable. It is composed of the solid borders of skin, yet these are soft, porous boundaries from which beads of sweat may leak out. The skin may become dry but it can absorb moisture and become soft to the touch again. It has a trajectory from birth and doesn't deform far from this shape. It stretches through growth becoming stronger and independent into adulthood and then shrinking again and becoming weaker and more precarious into old age. The swelling and weakening of a body through sickness that stretches back to its previous self once the infection drains out of the body. It goes through life, oscillating between these definitions. How then did the human body come to be so defined in binary constructs; man or woman, soft or hard, emotive or insensitive, strong or weak…?

Despite the roles assigned to it, the body leaks. For instance, the act of crying is bodily, so that the body acts before the brain can comprehend the reasons for tears. There is a knowledge ingrained in the body; a pain or sadness or happiness that leaks out before the person can understand their reasons for crying. These reasons often can't be represented through words, they exist somehow within the body. Telling the experience of living with her mother's pain Sara Ahmed writes '*through witnessing, I would give her pain a life outside the fragile borders of her vulnerable and much loved body. But her pain, despite being the event that drew us together (…) was still shrouded in mystery. I lived with what was, for me, the unliveable.*'[2] The borders of empathy can only extend so far when something is enclosed inside the other body.

To empathise stems from –*em-pathos*–, to be –*in-feeling*–, to step into another body's experience and try to share their feeling. How can one step into another body's experience when this experience can't be expressed through language? She can only attempt to translate the shaking or wailing of a body in pain. At such times the body acts outside of language; it finds other ways to express itself and to communicate with another. An embrace can convey the uncontrollable manifestations of the body; the shaking and sobbing that can't be explained in words. This close contact could transport us to a time we have felt hurt, and even if we are unable to empathise with the specific situation, we can recognise a pain or sorrow that we have felt before. The body is not enclosed in language and therefore shouldn't be stuck to its rigidity.

The human body is leaking and permeable. It sheds piss, semen, sweat and saliva, and may allow in and share semen and saliva with another body. In addition the female body functions for another potential body; shedding monthly blood and if the time comes sharing milk with her child. This porosity

1 All definitions that follow in this form –*example*– are taken from the Oxford dictionary.

2 Sara Ahmed, *The Cultural Politics of Emotion* (New York: Routledge, 2015)), 30

lends the human body an understanding of what it is to be a slippery object, particularly consistent in the female as these leaking fluids could be understood to give her wetter borders than that of the man. Perhaps this brings the connotation that her body is more easily emotionally manipulated, for she is used to being penetrated. She belongs to a wounded categorisation of people, her body is misunderstood.

The enclosed body

How has the female body been thrust into such a restricted category when she has seemingly fluid borders? She is stereotyped with words such as soft, delicate and sensitive, often in the derogatory sense of being weak, but perhaps these are her strengths. These wounds of misunderstanding give her more potential to empathise with other bodies.

Luce Irigaray says '*That we are women from the start. That we don't have to be turned into women by them, labeled by them, made holy and profaned by them. That that has always already happened, without their efforts. And that their history, their stories, constitute the locus of our displacement. It's not that we have a territory of our own; but their fatherland, family, home, discourse, imprison us in enclosed spaces where we cannot keep on moving, living, as ourselves. Their properties are our exile. Their enclosures, the death of our love. Their words, the gag upon our lips.*'[3] The oppressed female has an innate strength from having to shape her soft self around others, she is taught to compromise to other bodies. She must fight everyday to overcome and combat this feeling of displacement that seems enclosed inside her body, imposed by the rigid structures she is held within. This feeling won't leak out by itself.

Bodies as containers

I would like to use a broader term of *body*, generally defined as *–the physical structure (of something)–* particularly that of a human or animal, and often extended to include the physical structure of an object or a piece of writing, *a body of text*. A body therefore could be thought of as a container, a physical structure confined by borders which contains the physical attributes of something. If I were to then extend this definition to something somewhat immaterial, like language, how could I view this imaginary body? We know that language is made up of words, and these words can be compiled into a dictionary that visualises the extent of the English language, for example. Each word has a concise written definition that embodies a history and has a tendency to make references and connections to other words, often these references have different implications for different human bodies. How then would the borders of the language's body look? Are they hard or soft? Leaking or rigid?

The aura of a word

Words can hold a mysticism. The feeling you get from the verb *to wrap*, you can almost feel the tightness and warmth, touching on the memory of being swaddled as a baby, and being wrapped in bed as a child, later climbing into the comforting sweater of a lover, walking around day-to-day life with this body tight around you. The idea of a warm embrace with a loved one. These words hold a longing and a desire; *enclose, envelop, enfold, embrace…* the *en-/em-* meaning *–in–*, the feeling of being within something. The enchantment and image lays in the word, read silently or spoken out loud, the word dances in the imagination, it creates an aura, the same aura that a building can hold, that something exists in these spaces, these in-betweens. Between language and the thing. A silent memory that becomes history, something that is no longer present, so that to imagine it is to create something anew, something based on the memory of being within feeling. A word is like a cue to something that can't be fully defined in language.

The memory in a crease

A piece of clothing is as permeable as a human body. It can adjust to its wearer, absorbing and enveloping another body. It can be rinsed and wrung out and hung to dry. It will absorb and be affected by its surrounding bodies. The garment becomes a second skin, a wrapping that immediately takes the body's impressions and contains them in its fabric. A crease, in the human body, is a sign of ageing, *–a wrinkle or furrow in the skin–*, a temporary appearance resulting from an expression of emotion/feeling. As we age these temporary shapes become ridges in the skin that reference the expressions that have been pulled through the years. A textile acts in a similar way. It accumulates creases reminiscent of wrinkles in the skin. Stretches in the fabric which trace where the body has gestured are reminiscent of stretch marks in the skin, the body suiting to its environment. Tears are like bodily wounds. These textiles experience life with us as the closest object to our bodies, accumulating the moments of happiness and exaltation, and comforting us when we are hurt and upset. Clothing doesn't require us to explain, for the meaning is within the fabric, like traces in a landscape that changes over thousands of years, yet all remains either on the surface or buried just below.

As Virginia Woolf wrote in *Orlando*, '*it is clothes that wear us, and not we them; we may make them take the mould of arm or breast, but they mould our hearts, our brains, our tongues to their liking.*'[4] Clothing may be seen as an inanimate object but perhaps it is an object in the in-between state, halfway between object and body. When worn on the body it mimics the bodily form and echoes the movements of the human body that wears it, but when taken off it becomes a sort of object. It becomes still, hanging in the closet or folded neatly in the shelf, yet it continues to reference the human body. The body is recognisable in the sleeves and neckline and smell and creases. When thrown over the back of a chair, it slouches like a human body; the worn, tired expression it wears in this state is reminiscent of the human's expression at the end of a long day. These cues in the fabric make our own body visible in the garment, its permeable borders allow the human body to entwine with and hold its feelings and memories within the fabric. The material is outside of spoken language.

The vulnerable garment

To be vulnerable stems from the Latin word *vulnus* meaning *–wound–*. Clothing can become a protection, a way to approach the world with comfort and familiarity. The verb to *dress*, in the medical sense, can mean *–to treat or prepare something in a certain way–*, for example *–to treat or apply a dressing to a wound–*. You could see it as preparing a wounded body for an outside world, to conceal its vulnerabilities.

The act of dress becomes a front, at times a shield, for meeting the world. This can often be recognised in a person in mourning, they may hold close the clothing of a loved one, to feel the warmth of the body they are missing, they may wrap themselves in a knitted jumper of their loved one, to feel the body of this person holding them and fill the wounds that this loss has given to them. In the slow process of repairing after loss, the objects and belongings that once surrounded the deceased become emblems of comfort and care. The way a garment wore its owner is revealed in the stretches in the fabric and the stains of food and discolouring from sweat. The thinning threads reveal a love and comfort of repeated wear, taking on the person's bodily form.

The solid house

The soft, vulnerable body needs outer layers for comfort and protection. Clothing acts as a second skin, giving the body warmth and cover, thus not exposing the body in public. The house then gives a stable structure to support and protect the body, offering it a private space to dwell away from the public sphere. The walls of a house are hard, physical borders, they cannot be stretched or tightened to suit the human body, they

3 Luce Irigaray, *This Sex Which Is Not One* (Ithaca, NY: Cornell University Press, 1985)), 212 (from the chapter entitled *When Our Lips Speak Together*)

4 Virginia Woolf, *Orlando* (London: William Collins, 2014)), 123

stay firmly in place despite the body's hardest efforts, the most we can do is chip at these walls and alter their surfaces. We may cover them in wallpaper or fresh licks of paint and this can create the illusion of a bigger/smaller space without literally impacting the size or shape of the enclosed room. We may fill these enclosures with furniture and decoration or let them remain minimal and spacious. The interior is soft, alterable and if frustration arises from the way the body is moving around this space it can decide to rearrange or remove objects. The interior forms around us and contains us; it contains our habits and movements.

In one of Louise Bourgeois' etchings she handwrites '*I have spent my life washing dishes and vegetables — I have spent my life listening to the chirping of birds — the water dripping from the ceiling — I have spent my life smelling the burning from the stove.*' Her words reflect the many everyday repetitions and gestures that accumulate in a life. These accumulations become ingrained in the objects that surround us, our human imprint is held in their material. The house contains our memories and pasts and lives among us, ageing steadily, and holding traces of time passing. It may be constructed of hard materials like brick and plaster, yet the home moves within us, it shrinks around the body giving it a comfort equal to that of a loved one. The body moulds the building to fit around it, repairing the dripping tap and the missing shadow of curtains as the winter begins to creep in. It holds the body within its walls.

The home allows us privacy, an enclosed space to dwell and to loosen oneself from the restricted outside. It witnesses us in our most vulnerable states, observing us in acts traditionally only done in privacy; washing, excreting, copulating. A bedroom is often imagined as the most private space of a person, an invitation into the room can be like stepping inside the body, an invitation into a private sphere. Alternatively, the home can act as a front, a form of showing off to guests, something that constricts the visual elements to form an image of pride, a visual language that boasts for the inhabitant so they don't have to speak the words.

The home is an extension of the body, Elaine Scarry writes '*(the room is) an enlargement of the body: it keeps warm and safe the individual it houses in the same way the body encloses and protects the individual within; like the body, its walls put boundaries around the self (…) acting like the body so that the body can act less like a wall.*'[5] The boundaries of different bodies (human and non-human) can contort to the body's comfort. The garment and the house are both attempts to extend the body's borders and these bodies are in a constant state of expanding and shrinking in different contexts, to fill where the other bodies may be lacking. The home as a place of respite is important to the functioning of the body; the stability of architecture allows it a space to be grounded and thus able to move freely about the open world.

The political body

In this attempt to expand the possibilities of what a body can be and where its borders may lay, it is important to consider how human bodies treat one another. I am reminded of Spinoza's philosophy summarised by Deleuze, '*we don't even know what a body is capable of*'[6]. How we could expand the potential of a body by not thinking about what it is but what it can do. I wonder if this reframing could break the binary constructs we find ourselves within and challenge the dominant cultural perceptions. Instead of defining bodies by their sex, sexual orientation, the colour of their skin, the class they were born into or their abilities, we could simply recognise what they are or aren't capable of. To give all an equal opportunity; to commend them for what they are able to do and care for them where they are unable. This categorisation and mistreatment often drips down from the political body which influences how we behave toward the other.

In *The Cultural Politics of Emotion*, Sara Ahmed scrutinises the use of language in political discourse to separate and categorise bodies. Analysing this text from the British National Front '*We will reinstate the values of separatism to our racial kindred. We will teach the youth that one's country is the family, the past, the sacred race itself... We live in a nation that is historically Aryan*'. She writes '*This alignment of family, history and race is powerful, and works to transform whiteness into a familial tie, into a form of racial kindred that recognises all non-white others as strangers, as 'bodies out of place'. The narrative is addressed to white Aryans, and equates the vulnerability of the white nation with the vulnerability of the white body. 'YOU' will not be soft!*'[7] This vulnerability works by switching the narratives, by turning the white body and the wealthy nation into the damaged body, the body that must fear other bodies taking what is rightfully theirs. It instils fear into the white body by telling them that they are soft if they don't agree and fight for these beliefs.

The narrative suggests that this mixing with other non-white bodies will make the nation weaker and therefore before this wounding is possible we should create hard borders to protect the nation. The use of an us and them is clearly defined, marking two bodies of people; the body of the hard nation that must not be permeated by the *other* body *(the body out of place)*. It argues that the boundaries of the body must remain rigid and strong in order to protect its inhabitants who believe they deserve their place in it more than others.

The political body in Britain has forgotten too quickly about the many fatal bodies of the Grenfell tower block fire[8] and reduced them down to a number, and even worse an inferior number to the superior bodies who are in a position of power. The fatal bodies consisted of people in the categories of refugees and working class. Such bodies in political discourse are often degraded to a number rather than describing them as a friend, mother, child or lover. This number dehumanises them in some sense; it is still described as a tragic loss but the categorisation doesn't give space to humanise them or to imagine the individual loss of a body who died in the place that they should have felt most comfortable. These bodies are considered too singular or inferior to converse with the political body.

If we understand the human body to be soft and able to shape around another, we can wonder why the structures it has built around itself have become so hard and inflexible. The body needs outer layers to function as a being and as a society; clothing warms and covers it, the house gives it security and a private space to dwell away from the public realm, social infrastructure organises it so we may function together as a collection of bodies. The larger scale the layers, the less able the singular body is to control or suit them to its needs. Language when used on such a large scale becomes problematic, because it must deal with and talk about bodies as collectives rather than singular entities. This 'higher' position also trickles down and influences the way we discourse on a smaller scale. I wonder whether this constriction into categories is necessary and why it negatively impacts certain categories of bodies more than others.

The unwritten body

The female body is one category that has been neglected in many aspects of political discourse and history, but most fundamentally in the lack of understanding of her body. For example, a lack of research on menstruation and pre-menstrual syndrome means there is a lack of understanding of what the condition is and even a doubt of whether the pain actually exists, often brushed aside as an emotional fragility rather than a real physical problem. Communities such as the art school I am within facilitate an open, liberal attitude giving bodies more freedom and comfort to be able to share their difficulties and pains in a safe space. However in many other spaces women and teenage girls are suffering silently with the belief that there is something personally wrong with them. The female body

5   Elaine Scarry, *The Body in Pain* (New York: Oxford University Press, 1985)), 38

6   Gilles Deleuze and Martin Joughin, *Expressionism in Philosophy: Spinoza* (New York: Zone Books, 1992)

7   Sara Ahmed, *The Cultural Politics of Emotion* (New York: Routledge, 2015)), 2

8   The Grenfell Tower was a block of flats in West London where a fire broke out in June 2017, causing 72 deaths.

isn't exposed to discourses or words that are inclusive to her body and needs, and therefore often doesn't realise that her difficulties are valid since she hasn't heard them discussed in the public realm. Without conversation, menstruation remains bound up with stereotypes of being dirty and therefore she doesn't seek the care she desperately needs. The proof of these statements can be found by asking the majority of women about their experiences; even if they haven't suffered themselves it is likely that they have a friend that has, who has had to converse with other women to confirm that she is not alone.

The woman's words are ignored from the political body. The bodies that haven't traditionally been represented by our political body haven't the words to express the pains that have been inflicted on them. Anne Carson wrote '*the women of classical literature are a species given to disorderly and uncontrolled outflow of sound — to shrieking, wailing, sobbing, shrill lament, loud laughter, screams of pain or of pleasure and eruptions of raw emotion in general.*'[9] The woman's words are interpreted as shrieks and purely emotion rather than logic. Her voice is interpreted as a monstrosity, animalistic in its lack of ability to grasp the orderly construction of language. But perhaps she screams because the language she is given does not give her the words to express how she feels.

I'd like to weave in the voice of Theresa Hak Kyung Cha speaking toward her mother, Huo Hyung Soon. '*The tongue that is forbidden is your own mother tongue. You speak in the dark. In the secret. The one that is yours. Your own. You speak very softly, you speak in a whisper. In the dark, in secret. Mother tongue is your refuge. It is being home. Being who you are.*'[10] Her book Dictee introduces us to nine women who reject patriarchal roles and cannot have a voice for themselves due to various reasons; her mother couldn't use her voice as she was born in exile. She could only speak Korean in private, her mother tongue was denied to her. I consider how a language can be a home, it reminds me of when I return to England after a while spent abroad, and how natural it can feel to relax back into the surroundings of my mother tongue; understanding the conversations around me and the writing in public spaces, how much more at ease I feel. I wonder how it would feel to step outside of the English language into a softer form of language. How the whole body could relax without the constrictions of an unnatural language that tells the body how it can and cannot act.

Hysterical bodies and witches

The hardness that has been thrust upon her by society means the pubescent girl enters a world where her body is not talked about. She is silenced by her surrounding bodies. This silence has been the source of many misunderstandings around the female body; the restrictions of what she could be were so limited that she had to defy the definitions assigned to her body. This created a space for a misnaming and mistreatment of her body, both by others and by herself for she felt abnormal to not fit into the restricted *normal* role.

From a lack of recorded history (history often excluding marginalised bodies) grows myths and misunderstandings. The phenomenon of hysteria is a prime example of a damaging myth that still affects the discourse around female bodies. Female hysteria was a common incorrect diagnosis which dates back as early as 1900BC with the term eventually being dropped from the American Psychiatric association as recently as 1952. The symptoms included anxiety, shortness of breath, fainting, nervousness and sexual desire, among others. Hysteria stems from the ancient Greek root *hystera* meaning uterus and it was thought that women had a *wandering womb* that moved through the body of its own accord causing madness. The womb within the woman was imagined as '*an animal within an animal*'[11]. This connection between hysteria and the womb meant that for a long time it was believed that only women could be hysterical.

The word hysteria is now defined as –*exaggerated or uncontrollable emotion or excitement*–, and although the term is no longer exclusively used to refer to the woman, it is clear that this word still sticks to the stereotype of the female body unable to control its emotions, particularly whilst menstruating. The tendency to tell a woman she is being hysterical and to try to give reason to her manner by asking '*is it that time of the month?*' is still shockingly common and is often used as an act of diminishing the woman's position and state of mind. In this gap of knowledge, women have been made to search for alternative forms of medicine to care for their bodies and forced to hide or be ashamed to share their pain.

The myth of female hysteria was considered from two perspectives; both scientific and demonological, which leads to another myth — the woman as a witch. As Silvia Federici describes '*the surplus of animal presences in the witches' lives also suggests that women were at a (slippery) crossroad between men and animals, and that not only female sexuality, but femininity as such, was akin to animality. To seal this equation, witches were often accused of shifting their shape and morphing into animals, while the most commonly cited familiar was the toad, which as a symbol of the vagina synthesised sexuality, bestiality, femininity and evil.*'[12] This places a hierarchy between the superiority of the male body versus the inferior animal body, and how women were belittled in this supposed act of mingling between the lower form of life and her physical human body whilst deceiving the man by shapeshifting between these categories. The woman is not given a voice in this categorisation; her body is likened to that of an animal, a body that can't be understood by humans and must be tamed and domesticated if we are to live in harmony with them.

We are now at a point in history where women and queer bodies are getting recognition for the forms in which they have been repressed. Society is beginning to change to become more inclusive and repressors are being called out for mistreatment, yet there is still a long way to go until we can all converse equally. Luce Irigaray wrote '*If we keep on speaking the same language together, we're going to reproduce the same history.*'[13] The repressive categorisations of bodies are still inherent in the language we speak. The traditions of marriage, for example, still use vocabulary that puts the woman below the man. The father gives the bride away to the husband, implying she is an object that may be traded. The bride takes the man's name on as her own, therefore removing and replacing her past identity for her future with him. Traditions are argued to be important to history and convention, but surely we are at a point where we are realising the mistakes of our past and we should reformulate the structures we have been enclosed within.

Textiles as language

The language that we communicate within can be so forceful and direct that it can't express the physicality of pain or other emotions. Perhaps we need to open up our definition of language in order to exchange such emotions. One such language could be the language of textile. In *Zeros + Ones*, Sadie Plant describes the language of weaving and the messages and symbols that could be communicated through the cloth; '*cloths were woven to 'invoke magic' — to protect, to secure fertility and riches, to divine the future, perhaps even to curse.*'[14] She describes how this language was inherent in the very making of the material, in the process and the hands of the maker. '*Open diamonds are said to indicate fertility and tend to decorate (clothing). "These lozenges (…) rather graphically, if schematically, represent a woman's vulva." These images are quite unlike those which are later painted on the canvas or written on the page. The lozenge is emergent from the cloth,*

9   Anne Carson, *Glass, Irony, and God* (New York: New Directions Books, 2005)), 126 (from the chapter entitled The Gender of Sound)

10 Theresa Hak Kyung Cha, *Dictee* (Berkeley, CA: Univ. of California Press, 2001)), 45–46

11 Aretaeus and Francis Adams, The Extant Works of Aretaeus, the Cappadocian (London: Sydenham publications, 1856)) Aretaeus was an ancient Greek physician.

12 Silvia Federici, *Caliban and the Witch* (Brooklyn, NY: Autonomedia, 2004)), 194

13 Luce Irigaray, *This Sex Which Is Not One* (Ithaca, NY: Cornell University Press, 1985)), 205 (from the chapter entitled *When Our Lips Speak Together*)

14 Sadie Plant, *Zeros + Ones: Digital Women + the New Technoculture* (London: Fourth Estate, 1998)), 66

diagonal lines implicit in the grids of the weave.'[15] It is a visual language and a language of touch, one that transfers the hands of the maker to the hands of the beholder.

The textile language is one that can be shared between a community, for example the Moroccan Berber weavers. The Berber women weave together on an upright loom, knotting symbols that have often been passed on to them by their mothers or grandmothers, a material language that has been passed down generations through the fingers of the women. The motifs they use traditionally relate to fertility, sexuality, survival and protection. However these meanings often become lost or fractured from the verbal word that they represented as it is a language spoken through touch rather than through an explicit *writing* of a text in a carpet. Many of the women no longer know the meaning of the symbols as it is something they have always done through their hands, communicating their heritage rather than communicating a message. These examples represent the many histories that are unrecorded in the *language of words* as they don't fit into its restricted construction and the ways that bodies will always find a form to communicate and share their stories.

The elastic body

I'd like to return back to body language, the form of communication that is most primal and natural to the body, and consider the ways that this language has been morphed and categorised by the language of words.

The (heterosexual) sex act has been fantasised as an odyssey for the man to combat the woman, for she is the animal that must be slain and domesticated, the man penetrates her and deposits himself inside of her, a form of marking his territory. In our culture, women aren't expected to want or enjoy sex and it is something they must bear in order to tame the man's needs. This extreme rift between the expectations of man and woman divides the way men and women are allowed to act and separates the sex act from being a meeting and merging of bodies for both their pleasures, to being an act where both bodies are supposed to fill expectations presumed from whether their body consists of a penis or a vagina.

I feel I must explain myself at this point as words have a tendency to trigger only the ears and I'd rather open up their potential to illuminate the whole body. The verb *penetrate* is defined as –*go into or through (something), especially with force or effort*–. This suggestion of force often gives this word a negative connotation, especially when talking about sexual penetration. It can be imagined to wound the body that it acts upon, but perhaps we could rethink it as opening up the body or to imagine this wound as something positive. One definition of penetrate offers –*succeed in understanding or gaining insight into (something complex or mysterious)*–. When words trigger only the ears, the voice is triggered to shout back and defy these definitions. Sometimes this is necessary but at other times words may provoke an unnecessary response. The potential orgasm that results from sexual penetration could be the perfect example to counter this triggering, a feeling that seems to illuminate the whole body. It is beyond language. An ecstatic body that screams sound, not words. We could consider this penetration as giving bodies a porous quality that means they can mingle and understand one another more deeply. This definition can take into account the possible problems that can occur from the forceful aspect, but it can also expand our relation to the word. We can elasticate words so that our bodies can tune into them.

The words used to define bodies can implement expectations. As I have said, *feminine* and thus the female is attached to words such as soft, delicate and emotive, giving an often negative impression of her being malleable, vulnerable and lacking strength. However, on the other end of the spectrum, *masculine* and the male are attached to words such as strong, confident and assertive, making him vulnerable if he cannot fulfil these expectations. These expectations restrict the body, so that the act of living within the role of a specific body is confined

and it is harder for those who cannot connect with these definitions to break out of these conventional cisgender roles. Perhaps if we were to define our borders less rigidly, bodies could slip together and slide apart without being punished for not fitting into the categorisations they have been divided into.

The elastic female body is used to stretching to contain and hold another body, carrying a child in her womb lets the woman consider her two bodies simultaneously; she serves the needs of her child whilst caring for its outer body (her own body), so that she doesn't know where her breast ends and her child's mouth begins. The disassembled female body after giving birth must continue to service the child as if it were still a part of her. The elastic female body therefore stretches to suit the world imposed on it. She must seek new forms of strength in the bodies around her, to make up for her many wounds that she does not know how to treat or heal.

Perhaps we enjoy the shield of a wound, to be vulnerable, to be permeable. The tenderness of a wounded body (physically and emotionally) may allow the body to be open to encounters, to seek alliances with new bodies, to form strength in number. Often these new bodies aren't human bodies, she may seek refuge in objects that bring strength, or landscapes of nostalgia, reminding the body of a previous iteration of itself. Perhaps the lack of understanding coming from a human body when we are wounded and misunderstood leads the body to seek respite in non-human bodies, bodies that can reflect our pain, and affect and understand us in new ways to the human body, maybe the silent warmth of a jumper is easier company than another speaking body trying to comprehend our pain.

(Re)writing the body

I want to step outside of myself, and try to understand how I have come to define my body. I think of the women who have stuck to me; Virginia Woolf, Maggie Nelson, Luce Irigaray… who have flowed into my thoughts and continuously reform my outlook; of the world, of my body, of what my body can be. They mingle inside my porous borders and seep out of me. How they have used the very language that constricted them to stretch and expand it to include them. How they have used it, despite its flaws, to tell their own story. Maggie Nelson begins The Argonauts discussing the '*idea that the inexpressible is contained — inexpressibly! — in the expressed.*'[16] She states '*Its paradox is, quite literally, why I write, or how I feel able to keep writing.*' I recall similar sentiments from other writers and artists who conglomerate inside me; a frustration that language can't fully define the thoughts we want to express. Yet Maggie Nelson concedes '*words are good enough*'! — assumably along with many other writers, myself included; we have accepted this language as our own, as the form of which we want to express our thoughts, with the motivation that these words can't fully define the expressions within us but they can begin to scratch at those thoughts. And by scratching we can begin to flex the definitions and expand the hard borders of a word; by rewriting the histories of the oppressed from the bodies of the oppressed and reclaiming the words that have shaped us into small enclosures.

We don't stop at just language, we take up the tools of weaving and knitting and repairing to craft our stories into history, to not only soften language, but also the very forms with which we communicate and the bodies that these discourses will touch. If we think of the soft garment or the leaking body, we can understand it is possible to identify ourselves with multiple categories and histories that may entwine, and that it isn't necessarily negative to be shaped by others for it gives us a greater capacity for empathy. Louise Bourgeois said '*When I was growing up, all the women in my house were using needles. I've always had a fascination with the needle, the magic power of the needle. The needle is used to repair the damage. It's a claim to forgiveness.*'[17]

15 Ibid, 66–67

16 Maggie Nelson, *The Argonauts* (Minneapolis, MN: Graywolf Press, 2015)), 3

17 Louise Bourgeois, Marie-Laure Bernadac, and Hans-Ulrich Obrist, Louise Bourgeois: *Destruction of the Father Reconstruction of the Father: Writings and Interviews 1923-1997* (Cambridge: The MIT Press, 1998)), 222

In her artwork Bourgeois paved a way for bringing the domestic realm into a public space by expressing her emotion and life in art. Her works express many double-sided aspects of growing up in the early 20th century when women were still very bound to traditional roles; they seem to simultaneously hold in them the comforting protection and the caged existence of the domestic sphere and the role of the mother. Like the Berber women who weave symbols into their woven tapestries, an artwork can produce a visual language. The traditionally domestic duties of women (sewing, repairing, caring for the home and family) are incorporated into Bourgeois' sculptures becoming acts and items that leave the protected setting of the home and become seen on the outside, in public. In her late works, made in her 80s, her clothing often appeared; she sewed and attached these soft materials, the fabrics becoming like a diary, they recorded her body and her life encounters within her work, she said of this that it was an attempt to keep things together and make things whole. Personal memories were an important aspect of her work and the clothes gave a direct contact to her own body and its past, some still held the scent of her perfume. These artworks became a form of survival beyond the frail body and beyond the harsh reality of words, a softer less defined way to *write* about her suffering. This act of putting the domestic life into public view and discourse is one that has been done by many feminist artists since, as an act of reclaiming the woman's role from being one confined to the household. The private and public mingle together, dispersing the boundaries of how we should act where. Once again using the tools handed to us to re-craft our own stories.

Perhaps the pen could be language's claim to forgiveness, collectively we can rewrite the words that we feel limit us, due to the repressive histories that have stuck to them. To be soft is to know the feeling of fuzzy borders, to not know where the body ends and the landscape begins, to know the feeling of melting and converging with other bodies, to be able to understand and compromise with other bodies. We could experience the tear of a favourite jumper as if it were our own skin, stitch back this wound to make it whole so it can continue to embrace us. Or to think of a leaking ceiling like a leaking body, something to mend and give strength to while wiping away the tears. To repair the wounds inflicted by language and soften words to shape to our bodies, rather than allow our bodies to be shaped by words.

Conclusion

This is a beginning. An attempt to break out of the enclosures our bodies have been confined within. To make language correspond to the way bodies are composed: as open, porous structures. I continue to wonder if it is necessary to define ourselves through words, or whether our seeping, sticky, soft, hard, elastic, stiff, melting, conversing bodies are the tools that define our self; the way that we act and interact with other bodies, the way that we take up the tools of pens and needles or whatever we choose to shape our own stories. We are reclaiming our language so that we can speak through air that is breathable, that doesn't choke us with its myths that categorise our bodies.

I think that by approaching the body and its many definitions through different forms of language we may find new facades, hidden from the language of words. Language has enclosed me since I learned to name things, for as long as I can remember I have used words according to these definitions I was given as a child, but at times there are gaps in these definitions. These gaps in conversation are possibilities. Perhaps the attempt to translate other forms of contact to spoken language could create alternative definitions. We could begin to think through materials and gut-feeling, so that our slippery bodies could slide out of words, through new forms and return to words enlivened.

This text is an invitation to all bodies. To be ecstatic and scream and shriek and shake and to erupt, to not shrink into definitions. To elasticate words when we wish to speak, so that we can voice ourselves through our own bodies and not through the warped construction of language. To defy language when it is not enough and use other forms to interact. To not feel enclosed and have to act accordingly to other's expectations. To redefine the words so they envelop us in comfort yet stretch to contain our many definitions.

BIBLIOGRAPHY

Ahmed, Sara. *The Cultural Politics of Emotion*. Routledge, 2015.

Aretaeus, and Francis Adams. *The Extant Works of Aretaeus*, the Cappadocian. London: Sydenham publications, 1856.

Bourgeois, Louise, et al. Louise Bourgeois: *Destruction of the Father Reconstruction of the Father: Writings and Interviews 1923-1997*. The MIT Press, 1998.

Carson, Anne. *Glass, Irony, and God*. New Directions Books, 2005.

Cha, Theresa Hak Kyung. *Dictee*. Univ. of California Press, 2001.

Deleuze, Gilles, and Martin Joughin. *Expressionism in Philosophy: Spinoza*. Zone Books, 1992.

Federici, Silvia. *Caliban and the Witch*. Autonomedia, 2004.

Irigaray, Luce. *This Sex Which Is Not One*. Cornell University Press, 1985.

Nelson, Maggie. *The Argonauts. Minneapolis*, MN: Graywolf Press, 2015.

Plant, Sadie. *Zeros + Ones: Digital Women + the New Technoculture*. Fourth Estate, 1998.

Scarry, Elaine. *The Body in Pain*. New York: Oxford University Press, 1985.

Woolf, Virginia. *Orlando*. London: William Collins, 2014.

*All definitions in this form —example— are taken from the Oxford dictionary.

Morta Jonynaitė

Liquid Crystals and Blissful Dots

INTRODUCTION

Sally sells seashells by the seashore. I am inviting you to sail to the seashore to discover what a seashell might sell. This text is going to be a journey which swings from the sea to the shore and everywhere in between. Dwelling in a space that is so fluid might seem difficult, but a seagull above will guide you through the deluges and delusions that shall appear. If you manage to find the shell, gently press it to your ear, it will whisper the reason for the exploration — the search for tranquility.

The stories and the characters in this text will be connecting parts of a larger net I am trying to knot. Some words are inhabiting transformations, overlaps and clashes that are happening in the world, others are shifting the focus to a calm and peaceful state of mind. I became obsessed with the coast long ago, it has always felt so close and so far, just like those blissful moments of total serenity. It is a space constantly concealed and revealed by waters, always surprising with the unfamiliar textures, scents and beings. I am interested in creating a narrative that frees one from darkness and offers a cheerful break or a pleasant discovery.

SUNLIGHT

It is the sudden flap of a wave that wakes us up and lures us into the fluid zone that changes every single moment. We try to resist gravity, to reach the familiar and safe — but apocalyptic uncertainty is pulling us back. It is unclear whether the water is still ebbing, the flow might already be further away than harbours on the opposite side of the globe. The bare ground under your feet is mesmerising, the intense sea scent is making you feel alive and the soft spongy textures are caressing your body. This stillness, though, signifies that the sea is approaching somebodies' land with full force.

The sea will flood the sands, will wet the marble floors of history. Perhaps it will damage the colours of our cotton sheets, but when the next cycle comes — when water retreats to its deepest basin, new generations will arise, a seal will crawl out of the sea again and undecidedly chill on a sandy beach, rolling itself in the particles of fossils of those who lived there before.

The sea is a soup, boiling the biggest diversity of organisms on earth. All life started, and eventually ends, in waters. A dying body dries, releasing its liquids to the soil which connects all oceans above and bellow. We accept it as an inevitable part of our life, but it is troubling to imagine the apocalyptic scenario which shows our planet drowning altogether.

It is impossible to predict to what extent the changes will impact our lives, how high and how soon shall we have to climb to escape the rising waters. None of the engineering solutions can prevent the sea from spilling towards us. Despite having originated from the sea, we are becoming helpless as we see it approaching our contemporary lives. The paradoxical evolutionary path of mankind was noticed by marine biologist Rachel Carson who devotedly researched the seashore:

> "It is a curious situation that the sea, from which life first arose, should now be threatened by the activities of one form of that life. But the sea, though changed in a sinister way, will continue to exist; the threat is rather to life itself."[1]

Although she was observing this phenomenon in the middle of the last century, these days we are becoming more and more aware of the dramatic scenario that is influencing every being on earth. We are trying to take a step back, but changes only happen if one moves forward. I initially had the idea of writing a script for my art piece, which would be an invitation to escape the approaching tsunami in serenity, then some waves pulled me inside the Anthropocentric[2] thinking that deliberately

enhances the drama of our world today. It is not the way I want to tackle it, though. I am aware of things that scream about the catastrophe, but I also notice that people are anxiously looking for help. As religion retreats from Western thinking, people don't have a space to place their sorrows in, and 'nobody' to lean on. My attempt to create comfort by focusing on beauty might be a failed one, but I wish to open it up with different voices that perform alternative ways of looking at the world. I chose to move along the line between the sea and the shore in order to have the possibility of jumping from one matter to another, to shift perspectives and to enhance certain subjects in a metaphoric way. Some things are quite obvious if we try to talk about them, but they become visible if we shine a particular light on them.

My urge could easily be criticised as escapism, but that is how I wish to support humans during this whole cycle of catastrophe. I remember A. Camus' words: 'There is no country for those who despair, but I know that the sea precedes and follow me, and I hold my madness ready.' Is it possible to keep despair in suspense? While some people are trying to run away to outer space, I am inviting you to look for peace in the surroundings and observe the temporality of beauty. Perhaps it is time to adjust our position and focus on peace instead of chaos. It is both a passive and a neutral state. We become spectators of change, licking sweet metaphors of familiar imagery. Virginia Woolf, Walt Whitman and many other writers have always enchanted their readers with pictures from the seashore that wrap one in beautiful dreams. 'O madly the sea pushes upon the land, With love, with love.' Whitman writes[3]. In contrast, contemporary thinkers like Timothy Morton and Jeff Goodell mention the coast as a disastrous zone threatening our existence. 'Sea-level rise is one of the central facts of our time, as real as gravity. It will reshape our world in ways most of us can only dimly imagine.' states Goodell[4]. The sea is one of humanity's oldest metaphors for life, and a sea journey, as a journey through life. As noted by German philosopher Hans Blumenberg in his book 'Shipwreck with Spectator', he explores the metaphoric language of sea and shore throughout history and how human perspective is neutralised as we remain only observers recording events flowing in front of our eyes.

> "The contraposition of dry land and deep sea as the primary frame of reference for the paradoxical metaphorics of existence might, however, lead us to expect that, going beyond the ideas of storms at sea and sinkings, there must also be the, as it were, emphatic configuration in which shipwreck at sea is set beside the uninvolved spectator on dry land."[5]

In times when media is flooding everyday life, we must not forget to look for lucid shores that support one's personal vision. Our common knowledge about the space between the sea and the shore is driven by daily news about the rising waters, refugees leaving and arriving as well as our memories from holidays at the beach. The image of a lighthouse standing still or a fishermen pulling in their catch of the day. The shore is a place full of streaks which mark the passing of time, humans moving around and ecological changes in the world. It can be seen as a symbolic metaphor for the world, captured in each moment — groundless, fluid and rapidly changing, it affects our lives while we are the accelerators of all the change.

1   Rachel Carson and 'Silent Spring', https://www.independent.com/2019/08/29/rachel-carson-and-silent-spring/

2   Anthropocene – the current geological age, viewed as the period during which human activity has been the dominant influence on the climate and the environment.

3   Whitman, Walt. "Out Of The Cradle Endlessly Rocking." The Complete Poems: Penguin Books, London, 2004, p. 277

4   Not if the Seas Rise, but When and How High, https://www.nytimes.com/2017/11/22/books/review-water-will-come-jeff-goodell.html

5   Blumenberg, Hans. Shipwreck With Spectator : Paradigm of a Metaphor for Existence Studies in Contemporary German Social Thought. Cambridge, Massachusetts: The MIT Press, 1997, p. 10

Nevertheless, we can also make a positive impact. I believe it is not enough to raise the awareness, to emphasise the threats. It is more powerful to propose a solution which could be the 'lucid shore'. To me it means a serene moment, one which I am trying to create in my practice. I gather elements of everyday life that compose a situation where one can focus on the beauty of the mundane; a net becomes a narrator of the coastal events instead of an evil symbol of the fishing industry, the water is absent and reveals the tactile landscape, a lighthouse invites the spectator in and illuminates the hidden world.

STROBE LIGHT

Humans have always been enchanted by the seashore — its mysteriousness, power and magic — which evolved into a politically, sociologically and historically complex zone. The same tip of an iceberg that indicated the catastrophe of Titanic last century, is now becoming the Noah's Ark for polar inhabitants whose shoreline is melting with gradually increasing temperatures. At the same time there are new 'coastal' formations shaping in the oceans entitled 'the garbage patches'. Obviously those examples are concerning, but if one mindfully approaches and observes the strips of the seashore that are still vital and intimately unveiled by ebbing water, some stunning textures and colours will appear. Seaweeds, barnacles, mussels, crabs and other tough species are inhabiting the area that is always in flux, forcing them to adapt and evolve into an invincible army. One should stroll slowly there, bend the knees, come closer to the crystals of sand, transmitting whispers of invisible creatures. It is important to listen carefully, because this special moment may be disturbed by the chuckling baby having its first meeting with the sea, the shriek of a concerned parent observing that encounter or a radio report of a worried biologist tracking the changes in the marine ecotone.[6]

'Mum! It stole my sandwich! Bad bird! Ugly bird!' cries a little girl, who was having such an appetising lunch when a huge seagull noticed a vulnerable food source. She wipes her eyes with sandy hands and, half blinded, runs towards her family. It didn't take long for the joyful energy to return. A pink lycra suit was stretched over the body, inflatable wings were pressing her biceps — the girl was ready to play where sea meets land again. Although the elaborate sand castle, built over many hours, was already being beaten by powerful waves, the same water tongues were actively throwing out intriguing things. She noticed small yellow stones that looked like amber. There were so many stories that her mother used to tell about fossilised tree resin that holding the physical pieces in small palms felt magical. She particularly liked the Lithuanian legend about the goddess of the sea, Jūratė, who lived in an amber castle and a mortal fisherman Kąstytis. They fall in love, but their unity is impossible because land and water worlds can't mix. Jūratė gets punished by her father who uses lightning bolts to kill the man and destroy the palace. According to the legend that is why little pieces of amber keep arriving at the shores and beaches of the Baltic Sea.

My first encounter with the seashore was in Nida — a small village on the Curonian Spit, Lithuania. Every year, in the last week of August my family would go there on holiday. I learnt about the forceful nature of waves and the tranquility of sand on the beach of Nida. From time to time I would experience the temporality of my existence when a huge tongue of water sucked me inside a stream. Those moments might traumatise one, but if overcome it introduces the power of nature and makes you feel alive. It was mostly a careless and joyful time. I remember as kids we (my friends and siblings) would throw stranded jellyfish at each other or roll their slimy bodies in the sand, totally unaware they were 'beings'. We were also running to pee in the sea, encouraged by our parents. It felt more natural to release our urine into the massive 'soup' of different microbes instead of going further behind the dunes. The Baltic seaside often gets too dirty to dip sweaty holiday bodies into, partly due to the irresponsible behaviour of the holiday goers. On the opposite side of the globe tourists gather for (scuba)diving

sessions to look at the whitening coral reefs. Not all of them are aware that the monochrome colour palette is a warning sign from nature, showing the demand for non disturbance.

Beaches have always been places for recreation due to the healing properties of salty water and the chemical mixture of different substances in the seashore that provide soothing effects. Unfortunately, people don't only gather there to relax in serenity, but also abuse it as a picturesque setting for careless practices. This ends in colourful mountains of plastic covering the surfaces. It takes massive efforts from scientists to come up with solutions for this problem. Pornhub has recently released a provocative video showing typical porn scenes in plastic-flooded beaches aiming to draw the attention from sexual desire, to an urgent need for action.[7] Polluted beaches is only a small visible part of the whole surface that is causing trouble for sea dwellers as well as land inhabitants.

While most ecological changes are graspable, there are also discreet political actions that happen between aquatic and terrestrial zones. On the coasts of Africa, international forces are exploiting the area, leaving its inhabitants and the ecosystems disturbed. Local communities are not powerful enough to prohibit these environmental crimes. No wonder pirates of Somali have returned to their criminal activity. Originally making a living as fishermen, some men switched into piracy when foreign fishing ships started taking over their prey. They are mythologised and seen as Captain Hooks, but in most cases pirates are petty opportunists causing international concerns. Sympathising with them, one can understand that furious behaviour onboard is meant to protect the peace onshore.[8]

There are many factors that influence our understanding of the planet, the way we inhabit it as well as how we relate to other inhabitants. Humans perspective of the world has changed due to discoveries made and the advancement of technology — we know that our planet doesn't end at the horizon. It is interesting, though, that our knowledge of life below water is quite limited. Plato famously commented: 'We inhabit a small portion of the earth…living round the sea like ants and frogs round the pond'. The majority of the world's biggest cities are situated in coastal areas. It is a phenomenon that evolved due to the attractiveness and economical benefits for the residents of the coastline. Harbouring, fishing industries and tourism are some of the most profitable practices and ones that many people count on for their livelihood. It is inevitable, though, that such activities leave nature disturbed and often destroyed. Some problems occur in how inhabitants deal with the outcomes of their environment. While residents from richer areas tend to build massive concrete walls and blockades to protect their property from the rising sea and disastrous flooding, poorer communities have no power to fight the threatening waves approaching their homes and wiping out their livelihoods. Ten years ago I used to listen to Roisin Murphy's song 'Dear Miami', which announced the fatal future of the city, yet it is only now that I understand what 'disappearing under melting snow' means.[9]

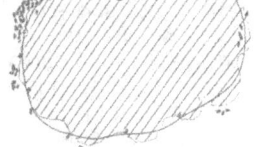

6   Ecotone — area where different plant communities transition from one to another. It contains characteristics of both bordering vegetations and often hosts species that inhabit neither.

7   https://www.youtube.com/watch?v=nskUHvjy1EA

8   https://www.youtube.com/watch?v=gH6AsRi4paU

9   Excerpt from lyrics:
     Dear Miami, you're the first to go
     Disappearing under melting snow"

DIM LIGHT

~~

slush blurp flip flop flap hug suck fuck phloop clurk

soft sofT sOoOft   so o o o ft

slip sliiiiip slippP sli p p p er y

        in in in in in side

disappear merge smerge

wow vowel slow shovel

touch retouch stretch reach

      s wa ll ow

look blink bling i eyes my mine glossy shine

this it big too big
small enough

skin itch ouch jell silk

stop front back care not

muscle tense tentacle tenser minced mouth beak crack more

pho egg noodle spaghetti sauce thick butter

~~

As bodies of water we ebb and flow across time and space. Crawling, swimming, walking we learn to live in the world. The joyful discoveries of the first tactile experiences of newborns recur during adult years when new or unexpected sensations are triggered. Our ten fingers are always alert to touch and grab, the nerves are quickly transmitting news to our brains — we get accustomed to our surroundings through similar explorations as those of the octopus. Eight tentacles are gathering knowledge while gripping undiscovered objects. The word tentacle originated from the Latin word 'tentare', which means 'to feel, to try'.

Crawling back and forth through wet and dry worlds octopuses are curiously exploring new places and objects. There are stories of them being found on carpets, along bookshelves and in teapots. They continue to surprise with their ability to blend in anywhere. Although humans usually judge other beings from their perspective or project anthropomorphic qualities on those that resemble themselves, it is interesting how the octopus remains an 'alien', despite sharing intellectual similarities. There are stories recorded of octopuses taking humans by the hand and showing them around the sea or even inviting them to visit their dens. Holding hand in tentacle, tentacle gripping hand, we could blur the transition of marine ecotone and acknowledge our interconnectedness.[10]

Cultures that worship nature and animals, respect their presence and habits, they manage to cultivate a peaceful linear relationship that doesn't elevate some beings above or detach from others.[11] People knew that the sea gods must be respected to maintain harmony in the world. In Greek mythology many characters have to cross the mysterious sea and reach unfamiliar lands in order to face the most powerful gods or their own destiny. Those stories evolved into traditions that continue to this day. In 1492 Cristopher Columbus left the coast of Castile to find new paths around the world. He was looking for the fastest way to ship foreign goods to his homeland, which laid out routes for future colonialism. Recently, everybody observed Greta Thunberg as she sailed across the Atlantic Ocean to attend 2019 UN Climate Action Summit. The trip was a demonstration of her belief in the importance of reducing emissions. The young heroine believes that it is a way to fight for a peaceful future.

People onshore are waiting for the Argonauts[12] and the changes they bring to the coasts. What looks like an achievement in the moment, may later develop into complex histories. Both Columbus and Thunberg were conquering waves motivated by a genuine urge to bring positive results to the land. Contrary to their stories there is a silent flow of people, to whom arriving at a distant shore is a life changing event, an escape from chaos. Citizens from extreme political areas are ready to leave their homes hoping to find safety elsewhere. The path of a refugee often crosses vast waters, the desperate hope of jumping over an abyss pushes them offshore. Their life is without a shoreline and the only mark of navigation is the horizon ahead with the rising and falling sun. The sounds and the figures familiar to the life on-shore are usually the signs of mission accomplished and the peaceful ground awaiting. There is a whole generation of Lithuanians, who escaped Soviet occupation by crossing the Atlantic. One of them was the filmmaker Jonas Mekas, who recorded memories from the trip in his diary:

> "We are beginning to pass some ships. Must be some islands nearby. I am standing on the deck watching seagulls, I listen to their sad screeching cries. I am also sad, but I am not crying. I am trying to keep my seagulls locked inside."[13]

For Mekas, arriving at the coastal waters of America meant both salvation and alienation. Far from the native Baltic Sea it signified that he would step on the land of new life. Nevertheless, he suspended the drama and managed to find peace, silently accepting his fate. Later in life he made a biographical film, capturing the sublime fragments of living in fluidity. It was entitled 'As I Was Moving Ahead Occasionally I Saw Brief Glimpses of Beauty'.

These days a trip does not mean a lifetime journey anymore. Living in mobility has become easy and accessible for the majority of people. Everybody has a certain knowledge of how various systems function in totally different parts of the world. It is still questionable, though, if the evolution has taken a second loop and we as humans are back to a nomadic way of living. Being in flux all the time asks for a certain alertness just like walking alongside the sea. Beware of the waves crashing towards you.

To continuously move around is to live life without banisters. Nevertheless, we need to hold onto something to prevent ourselves from an endless fall. Coasts have blinking lights which direct and help travellers to navigate and avoid. The lighthouse is a spine for the horizon. The axis that pierces the sea in order to illuminate the end of an empty field of water. It exists on the edge of the horizon, almost in one's imagination. It is a floating structure that neither reaches the land, nor is completely isolated from the waters. The life of a lighthouse keeper is often either romanticised or seen as a desolate life for those who prefer the solitary confines of the role, away from the social rigours of mainland life. It stands still under the moon — the other light that stretches from as high as our galaxy and reaches underwater ecosystems. The moon might be the only companion for the lighthouse keeper — no matter whether full or crescent it measures the time and pushes or pulls the waters around. The modernised automatic blinks of the lighthouse dance in line with, or cross the moonlight. Although nowadays a human is not needed for the lighthouse to lead the way, there are still some places around the world where a person in charge observes the shoreline from above, notifying about the shipwrecks, the lost souls of the oceanic world and those humans who didn't make it across the sea or back to the coast. The lighthouse is a concrete symbol of direction, but the horizon in which we try to find our path remains unstable. Hito Steyerl writes:

10 Reference to D. Haraway's concept of 'Tentacular Thinking' from her book "Staying with the Trouble"

11 Ingold Tim. The Perception of the Environment. Routledge: London and New York, 2000

12 Argonauts — heroes in Greek Mythology who assisted Jason sailing the ship Argo to fetch the Golden Fleece

13 Mekas, Jonas. I Had Nowhere to Go. Leipzig: Spector Books, 2017, p. 291

"Our traditional sense of orientation — and, with it, modern concepts of space and time — are based on a stable line: the horizon line. Its stability hinges on the stability of an observer, who is thought to be located on a ground of sorts, a shoreline, a boat — a ground that can be imagined as stable, even if in fact it is not."[14]

A human eye can only see a maximum 4,5km in front of it, which means that physically our sense of space remains relative. It is the pre-knowledge and the imaginary that reassures us and situates our location on a map. That is perhaps the psychology of a person that is mostly standing vertically and facing the horizontal. While a horizontal body pressed down by gravity is soaking up the immanence of the surroundings, one's mind may experience transcendental sensations, triggered by sounds, smells and the vastness of space.

We are accustomed to living erect, therefore, it is easy to thrive on the shore, but we become vulnerable in the midst of deep seas — the unstable terrain, which asks to adjust both the body and the mind. Yet there are some people who get empowered by living with water. One extraordinary example is the Haeneyo women who work as divers collecting underwater treasures. These South Koreans known for their independent spirit, iron will and determination, represent the semi-matriarchal family structure of Jeju island. Covered in neoprene suits they swim between seaweed bag and the sea floor, living under different pressures. As they surface, each women utters a distinctive cry — a determined groan of endurance and an ancient technique to expel carbon dioxide from the lungs. By working under water Jeju women ensure themselves a stable position in the society on the coast. Living aligned with the horizon they are immersed in the world unlike the majority of contemporary people who have a detached vertical perspective as described by Steyerl.

Haeneyo women show that the ever moving shoreline may empower, but one has to adapt to the surroundings. One's corporality ought to be experienced in a different way — engaged with the environment. Such human relations to the seashore were researched by scientist Anna Ryan in her book 'Where Land Meets Sea':

"People are drawn to the coast — to the paradoxical regularity of its ever-moving and elusive characteristics. This flowing mobility of the meeting of land and sea draws attention to multiple spatial sensations: as well as making the physical mobility of the world materially and visibly apparent, the coast also emphasises the flowing nature of the relationship between body and world."[15]

Standing on the shore for some time, one starts noticing how different elements rhythmically shape a beautiful and gentle dance; a choreography of rockweeds slowly waving during a rising tide, the movement of waves spilling, plunging, collapsing and surging towards the shore, birds traversing aerial space and piercing deep waters, wind combing the beach. Human presence is relatively small — no matter how hard a surfer tries to stand on the board, it is difficult to achieve such an attuned state with the powerful forces around. At the same time, both physical and mental freedom may be experienced there. In the film 'Beau Travail', Claire Denis has shot French Legionnaires on the coast of Djibouti. The paradoxical blurry space is a perfect landscape to place men with erased pasts distancing themselves from their memories. They perform a choreographed training ritual, which is graceful, yet passionate and builds up a lot of tension. Muscular bodies are approaching others with full force. The dusty deserted edge of the land is shot in contrast with the soft waters. It's only when the men swim naked in the sea that they loosen up — their actions become joyful, playful and less cautious, it becomes visible that some have a desire to share intimacy with each other. The coast, though, brings Legionnaires back to reality — controlled and empty lives have to be performed there.

JUST A BLINK

What is it that we are looking for in the sea, standing on the edge of the land? Are we merely mesmerised by the beauty of the natural rhythm, the ephemera of the moment, or is it that attraction of the undiscovered zone that enchants with its mysteriousness. Since this space appears in so many narratives, it is clear that humans tend to romanticise the beauty and the darkness of immense waters. A shelter for the majority of our planet's inhabitants. R. Carson proposes:

"The shore is an ancient world, for as long as there has been an earth and sea there has been this place of the meeting of land and water. It is the elusiveness of that meaning that haunts us, that sends us again and again into the natural world where the key to the riddle is hidden. It sends us back to the edge of the sea, where the drama of life played its first scene on earth and perhaps even its prelude; where the forces of evolution are at work today, as they have been since the appearance of what we know as life; and where the spectacle of living creatures faced by the cosmic realities is crystal clear."[16]

Despite the fact that there is so much negative information circulating around the damage that people are accountable for, it is important to create conditions to avoid the drama. I believe that by noticing and emphasising the beauty of life on earth we could establish an affectionate and respectful relationship with the surroundings and oneself. The seashore is one of the places that can comfort and calm down the tension. Therefore, I wish to represent it in my work as a guardian rather than a threat. It has been the (back)ground in the imagery of art, to situate people looking for hope. The sea is like a warp that stretches in front of ones eyes. It is the given in life and the waves that flow in all directions, go over and under like a weft. It is what happens in life.[17] Edward Munch's painting 'Two Human Beings (The Lonely Ones)' unveils this fluid weave. We see people who face the water that reflects their existence.

I had my first cigarette near the harbour of Reykjavik. Sitting on the lava rock I was watching the pink sky and the never landing summer sun reflected on peaceful waters. Such beauty made me consider paganism and think of the Vikings. It was magical and gave me strength to ebb from Iceland in order to flow further. V. Woolf writes:

"…the monotonous fall of the waves on the beach, which for the most part beat a measured and soothing tattoo to her thoughts and seemed consolingly to repeat over and over again as she sat with the children the words of some old cradle song, murmured by nature, 'I am guarding you — I am your support'."[18]

Try again, board a boat that is leaving your past and heading for the unforeseeable future. Try to escape the burdens the world has put on your shoulders. The waves will help you, they will peel it off your soul and you will reach the lighthouse that is waiting, lonesome, whispering of hope. A moment I am building for is like a second in meditation — there is nothing but the silent death of one's troubled presence in search for bliss. Everybody onshore is mourning the world, but the seagulls above are screeching louder, you are leaving the voices behind, swaying on a boat that is carrying you further. We can't swim together, but we can teach each other to float on the surface. You flip your body and look at the sky, feathery clouds, pale blue sheets above you. You are in the middle of the world and it is a beautiful place to be.

14 Steyerl, Hito. In Free Fall: A Thought Experiment on Vertical Perspective. E-flux Journal #24 – April 2011

15 Ryan, Anna. Where Land Meets Sea. London: Routledge, 2012

16 Carson, Rachel. The Edge of the Sea. London: Staples Press Limited, 1955

17 Interpretation of Richard Tuttle's quote: The warp is what is given in life and the weft is what happens in life.

18 Woolf, Virginia. To the Lighthouse. London: Penguin Books, 1996

Liquid Crystals and Blissful Dots

Morta Jonynaitė

BIBLIOGRAPHY

Blumenberg, Hans. Shipwreck With Spectator : Paradigm of a Metaphor for Existence Studies in Contemporary German Social Thought. Cambridge, Massachusetts: The MIT Press, 1997,

Carson, Rachel. The Edge of the Sea. London: Staples Press Limited, 1955

Haraway, Donna J. Staying with the Trouble. Durham and London: Duke University Press, 2016

Ingold Tim. The Perception of the Environment. Routledge: London and New York, 2000

Mekas, Jonas. I Had Nowhere to Go. Leipzig: Spector Books, 2017

Not if the Seas Rise, but When and How High, https://www.nytimes.com/2017/11/22/books/review-water-will-come-jeff-goodell.html

Steyerl, Hito. In Free Fall: A Thought Experiment on Vertical Perspective. E-flux Journal #24 — April 2011

Rachel Carson and 'Silent Spring', https://www.independent.com/2019/08/29/rachel-carson-and-silent-spring/

Rachel Carson and 'Silent Spring', https://www.independent.com/2019/08/29/rachel-carson-and-silent-spring/

Ryan, Anna. Where Land Meets Sea. London: Routledge, 2012

Whitman, Walt. The Complete Poems: Penguin Books, London, 2004

Woolf, Virginia. To the Lighthouse. London: Penguin Books, 1996

https://www.youtube.com/watch?v=nskUHvjylEA

https://www.youtube.com/watch?v=gH6AsRi4paU

Matilda Kenttä

A Mouth Has More Flesh Than a Butterfly Can Carry

ELINA'S ROOM

Imagine rooms, chambers and entering vaults. Women sitting around blue tables on chairs and in each others beds. A woman lying down on the soft carpet. A hurting back, a broken foot, a healing heart, a hand that no longer obeys. Red tea and pink liquor are passed around the room on trays filled with fruit. A plastic box with homemade jam, fresh bread and some leftover cake. A woman shows a text message from a lover. Her lover works too hard, he is too tired to fall in love. Phones make sounds as Elina sends a text around in the messenger group. Linnea's antibiotics for her infection in her uterus does not work, she is in pain. We're searching the internet for recipes to calm the pain. We read: dandelion and garlic. Someone sighs, while Morta gets up to walk around. Klara enters. Women talking to each other, mouths to ears. Someone wants to expel all men, others object, some of us become Marxists, some desire collectivity. Pernille calls from the kitchen, it's time to start cooking together. We do that a lot. We cook, we eat, while gossiping. The room is moist with our breath. Her voice is becoming moist by the touch of mine.

The technical connotation of a vault is a structure that provides a space, and holds it and opens. It gives form by producing an inside separate from the outside and providing supported cover for those underneath it.

```
To write.
I can't.
No one can.
We have to admit: we cannot.
And yet we write.[1]
```

Marguerite Duras writes this from her vault, her house in the north of France. On the outside of the house was a park with cats, birds and one squirrel but on the inside she was alone. Both she and Virginia Wolf has written from their rooms about the need for solitude to be able to produce text.

In my own solitude I am word blind, its hard for me to write and to read. Because of this I have to leave my room. This essay is written collectively around kitchen tables carving in thought into text together with my friends. My friends give written words to the word blind, reading text out loud. I bring them banana bread and gossip as return. How economic. Economic has its Greek root in *oikos*, indicating a domestic habit, house, or family — a familiar ecosystem. Often this domestic landscape is a site that is thought on historically as being voiceless. Anne Carson writes in her essay "The gender of sound" describing echo; as a girl with no door to her mouth[2]. I write in a landscape without doors where the echo of my voice bounces down to the pages through my friends fingertips.

Dear Linnea, Pernille, Morta, Bronwen, Klara, Amanda, and Elina this essay is written by and for you.

Lisa Robertson writes: *"The domestic, that urgent foundation for natality, will here be considered in terms of a mediating skin, rather than in term of a private interiority conceptually opposed to a social outside. This mediating condition will be inflected temporally, rather than spatially, since its limit is less structurally architectural than flexibly transformative: the taking in preparation of food, of erotic encounter, of various modes of work, of reproductive labor, of the production of an affective surplus and the constant re-initiation into a freshened verbal motility — the Domus is the place of rhythmic protection of the vulnerable body, while sleeping, in illness, age, and childhood. Often while eating and washing, while resting while talking and working. So the domestic sphere isn't private just as the body and the models of conviviality, reproduction and care aren't private…"*[3]

Bell Hooks answers in her essay *The homeplace as a site of resistance*: "we could not learn to love or respect ourselves in the culture of white supremacy, on the outside; it was there on the inside, in that "homeplace", most often created and kept by black women, that we had opportunity to grow and develop, to nurture our spirits. This task of making a homeplace, of making home a community of resisters, has been shared by black women globally, especially black women in white supremacist societies."[4]

Quinn Latimer adds: *"Well, food and meals-whom we take them with, cook them for-can also be a kind of style. A kind of criticism. A kind of daughterhood, also…"*[5]

I believe it is on the inside that our care is nurtured and generated. Through our gatherings we practice radical care on a daily basis. Our gossip develops strategies and forms of resistance; for how we, as more or less, females can take care of each other in precarious times. How can we take care of one another so that we survive: mentally, financially, physically and politically?

CRY-CALL

The last time I was heartbroken I pushed a Helen Marten vase off it's pedestal onto the floor and it broke, it was an accident, the vase and the heart. The vase spelled out shame and left me crying outside the König gallery. I had gone from Amsterdam the day before, with the mission to get over a long love and meet an old one in Berlin. Between the time that I bought the ticket the night before and when I was standing at the airport some hours later, the old lover who had invited me had changed his mind. When I cry—I call Lovisa. Lovisa has the ability to cook up some sort of conspiracy theory that suits my failures and shames. She instructed me to go to a bar, to drink and read. For the next four days, Morta sends maps that lead to Surinamese food, she asks how I am doing, I reply by sending a picture of the blue jeans I bought. I follow Lovisa's advice, wasting time at bars reading. The book that I brought is *Caliban and the Witch: Women, the Body and Primitive Accumulation* by marxist, feminist theorist Silvia Federici. The book came to me from Elina, it came to her when she attended a reading group with Amelia Groom at the Rietveld some years ago. On page 186 I underline with blue ink: *"it was also in this period that the word "gossip" which in the middle ages meant "friend" changed its meaning, acquiring a derogatory connotation, a further sign of the degree to which the power and communal ties were undermined."*[6]

Nearly 500 years or so have passed since gossip meant friend. Nearly a year has passed since my heartbreak. This year that I have spent thinking about and with my gossips, slowly redefining "friend" as not a full enough definition for a close female friend. The word gossip carries another layer of expectation, like the term "girlfriend" or "comrade" or "mother". I couldn't help but wonder: how have we settled on calling each other "friends", and why has "gossip" ("close female friend") come to have such a negative connotation.

GOSSIP GIRL

In another bar in Amsterdam late last fall Pernille and I were drinking in her honour. Next to me at the table sat a guy that works at the Rietveld, he remembered that I was graduating and asked me what I was writing about for my thesis. I told him that I was trying to write about gossip. He seemed amused by my topic and asked if I was going to have any good gossip in it. I asked if he had any good gossip that he would like to share and he said that he did not. I once again referred to Silvia Federici, of how gossip once meant friend, and how the highly gendered meaning of gossiping had changed over the last centuries. I had a speech ready for the guy; that over the centuries patriarchy

1 Duras, Marguerite: Writing, Éditions Gallimard, Paris, 1993. p. 43

2 Carson, Anne: Glass, irony, and God, New York, 1995. p. 121

3 Robertson, Lisa. Nilling : Prose Essays on Noise, Pornography, the Codex, Melancholy, Lucretius, Folds, Cities and Related Aporias. Toronto, Bookthug, 2012. p. 75

4 Hooks, Bell. *Yearning : Race, Gender, and Cultural Politics.* New York, Routledge, Taylor & Francis Group, 2015. p. 384

5 Latimer, Quinn: Like a Women, Essays, Redings, Poems. Berlin, Sternberg Press. 2017. p. 45

6 Federici, Silvia. Caliban and the Witch : Women, the Body and Primitive Accumulation. New York, Autonomedia, 2014. p. 186

has managed to completely erase the solidarity that the gossips once generated. The meaning of gossip we know today has been shaped by the patriarchal regime, creating the idea of women being stupid and lazy and wasting their time together gossiping. Spreading rumours and spreading lies, irrational thoughts. Somewhere here I stop for a bit of air and end the monologue with how the hatred of gossip is hatred of women talking to each other.

Marie Thompson writes; "To be sure, gossip carries with it the idea that women talking together makes trouble for men... since men and their wrongdoings are often suspected to be the subject of women's idle chatter"[7].

Gossip is seen as talk with the potential to cause trouble and bring about disorder. But maybe this potential is what makes it powerful for women, it disrupts normative forces and brings women together.

Gossip was a form of resistance to being controlled. During 16th century torture devices were shaped to tame the female tongue. Women were the targets during the witch hunt. They stood in front of courts in trials accused, forced under torture to denounce each other[8]. Daughters turning on their mothers and mothers on their daughters. Gossips turning their backs on gossips. Women were accused of being unreasonable, vain, wild, wistful. The female tongue was particularly blamed. A women could be punished for any demonstration of independence and criticism against her husband and was increasingly expected not to speak. One way of punishing and attempting to tame the female tongue was the *gossip bridle or scolds bridle*[9]. The same devices were used on the mouths of slaves who were insubordinate, when they were kidnapped and forcibly transferred over the the Atlantic Ocean under colonisation. It was a sadistic torture device of metal and leather with a framework that enclosed her head. A metal curb-plate with spikes on the top was slipped into her mouth to press down her tongue or to lay her tongue flat on the spikes. If she attempted to speak her tongue was torn apart. The *gossip bridle* was to be worn in the public sphere as a warning for other women in the community to keep their mouths shut.

Pernille and the guy at the bar continue our conversation which leads to gossip-magazines, the shiny sticky ones. He said that he didn't understand people's interest in other people's business. Pernille reminded him that gossip means friend, that gossiping is something she does alongside close friends. She points out the need of gossiping as a way of washing or cleansing her shame. A stain, a mark of: sticky saliva, wine, oil, mucus, sweat, sperm, lipstick etc. Something small but permanent that ruins the whole skirt.

On the bike home Pernille and I chat about those nights that cause stains and how we have a need in the morning to call each other so her words can rub the stain off my skirt.

Gossip is a protection against shame and a carrier of warnings, it is needed because women are more commonly victims of sexual and domestic violence.

I begin to imagine gossip as a network. A net that ties information. It's a net woven inside rooms, but it can leak to the outside. The construction of gossip is that you take your own shame and weave it into a net together with theory and experience, battling old warnings and suffering new longing. You bring it outside as a security net in which you can fall into. It can betray when it leaks. When ambition and relationship fails, then you also have this net of security that you can lean on and fall on. It both leaks and carries you.

Hanna Black writes: "Communities of gossips nurse each other through the degradations that partners, bosses and families inflict on us. Without the love of gossips, most of us would be either dead or dead inside."[10]

Elina answers: "We have to tell, otherwise it doesn't exist. We have to tell to be able to understand and relate. It has to be given a tongue and a voice—it has to be received by an ear. It exists when someone listens. It changes, improves, strengthens, worsens, undermines, destroys and sublimates as it travels. Always alive. As long as it's alive it's gossip, as long as it's gossip it's alive."

(THE MAGIC WORDS: 'YES, DARLING, YOU ARE A REAL WOMAN')

In Silvia Federici's essay On the Meaning of 'Gossip', she continues her work tracing the herstory of the highly gendered concept of the meaning of gossip. "In the 16th century it was a neutral or even positive term of female companionship. Federici writes "In the 16th century, the English terms God and sibb (akin), 'gossip', originally meant 'godparent'—one who stands in a spiritual relation to the child to be baptized. In time, however, the term was used with a broader meaning. In early modern England the word 'gossip' referred to companions in childbirth not limited to the midwife. It also became a term for women friends."[11]

During The Middle Ages the woman had gossips. She shared her life and labour alongside the women of her neighbourhood. Women as gossips moved freely between the communal land and domestic spaces. Her movement was independent from the man in the neighbourhood. Federici continues: "for neither in rural nor urban areas where women were dependent on men for their survival; they had their own activities and shared much of their lives and work with other women. Women cooperated with each other in every aspect of their life. They sewed, washed their clothes, and gave birth surrounded by other women, with men rigorously excluded from the chamber of the delivering one."[12]

In Europe in the late 16th century during the beginning of capitalism, gossips could see the common land being taken away from them. Before, the land was consolidated by small farms and public land (the commons). This all changed when the state and church stole this land converting it into private property, making them landlords with sole rights to the land's produce. The working class could rent land or work on it. It was necessary for the landlords that the vast majority of the population would be dependent on a wage for survival.[13] The workers that cultivated the fields received a wage. Both men and women worked on the fields together, but the the wages were received by the men. The women found themselves dependent, firstly on their fathers as daughters, and later on their husbands as wives. This hid their status as workers, while giving men free access to their bodies and labour. A woman was dependent on her husband while working in the fields, but at the same time, her husband depended on her to perform unwaged labor of social reproduction within the home. The separation of commodity production from the reproduction labour made the accumulation of unpaid labour possible — labour done within the domestic sphere. To card and comb wool, to patch and to wash, to rub flax and reel yarn, to peel rushes, to weave the cloths.

In Sadie Plant's book *Zeros+Ones* she writes: "The weaving of complex designs demands far more than one pair of hands, and textiles production tends to be communal, sociable work allowing plenty of occasion for gossip and chat. Weaving was already multimedia: singing, chanting, telling stories, dancing, and playing games as they work, spinsters, weavers, and needle workers we literally networkers as well."[14]

7   Thompson, Maria. Gossips, sirens, Hi-Fi Wives: Feminizing the Threat of Noise, in Resonances: Noise and Contemporary Music. New York, Bloomsburg, 2013. p. 301

8   Federici, Silvia. Caliban and the Witch : Women, the Body and Primitive Accumulation. New York, Autonomedia, 2014. p.197

9   Federici, Silvia. Witches, Witch-Hunting, and Women. Toronto, Between The Lines, 2018. p. 58

10 Black, Hanna. Gossip has always been a secret language of friendship and resistance between women. The Gossip Issue. The TANK Magazine. 2017.p.56

11 Federici, Silvia. Witches, Witch-Hunting, and Women. Toronto, Between The Lines, 2018. p. 56

12 Federici, Silvia. Witches, Witch-Hunting, and Women. Toronto, Between The Lines, 2018. p. 59

13 Federici, Silvia. Caliban and the Witch : Women, the Body and Primitive Accumulation. New York, Autonomedia, 2014. p.75

14 Plant, Sadie. Zeros and Ones : Digital Women and the New Technoculture. London Fourth Estate, 1998. p. 65

Women's labour has been exploited since the middle ages. Centuries later, in 1974, the campaign *Wages Against Housework* writes in their manifesto of the exploitation: *"We must admit that capital has been very successful in hiding our work. It has created a true masterpiece at the expense of women. By denying housework a wage and transforming it into an act of love, capital has killed many birds with one stone. First of all, it has got a hell of a lot of work almost for free, and it has made sure that women, far from struggling against it, would seek that work as the best thing in life (the magic words: 'Yes, darling, you are a real woman')."*[15]

The private ownership of the land encouraged labour power, entailing the demise of bodily power, just as nature diminished through cultivation. As a form of resistance to this irreversible change women often practiced forms of magic. The magic practice was a communal practice and knowledge, it was gossip among friends. The basis of magic was an animistic conception of nature that imagined the cosmos as a living organism[16]. She knew the apron she wove was once flax on the field and that wheat creates bread, that bread stills hunger, that three leaves on the tongue becomes a potion for abortion. The conflict was that womanhood also longed for a knowledge not only to bring up life, but also to use the advantages of wild nature. To create agency. To provoke abortion and sterility. A knowledge about the ability to not become mothers. And most importantly to share this knowledge with fellow women — to relate to nature and each other.

That was the disruptive force. This force was what led to the barbarity of the witch hunt, which emerged as a way to police women and their potentially subversive activities; from the refusal to pay rents and taxes, to exercising reproductive control. During this hunt on women and the communal land, one starts to see a change in the meaning of gossip in the public sphere where gossips once dwelled — wasting time and sharing time. During the hunt on women the squares in villages became stages for burning women, accused by courts of performing/ spreading magic and cooperation with the devil[17]. Women were shamed and the communal bond was broken. Women started policing each other, this resulted in rumours which made women have to act within their restricted roles of the nuclear family, so that they weren't accused of being witches. Gossip became rumours and female friendships became an object of suspicion, denounced from the pulpit as subversive of the alliance between husband and wife.

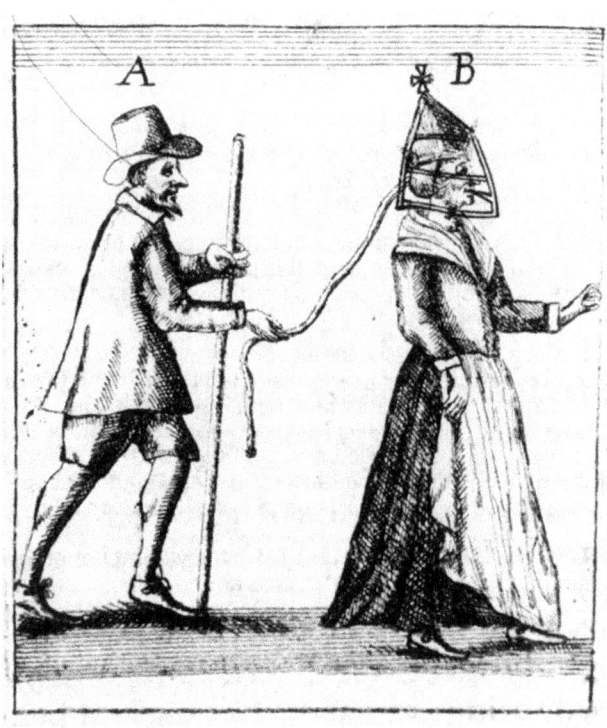

English School, 17th Century. Medium: engraving. Ancient punishment in use at Newcastle in the North of England.

15 Federici, Silvia. Wages Against Housework ,Montpelier, The Power of Women Collective and the Falling Wall Press,1975. p. 3

16 Federici, Silvia. Caliban and the Witch : Women, the Body and Primitive Accumulation. New York, Autonomedia, 2014. p. 141

17 Federici, Silvia. Caliban and the Witch : Women, the Body and Primitive Accumulation. New York, Autonomedia, 2014. p. 102

MACHINES REMIND ME
OF MY LONELINESS

When iron interacts with oxygen it turns red, Amanda tells me. I note a red stain on my skirt. I have leaked, bled through my skirt. Elina instructs me: Let the skirt soak in cold water for one hour. She borrows me her gall soap that she got from her mother. A gall soap is made from the bile of mammals. Rub the gall on the blood stain and the stain turns light pink. Leave the pink stain for one hour, then rinse it under cold water. It is like a potion. My washing machine starts to remind me of my loneliness while reading about communal living at the time when women were gossips. Women were not doing maintenance work separate from each other. They washed once a month on the riverbanks alongside the women in their neighbourhood. Rubbing soap against blood stains from war, labour, hunt. To make the hard labour smoother they sang, talked, laughed, maybe smoked cigarettes together as the laundry was drying in the wind. That was how they shared lives, shared linen. Silvia Federici adds: *"All over Europe you can see the signs of this collective way of washing, in many places with big seminar tubs, where women collectively washed. You had festivals, everything, every aspect of lives was collective, that was a great power."*[18] While thinking about this particular power I read Hanna Arendt's words in The Human Condition, *"The only indispensable material factor in the generation of power is the living together of people. Only where men live so close together that the potentialities of action are always present can power remain with them…"*[19]

Along the course of history washing has become more and more isolating. From the medieval washing together, to becoming a wife and the washer of the nuclear family on the so called *"Blue Mondays"*[20],. After the second world war, architecture historian Beatriz Colomina writes in her book *Domesticity At War* about how American and European manufacturers adapted the techniques and materials that were developed for military applications to domestic use. Just as manufacturers were turning wartime industry to peacetime productivity — going from missiles to washing machines[21]. This meant washing machines became cheaper and many households were able to purchase one. The story has been told that the washing machine played a part in the second wave feminism in the 60's. It was told that it saved women's labour power and gave them the time to enter the labour market and receive a wage, and in that way gain independence. This created a double exploitation for women doing wage work and housework. This was a domestic exploitation which created isolation, friends were replaced by washing machines. Federici describes how by doing work together one builds strong ties and solidarity, but washing, in the same way as gossip, has never been connected with power or solidarity.[22]

Gossip is not seen as an act of solidarity, but an integral part of the devaluation of women's personality and work, especially domestic work. In the labour performance upon the domestic terrain, the act of gossip flourishes. I want to think about washing as a generator of power, generating powerful hands, doing meaningful labour. The potion of cleaning with the hands soaked in soap, rinsing out the: glass, plate, tile, bamboo, plastic, violence, desire, debt, metal, minerals, sex and leave the room smelling of lavender.

Once I worked in an elderly care facility in a miner town. Many retired miners lived there, their bodies had become soft from the iron in the mine. The soft heavy bodies are filled with fluid, the bodies are thirsty and they are leaking. That generates a lot of laundry. The maintenance work never dried, it's wet. My hands made circulating movements, holding wet rags that have sucked up coffee on t-shirts and tables. The textile fibres of the cloth swell in contact with water, opening and sucking. The stains do not dissolve, they move from one to the other. Cleaning is invisible when one performs it well. In the afternoon was my favourite part of the day, when I worked in the washing room. A room with four washing machines and one drier, where you washed their clothing and linen. The room was always warm from the machines and the sounds of the drum beating made it a good place for gossiping. Our break room was very close to our boss's office so on our breaks we also went to the washing room to gossip. Sometimes, while one was folding laundry, a colleague could come in with a cup of tea to share information from the morning or their weekend plans. Everything was intertwining; the clean and the filthy linen, the break chatting and the labour. On one of these afternoons I take a seat around the table and drink coffee with one of the retired miners. He speaks of legends from 1968 and the wild strike in the mine, how they read Marx and Engels and dreamt of reclaiming the means of production. At the end of the day I can see my workday on the apron I borrow from the municipality. I put it in a speckled cleaning basket for the night staff. The next morning my apron is folded and clean. All production leaves behind maintenance.

THE MAINTENANCE WORK
NEVER DRIED, IT'S WET.

In *The German Ideology*, written around 1845-1846 by Karl Marx and Friedrich Engels caricatured socialism as utopian and described their own strategy of organising industrial workers as scientific socialism. They lost sight of the female half of the human race, whose household labour was essential to society and was also shaped by industrial capitalism[23]. Having developed a much more incisive critique of capital and its workings than the communitarians, Marxist socialists talked persuasively to male industrial workers about seizing the means of production and ignored women's work and reproduction. Socialists such as Engels and Lenin argued that women's equality would result from their involvement in industrial production, which would be made possible by the provision of socialised childcare and food preparation. Socialised domestic work was, for them, only a means to this end. They did not consider socialised domestic work to be meaningful work, and they assumed that it would be done by low-status women.

During the same period of time in the beginning of the new century. A wave of American women moved from the countryside to the cities. They saw the urban landscape get lit up with electric vacuum cleaners, mechanical dishwashers and steam washing machines. These were made for use in large enterprises such as hotels, restaurants, and commercial laundries. This technology was first developed at a scale suitable for fifty to five hundred people. In one of these brightly lit cities, Susan B. Anthony wrote in 1871 : *"Away with your man-visions! Women propose to reject them all, and begin to dream dreams for themselves."*[24]

I find this calling for new reclamation and dreams in Dolores Hayden's book *The Grand Domestic Revolution* published in 1981. The first line in the book: *"Cooking food, caring for children, and cleaning house, tasks often thought of as "woman's work" to be performed without pay in domestic environments, have always been a major part of the world's necessary labor."*[25] The book moves around the first feminists in the United States to identify the economic exploitation of women's domestic world in the beginning of the new century. Hayden names this feminism, Material Feminism.

18 2019-09-13, The Dig, Podcast, The Dig ,https://www.thedigradio.
    com/podcast/silvia-federici-on-women-and-capitalism/

19 Arendt, Hannah. *The Human Condition. (Fifth Impression.).*
    Chicago & London: University Of Chicago Press, 1969. p. 221

20 Wikipedia Contributors. "Blue Monday (Term)." Wikipedia,
    Wikimedia Foundation, 30 Aug. 2018, en.wikipedia.org/wiki/
    Blue_Monday_(term). In literature of the 1830s, Blue Monday
    referred to the hungover state of the labor workforce after a
    weekend spent drinking, and the association of the color blue
    with a depressed state of mind.[1] In the 1860s, the term began
    to be applied to a weekly home "wash day." White clothing was
    sometimes rinsed with bluing.

21 Colomina, Beatriz. *Domesticity at War.* Barcelona,
    Actar, 2007. p. 12

22 Federici, Silvia. *Witches, Witch-Hunting, and Women.*
    Toronto, Between The Lines, 2018. p. 51

23 Marx, Karl, and Friedrich Engels. Collected Works / Vol. 5,
    Marx and Engels: 1845-47. New York, International Publishers,
    1976. p. 47

24 Hayden, Dolores. The Grand Domestic Revolution. S.L.,
    S.N.1982. p. 3

25 Hayden, Dolores. The Grand Domestic Revolution. S.L.,
    S.N.1982. p. 1

Hayden continues: "*The material feminist argued that women must assert control over the important work of reproduction which they were already performing, and reorganize it to obtain economic justice for themselves. They demanded both remuneration and honor for woman's traditional sphere of work, while conceding that some women might wish to do other kinds of work. They were not prepared to let men argue that a woman's equality would ultimately rest on her ability to undertake "man's" work in a factory or an office.*"[26]

The Material feminists that worked in these enterprises with the big bright machines, realised that they could also use these large scale domestic apparatuses to break the traditional solitary housework by socialising it, and plan for collective domestic consumption by organising. In contrast to the marxist thought of mechanising the means of reproduction the material feminists wanted to mechanise the domestic work by socialising it and breaking the binary boundaries between the public and the domestic sphere.

I imagine: their aim as a way to bring tender, loud gossip back from the secret interior into the public domain. On every other Wednesday the gossips bring the big washing machines to the park as they are portable. This Wednesday it is a sunny morning, they plug the machine into a wall. At ten o'clock more gossips arrive from the neighbourhood carrying their white linen. They place the linen in the washing machine and pour soap inside and the park starts to smell of lavender, even in early May. While the machine cleans the linen with waves, the gossips wash by hand the tender animal fibres in the fountain, the water is warmed with sunshine. When the work is done the gossips hang the white linen out to dry with the wind and drink orange juice.

```
Like linen, like mouth
We dip our hands in to each others
Mother lays linen in boiling water
I am always dressed in boiled linen
I wake up in boiled linen,
I fall asleep in boiled linen
linen like mouth would not dry —
It was wet
The mouth is wet as long as we live,
the linen drips as long as it boils.
```

LESSON FROM THE KITCHEN

A mouth is wet. It swallows the spit which produced language. The mouth made *the bread into dough again*. We have moisture within us, we lick off stains with our tongues. The cat licks its babies to make them clean — that is a way of washing. The moisture keeps it moving and flowing. It produces tender gossip and sharpens the tongue.

My grandmother Inger was born on one side of a river. Before she was born the river became a line in the Northern landscape. Like all lines in landscape they produce ownership over the land. The river *Torneälven* became, in 1809, a separation between the national state Sweden from Finland. On both sides of the river the mother tongue was spoken and some still speak Meänkieli, a language that leaks between Swedish and Finnish. Women gathered water on both sides of the river for boiling linen, they spoke through the river. Mother tongue shouted, "Come over the river", "Come home it is time for dinner". Mother tongue is an endless landscape.

By the river was a kitchen. The kitchen was surrounded by mountains and forest. Baked bread feeds a greedy daughter who receives it at the table when it is still steaming warm from the oven. The butter drips from her mouth, of her mother's work. 2 slices of whole grain bread contribute 10% of a young woman's iron needs.[27]

In the beginning of the 20th century the Swedish state began to mine iron in these mountains. Laying the railway from the south to the north. Bending the forest into timber, turning mountains into iron and minerals, exploiting the land and transporting the goods to the south. The Swedish state also placed its schools where the railway line was drawn. The Meänkieli-children had to start the Swedish state school and were forbidden to speak Meänkieli there, instead having to learn Swedish. Bending mother tongue into Swedish is a punishment.

She will have to grow into a voice, mould the tongue to make it hers. Elma spoke Meänkieli to her daughter, she named her Inger. Inger was the first daughter to attend a Swedish school and learn to speak Swedish. Inger spoke Swedish to her daughter, she named her Anette. Anette aimed to understand her mother's gossip in the kitchen, she learned to mend her ears but never to speak in her mothers tongue. Anette spoke Swedish to her daughter. I am the first one who doesn't speak nor understand this mother tongue.

Still I get very happy whenever I listen to Meänkieli during a summer spent in the kitchen. My aunts enter the kitchen where Inger is baking bread, in domestic architecture. I boil coffee and find some leftover cake, we take a seat at the table. The gossip crosses back and forth around the table. I hear names passing by. Lilly goes out for a smoke, Inger gets up and turns on the oven. When the smoker comes in again she's carrying items to trade: shared knowledge, insight. Lilly asks me if I understand what they are saying, I say that I don't. One aunt apologises, while another aunt starts: "*We were forbidden to speak Meänkieli in school, even on our breaks. But of course we broke the rules, we had to talk. Talk to each other. We had to speak the language that we could speak. Meänkieli was the only language I could speak when I started school.*"

Gossip crosses back and forth across tables, between homes and worlds, between domestic and public, carrying items to trade in confinement. When we gossip it is generally women who do this work of love. When we gossip, we share vital information: this one is sad, this one is in love, this one is dangerous.[28]

When my gossiping aunts have gone home, me and my grandmother return to the bread, in the kitchen surrounded by forest and mountains. We continue to gossip. She tells me the first sentences of Swedish she learned in school.

```
Far är rar
Father is sweet
Mor är en orm
Mother is a snake
```

(in Swedish it rhymes)

A snake has a split tongue. The snake is flexible and can fill out cracks. The gossip sits at the window, fills it out, the tongue wants to find an escape — a crack. It leaks. The crack is also an opening, like the door and the window. Gossip also cracks walls open, it is commu- nication between the houses that women gossip in. The house is whole and concrete, but gossip leaks through, it leaks and cracks. The domestic house, if it is made of stone it cracks. If it is made of wood it leaks. Gossip always finds a way out.

26 Hayden, Dolores. The Grand Domestic Revolution. S.L., S.N.1982. p. 6

27 Brödinstitutet Kommunicerar Bröd & Hälsa, Klimatsmarta Val Och God Mat." Brödinsti- tutet, 2019, www.brodinstitutet.se/om-brodinstitutet/.

28 Black, Hanna. Gossip has always been a secret language of friendship and resistance between women. The Gossip Issue. The TANK Magazine. 2017.p.55

BIBLIOGRAPHY

Arendt, Hannah. The Human Condition. (Fifth Impression.).
Chicago & London: Universi- ty Of Chicago Press, 1969.

Black, Hanna. Gossip has always been a secret language of
friendship and resistance between women. The Gossip Issue.
The TANK Magazine. 2017.

Carson, Anne: Glass, irony, and God, New York, 1995. p. 121
Colomina, Beatriz. Domesticity at War. Barcelona, Actar, 2007.

Duras, Marguerite: Writing, Éditions Gallimard, Paris, 1993. p. 43

Federici, Silvia. Caliban and the Witch : Women, the Body
and Primitive Accumulation. New York, Autonomedia, 2014.

Federici, Silvia. Wages Against Housework ,Montpelier,
The Power of Women Collective and the Falling Wall Press,1975.

Federici, Silvia. Witches, Witch-Hunting, and Women. Toronto,
Between The Lines, 2018. Hayden, Dolores. The Grand Domestic
Revolution. S.L., S.N.1982.

hooks, bell. Yearning : Race, Gender, and Cultural Politics.
New York, Routledge, Taylor & Francis Group, 2015.

Latimer, Quinn: Like a Women,Essays, Redings, Poems.
Berlin, Sternberg Press.2017.

Marx, Karl, and Friedrich Engels. Collected Works / Vol. 5, Marx
and Engels: 1845-47. New York, International Publishers, 1976.

Plant, Sadie. Zeros and Ones : Digital Women
and the New Technoculture. London Fourth Estate, 1998.

Robertson, Lisa. Nilling : Prose Essays on Noise, Pornography,
the Codex, Melancholy, Lucretius, Folds, Cities and Related
Aporias. Toronto, Bookthug, 2012.

Thompson, Maria. Gossips, sirens, Hi-Fi Wives: Feminizing
the Threat of Noice, in Reso- nances: Noise an Contemporary Music.
New York, Bloomsburg, 2013.

WEB AND PODCAST

The Dig, Podcast, 2019-09-13, The Dig,https://www.thedigradio.com/
podcast/silvia-fede- rici-on-women-and-capitalism/

Wikipedia Contributors." Wikipedia, Wikimedia Foundation,
30 Aug. 2018, en.wikipedi- a.org/wiki/Blue_Monday_(term).

"Brödinstitutet Kommunicerar Bröd & Hälsa, Klimatsmarta Val
Och God Mat." Brödinsti- tutet, 2019, www.brodinstitutet.se/om-
brodinstitutet/.

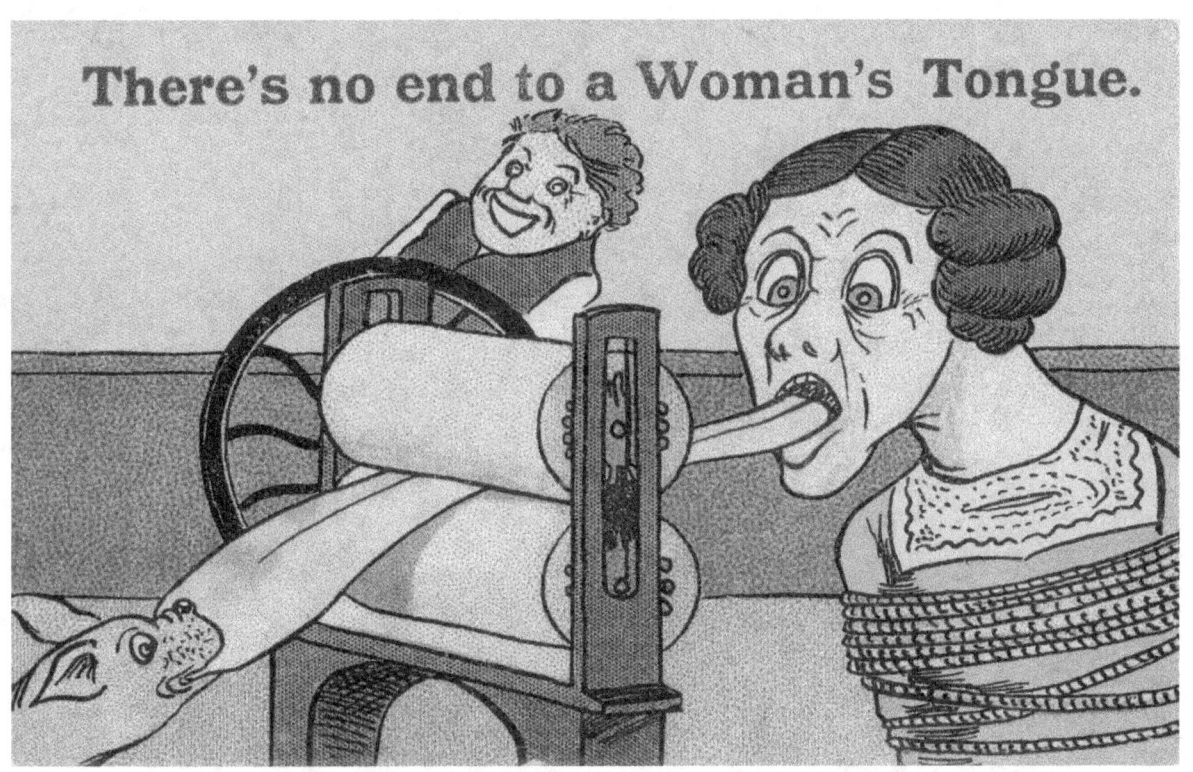

Anti suffragette, There's no end to a Women's Tongue,
Corona Publishing Co. 20th Century, Glasgow Women's Library.

Vera Laarakker

Een vaas
Een schoen
En de zee

*Een vaas
Een schoen
En de zee*

Dera Laarakker

Onlangs ben ik in het bezit gekomen van een Egyptische thee set. Een theepot, suikerpotje en een melkkannetje van keramiek met daarop Egyptische symboliek. Van mijn kant was het liefde op het eerste gezicht. Het object zelf hulde zich in mysterie. Het lijkt fabrieksmatige keramiek, maar doordat er oneffenheden en afgebroken stukjes duidelijk zichtbaar zijn, creëert het een gevoel van authentiek handwerk. Ik begon symbolen te herkennen en realiseerde ik me dat ik helemaal niet naar hiërogliefen aan het kijken was, maar naar een verzameling van bekende Egyptische symboliek en afbeeldingen die mensen vandaag de dag linken aan de Egyptische oudheid. Aan de zijkant van de theepot staat bijvoorbeeld een Ankh afgebeeld.

In de oudheid droegen de Egyptenaren de Ankh bij zich als teken van hun onsterfelijkheid, als een sleutel voor het eeuwig geluk; wanneer mensen het dragen, wordt daarmee aangegeven dat zij deze wereld voor het hiernamaals hebben ingeruild. Het werd geacht bescherming te bieden aan hen tegen allerlei gevaren. Interessant, maar dit geeft echter geen duidelijkheid over wat er dan wel mee bedoeld wordt in de context van deze thee set. De set hult zich in mysterie. Het doet zich voor als iets met toch zeker een gedachte achter de plaatsing van de symbolen. Een soort simulatie van betekenis. En alhoewel ik nog steeds tevreden mijn kopjes thee uit deze thee set drink heeft het wat stof doen opwaaien. Ik begon me af te vragen welke rol heeft materiaal zoals keramiek maar ook textiel bijvoorbeeld in het overdragen van boodschappen, levenslessen en verhalen uit het heden en verleden? En zijn er verschillen tussen deze media in de manier waarop zij deze overdragen en het verleden laten voortbestaan?

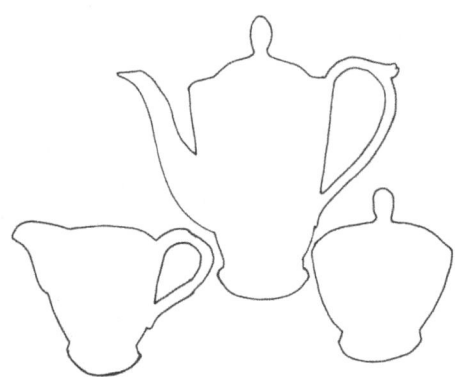

Afbeelding 1 –
Een visualisatie van de thee set

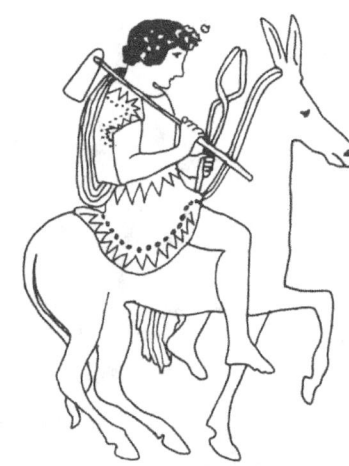

Afbeelding 2 –
Detail uit het verhaal 'de terugkeer van Hephaistos'

FAMILIE

Op een hoge berg in Griekenland, de Olympus, werd heel heel lang geleden een jongetje geboren. Een god, die later zou uitgroeien tot een van de meest befaamde ambachtslieden ooit: Hephaistos. Hera, godin van het huwelijk en de vruchtbaarheid, is zijn moeder. Wie zijn vader was? Het werd in de loop van de eeuwen een redelijk ingewikkeld verhaal. Er gaan twee theorieën de ronde. Allereerst een verhaal afkomstig uit Homerus' Ilias. De vader van Hephaistos zou Zeus zijn, hij wordt gezien als de oppergod van de Griekse oudheid. Zeus is de broer en tevens de echtgenoot van Hera. Incest was op dat moment niet zo controversieel. Tijdens een echtelijke twist tussen zijn ouders zou Hephaistos zijn moeder te hulp zijn geschoten, om haar te beschermen tegen de wrok van zijn vader, die snel aangebrand was. Zeus, inmiddels woest, pakte Hephaistos bij zijn been en wierp hem van de berg Olympus af. Hij kwam helemaal terecht op het eiland Lemnos. Een volk uit Thracië, de Sintiërs, die met een volksverhuizing op Lemnos terecht zijn gekomen, verpleegde hem maar hij bleef zijn hele onsterfelijke leven mank.[1]

In de tweede versie had Hephaistos helemaal geen vader. Volgens Griekse dichter Hesiodus kreeg Hera het kind omdat Zeus alleen een dochter kreeg, Athena. Hera zon op wraak en kreeg zelf ook een kind, Hephaistos. Bij de geboorte was Hephaistos mank, vaak daarbij omschreven als lelijk. Hera bekeek vol afschuw het kind dat ze gebaard had. Uit schaamte wierp ze hem van Olympus, wat ook werd gezien als het huis van de goden. Dit kwam zijn mankheid echter niet ten goede. Hij belandde in de oceaan en werd later opgevist door Tethys (een Titaan maar tevens de godin van de zee en ondergrondse rivieren, wordt ook vaak gezien als de beschermheilige voor de zorg van kinderen) en Eurynome (een waternimf). Zij namen hem onder hen hoede en voedden hem op in een diepe grote donkere grot bij de zee.

Voortbordurend op de tweede versie blijkt dat, toen hij ouder was, hij zich besloot te wreken door aan zijn moeder een door hem gesmede gouden troon te schenken. Wanneer zij daar echter plaats op nam, was ze er plotseling aan vast geketend en niemand behalve Hephaistos zelf kon haar bevrijden.[2]

Al vanaf zijn geboorte, welke van de twee verhalen je ook geloofd, had Hephaistos een moeilijke relatie met de andere goden van Olympus. Op het moment dat het verhaal uit uitkwam wat hij met zijn moeder gedaan had, smeekte de goden hem om haar vrijlating. Hij weigerde om met alle andere goden te praten, behalve Dionysos (vooral bekend als god van de wijn), die vertrouwde hij blindelings. Achteraf gezien had hij dit beter niet kunnen doen. Dionysos voerde hem erg dronken waardoor hij niet meer op zijn eigen benen kon staan.[3]

De vaas uit het hoofdstuk 'de terugkeer van Hephaistos' visualiseert wat er zich vervolgens in het verhaal afspeelt. Hephaistos, te dronken om te lopen, zit achterop een ezel en houdt zijn hamer en tang vast. De ezel wordt geleid door Dionysos, die een Thyrsus (een staf met een dennenappel aan het einde) vasthoudt en een drinkbeker. Voor hem loopt een Satiricus (een Satyr kind). Een Satyr is een menselijk wezen met bokkenstaart, -oren en soms ook -poten.) Dat is waar het verhaal op deze vaas stopt. Er zijn echter versies waarbij Hera te zien is, vastgebonden aan de troon, wachtend om bevrijd te worden door de zoon die ze nooit gewild had.[4]

1 The Greek Myths ,Robert Graves –
   Penguin Books Ltd, 2012 – p. 63

2 https://www.greek-gods.info/greek-gods/
   hephaestus/myths/hephaestus-revenge/

3 https://www.theoi.com/Gallery/K7.1.html

4 ibid

Hephaistos is een mooi voorbeeld als het over materialen en boodschappen gaat. Naast dat hij al vanuit de oudheid gezien wordt als een befaamd ambachtsman, is hij uiteindelijk de overdrager van een boodschap. Zijn hele bestaan is een balans tussen het verhaal en de manier waarop het verteld wordt. Enerzijds vanuit zijn eigen visie en afbeelding in de oude teksten, anderzijds als visualisatie van de ambachtsman.

De ambachtsman creëert, maar vertelt ook een verhaal. Hoe hij iets maakt, is een verhaal op zichzelf. Voor zijn creatie geldt dit ook. Voor mij geldt dit als een reden, waarom ik mij verbonden voel met deze mythologische figuur. Zelf zie ik mij als ambachtsvrouw, kunstenaar en verhalenverteller. Wat relevant is om hierbij te vertellen, is dat ik een 4-jarige beroepsopleiding keramiek heb gevolgd en dit is nog steeds de hoek waarin ik me het meeste op mijn gemak voel. Het mooie van wat er over Hephaistos wordt geschreven, door bijvoorbeeld Richard Sennet, een Amerikaans socioloog, is dat Hephaistos als figuur een universele boodschap bij zich draagt:

'Er is iets sociaal consequent aan de horrelvoet van Hephaistos. De horrelvoet symboliseert de sociale waarde van de ambachtsman. Hephaistos maakt sieraden van koper, een gewoon materiaal; zijn strijdwagens zijn gevormd uit de botten van dode vogels. Homerus omhelst Hephaistos te midden van een verhaal over helden en heroïsch geweld' de huiselijke deugden van huis en haard liggen onder de minachting van onze helden. De misvormde figuur van Hephaistos is bedoeld om te suggereren dat de materiële huiselijke beschaving nooit het verlangen naar glorie zal bevredigen; dat is zijn fout'

Richard Sennett – The Craftsman[5]

Er bestaat een soort muur tussen de ambachtsman en de westerse samenleving. De hedendaagse materialistische samenleving heeft simpelweg minder interesse in de afkomst van het werk. De kracht van de ambachtsman staat tegenwoordig lijnrecht tegenover de hedendaagse samenleving. De ambachtsman die producten maakt die de moeite waard zijn voor het dagelijks leven en van goede kwaliteit zijn, maar vooral de ambachtsman die het hele proces van een voorwerp beheerst. Een voorwerp, bijvoorbeeld een spijkerbroek gaat door honderden verschillende handen voor het in je kast ligt. We leven in een samenleving die vooral om geld draait.

Iemand knipt de stof, weer iemand anders naait de stof, dan is er nog iemand voor de zakken op de achterkant, dan nog iemand voor de knopen, de ritsen en later voor het verzenden en de verkoop. Iedereen raakt vervreemd van het proces en er is weinig tot geen sprake van vakmanschap en een 'materiaalbeleving'.

Het lijkt alsof de ervaring en kunde van de ambachtsman meer waard is dan datgene dat hij uiteindelijk maakt. Als ik vanuit eigen ervaring spreek kan ik dat wel begrijpen; als ik een vaas maak dan is de vaas die uiteindelijk op tafel staat als het ware een lege huls van het proces dat ik heb doorgemaakt als maker. Zeker als je mij of mijn inspiratie niet kent. Dat betekent dan zeker niet dat het niet nog steeds mooi, inspirerend of aantrekkelijk zou kunnen zijn. Er is een bekende quote van Marshall McLuhan, Canadees filosoof en wetenschapper: 'het medium is de boodschap'. Bijvoorbeeld in kunstgeschiedenis interpreteerde McLuhan het kubisme als duidelijk voorbeeld waar het medium de boodschap van is. Voor hem vereiste de kubistische kunst 'onmiddellijk zintuiglijk bewustzijn van het geheel', in plaats van bijvoorbeeld alleen het perspectief van het werk. Met andere woorden, met kubisme kon men niet vragen waar het kunstwerk over ging (inhoud)[6], maar het juist in zijn geheel beschouwen. De Canadese Universalistische minister en theoloog Angus MacLean bedacht de uitdrukking 'de methode is de boodschap'. Maclean beweert bijvoorbeeld dat de manier waarop religie wordt onderwezen belangrijker is dan wat er precies wordt onderwezen.[7] Beide stellingen geven een interessante kijk op hoe we sommige onderwerpen het beste kunnen benaderen en er vervolgens er het meeste uit kunnen

halen. Het lijkt nu een duidelijke verdeling; ofwel is de methode de boodschap, ofwel het medium. Is dit in de praktijk ook zo duidelijk?

Maar hoe zit dit dan met de maker in het gehele verhaal? Zelf zou ik daar misschien nog wel eens schepje bovenop willen doen. Ik zie hoe het medium en de methode de boodschap kunnen zijn, maar hoe zit het met de hand en die het voorwerp leven geeft, deze zal toch zeker ook iets overdragen met zijn werk? Als we het voorbeeld van Hephaistos gebruiken zien we duidelijk dat hij als persoon een boodschap doorgeeft in zijn manier van doen. Hij werkt vol passie aan prachtige functionele objecten. Maar desondanks wordt hij door vele mensen afgerekend op zijn handicap. Gewone stervelingen maar ook de goden kunnen niet door zijn mankheid heen kijken.

Begrijp me niet verkeerd want ik bedoel dit zeker niet als een 'performance' of optreden, dat maakt het naar mijn gevoel niet oprecht. Een kunstenaar-ambachtsman en zijn praktijk, als vorm, zijn ook een boodschap.

Methode en praktijk lijken heel dicht bij elkaar te zitten qua betekenis en enerzijds klopt dat ook. Woorden als 'aanpak' en 'manier van doen' kunnen worden gebruikt om beiden te omschrijven. Maar een praktijk, bijvoorbeeld de kunstenaars praktijk, is meer een verzameling van verschillende methodes, meerdere verhalen.

Hoewel sommige van McLuhan's stellingen als omstreden worden gezien, twijfel ik niet aan zijn kernbewering: 'Om de huidige wereld te begrijpen, dient men de media te begrijpen'. Oorspronkelijk, met de opkomst van het internet bedoelt hij media zoals televisie, internet en kranten. Maar een medium, wat in het latijn 'het midden' betekent, een drager of overdrager van iets anders is. Dit "iets anders" kan zowel stoffelijk als onstoffelijk zijn. Het meervoud is dan weer media. Dit stoffelijke en onstoffelijke medium is een interessant fenomeen. Het omschrijft eigenlijk alles, maar ook weer niets. Hoe werken deze samen? Geeft een stoffelijk medium een onstoffelijke boodschap door? En hoe werkt dat andersom?

5   The Craftsman ,Richard Sennet, Penguin Books Ltd – 2009, p 292
6   Understanding media, Marshall McLuhan,
    Taylor & Francis Ltd, 2001, p.13
7   http://uudb.org/articles/angusmaclean.html

DE TERUGKEER VAN HEPHAISTOS

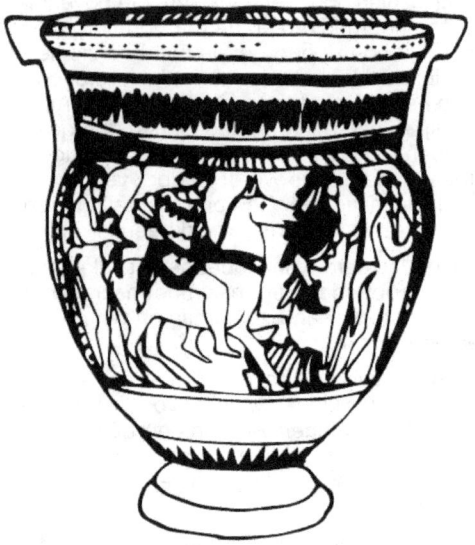

Afbeelding 3 –
Vaas met de titel: de terugkeer van Hephaistos

Een van mijn favoriete stoffelijke media is keramiek. Zoals ik al eerder vertelde, heb ik een opleiding tot keramist gevolgd en mijn wortels van mijn kunstenaarspraktijk zitten diep in de klei, ook al is mijn medium op het moment textiel. Als we het hebben over materialen en boodschappen, stoffelijke en onstoffelijke boodschappen en materialen en mythologie dan mogen we klei en keramiek niet vergeten.

Klei, al vanuit de oudheid een populair materiaal en tot op de dag van vandaag nog veel gebruikt, voor kunst en voorwerpen maar zeker ook voor praktisch gebruiksgoed. Door zijn stevigheid en standvastigheid zijn er veel voorbeelden bewaard gebleven van deze oude samenlevingen.

Wat dat betreft is het een erg verhalend materiaal. Het geeft boodschappen en verhalen door maar ook zeker de manier hoe je met de klei omgaat geeft een boodschap.

Bovenstaande vaas heeft de titel 'de terugkeer van Hephaistos'. Deze vaas is vermoedelijk in circa 425-430 voor Christus gemaakt in Attica, Griekenland.[8] Vazen waren in het oude Griekenland erg belangrijk en besloegen een groot deel van het dagelijks leven en werden vooral gebruikt voor het opslaan of vervoeren van bijvoorbeeld graan en water, maar ook om dingen met elkaar te vermengen, serviesgoed om mee te eten of te drinken, speciale vazen voor olie of parfum en zelfs vroege vormen van cosmetische schoonheidsmiddelen. Daarnaast waren er ook bepaalde vazen die gevuld werden met olijfolie van de 'heilige olijfboomgaard van Athena' en daarna uitgereikt werden als prijs aan winnaars van wedstrijden als bijvoorbeeld 'Grote Panathenaia'. Een Oud Griekse vorm van boksen.[9]

Wat ik zo interessant vind aan deze vaas, naast het verhaal, is de manier hoe er in die tijd met een materiaal als keramiek werd omgegaan. In onze moderne tijd is hand vervaardigde keramiek een luxeproduct geworden. Vroeger was de ambachtsman de enige die deze kennis en kunde had en werd alles met de hand vervaardigd. Er werd beter geluisterd naar wat een medium als klei wil en nodig heeft, omdat men er meer afhankelijk van was. Het maakproces van een vaas vind ik erg inspirerend. Dit geldt vooral voor een vaas van 2000 jaar geleden. Maar kunnen we nu zeggen, in het heden en kijkend naar deze vaas nu, dat het medium de boodschap is of de methode? Is de klei zelf de boodschap of de manier waarop de vaas gemaakt is?

Handwerk

Stel, we maken nu een vaas. We draaien een gipsen vorm en maken hier een mal van. Deze gieten we in met witte gietklei en zie daar, we hebben een vaas. We bakken deze op 1050°C en daarna glazuren we hem, eventueel met een zelfgeschilderd design. Merk je wat er gebeurt? We maken dus een oppervlakte en leggen daar als het ware weer een extra oppervlakte op. De lagen zijn misschien in combinatie met elkaar een mooie uitkomst maar ze zijn nog steeds enigszins apart van elkaar. Versmolten op elkaar in plaats van in elkaar. Dit is niet erg, maar het mist de poëzie uit het maakproces van een oud Griekse vaas.

Grieks aardewerk werd gestookt op temperaturen tussen de 750-950°C. Hierbij werd zowel zwart als roodkleurig aardewerk gebruikt. Zwart en rood bevatten beide metaaldeeltjes, welke hen kleur geven. Dit verschilt in de plaats waar je de deeltjes, de klei, uit de grond haalt. Vazen werden gemaakt op een pottenbakkersschijf, en voorzien van afbeeldingen. Door een dunne laag van een andere kleisoort te gebruiken, die door het bakken op verschillende temperaturen rood of zwart kleurt, kwamen de afbeeldingen tot leven. Lijnen werden ingekrast, en later geschilderd. Het beschilderen van vazen met deze kleiverf maakte dat de vaas uiteindelijk drie stookfasen had:

Allereerst de eerste oxidatie fase: Tijdens de oxidatie fase is er een continue luchtstroom door de oven. Niet zoveel dat het afkoelt, met temperaturen van 750-950°C, maar zodat er genoeg zuurstofdeeltjes in de oven zweven. Deze ijzerdeeltjes reageren op de ijzerdeeltjes in de klei. We hebben rode klei gekozen voor onze vaas en in deze fase wordt de gehele vaas, inclusief beschildering een soort terracotta rood.

Vervolgens de reductie fase: In de oxidatie fase is er veel zuurstof in de oven te vinden maar in een reductie stook is dit het tegenovergestelde. Alle klepjes gaan dicht en er is geen zuurstof te vinden. In combinatie met de temperaturen leidt dit ertoe dat de gehele vaas zwart kleurt. De plekken die zijn beschilderd met de kleiverf sinteren dicht. Dat wil zeggen dat de deeltjes dichter tegen elkaar gaan liggen op die plekken en als het ware vast komen te zitten in die positie.

Als laatste de tweede oxidatie fase: Er is opnieuw een luchtstroom in de oven, alle klepjes zijn weer open en wat er hier gebeurt vind ik bijzonder. De beschilderde onderdelen die in de reductie fase zijn dicht gesinterd blijven de zwarte kleur behouden maar de rest van de vaas gaat terug opnieuw zuurstof opnemen en kleurt weer rood.[10]

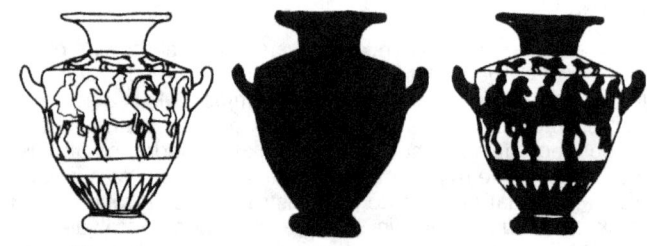

Afbeelding 4 –
Een visualisatie van het stookproces.
Van links naar rechts: eerste oxidatie fase,
reductie fase en de tweede oxidatie fase.

In dit geval is voor mij de methode de boodschap, en het materiaal meer de boodschapper. Het mooie aan dit proces is de samenwerking tussen mens en materiaal. Er wordt klei gegraven uit de grond en het hele proces is een wisselwerking tussen wat het materiaal al in zich heeft en wat de mens het kan bieden. Kortom, het 'opplakken' van een extra laag is anders dan werken met de metalen en mineralen in de klei om dan een synergie te bereiken. Veel kennis is verloren gegaan en daarmee ook deze bijna poëtische vorm van omgang met materiaal. De methode is dan wel grotendeels verdwenen maar de vaas is nog steeds hier, in een prachtige staat. Dat zegt ook iets over de kwaliteit en kunde van deze ambachtsman.

8 https://www.jbagot.com/obra/krater-of-columns-with-the-return-of-hephaestus-to-olympus-accompanied-by-dionysus

9 http://griekse-kunst.blogspot.com/p/de-griekse-schilderkunst-is-op-de.html

10 Vaste tentoonstelling van het Allard Pierson museum.

We hebben het over boodschappen en hoe deze overgedragen worden in de media, maar wat is een boodschap nu eigenlijk. Waarom hechten we zoveel waarde aan deze boodschappen uit het verleden en helpt het ons eigenlijk wel? En speelt het medium daar een grote rol in? Kan het ook zonder?

Waar we in de Egyptische geschiedenis onze kennis alleen konden uitbreiden door het vinden van graven werden er van de Grieken juist heel veel alledaagse objecten teruggevonden, waardoor we nu zo'n 2000 jaar later ons iets kunnen inbeelden van hoe de Grieken waren in het dagelijks leven. En als er een onderwerp is dat tegenwoordig nog altijd populair is dan is het de Oud-Griekse wereld wel. Niet alleen als onderdeel van een literatuur curriculum of geschiedenislessen op school maar ook in de moderne media en in ons taalgebruik. Ik vraag me af: wat is het in deze Oud-Griekse wereld dat mensen, inclusief mezelf, nog steeds, anno 2020, aantrekt in deze wonderlijke wereld. De mythes zijn toch eigenlijk oude volksverhalen die duizenden jaren geleden relevant waren? Waarom komt er dan regelmatig toch weer een film over een Griekse mythe of gevecht? Waarom gebruiken zo veel plaatsen en bedrijven Oud-Griekse beeldtaal?

Wat de Grieken interessant maakt is dat zij aan de wieg van onze moderne beschaving stonden. Maar voor de Grieken begonnen te filosoferen en te kleien waren er vele volkeren voor hen op deze aarde. Boeddha en Confucius waren beide al overleden voordat Socrates geboren werd. Dit betekent dat de Grieken niet kunnen claimen dat ze filosofie hebben uitgevonden. En als je ooit een tentoonstelling over Toetanchamon of het oude Egypte hebt gezien dan weet je wellicht dat de Egyptenaren al best behendig waren met goud en keramiek in de 14e eeuw voor Christus en het bouwen van piramides zelfs al 1000 jaar daarvoor. De Babyloniërs creëerden in 2000 voor Christus immense terrasvormige piramides genaamd Ziggoerats. Voordat de Grieken ook maar iets geschreven hadden waren daar de Assyriërs met hun prachtige paleizen in 800 voor Christus en de Hethieten 200 jaar later. Dit was nog zeker 600 jaar voor het eerste Griekse schrift. Ze zijn niet de eerste geweest maar waren wel de fundering waarop onze kunst, architectuur en cultuur werd gebouwd.[11] De oude Grieken hadden veel kennis overgenomen van het oude Mesopotamië en Egypte. Deze kennis verbeterden ze en breidden ze uit. Vervolgens nam het Romeinse Rijk de kennis van de Grieken over en verspreidde deze in heel Europa.[12]

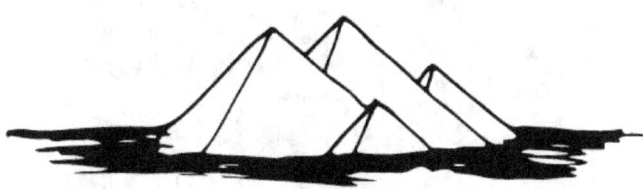

Afbeelding 5 –
Egyptische piramides

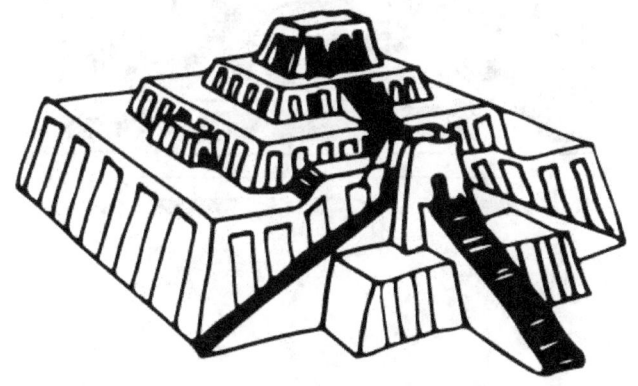

Afbeelding 6 –
Babylonische ziggoerat

Nieuwe media, oude boodschap

Op dit moment is er een enorme hoeveelheid aan media met oud Griekse thema's en daaruit concludeer ik dat het mensen nog steeds fascineert. De een om de Spartaanse gevechten, in films zoals 300 (2006) over de slag bij Therpolae waarin de koning van Sparta, Leonidas I, die samen met 300 spartanen vocht tot de laatste man, tegen de koning van Perzië, Xerxes I.[13]

De ander is geïnteresseerd in het drama in het keizerrijk met films als Gladiator (2000), een fictief verhaal geïnspireerd op keizer Commodus en zijn vader Marcus Aurelius.[14] En er zijn ook de mensen die, net zoals ik, van de Oud-Griekse mythes houden en misschien meer houden van films als Hercules (2014). Gebaseerd op de Radical Comics' Hercules: 'The Thracian wars' door Steve Moore.[15] Wanneer geen enkele je bevalt zijn er nog altijd videogames als Assassins Creed Odyssey (2018), waarin spelers een scala aan politieke en wetenschappelijke thema's te verwerken krijgen zoals democratie versus tirannie, mythe versus wetenschap en orde versus chaos. Dit spel speelt zich af in Griekenland tijdens de Peloponnesische oorlog (431 – 404 voor Christus).[16]

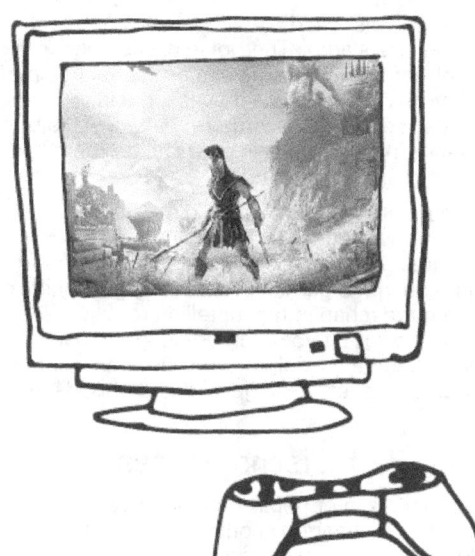

Afbeelding 7 –
Het spel 'Assasins Creed Odyssey'.

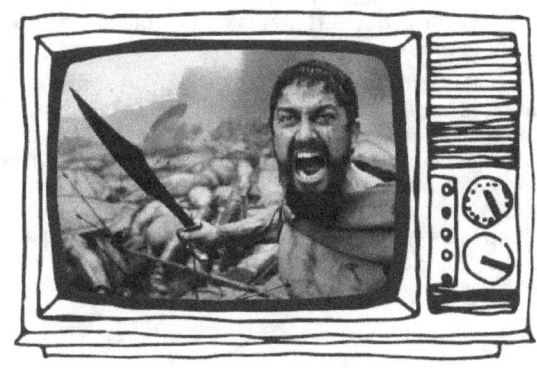

Afbeelding 8 –
Bekend beeld uit de film '300' waarin
Gerard Butler 'This is Sparta!' schreeuwt.

11 A Classical Education: The Stuff You Wish You'd Been Taught At School, Caroline Taggart, Michael O'Mara, 2009, p.11

12 http://breinwekker.blogspot.com/2016/11/griekenland-de-bakermat-van-de-westerse-beschaving.html

13 300 – film – 2006 – regie: Zack Snyder

14 Gladiator – film – 2000 – regie: Ridley Scott

15 Hercules – film – 2014 – regie: Brett Ratner

16 Assassins Creed Odyssey – videogame – 2018

Wat deze films en videogames met elkaar gemeen hebben is dat ze de media vertegenwoordigen die verhalen van duizenden jaren geleden levend houden, net als de vaas uit 'de terugkeer van Hephaistos'. Je zou kunnen zeggen dat een vaas meer tot de verbeelding spreekt dan een film of videogame. Een afbeelding op een vaas is een representatie van een verhaal. Er kan gegist worden naar wat er zich nog meer rond dat verhaal afspeelt maar uiteindelijk is de afbeelding een soort 'snapshot' uit een bewegend beeld. Er wordt wel eens gezegd dat een afbeelding meer zegt dan 1000 woorden, en in veel gevallen is dat zo. Maar hoe zit echter met een bewegend beeld, zoals films of videogames?

Met een film of game kun je beter voorstellen dat je in een gevecht of verhaal zit. Je zit in een simulatie van de omgeving van het verhaal, je maakt mee wat er in de kampen tijdens de gevechten gebeurde, je ondervindt wat de commandostructuur was en volgt het verhaal van je gesimuleerde familie en vrienden. Het is een andere werkelijkheid die je de kans geeft om meer diepte te creëren in het verhaal. We hoeven niet alles aan te nemen als waarheid. De makers van de film '300' leefden niet toen de slag bij Therpolae plaats vond, maar hebben geprobeerd een vertaling van het verhaal te maken. Dit geldt ook voor de maker van de vaas, die in zijn tijd een vertaling van dat verhaal probeerde te maken. Dit leidt mij tot een eerdergenoemde vraag: Is in dit geval de methode de boodschap? Of toch het medium?

Bewegend beeld brengt een nieuwe dimensie in. Het opent een deur naar een nieuwe wereld, een gesimuleerde wereld, waarin we kunnen tijdreizen en andere werelden kunnen ontdekken. De methode, een video game bijvoorbeeld, geeft hiermee een duidelijke boodschap in tegenstelling tot bijvoorbeeld een vaas. De game nodigt uit voor een ervaring, en daaruit volgend, misschien wel nieuwe mogelijkheden voor ons leven in de 21ste eeuw. De methode geeft in dit geval dus de boodschap.

Historische fantasie

Door de jaren heen zijn er bepaalde dingen van oude beschavingen blijven hangen in onze cultuur. Denk hierbij bijvoorbeeld aan invloeden in onze taal zoals 'status quo' en 'cum laude', of het feit dat onze democratie afstamt van de democratie van Athene twee duizend geleden. Deze natuurlijke historische voortzetting is meer dan logisch. We nemen een paar mooie ingrediënten en gebruiken deze in onze eigen recepten voor een samenleving in de 21ste eeuw. Niet dat dit bewust of opzettelijk gebeurt, het is een natuurlijke samenloop van omstandigheden.

Wat me tegenwoordig opvalt is dat er vaak een soort kunstmatige fantasie aan mensen wordt verkocht, denk bijvoorbeeld aan een kledingstuk of gebouw waar soms letterlijk iets van de klassieke oudheid opgeplakt is, de maker wil iets uitstralen en haalt er dan beelden bij van andere culturen of tijdsperiodes om dat doel te bereiken zonder echt in te gaan op wat een bepaalde mythe of gebruik van materiaal betekende in die tijd of cultuur. Een beetje dezelfde gedachten als mijn thee set in het begin.

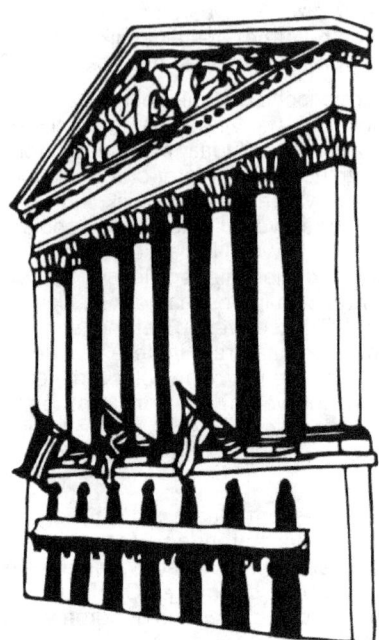

Afbeelding 9 –
Effectenbeurs op Wall Street

Een voorbeeld van deze kunstmatige fantasie is de effectenbeurs op Wall Street in de Verenigde Staten. (Zie afbeelding 7) Het gebouw zoals het er vandaag de dag uit ziet werd geopend op 22 April 1903. Meerdere pertinente zuilen ondersteunen een groot fronton waarin enkele figuren staan afgebeeld. De ontwerpers van dit gebouw noemen het zelf de 'Greek Revival Look', en werd in hun ogen gebruikt om de oude beschavingen die integriteit belichaamden en morele filosofie uitvonden, weer tot leven te wekken.[17]

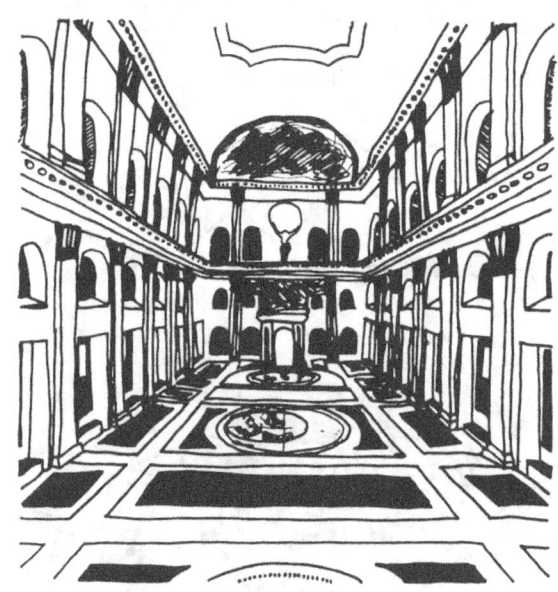

Afbeelding 10 –
Burgerzaal in het Paleis op de dam

17 https://www.wentworthstudio.com/historic-styles/greek-revival/

Een voorbeeld in Amsterdam is het Paleis op de Dam. In de gouden eeuw lieten de burgemeesters van Amsterdam hun nieuwe stadhuis (later op 20 april 1808 omgedoopt tot paleis) bouwen naar voorbeeld van een antieke tempel. Er was op dit moment genoeg welvaart, bovendien wilden men hun macht en prestige laten zien aan de bevolking en dit leek een uitgelezen kans. Aan de binnen en buitenkant zijn overal ten overvloede Griekse en Romeinse goden, mythes en verhalen uitgebeeld. Deze zijn bedoeld om uit te drukken wat het stadsbestuur van Amsterdam destijds wilde zijn en uitstralen maar ook hoe ze over zichzelf als Amsterdammers in de bloeiperiode van de Nederlandse geschiedenis over zichzelf dachten. Zij wilden hiermee onoverwinnelijkheid uitstralen.[18]

Een voorbeeld hiervan staat in het paleis, destijds stadhuis, in de burgerzaal. In de vloer van de burgerzaal zijn drie cirkels ingelegd met kaarten van het oostelijk en westelijk halfrond en een sterrenkaart. Er wordt gezegd dat men destijds (jaartal, rond bijv 1650) hiermee wilde uitstralen dat voor de burgers van Amsterdam, de hele wereld en de hemel aan hun voeten lag. De burgerzaal zou uitstralen dat ze het centrum van het universum waren.

Een ander voorbeeld van deze kunstmatige fantasie is het symbool van de Britse landingsdivisie in de Tweede Wereldoorlog. Te zien is dat Bellerophon op een Pegasus zit, met zijn speer in de aanslag. In de mythe werd Bellerophon door koning Proetus op een queeste gestuurd waarvan hij normaal gesproken nooit levend van zou kunnen terugkeren: hij moest een vuurspuwende Chimaera doden, een beest dat samengesteld was uit drie verschillende levensvormen. De kop van een leeuw, het achterlijf van een slang en het lichaam van een geit.

Uiteindelijk, met hulp van de godin Athena en de Pegasus lukt het hem de Chimaera te verslaan, zonder die goddelijke interventie was hij nooit levend teruggekeerd. De moraal van het verhaal komt later. Bellerophon keert als een echte overwinnaar terug, krijgt een mooie vrouw en de helft van het koninkrijk van Proetus. Terwijl zijn faam groeide, groeide ook zijn ego. Bellerophon wilde met de Pegasus naar de Olympus vliegen, de berg waar de goden woonden. De vlucht was veel te zwaar voor het arme beest en op het moment dat Bellerophon en de Pegasus er bijna waren stuurden de goden een vlieg, die de Pegasus prikte waardoor hij steigerde. Bellerophon viel naar beneden en raakte mank en blind aan één oog. Op deze manier werd hij bestraft door de goden voor zijn eerzucht en hybris, wat hoogmoed betekent. Hij trok zich terug en leefde verder als kluizenaar.[19] De uitdrukking 'Hoogmoed komt voor de val' zou een verwijzing kunnen zijn naar dit verhaal. Zou het ook hoogmoed bij de Britten zijn geweest die ze dit symbool deed kiezen?

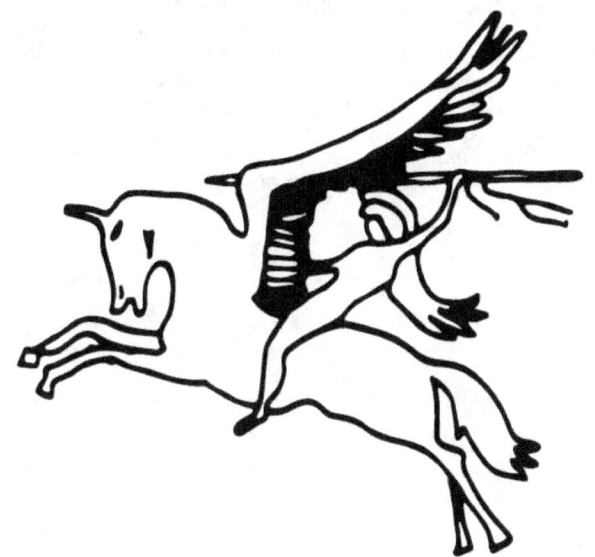

Afbeelding 11 –
Bellerophon op de Pegasus met een speer in de aanslag

MYTHES EN DEFINITIES

In de vorige hoofdstukken is gekeken naar media en boodschappen, bijvoorbeeld in de mythologie. Heeft de manier waarop een boodschap wordt aangeduid, bijvoorbeeld als mythologie, sprookje, legende of religieuze tekst invloed op de manier hoe dit wordt doorgegeven, en is het veel veranderd door de jaren heen? Is dit dan altijd alleen maar positief? Of betekent dit dat het ook gebruikt kan worden voor negatieve doeleinden?

Het woord mythologie is afkomstig uit het oud Grieks en kwam als zodanig in de klassieke oudheid al voor. Het is een samenstelling van mythos, 'het gezegde', 'het opgezegde verhaal', en logos, 'woord' of 'wetmatigheid'. In mythos zit de stam(mu), 'spraak'. Zodoende betekent dit letterlijk enerzijds het mondeling navertellen van mythen en fabels, of de studie van mythen.[20] Hoe men hier ook naar kijkt, mythes zijn niet zomaar verhalen zonder moraal of kern van waarheid.

Misschien zijn ze beter te bekijken als een vertelling die uitlegt.[21] In onze geschiedenis als mensheid, of je nu kijkt naar het oude Egypte, de oude Grieken en Romeinen of naar de godsdiensten van onze moderne tijd zoals Katholicisme, Protestantisme of de Islam, deze verhalen smeden ons besef van wie we zijn, hoe we hier zijn gekomen en hoe wij in een wereld passen die vol zit met aan de ene hand de prachtigste bloemen maar ook diepe valkuilen verstopt in het zand.[22] Daarmee raakt 'de mythe' van allerlei vragen aan waar de mensheid al vanaf het begin van zijn bestaan een antwoord op zoekt, denk bijvoorbeeld aan scheppingsverhalen. Dit verklaart waarom er vaak overeenkomsten tussen thematiek tussen mythes uit verschillende culturen zijn die ver van elkaar verwijderd zijn. Niet alleen in afstand, maar ook in tijd. Mythen die binnen een bepaalde cultuur belangrijk geacht worden, zijn vaak richtinggevend voor vragen betreffende de geschiedenis, toekomst, gebruiken en leefwereld van de desbetreffende cultuur.[23] In aanvulling hierop dient het onderwerp van een mythe uitzonderlijke karakteristieken te hebben, zodat de personages, bijvoorbeeld dieren, mensen en goden, in de mythe bijvoorbeeld vaak bovenmenselijk worden.[24]

In bovenstaande termen wordt mythologie en mythe eenduidig gebruikt. Dit heeft verschillende redenen. Allereerst hebben mythen verscheidene betekenislagen en functies. Deze kunnen in de loop der tijd veranderen, en kunnen op verschillende manieren geïnterpreteerd worden.

Wie alle mythen op een enkele wijze wil verklaren, en ze als statisch beschouwt doet geen recht aan de complexiteit en de dynamiek die mythen en mythologie hebben.[25]

Ook de overgang tussen de begrippen mythe en mythologie is vaak vloeiend, zowel voor degenen die met mythen leven en erin geloven als voor onderzoekers of buitenstaanders die de mythen bestuderen. Ditzelfde geldt ook voor de relatie met begrippen als folklore, legenden, sagen en sprookjes. Het blijkt ook uit de literatuur over het onderwerp, waarin auteurs dergelijke woorden ook vaak vloeiend gebruiken. Taal lijkt in een constante staat van verandering te zijn, waardoor woorden in de loop der jaren kunnen veranderen. Als je een boek over mythologie oppakt kan dit verhalen bevatten waarin de focus bijvoorbeeld op folklore ligt. Een mythe is dus niet iets wat op zichzelf staat. Dit roept vragen op over mythe in samenhang met het geloof in de mythe. In hoeverre is folklore nog een blijk van oprecht geloof in een bepaalde mythische 'overlevering'?

18 https://www.paleisamsterdam.nl/over-het-paleis/
19 The Greek Myths, Robert Graves, Penguin Books Ltd, 2012, p. 240

20 Beknopt Grieks – Nederlands woordenboek door
   Fred Muller en J.H Thiel, Wolters-Noordhoff, 1958
21 The place of religion in modernity, Robert Segal, 2004 p.5,
   https://journals.sagepub.com/doi/10.1177/0952695104048077
22 Humankind: A brief history door Pelipe Fernández-Armesto-
   Oxford University Press- 2004 - p.7
23 The place of religion in modernity, Robert Segal - 2004 - p 5-6
24 The place of religion in modernity - Robert Segal - 2004 p 55
25 The nature of Greek myths - G.s Kirk - Penguin - 1974

56   *Een vaas*   *Vera Laarakker*
Een schoen
En de zee

Een enkeling plaatst mythe zelfs onder folklore, dat wil zeggen vertellingen van het volk. Hoewel fabels een uitgesproken didactische functie hebben, vermeldde bijvoorbeel de Griekse dichter Aesopus in zijn fabels diverse goden.[26]

Folklore is een belangrijke bron van informatie over oude godsdienst en mythologie. In de 19e eeuw was er een toenemend nationaliteitsbesef in Europa, waarbij landen of taalgemeenschappen de eigen cultuurgeschiedenis zelf begonnen te onderzoeken. De gebroeders Grimm, twee broers uit Duitsland die tevens taalkundigen waren, verzamelden bijna hun hele leven Duitse volksverhalen en schreven deze op. Ze reisden door Duitsland en legde zo deze verhalen vast voor de volgende generatie.[27]

Oude helden in een nieuw jasje

In Nederland is er een figuur dat door vele nog als nationale volksheld wordt gezien en daardoor soms verheven wordt naar een soort mythologische heldenstatus. We hebben het dan over een van de beroemdste 17e -eeuwse zeehelden: Michiel de Ruyter. In de Tweede Engelse Zeeoorlog (1667), beleefde De Ruyter een moment wat hem enorm beroemd heeft gemaakt. Hij moest Engeland een grote slag toebrengen en daarbij verwoestte hij een groot deel van de Engelse vloot. Het leverde hem een heldenstatus op en hij werd vereerd als de nieuwe Hannibal. In 1676 overleed De Ruyter in een zeeslag en kreeg hij in de Nieuwe Kerk in Amsterdam een marmeren praalgraf op de plek van het voormalig hoogaltaar.[28]

In 2015 kwam er een film over Michiel de Ruyter uit. Na een voorvertoning in het Scheepvaartmuseum te Amsterdam betoogde scheephistoricus en conservator Remmelt Daalder dat elke tijd zijn eigen versie van Michiel de Ruyter creëert.[29]

Nederland was in 1830 op zoek naar helden waarmee het volk zich kon identificeren. De Belgische opstand (1830) zorgde ervoor dat Nederland flink gekrompen was en niet meer de macht had als daarvoor. Burgers in Engeland konden teruggrijpen naar Nelson en in Frankrijk naar Napoleon voor wat nationale trots. Er werd in Nederland gezocht naar eigentijdse helden maar werd er teruggegrepen op grote namen van de 17e eeuw, zoals Piet Hein, Rembrandt en Michiel de Ruyter.

In de 19e eeuw werd De Ruyter als schoolvoorbeeld gesteld aan de Nederlandse jeugd. Er werd De Ruyter allerlei eigenschappen toegewezen die in die tijd paste binnen de opvoedingsidealen, bijvoorbeeld vaderlandsliefde, moed en bescheidenheid, godvrezendheid en politieke neutraliteit. Begin 20ste eeuw verandert dit. Nederland heeft zijn zelfvertrouwen herwonnen en Michiel de Ruyter veranderd naar een onverschrokken zeeheld. Zijn onberispelijke karakter is niet meer nodig.[30]

In de Tweede Wereldoorlog doet De Ruyter weer een intrede en niet aan de kant van geschiedenis waar je het zou verwachten. Deze nieuwe periode van ongekende populariteit zit niet bij de gewone Nederlandse burger voor steun in moeilijke tijden maar bij de nationaalsocialisten (NSB). De Ruyter werd gezien als de ideale bondgenoot voor de nazi's. Een heldhaftige onverschrokken held die zijn hele leven tegen de Engelsen vocht, en vaak won. Ze zagen dit alsof Nederland en Duitsland een gemeenschappelijke vijand hadden.

Het wervingsaffiche uit afbeelding 10 gebruikt een visualisatie van de Slag bij Kijkduin voor nazipropaganda. We zien een U-boot samen met de Zeven Provinciën (het vlaggenschip van de Ruyter) optrekken naar Londen onder de tekst 'Steeds Dezelfde Vijand 1673-1943'. Zijn karakter wordt op deze manier gekoppeld aan de oorlog die de Duitsers voeren en de strijd tegen Engeland.[31]

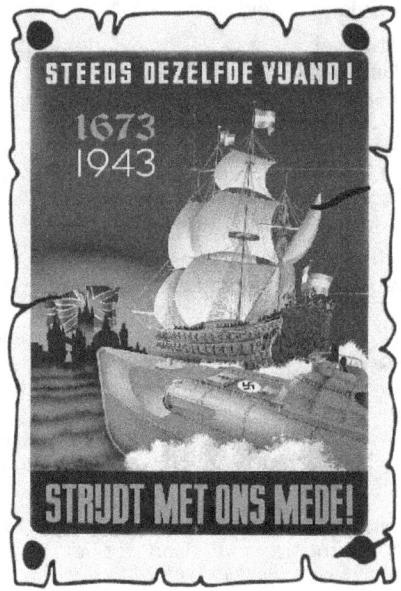

Afbeelding 12 –
Wervingsaffiche en tevens nazi propaganda

Achter elk ontwerp zit een idee, vooral in het geval van nazi-Duitsland. Deze zwarte bladzijde uit de geschiedenis is een voorbeeld van de manier waarop boodschappen, verhalen en mythes gebruikt kunnen worden voor een totalitaire verleiding. Er werd gebruik gemaakt van propaganda waarin bewust eenzijdige en ook verzonnen informatie stond. Materiaal en boodschap kunnen dus ook ingezet worden voor minder nobele en onschuldige doeleinden.

De nazi's spiegelden zich graag aan de Griekse en Romeinse cultuur. Door Hitler en zijn volgelingen werd deze cultuur en kunststijl gezien als kunst waarvan de uiterlijke vorm een innerlijk raciaal ideaal belichaamde. De nazi's streefden naar het creëren van de perfecte mens, en de mensen die niet in dit perfecte beeld paste, werden weg 'geselecteerd'. Ze misbruikten de evolutietheorie om eigen theorieën goed te kunnen praten. Daarnaast kon de gewone burger de Griekse en Romeinse cultuur begrijpen. Geen ingewikkelde concepten of volgens Hitler 'besmette' modernistische kunst en vormgeving, maar heroïsche en romantische media.[32]

26 Fabels – Caius J. Phaedrus , vertaald door John Nagelkerken – Singel Uitgevers – 2002 – Hoofdstuk 17

27 https://kunst-en-cultuur.infonu.nl/biografie/78505-de-gebroeders-grimm-en-hun-sprookjesboek.html

28 https://www.hetscheepvaartmuseum.nl/michiel-de-ruyter

29 https://nos.nl/artikel/2015467-met-de-ruyter-trots-op-nederland.html

30 https://www.hetscheepvaartmuseum.nl/collectie/artikelen/680/ieder-tijdperk-zijn-eigen-de-ruyter

31 idem footnote 29

32 https://www.parool.nl/kunst-media/overzichtstentoonstelling-design-van-het-derde-rijk~b30894e8/

Uiteindelijk, terugkijkend op de ontwerpen en verhalen zijn ze vaak onpersoonlijk en stereotyperend. De identiteit van mensen werd ontnomen. Zij waren geen individu meer, maar eenvoudige emblemen die de indruk gaven een universele eeuwenoude waarheid te vertellen. Dit was echter niet het geval. Men ging hier nog verder in, mensen werden in sommige gevallen zelfs gereduceerd tot alleen een nummer. Kijkend naar nazi architectuur, kunst of schilderkunst krijg je al snel het gevoel dat achter elk idee, ontwerp, vorm, kleur en gezicht een propagandistisch doel zit. Denk bijvoorbeeld aan de naakten die het ideale mannelijke en vrouwelijke lichaam moesten voorstellen. Meters hoge beelden die ter ere van de Olympische zomerspelen van 1936 in het straatbeeld van Berlijn verschenen. Het zijn uiteindelijk vaak allemaal dezelfde gestileerde vertalingen van nazi-deugden – macht, kracht, stevigheid, (Arische) schoonheid.[33]

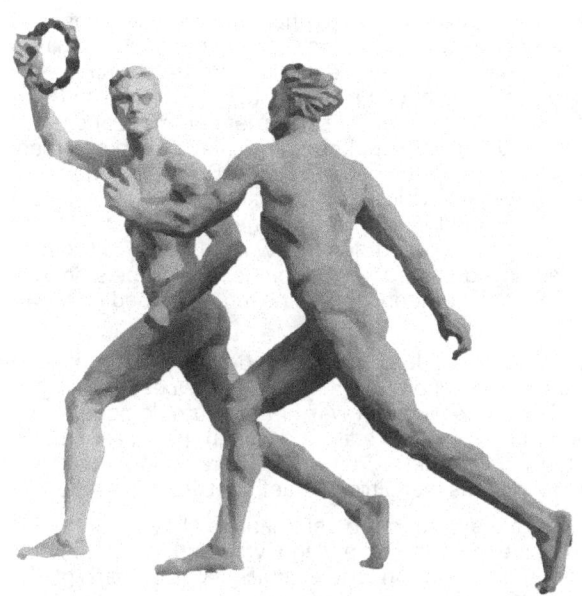

Afbeelding 13 –
Standbeelden ter ere van
de Olympische zomerspelen van 1936

We zitten eigenlijk op een grote zee van media en verhalen. Soms vang je iets op en soms gaat het compleet langs je heen. Als we kijken naar Griekse mythes bijvoorbeeld, is het dan ons 'geluk' dat veel mensen dit hebben opgepikt en dat we er daarom nog van kunnen genieten? Het is in ieder geval niet zo onschuldig als het lijkt. De nazi's zijn met veel klassieke idealen aan de haal gegaan om hun eigen wanpraktijken te verheerlijken. Alsof zij wel een fundament voor 'de waarheid' hadden.

Of het nu over stoffelijke of onstoffelijke media gaat, het medium heeft vaak een boodschap of voegt een extra laag toe aan de ervaring ervan. Kijkend naar de stoffelijke media keramiek en textiel hebben ze beide enorme kwaliteiten in hun verhaal vertellend vermogen. Maar ook als materiaal zelf en de wisselwerking die tussen mens en materiaal kan ontstaan. Wat zet textiel dan apart? Het heeft in ieder geval een grotere vergankelijkheid en zal niet zo snel duizenden jaren kunnen overleven. Wellicht delen van een groter stuk textiel, maar zelden hele kledingstukken of garderobes.

Over het algemeen, als je het bijvoorbeeld vergelijkt met keramiek, de vaas en de thee set, is de herinnering van textiel veel breder, maar de levensduur vele malen korter. Met herinnering bedoel ik dat textiel alles om zich heen kan absorberen. Denk aan water dat gemorst wordt op een kleed, parfum in kleding, voedsel dat blijft kleven aan de vezel of droogte en warmte van het weer dat zorgt dat de vezel fragiel wordt. Keramiek zal tot op zekere hoogte ook zijn historie met zich mee dragen. Denk bijvoorbeeld aan stukjes die eraf springen, letterlijke verhaalvertellingen op de scherf of de manier van hoe het gemaakt is. Uiteindelijk is textiel toch wel de perfecte conservator van het dagelijkse leven.

TIBETAANSE SCHOENEN

Om erachter te komen hoe een stoffelijk materiaal als textiel de historie voortzet, zocht ik hulp bij mijn speurwerk. Het Textile Research Center in Leiden, leek de geschikte kandidaat.

Het TRC is een onafhankelijk onderzoeksinstituut op het gebied van textiel en kleding. De huidige directeur is Gillian Vogelsang-Eastwood, een kleding historicus en textiel archeoloog. Het TRC wil graag antropologisch en archeologisch onderzoek in textiel en kleding stimuleren in de breedste zin van het woord. Het enorme archief bestaat uit bijvoorbeeld preïndustriële textieltechnieken en daarnaast veel kledingstukken van over de hele wereld. Het komt over als een hele menselijke manier om een tijdsgeest weer te geven. Je kunt een stukje chinees textiel zien liggen dat eeuwen geleden gedragen werd, en daarnaast een geel hesje van de demonstraties een paar jaar geleden. Beide hebben een cultuurhistorische waarde, elk op een eigen manier.

Het was enorm fascinerend om hier textiel te kunnen onderzoeken. De ene dag prachtige danskleding uit Indonesië, de volgende een zakdoekje dat met de hand geborduurd werd in één van de kampen opgezet na de Tweede Wereldoorlog voor vrouwen die aan de kant van de Duitsers hadden gestaan. Textiel, in de vorm van een zakdoek, kan ineens zo'n beladen object worden als het bijvoorbeeld gelinkt wordt aan de Tweede Wereldoorlog, maar tegelijkertijd is het ook een heel luchtig, lief uitziend zakdoekje. Zo liggen er honderden, zo niet duizenden alledaagse en gebruiksvoorwerpen in het magazijn van het TRC. Als een soort tijdcapsules zullen zij altijd de geur, structuur, textuur en sfeer van hun tijd en omstandigheden bij zich dragen en weer doorgeven naar een volgende generatie.

Op een dag kwam ik tijdens mijn zoektocht een paar prachtige Tibetaanse schoenen tegen, afkomstig van een stam die de Drokpa wordt genoemd. Drokpa betekent 'mensen van de eenzaamheid'. Ze staan bekend als nomaden en zorgden tot voor kort voor ongeveer 25 tot 40 procent van de Tibetaanse bevolking. Ze zijn echt een bergvolk die hun vee houden op enorme hooggelegen weides in China. De manier van leven is hier eeuwenlang onveranderd gebleven, waardoor ze de natuurlijke meesters zijn van de graslanden van Tibet en tevens de levende voorbeelden van de originele Tibetaanse cultuur. Langzamerhand verdwijnen deze kampementen echter en nemen steeds meer stammen de traditionele Chinese stijl over.

Paarden, vroeger een van de pilaren van de samenleving, verdwijnen en er komen motorfietsen voor in de plaats. Waar er vroeger uren, zo niet dagen aan een paar schoenen werd gewerkt komen ze nu liever voor de dag in goedkope schoenen uit een Chinese fabriek.[34]

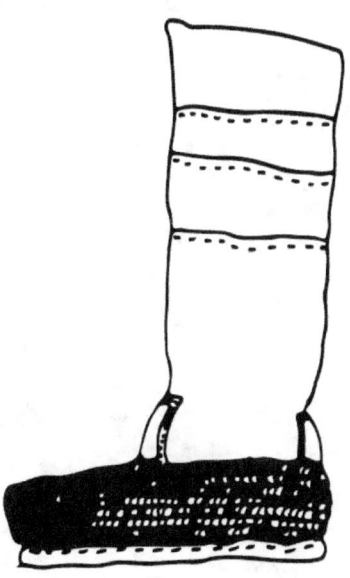

Afbeelding 14 –
De Tibetaanse schoen

33 http://www.brabantc.nl/site/wp-content/uploads/2019/10/
projectplan-derde-rijk.pdf – pagina 9

34 https://www.globalonenessproject.org/library/photo-essays/
drokpa-nomadic-mountain-people-tibet

Een vaas
Een schoen
En de zee

Vera Laarakker

DE MATERIALEN KAMELEON

"De top van de berg,
Draagt sneeuw als een lamsvacht.
Kom mijn lichte, schitterende zon
En ik zal die lamsvachten hoed afzetten.
De berg draagt een gordel van mist.
Kom zachte wind
En ik zal de riem losmaken.
De voet van de berg
Draagt een schoen van bevroren rivier.
Kom lente, met je warmte
En ik zal mijn schoenen uitdoen. "
    Nomadenlied van de Drokpa[35]

Deze schoenen zijn in de jaren zeventig verkocht aan een reiziger die ze mee heeft genomen naar de Verenigde Staten. In 2019 zijn ze gedoneerd aan het Textile Research Center in Leiden. Het voelt echt als een natuurlijke historische voortzetting, dat ik deze schoenen in mijn handen kan houden. Een natuurlijke doorstroom van deze techniek, materie en verhalen. Een soort tijdscapsule die de traditie van de Tibetaanse Drokpa levend houdt in de vorm van deze paar schoenen. De zachte, handgeweven stof en de geur is mij nog lang bijgebleven. De geur deed mij denken aan het beklimmen van een berg, waar de schapen lekker op een nieuw weiland gras stonden te eten. Het rook alsof we zweterig van deze tocht over de rijke grasweides in de bergen uitkeken. Deze essentie zit helemaal in de schoen genesteld. De zool van de schoen is een stuk leer wat er grof aan is gezet, met grote steken en overal op de schoen zijn plekken van gebruik te zien. Als je de schoen helemaal inspecteert, binnen en buitenkant, krijg je een beter idee van de functie van deze schoen en de synergie die deze mix van materialen en technieken creëert.
Een 'onmiddellijk zintuiglijk bewustzijn van het geheel', om McLuhan te citeren. Het materiaal vormt hier een duidelijke boodschap, een verhaal dat op meerdere manieren geïnterpreteerd kan worden.

Hoewel deze schoen een goed voorbeeld is van de natuurlijke historische voortzetting kan ik hieraan toevoegen dat dit verhaal, deze historie, nu kunstmatig in leven wordt gehouden in het Textile Research Center. Het verhaal van deze schoen in zijn oorspronkelijke leefomgeving is eigenlijk al gestopt in de jaren 70, toen het meegenomen werd door die reiziger uit de Verenigde staten. Nu ligt deze schoen in een doos op een plank ergens in het archief van het TRC, en sijpelen langzaam de laatste geuren uit de stof.

De Tibetaanse schoen voelt authentiek aan. De traditie van het maken van deze schoen zal weliswaar niet meer zo lang bestaan maar ik ervaar dit echter als een natuurlijk proces. Er sterft een traditie uit en misschien komt hier ooit een andere traditie voor in de plaats.

In Nigeria pakken ze dit anders aan. Er wordt geleefd en gewerkt met een kunstmatige fantasie, en iedereen speelt erin mee. Nigeria wordt op het moment overspoeld door smokkelaars en hun waar, onder andere een enorme hoeveelheid aan textiel.

De textielindustrie, vroeger het hart van de Nigeriaanse samenleving, begint tegenwoordig in een fabriek in China. Als een echte materialen kameleon transformeert een lap stof zich constant. Beginnend als goedkoop stuk textiel in China, vervolgens transformeert het zich met een merk of opdruk. Dit gaat gepaard met met spelfouten om niet in de problemen te komen met copyrights en trademarks. Denk bijvoorbeeld aan Dolce and Banana (Dolce and Gabbana) en Abidas (Adidas). Later, na een tocht van 10.000 kilometer krijgt het vaak van de verkoper op de markt een nieuw label: made in Nigeria. Verkopers van de producten kopen deze nep labels om het toch wat meer 'authenticiteit' te geven, wat goed uit komt voor onze kameleon.[36]

Wat jammer is aan deze fantasie, is dat het naast het culturele aspect ook de economie van het land verwoest. In het geval van de Tibetaanse schoen was het medium de boodschap. Het straalde zijn afkomst letterlijk af door zijn geur maar ook door het uiterlijk. Een stuk stof uit Nigeria spreekt juist weer door de methode, die dus niet altijd positief hoeft te zijn.

Een lap stof die je koopt op een markt in Nigeria kan gezien worden als een soort camouflage, waaronder het ware verhaal van de Chinese textielindustrie schuilgaat. Deze lap ligt echter niet in een kunstmatige omgeving opgeslagen, zoals de Tibetaanse schoen, hij ligt midden in het leven. De lap ligt op de markt in Nigeria en absorbeert daarom nog steeds het leven, de geuren en natuurlijke invloeden die hij opdoet door zijn omgeving. Misschien zal deze stof gebruikt worden voor traditionele Nigeriaanse kleding, of komt deze stof terug met een reiziger in China terecht, verwerkt in traditionele kledij. Er kan nog van alles gebeuren, het verhaal dat schuilgaat onder deze camouflage lijkt nog niet af te zijn.

35 Vrij vertaald naar het Nederlands
   https://www.globalonenessproject.org/library/photo-essays/
   drokpa-nomadic-mountain-people-tibet

36 https://www.ft.com/content/b1d519c2-b240-11e4-b380-00144feab7de

Textiel als fysiek, stoffelijk ambacht is langzaam aan het uitsterven. Het echte handwerk wordt steeds meer een luxeproduct, dit is ook zo bij keramiek. Het lijkt een natuurlijk proces te zijn aangezien computers en robots steeds vaker verkozen worden over het werk van de ambachtsman. Maar kan een medium zoals textiel voortleven in een andere vorm? Misschien als een immateriële, onstoffelijke vorm?

Als we terugkijken naar de Tibetaanse schoen en de Nigeriaanse stof leek het best duidelijk; beide stoffelijke objecten met elk hen eigen verhaal. Textiel is minder standvastig als keramiek en zal niet oneindig geconserveerd kunnen worden. Stel dat de schoen vergaan is, leeft deze dan nog voort? En hoe vertelt deze zijn verhaal? Textiel is wat dat betreft een erg flexibel materiaal. Enerzijds in zijn stoffelijke vorm maar ook zeker in zijn onstoffelijke vorm. De textiel kan zich verplaatsen tussen deze twee en kan beide vormen aannemen. Neem bijvoorbeeld een weefsel. Tegenwoordig wordt er zo vaak over 'the social fabric, het sociale weefsel' gesproken, maar wat is het nu eigenlijk, dit immateriele onstoffelijke weefsel?

Het Engelse 'fabric' wordt vaak in het Nederlands vertaald naar weefsel maar zou ook vertaald kunnen worden als stof. Stof is een synoniem voor textiel. Het is een netwerk van de garens, omgezet in een nuttige stofstructuur. Weefsel en stof hebben hebben overeenkomsten maar uiteindelijk mist stof de beweging die het weefsel wel heeft. De beweging van de draden, maar ook zeker van de samenleving die het weergeeft, als we het over het sociale weefsel hebben. Dit zou een metafoor kunnen zijn voor de manier waarop mensen van een gemeenschap met elkaar omgaan. Als je alle individuele mensen als draden beschouwt, wordt het 'sociale weefsel' gemaakt door die mensen te laten communiceren en bewegen, waardoor de draden samen worden geweven. In dit geval geeft textiel, een weefsel, een krachtige boodschap door, zonder dat je werkelijk fysiek een weefsel hebt hoeven maken. Is dit een volgend stadium van de ontwikkeling in textiel? De onstoffelijke stof?

Het is een mooie en geruststellende gedachte dat een materiaal als textiel zich volop aan het transformeren is. Er hoeft geen fysiek weefsel op tafel te liggen om uren te kunnen praten over weefsels en hun toepassingen. Deze weefsels zijn meer dan dat. Deze weefsels die in feite niet fysiek bestaan op onze wereld zijn daarvoor zeker niet minder belangrijk. Het medium is de boodschap. Praten over sociale weefsels verlangt die zintuigelijke bewustzijn van het geheel en daagt je daarmee uit.

Deze uitdaging is voor de ambachtsman en kunstenaar levendiger dan ooit, die net als in het geval van Hephaistos toch staan voor handwerk en het fysieke materiaal? Ik blijf me afvragen, hoe blijf je fysiek tastbare dingen maken in een wereld die dit langzaam verruilt voor niet-tastbare materialen?

We hebben het gered! De zee van media is getrotseerd en het einde van mijn scriptie is in zicht. Nu ik met mijn gedachten terug in de tegenwoordige tijd ben, realiseer ik me pas hoe zeer ik bewonder dat Richard Sennet, een auteur uit de 21e eeuw, kan schrijven dat een mythologisch figuur als Hephaistos een universele boodschap bij zich draagt.

De boodschap blijft vaak hetzelfde, ondanks de verandering van de media of van het verhaal, zelfs door de eeuwen heen. Hier moeten we echter ook mee oppassen. Soms kan een bepaalde opvatting of oorspronkelijk onschuldige zin, afbeelding of deugd in een compleet andere context gebruikt worden. Bijvoorbeeld voor racistische of fascistische doeleinden. Het verbaasde me hoe gemakkelijk dit gaat, historisch gezien, om een verhaal of bepaalde eigenschappen ervan je eigen te maken en op een aangepaste manier te verspreiden, bijvoorbeeld als propaganda.

De boodschap kan leidend zijn in een verhaal, maar kan ook enkel een onderdeel van het geheel worden. De methode waarop, of het medium zelf, heeft ook een verhaal en de boodschap hiervan kan soms luider zijn dan wordt bedoeld door de schrijver of maker. Het is soms belangrijk je hier bewust van te zijn, ook al is je verhaal nog niet helemaal geschreven, of je vaas niet helemaal gebakken.

Materialen en media zijn aan het veranderen van vorm. Niet alleen door de menselijke hand die het medium vormt, maar ook door de samenleving die andere mogelijkheden ziet voor een materiaal in vergelijking met 2000 jaar geleden.

Terugkomend op de vraag welke rol materialen als keramiek en textiel hebben in het overdragen van boodschappen en welke verschillen er tussen deze twee bestaan, heb ik ontdekt dat ze beide op een heel eigen manier gebeurtenissen opslaan en verwerken. Keramiek maakt het verleden meer tastbaar en fysiek. Textiel creëert een meer zintuiglijke bewustwording van het geheel.

Uiteindelijk lijkt het allemaal om balans te gaan. Een balans tussen realiteit en de mythe, fysieke en denkbeeldige materialen, en voor mij persoonlijk, tussen keramiek en textiel. Hoe zou deze balans eruit kunnen zien?

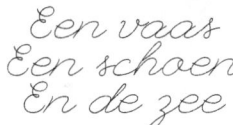

AFBEELDINGEN

1   Eigen beeld

2   Originele afbeelding: http://theconsummatedabbler.com/2016/06/25
    of-the-worlds-most-famous-blacksmiths/

3   Originele afbeelding: https://www.jbagot.com/obra/krater-of
    columns-with-the-return-of-hephaestus-to-olympus-accompanied-
    by-dionysus

4   Originele afbeelding: https://fr.123rf.com/photo_42059385_vase-
    peint-avec-des-chiffres-noirs-illustration-vintage-gravé-.
    html?fromid=cjZ2aTJUUE1MOW5WSWNka2i1bnc1Zz09

5   Eigen beeld

6   Originele foto: https://www.gettyimages.nl/detail/illustratie/
    reconstruction-of-ziggurat-of-ur-drawing-mesopotamian-stock-
    afbeelding/479643835

7   Originele afbeelding: https://gamemag.ru/news/129816/assassins-
    creed-odyssey-razrabotchiki-rasskazali-o-settinge-drevney-
    grecii-i-ego-dostoinstvah

8   Originele afbeelding: https://filmkrant.nl/recensies/300/

9   Originele foto door: Reinhard Jahn, Mannheim (Wall Street, New
    York 1999)

10 Originele afbeelding: https://www.paleisamsterdam.nl/opdekaart/

11 Originele afbeelding: http://www.petergh.f2s.com/flashes.html

12 Origineel beeld: https://collecties.stadsarchief.rotterdam.nl/
    detail.php?id=76946&titel=Steeds%20dezelfde%20vijand!%201673%20
    -%201943.%20Strijdt%20...

13 Originele afbeelding: https://historycollection.co/a-look-inside-
    hitlers-1936-nazi-olympics-through-amazing-photographs/

14 Eigen beeld

Kim Lang

Thriveability Flowers in the Grey

IN TOGETHERNESS WE CARE,
A LANDSCAPE WE SHARE
BY WORKING THE GROUND
FOR SEEDS TO BE SOWN,
AND PLANTS TO BE GROWN
PEOPLE TO BE NOURISHED,
BY THE GARDEN, THAT THEREOF FLOURISHED

PREFACE

How to read a text, that is cut and pasted, cut and pasted, by hand, heart and mind? Maybe do what she did, follow your curiosity, your intuition, your rhythm and it will lead you through a landscape of questions, atmospheres and attempts to answer. Thank you for part-taking.

INTRODUCTION

This is a text full of beginnings, without ends, of invitations and meeting points, of adaptations and antagonism, of togetherness and transformation. A re-learning to re-search how to live together on this planet, not in a complex global-future-thought-construct but rather here, very close to your own body, the local.

These words strive to reconnect the excluded to the whole, depletion to abundance, the individual to the community, the food we consume to the place where it grows. In the belief, that by finding new ways to relate to each other (again), we, in togetherness have a thriving impact. Biocentric. Us amongst the other. Other beings. Us embedded in nature. It is nothing new. Interweaving ourselves back into the landscape we inhabit. By caring. sharing. grounding. sowing. growing. nourishing. flourishing.

She/Her

One of her favourite things to do is to pull forwards a sleeve, which crawled back to the elbow. By moving it down to the wrist her elbow suddenly has more space to move, her forearm is warm again. This sensation, this regained possibility to move, is what she wants to share. With You. She is willing to offer flowers and stories to this text, which she carries in her container from one place to another. Stories about her growing up, surrounded by wild flowers and other life-affirming creatures. Stories about her encounter with grey concrete poured over living matter — and ways of dealing with these materials and their characteristics.

Inviting the world into our houses - our bodies

Our urgency should not be sustaining the earth, but to make things thrive (again). I can recall the situation where this has been said very well. It was while watching a documentary. The green, the sun, the message that came through the screen, seemed to reach me, where I was sitting on my bed. A moment which Hartmut Rosa would describe as 'resonance'.

Our urgency should not be sustaining the earth, but to make things thrive (again).

Nature as an organism has a very caring attitude. Not only a caring one, but also a regenerative, flourishing, blossoming one - nature thrives, it shares benevolence — it is abundance. Could this be the attitude, the direction, the path to step on? Thriveability. The possibility of thriving.

But, who can afford to thrive?

Many inhabitants on this planet live a life in poverty, in isolation — in a fight for survival. Pursuant to the 'Global Multidimensional Poverty Index'[1] about 77% of our global population live in circumstances rated as poor. And this poverty is mostly provoked by the exploiting lifestyle the Global North[2] performs with the resources (still) available. The exploitation and

deprivation leads to the climate crisis which effects the Global South the hardest! And not only human beings are suffering, animals are traumatised, tortured.

Exploitation. We exploit our all mother. We dig substances we call "resources" out of her belly. We exploit one each other by extreme labour. This exploitation, this injustice[3] causes a lot of world pain.

So, what if the "world's pain" knocks on your door and asks, if it could come into the warm for a while? Be my guest. The doors are open. The world pain enters.

World pain makes me feel swooningly - on the edge of fainting. Fainting forward, into the alarming, shocking and painful circumstances other beings are experiencing — right now. The skin, that first seemed to separate me from "the other" cracks open and the world pours in. Thunderous floods of pain of suffering, of worldliness, of pluriverse[4]. No hold — all in. Be my guest. Any sense of separation is washed away. Washed away. Into one. big. ocean. We. are. one, big, ocean. Stutter.

I. stutter. when I. write. these words. I stutter.

Because. it seems. so alien. it seems. so pain-full. so wrong. so unjust. so unfair.

What. on earth. what. on earth. are we doing? Human. species. Human? Is this human?

The pain. the trauma. is. present. embodied. in the world. the earth. within. me.

We could treat the world pain in our bodies like a disease. It being something we want to get rid of. Something alien, distant, unwanted. Or, are we able to live with the world pain, to accept it as part of us and even take care of it. In a next step, could we even appreciate the qualities of the effects the world pain has on us: becoming compassionate, sensitive, open, permeable to "the other", the worldliness, we might feel close to something that is happening somewhere else, sometimes far away.

I'm not fainting. So far I've never fainted from world pain. On the contrary, it grounds me, makes me aware of where and how I am standing on my feet. It lids a fire within me, a force. The fuel is called responsibility. Responsibility drives me, to act upon the current situation, by the means given to me.

Nature wants to thrive, and we as part of nature, want to thrive as well. Every being on earth. I believe. This is our nature. But due to different causes we touch upon the inability to thrive. Every-body is on their journey towards the thriving. In different bodies, different places and different tempos.

In the following chapters I would like to travel with you through the landscape of the following words. In order to locate questions and 'answering voices' on historical, present and future practices.

```
«in togetherness we care
a landscape we share
by working the ground
for seeds to be sown
and plants to be grown
people to be nourished
by the garden, that thereof flourished»
```

1   Global Multidimensional Poverty Index: *"Human Development Reports."* The 2019 Global Multidimensional Poverty Index (MPI) | Human Development Reports. 2018.

2   Global North/Global South

    Global South is what was called third world countries, most of them are located in Asia, Africa, Latin America and the Caribbean. While the Global South had have little responsibility for the current climate crisis they feel the effects the most. The climate change is mainly caused by the Global North.

3   Climate Injustice: Climate injustice refers to the fact that those who have done least to cause climate change (Global South) are suffering the most from its effects, like e.g. flooding, drought, heat-waves, forest fire, storm, cyclone...

4   pluriverse: the world as conceived according to a theory of pluralism, "a world where many worlds fit" Escobar, Arturo. *Designs for the Pluriverse: Radical Interdependence, Autonomy, and the Making of Worlds.* Durham ; London: Duke University Press, 2018.

CHAPTER 1
IN TOGETHERNESS WE CARE,
A LANDSCAPE WE SHARE

1.1
A world full of
adaptations and antagonism

Some of us grew up in a garden of flowers. I did and She did as well. Surrounded by the blossoming, flowering, thriving she could not imagine that there are others without. She grew up with a feeling of being embraced by the living surrounding her, consisting of trees, meadows, bees, small lakes, flowers, the sun, a mother, a father, a sister, animals, a garden which faded out into meadows and little paths, crossing over with streams of clear water. Within this embrace she experienced a lot of freedom to move, into all directions, to run, jump, fall and get dirty.

When she was 17 she exchanged the romantic, rural landscape for one dominated by concrete, by severity. Not only the landscape had a different tone of colour but as well the people inhabiting it. The poverty and suffering of both landscape and inhabitants was inescapably present. It was then, when she experienced how loaded and heavy peoples baggage can be. How they are de-pressed by the weight of their their grief, their pain, their fear. The weight so heavy and unbearable that they almost collapse.

Collapse.

Collapse on concrete.

Collapse into the grey.

A grey room. She finds herself sitting on a table, with everyone else. The room is dark and the lamp only spots the plates on the table. All participants sit in the dark. She tastes the meal that is served. It is very quiet. She startles by the intensely bitter taste and the size of the chunks, they are huge. Way too big for one bite. Way too big for some-one to chew on. Who want's to eat this bitter meal? And how to swallow it? She looks around in the room. Hesitating spoons, bodies in the dark. It is not the food she has prepared, neither is she the only one suffering from it's bitter taste. No. So many are here and so much skin and flesh of the earth. It hurts. It hurts to see everyone struggling. She bites and tries to swallow it with the others. They can't handle it either. She stands up. The others sit still. They can't move. She, standing behind her chair, looks at the scenario. Observing. Unlike the others, she can leave and enter the room freely, as she wants. She finds it wrong to just leave this room behind her, close the door. Ignore. On the other hand her participation in this dark room, this bitter meal can't be an innocent one, it asks her to know about her approach, her attitude, her role within the situation, this is the responsibility she feels as an artist.

1.2
Different modes of living

The system in the Global North amplifies competition and self-expression. It is a constant musical chairs game[5]. The moment the music plays we all run around the room, alert, elbows out — ready to jump on one of the chairs and push the other away. While some earthlings are afraid of freezing to death over night, others don't have enough lifetime to spend their money. Each individual lives in different circumstances.

If we humans are part of nature, we are part of its thriving qualities as well. But many people experience suffering by different causes and circumstances which keeps them away of this thriving motion. When describing different modes of living, I don't refer to how rich or poor someone is money-wise, but rather to how free we are to share ourselves?

Survival

In the survival mode life is a constant fight to stay alive.

To survive, to "not die" is the main concern. The very basic needs are not met. Fear is present. You eat the bitter meal. There is no other option.

— The hands baled to fists.

Life Sustaining

It is a bumpy road. To keep the wheel turning a lot of effort is needed. Life is a rat-race. There is no option to take a break, a short standstill, the only way is to keep on moving, running with a heavy container. The needs of the present and the near future are heavy.

— Nervous, busy fingers, sweaty palms.

> «clean your desk, wash the dishes, clean the floor,wash your clothes, wash your toes, change the baby's diaper, finish the report, correct the typos, mend the fence, keep the customer happy, throw out the stinking garbage, watch out don't put things in your nose, what shall I wear, I have no sox, pay your bills, don't litter, save string, wash your hair, change the sheets, go to the store, I'm out of perfume, say it again— he doesn't understand, seal it again—it leaks, go to work, this art is dusty, clear the table, call him again, flush the toilet, stay young.»[6]

Equilibrium

Life is rolling, sometimes on its own. Sometimes the concerns overweigh, other times the sweetness of life. The swing is the security. It goes up and down like a pendulum.

— The arms move as extensions of the body, spacious movement, the palms are sometimes visible.

> "We are neither poor nor rich, we are something in between, we have everything that we need, but not everything that we wish for."[7]

Thriving

There is no fear of having too little. Abundance is present. Fear absent. The backpacks are open, everyone is able to take. It is a direction. A movement. Branching forwards, upwards to the infinite.

— Soft, giving hands, no clinging, the palms open.

1.3
What does care taste like?

When in the survival-mode, there is little space to think about the wellbeing of "the other". There is just no capacity for that. In order to care about somebody or something else, the very basic needs must be fulfilled. Still, greed could keep us busy and therefore lonely. But if your subjectivity is not overpowering, "the other" receives space, where care can be shared. By care I refer to the actions we undertake to sustain or uplift the wellbeing of ourselves, someone or something else.

---

5 musical chairs game
    There is always one chair less than people playing the game. When the music plays participants move around in the room. When the music stops everyone tries to catch a chair. The one person which was not able to get a chair is out of the game. One more chair is removed and the game continues.

6 Laderman Ukeles, Mierle. *"Manifesto for maintenance art 1969! Proposal for an exhibition «CARE»"*. Philadelphia, 1969.

7 *«Gestern ist Heute – Lebensraum Rumänien (1996) III.»* YouTube. hanshedrich, 2017.

1.4
Gift economy

To step over into a caring network Charles Eisenstein promotes the "gift economy". A system which is quite opposite from the current money driven system we are living in. Capitalism keeps us very busy with earning, owing and spending money. It asks a lot of investment of our time and energy (and resources) in order to receive a number on a bank-account, with which we are forced to pay for life-surviving and life- sustaining things. It seems that no one thought of care when setting up this system. Capitalism has a bitter taste, it is greedy and hierarchical. With these conditions we are very much in a mindset of: "What can I get from this life, this world?" The gift economy is an alternative in which actions that "nourish" someone or something else are acknowledged. The more you give, the richer you are. And this is done by resources that are freely available to us. So much has been privatised over the last few decades. In order to care for each other and for the landscape we inhabit, we need access to resources, such as food, water, land. My assumption is, that if you are close to the "sources", if you are connected to what is thriving, if you feel taken care of by others, attitudes needed in a competitive money game are not of importance anymore. You won't have less if you help others, or help the landscape to thrive. Even the opposite. The more you give, the richer you are. You add to the thriving motion. And once this starts rolling, selfish and greedy people are no longer served by the gift-economy. It is quite the opposite of what we are undergoing now, here in the Global North. Charles Eisenstein emphasises therefore the 're-skilling' of people in order to be able to support and care for one another outside the money-game. A big value shift takes place when your ability to share, care, listen, fix, build, heal and grow is the currency that you make your living from.

She finds herself in a gathering, high up in the mountains. Many come and sit around a fire in a big tent, crossed legged, one person behind the other, in a circle — of course. Beautiful, uplifting melodies are sung, offerings are made, to all the elements. Rice thrown into the fire. Rhythmically. "Sv h", "Sv h", "Sv h" — over and over again. Everyone sings when lining up to get holy food. A big wooden spoon serves the meal into her palms out of a big round ceramic container. The warm and soft food rests in her palms. She shares gratitude towards mother earth, the people who cultivated and harvested, the journey the food had until arriving here, gratitude towards the people involved in cooking this meal. Then out of her palm she eats. "Oh, so sweet. So sweet." She closes her eyes and the 'prasat'[8] takes her on a journey, to the most familiar place, to the breast of her mother. Small she is, held in loving strong arms, lying on her lab. She remembers the taste of breast-milk. Tears run down her face. She nourishes her — all-embracing mother.

1.5.
Landscape and the human body, an interwoven relationship

We all are, born through a mother, into this world. Born into different modes of living. What do we all share? Each of us carries a different baggage, another container on their path, throughout life. The ideas that we have about life, values and dreams or visions are as diverse as the character of each individual. In this there is nothing overall in common. But what we do have in common may be the actions that we undertake to stay alive — such as eating. The act of eating is not only connecting human to human through an activity, but it also connects us to the landscape which we inhabit, the place where the food comes from. All the knowledge of the soil, the bacteria, the pesticides, herbicides, the machine work, the humans and animals involved in the growing process of the food are transported to the (super)market and from there to our plates, into our mouths, becoming our bodies. Eating is the occasion where the landscape merges with the human body — the food (the former landscape) takes the shape of the human body. The act of eating, the transformation from landscape into human body connects all humanity.

To sustain the human organism we nourish it with liquids and solid food. Often unconscious about the fact that these materials have been segregated elsewhere. «What we eat shapes the landscape we live in.»[9] It might seem absurd that the coffee we drink, actually grew on the other side of the planet, somewhere in the earth, at a location, a specific place in the landscape, with certain weather and climate conditions and so many human and other interactants. Most of the time we are not in touch, nor confronted with the landscape, the system, the rhythms of the place where our food actually grew. The supermarket is the place where we meet this often foreign landscape for the first time. Nicely packaged, in order to maximise the probability of the product being sold, all kinds of marketing tricks are used.

The romanticisation of the landscape, the romanticisation of the heritage of the product, the romanticisation of the narrative behind the food we consume takes place in the supermarket. Depending on what food we consume, a certain system is supported. The product bought, leaves an empty spot on the shelf and will therefore (most likely) be replaced by a product that has already been produced. The consumer is therefore influencing its direct or distant landscape. The impact is not only visual, but multilayered. By consuming certain products, we are keeping production chains alive - or not. These production chains start in the very earth itself. Where on earth is the soil we are talking about? I want to know.

«We are makers, among much else, of landscapes. The land under our hands is shaped by the food we eat; by farming methods and ways of preparing and rotating fields; by the ways we hedge or wall or fence them; and by the laws we make for passing them on. We remake the land in our own image so that it comes in time to reflect both the industry and the imagination of its makers, and gives us back, in working land, but also in the idealised version of landscape that is park or garden, an image both of our human nature and our power. Such making is also a rich form of possession.»[10]

Our knowledge and awareness grows of which kind of nourishment supports a healthy, thriving, natural environment. But most often healthy, thriving food comes at a high monetary cost for the consumer. And some, even with goodwill, don't have the possibility to pay for this healthy, thriving landscape on the shelf... But maybe the garden, your own or the garden of your neighbour, the garden in your neighbourhood is the place to practice the thriving relationality of landscape and its inhabitants.

«The soil, the garden is
an extension of the house.
Or reversed.
The house is an extension of the garden.
The garden is entering the house through the kitchen, into her body. And all this in circles.
All year round.
Pataa Pataa Pa ua ua u. Pata taa Pata Pa ua ua u.
Plates are turning in circles. Food is shared.
We chant to the mother. The mother generously feeding us - with love and care - beautiful mother. Pataa Pataa Pa ua ua u.
Pata taa Pata Pa ua ua u.»

8 Prasat or Prasadam literally means a gracious gift. It denotes anything, typically an edible food, that is first offered to a deity, saint, Perfect Master or an Avatar and then distributed in His or Her name to their followers or others as a good sign.

9 Jorge Menna Barreto is a Brasilian artist who lives and works in Rio de Janeiro. He creates site-specific projects which investigate our delicate relationship with food, society and nature. By asking audiences to engage through the act of eating, he questions complex environmental issues regarding our unsustainable dependence on a global food system. www.cargocollective.com/jorgemennabarreto

10 Galligan, Brian. *Australian Citizenship*. Land and Heritage. p. 119. Melbourne, 1997

2.1.
Where on earth is the local?

In a vast valley, surrounded by high snow-topped mountains, in northern Italy a wise man told me how his local tastes like:

> «To define the space in which I practice, I use the following measurement. As far as I can cycle with my bicycle in one day. As far as my good reputation reaches. And as far as my eyes can see.»

We can't be and act anywhere else than here. But this does not mean that we don't "sense" the rest of the earth. A balancing act. To practice locally with the awareness of "the whole". When taking the local into consideration it seems absurd to deny the existence of the rest of the planet. The global. The global being something bigger, the global being always somewhere else, never here, the global being this all-encompassing fabric spun over the globe. Unreachable. Untouchable. There are no "global solutions". The whole world is made from local skills. And this is what I'd love to emphasise. The idea that the whole world, the global, can learn from locally embodied skills and solutions.

2.2.
Agriculture + Horticulture

Agriculture is a very young phenomenon. It derives from the latin word «agro», meaning field. which hypothetically sources from the Sanskrit word «ajras», meaning "plain and open country". This refers to the fact, that agriculture cultivates food on fields. But before cultivating anything the space needs to be made "plain and open" which means: cleared, flattened, to be accessed by big machines. Especially in industrial agriculture[11] this means not to work with, but on, the land. Agriculture began only 10'000 years ago, whilst human culture already exists for around 2 million years. Before agriculture we lived in a horticultural period, «hortus» meaning garden. And in horticulture the idea of the garden is a wild one. The human is really just a part-taker in the landscape by helping certain plants to grow using very simple techniques. What was practiced differently in horticulture as in agriculture of today, is that horticulture involved an active participation of individuals in life sustaining and life giving activities such as observation, cultivation, care and maintenance, this is, with industrial agriculture surely not required anymore, here in the Global North. The meaning of "the life giving" in the Global North is closely connected to a job that ensures the earning of money, which makes it possible to access the food-supply. This concludes in the idea: 'food comes through money' and not from a landscape.

Working the ground could therefore refer to the need to bring soil back to life. To reconnect to this life-giving ground we live on. "For many of our challenges, we don't need new technologies or new ideas; we need the will, foresight and courage to use the best of the old ideas," Shoshanna Saxe says. The ground is here, surrounding us, I hear a call, I sense the responsibility to free the soil, to shine light on it and gather around this piece of landscape to practice new ways of cultivation.

The local can taste of reachable distances, familiar faces and places, feasibility, embodied knowledge of the landscape we inhabit.

CHAPTER 3
FOR SEEDS TO BE SOWN,
AND PLANTS TO BE GROWN

3.1.
Growing participation

Vandana Shiva promotes, if young people recognise, that working with the hands is an act of sowing the seeds for a possible future world. «Working with the hands is not a degradation, it is our real humanity — start a garden...»[12]

Our body, mind and the senses are asked to collaboratively participate. It is us and the landscape. In togetherness. It is shared cultivation, care and maintenance labour that allows us to support and afford a healthy, thriving, natural landscape that nourishes us in return. Participation creates community and this is what the cultivation of a garden represents to me.

3.2.
CSA (community supported agriculture)

'Radiesli'[13] (radish, in Swiss German) is the name of a project in Switzerland which follows the principles of CSA (communally supported agriculture). By means of participation, CSA projects soften the border between production and consumption. This means it is not possible to pay money and get food, participation is mandatory, but there are various ways of part-taking. When visiting 'Radiesli' I was so astonished by the diversity of this small scale farm. The site is so romantic, colourful, small and packed with shrubs full of berries. There are trees loaded with apples, fields full of salad, corn, wheat, rye, buckwheat and more. Of course they also cultivate parts of their vegetables on fields, but the whole area seems more like an enlarged garden (referring to Horticulture) than an industrial agriculture landscape. Marion, one of the two gardeners working for 'Radiesli', brings me to the fields where I meet other participants. One of the first things I hear from them is how much they love to work here. "We are only supposed to work 8 times a year 3, hours a day on the farm. But I could imagine coming more often! Most of us come here by bicycle, it is only 20 minutes from Bern (capital of Switzerland) and to work with the soil, the vegetables, the hands, is such a good alternation from the other work we normally do..." Marion and another gardener work for a paid job. All the costs of 'Radiesli' are covered by a small annual fee paid by the participators and their labour. The structure seems very inclusive. Families bring their children to the farm, they have their own corner in the garden where they have flower-beds and tipi-tents. Participators with difficulties paying the annual fee are able to give more of their time to help on the fields to compensate. Marion is very patient with us. "What are you planting?" she asks a young woman next to me, we are four, working body on body, in silence, some words, some laughter, planting 1'500 little seedlings into the good smelling earth. "Salad", she answers. Marion laughs, "What kind of salad?"

---

11 To sustain industrial agriculture a huge amount of water and other resources are needed and hard chemicals are used, which is exploiting and drying out the landscape. The world population continues to increase, while the topsoil (the outermost layer of soil, the first 13-25cm, very crucial for plant growth, water filtering and absorbing carbon out of the air) is decreasing intensely. Intensely means, if we would sustain the cultivation of industrial agriculture just the way we do now, we would have about 50-60 years of harvesting left until all the topsoil of the earth is gone. This would, of course have quiet life diminishing impacts on this planet. If the topsoil is gone, it will get pretty hot here, since topsoil cools our whole climate, there will be none of the plant-harvest possible anymore which now makes 95% of our all food.

12 Shiva, Vandana. Video. *Phycisist and Thinker*, 2018.

13 www.radiesli.org

3.3.
What does hope taste like?

She looks at their hands. Closed and tight fists. «What is it that you wish for the most?» Her hands become a bit nervous. He looks at her, straight. All hands hold a warm glass of tea. Silence. Lemon and Verbena in Arabic letters. «We are not in a position to wish for anything.» Silence. Lemon and Verbena. She takes a sip. «Mmm. So what would you need?» He looks at the stony ground. «Hope — this is what I' lost on my journey from Chad to Amsterdam.»

Hope.

How does hope taste like?

Her hands relax again. She remembers a story.

The Stone soup (also known as nail soup, axe soup, button soup, wood soup) is a folk tale, first published in 1720 by Madame de Noyer. It is a story about a traveler entering a village with nothing else than a metal vessel. The traveler is hungry and has nothing to eat, but carries an idea. The vessel is filled with water from the nearby stream, a fire is prepared, the container placed on the heat. The traveler adds a stone into the container and stirs. A villager passes by and examines the happening and asks with curiosity what is boiling in the container. «A stone soup, a very delicious soup that will be shared with everyone in the village later». The villager looks enchanted. «We only need a little bit of salt it seems, would you have some salt at home to add to the stone soup?» The villager does not hesitate and walks off to get the salt. Another villager passes by and is involved in the preparing of the soup by adding a few carrots s-he has at home. Another one adds onions and so it continues until the soup is enriched by all the curious villagers who help cooking the soup even though this was not their first intention. The stone is removed and the soup ready to be shared with the villagers.

This is the story of the stone soup. Her hands unfold. The palms open towards the ceiling. Then, she brings them slowly together, to a little bowl — a container. She fills the container with wishes for him and for the other him.

3.5
What makes us human?

If we follow the human lineage back to its beginnings, we find activities that have been practiced for around 1'000'000 years! Over this period of time we gathered around fire, made baskets to contain things, tended and harvested food, raised children together, made music and built shelters. This sits so deep in our genes, whereas agriculture with its many consequences to our society is only about 10'000 years old. What if being human has not much to do with money-earning, being competitive, individualistic and greedy but is way more focused on the aspects of sharing, togetherness, crafting, nourishing and caring?

Once she got washed by a Sri Lankan mother, in a backyard. She made her lay, naked on a big warm stone. The mother scrubbed her, washed her, dried her with a soft towel and oiled her skin. She was crying like a baby.

3.6.
What do we want to cultivate?

Cultivation (from Latin 'colere')[14] after all, is about taking care of life; the cultivation of life is concerned with forms of living as much as it is with life itself.

We can find it all in the garden. A caring, engaged and encouraging sociality; a constant re-learning of interaction; a holistic approach[15]; working in togetherness; the interaction of human(nature) with thriving nature; the coming home to a landscape over and over again; a nourishing aspect that goes in both directions, from the ground to us humans and from us humans into the ground; and last but not least the thriving aspect that you, as a part-taker, are part-of.

```
«'to flourish' - be vigorous, prosper, thrive
I want to be someone who reminds You, that flowers
exist and that you are able to plant them
I don't want to close my heart, my eyes and ears
for the bad, the pain, the fear, the anger
I want to be open and receptive
I neither want to force things into existence
You can't force flowers to grow
We might not be able to shut down voices that
want to mute our hope, our trust our love, our
flourishing shut up. No.
Let them talk
Let them be
Turn up the volume
of Your inner voice
Your inner magic
Your inner flourishing process
Let's remind each other, that flowers exist
and we are able to plant them»
```

14 Petti, Alessandro, Sandi Hilal, and Eyal Weizman. Architecture after Revolution: Decolonizing Architecture Art Residency. p. 183. 2013.

15 a 'holistic approach' aims to consider all cooperating and influencing aspects of a person, a landscape or situation

CHAPTER 4
PEOPLE TO BE NOURISHED,
BY THE GARDEN,
THAT THEREOF FLOURISHED

4.1. Support structures

```
What are we nourished by? Embedded in grey, the
sun becomes very crucial for the inhabitants of
a city. When there is no green, there has to be
yellow, otherwise everything gets the qualities
of concrete — grey, hard, silent, rough, heavy.
Attempts to eat the greyness away ended in pain.
It was not the diet that made her flourish. No.
She wonders, how to arrange a table to nourish
people through a healthy thriving landscape,
not only to meet their need of being fed in
the belly, but including the hidden needs as
well. She thinks of warm soap-water. Of oil
and soil, of food with the characteristics of
a giving mother.
```

Around 30'000 years ago, our brains evolved with some extra layers of cells in the neocortex, making it possible to see meaning and symbols in the world. This is when we find first evidences of spiritual practices in human culture.

Before constructed sites were built, people gathered in natural locations, where trees, stones, bodies of water and other natural objects were venerated, in the belief that these places were hosting spirits and gods. Steadily these natural sites became areas for constructed places of worship (such as temples and churches) which can be seen as effigies of what has been worshipped before. Natural elements were then gradually incorporated in rituals and cults.

These places of worship were large-scale community-projects on which hundreds of people worked on for many years. This occasion asked for structures which brought about very hierarchical systems, notions of control and power. When agriculture came into existence, around 10'000 years ago, it was developed to feed the community that gathered around these places of worship. Agriculture means civilisation. «You don't get civilisation, cities, civis - city life until you get agriculture.» Or in the words of excavator Klaus Schmidt: "First came the temple, then the city."

Agriculture, despite Horticulture was able to nourish big groups of people on location in a very efficient and controlled manner. But agriculture brought in many faults to our relationship with the landscape. "Agriculture turns ecosystems into people."16 What Toby Hemenway means by that, is, that agriculture does not support an ecosystem's function, but rather destroys it by our flattening of the landscape and forcing crops to grow, mono. Mono, solitary, remote from a functioning ecosystem.

And nowadays we still build temples, for things we worship. They are directed to values we rate highly in our culture. Here in the Global North this means: insurance buildings, banks and other finance temples. They glorify a wealth invented by humans, for a very exclusive group of people. They nourish a competitive, outsmarting, overpowering attitude — the genius of men.

In Quechuan, the language spoken by different indigenous groups in South America, they have a word for for a functioning, thriving ecosystem — 'Sumak Kawsay' or 'La Pachamama'16. It refers to wellbeing, which means to live in harmony with ourselves and each other within the living and breathing environment. It describes a way of doing things in a community-centric, ecologically-balanced and culturally-sensitive way. This creates a support structure17 for all of us, humans and non-humans, when we find a humble and healthy way of relating to our ecosystem.

16 «Within Pachamama, human beings are but minuscule elements. They are guided by certain elements, one of them being the principle of "relationality". We believe everything is interrelated. Nothing is disconnected, nothing is separate.» Marques, Pedro. Book. The Forest & the School: Where to Sit at the Dinner Table? Paulo Tavares. p.498, 2014.

17 Celine Condorelli and Gavin Wade wrote a book called "support structures", «It is a manual for those things that encourage, give comfort, approval, and solace; that care for and provide consolation and the necessities of life.»

4.2.
The fabric of elaborated care

I feel driven by a sense of responsibility to serve the world with the means given to me.

To observe how our species is co-inhabiting and co-relating with its direct surrounding.

To scrutinise local circumstances with their multi-complex issues and to pull on certain strings in order to activate potential which can enhance the life quality of the ecosystem as well as its inhabitant's.

While art shown in galleries and museums only speaks to a very specific group within our society, I feel challenged to have a hands on approach, to practice the accessible and inclusive, to create sites or situations where these qualities are outlived.

As an artist I wonder how contemporary occasions for rituals and ceremonies would look, taste, sound and feel. And how this could help us reconnect to the landscape surrounding us, to increase health, wellbeing and relation. Therefore I see a lot of potential in the garden as a local support structure, a site for reconnection. The garden as an effigy of nature, where rituals of care and maintenance can be practiced. The garden as a place for education, de-learning, a re-learning, a place of 'growing participation', a site for practicing co-inhabiting and co-relating with the direct surrounding we are living in. And not a garden where we humans are overpowering the landscape but rather a place where we practice to weave human and thriving nature together, a re-learning of relating to each other (again) — in one big fabric, a 'construct of elaborated care'18.

```
                                      in togetherness»
                                            flourish

                              flourish
                              nourish

                    plants to be grown
                    for seeds to be sown
                    by working the ground

              we share
              we care

           from where the flowers grow
           this is the beginning,
           the nourishing ground

      «This is not the end
```

18 'texere'
Latin for:
1 'construct with elaborate care'
2 plait (together)
3 weave.
   'We-ave' draws the attention to the intersections in life. The moment where two separate fields meet, join and merge. Two different colours converge. Each of them with their qualities, their histories, their needs, dreams, visions. Weave. After the crossing over, the moment of separation follows. We never leave as we arrive. We grow, store, share, nourish, stain each other. When separating we wish each other well. 'We-ave'. What would we be without each other? A loose thread — dreams, potential would fray out. By meeting and separating, meeting, separating, meeting, separating, wishing each other well, over and over again, we create a web, a fabric. 'We-ave' could therefore stand for these procreative, foster occasions which creates a network, a fabric of elaborated care.

CONCLUSION

Thriving has, same as this text, the qualities to branch out, to the infinite, the 'yet unknown'. As an artist I'm interested in working the ground, creating circumstances and situation in which the potential for thriving is created. Thriving is nothing singular. Same as this text. It is nothing I am able to push into existence myself. No, it is plural, it is alive. It is an attitude, a movement, a direction of an organism. I am curious of the undertakings after this text, of myself and others.

Epilogue:
A house of six floors

«Dear Sister, dear Friend, dear Brother, Lover and Father, dear Yet-Unknown

A few years ago we shared a vision. Something we all sensed but could not give words to. And in the meantime it continued to grow, into something bigger — something more tangible. This is an attempt to draw this vision using words.

We have been talking about a house. Of six floors. A house in the city, in the midst of madness. In society and not off it. A container wherein things are carefully cultivated, ritualised, crafted and harvested. A house in which nourishment transforms into meals through many hands, into many bellies. Pouring liquid from one container into the other. With care, with joy and some splashes. We shared the idea of the house being open and safe at the same time. Where strangers turn into participants and friends. Where people are able to retreat, recover, nourish, cleanse, practice, educate, rest and thrive.

You enter the house through the kitchen, one long table, big windows, plants, a wooden kitchen counter in the middle of the room. Food and people are able to circulate, in the room, around the table, through the kitchen, through their bellies.

One floor above the kitchen things are stored. The landscape in jars, simple food, simple cleaning products and tools for maintenance.

When walking up to the second floor the shoes are taken off. We have been talking about «the Academy of the thriving». Smaller tables, books on the walls, access to internet, printers, bookbinding, a space to meet and exchange, to educate each other, in what we think helps us and the landscape to come to a thriving motion.

The third floor is empty. A big spacious room. Wooden floor. Next to the window are, carefully placed, some sacred objects, candles, incense, stones, a wooden board, flowers. There are mats in the room, some cushions and blankets. It is a room to practice, to rest, to meditate.

The fourth floor is simply equipped with wooden loft beds. A wall of shelves to store personal belongings. A room for guests, long or short-term, the participants of the house and its rhythms. It is quiet, simple and clean. There are textiles hanging in the space, light colours, to divide the shared space in private pouches. From here you reach the fifth floor. It is a space for cleanliness, water, earth and soap sets the tone. One separation in the room is furnished with a massage bed — for treatments of different kinds. It is a space where the water flows on, and in our bodies.

And now, do you remember what the sixth floor was for? Was it the space where we weave the common fabric? On one big loom? Was it the void, the space we need for the 'still-to-come'? Dear, Sister, Friend, Brother, Lover, Father , dear Yet-Unknown, do you remember? What did I forget?»

«... Your house is
your larger body... »[19]

If the house of six floors is my enlarged body, a container to serve from. a kitchen, where you transform the landscape into nourishing meals
a storage full of delights
an academy of the thriving
a spacious room, a void for things to arise
a guesthouse for resting
a space for cleansing and caring
and of course, a loom to weave the common fabric on.

Then I ask myself if my body and all the actions coming from it, is able to cultivate, carry and share these qualities as well. To practice them in the everyday life. For the everyday landscape, the everyday people. By embodying, materialising and ritualising these qualities they get in touch with the world surrounding me. While certain issues on this planet seem to have clear applicable solutions (as for example the step towards fossil free energy) other intersections such as the lost connection with our landscape, the sources of the food we eat and the therewith connected injustice of nature and its inhabitants asks for a more interdisciplinary, multilateral approach. And this, close to my own body, close to the everyday, is where I see so much potential to embody, materialise and ritualise research into an artistic practice. Through different medias, in different occasions and formats to nourish the landscape and people with what we have lost to re-discover our thriving nature.

```
«and into this pouch, into this pocket you are
taken a warm and caring place
a scent of
boiled rice
coming from the earth
yellow curcuma
golden saffron flower
growing under the sun
you are embedded in warm soil
deep securing roots
an opening facing the sky
golden light pouring in
into your body
your body is warm
embraced, enlaced
held — caring, loving
by woven threads»
```

19 Gibran, Kahlil. *The Prophet*. p. 42, 1923.

During the summer 2019 I was able to make a research trip throughout Europe to visit different locations where people de-learn or re-practice their relationship and interaction with each other and their environment. The documentation of this research is bundled in another independent publication.

If you are interested in ordering a copy of it, get in touch with me: plantanism@gmail.com

Andersen, Kip and Kuhn, Keegan. Movie. _Cowspiracy. The Sustainability Secret._ Los Angeles, 2014

Choi, Binna, Annette Krauss, Yolande van der Heide, Liz Allan. Book. _Unlearning Exercises. Art Organizations as Sites for Unlearning._ Co-published by Casco Art Institute: Working for the Commons, Utrecht and Valiz, Amsterdam, 2018.

Condorelli Céline, Gavin Wade, and James Langdon. Book. _Support Structures._ Berlin: Sternberg Press, 2014.

Dass, Ram. Book. _Be Here Now._ Lama Foundation, San Cristobal, New Mexico, 1971.

Dass, Ram. Video. _Sacred in the Everyday – Ram Dass Full Lecture._ Baba Ram Dass, 2014.

Eisenstein, Charles. Video. _Systems Of The Damned | Russell Brand & Charles Eisenstein - Under The Skin._ Russel Brand, 2019.

Eisenstein, Charles. Video. _A New Story of Climate Change – Charles Eisenstein at New Frontiers._ Edmund Hillary Fellowship, 2018.

Eisenstein, Charles. Book. _More Beautiful World Our Hearts Know Is Possible._ READHOWYOUWANT COM LTD, 2017.

Escobar, Arturo. _Designs for the Pluriverse: Radical Interdependence, Autonomy, and the Making of Worlds._ Durham ; London: Duke University Press, 2018.

Gibran, Kahlil. Book. _The Prophet._ Alfred A. Knopf,1923.

Haraway, Donna J. Book. _Staying with the Trouble Making Kin in the Chthulucene._ Durham: Duke University Press, 2016.

Hemenway, Toby. Video. _How Permaculture can save Humanity and the Earth, but not Civilization._ Duke's Nicholas School of the Environment, 2010.

Laderman Ukeles, Mierle. Essay. _"Manifesto for maintenance art 1969! Proposal for an exhibition «CARE»"._ Philadelphia, 1969.

Marques, Pedro. Book. _The Forest & the School: Where to Sit at the Dinner Table?_ Berlin: Archive Books, 2014. Menna Barreto, Jorge. Artist. cargocollective.com/jorgemennabarreto

Petti, Alessandro, Sandi Hilal, and Eyal Weizman. Book. _Architecture after Revolution: Decolonizing Architecture Art Residency._ Berlin: Sternberg Press 2013.

Rauterberg, Hanno. Book. _Die Kunst Und Das Gute Leben. Über die Ethik der Ästhetik._ Berlin: Suhrkamp, 2015. !17 of !19

Rosa, Hartmut. Video. _Harmut Rosa talks about his concept of "Resonance" – Degrowth Leipzig 2014._ ecapio. 2014

Shiva, Vandana. Video. _Phycisist and Thinker._ Gulab Jamun, 2018.

Shiva, Vandana. Video. _A message from Dr Vandana Shiva for the New Year 2020._ NAVDANYA, 2019.

Van Heeswijk, Jeanne. Essay. _Preparing for the Not-Yet._ Slow Reader, A Resource for Design Thinking and Practice, 2016.

REFERENCES

Auboyer, Jeannine. _"Ceremonial Object."_ Encyclopædia Britannica. Encyclopædia Britannica, inc., December 9, 2015. https://www.britannica.com/topic/ceremonial-object.

"Agriculture (n.)." Online Etymology Dictonairy. https://www.etymonline.com/word/agriculture?ref=etymonline_crossreference.

Busch, Henner, and Department of Human Geography at Lund University. _"Green Transition: The Whole World Can Learn from a Small Town in Iceland."_ SNORDIC-FRONT, August 22th 2019. https://sciencenordic.com/co2-environment-forskerzonen/green-transition-the-whole-world-can-learn- from-a-small-town-in-iceland/1555021.

"Climate Justice: 5 Inequities of Climate Change, Explained." Olivia Giovetti. Concern Worldwide. 2019, https://www.concernusa.org/story/climate-justice-inequities-climate-change/.

"Connecting Art, Food and Nature – Jorge Menna Barreto." Connecting Art, Food and Nature – Jorge Menna Barreto | Liverpool Biennial of Contemporary Art. 2019. https://www.biennial.com/blog/2019/05/08/connecting-art-food-and-nature-jorge-menna-barreto.

"Education Transforms Lives." UNESCO. 2019, http://www.unesco.org/education/tlsf/mods/theme_c/popups/mod19t04s01.html.

Galligan, Brian. _"Australian Citizenship."_ Land and Heritage. Carlton, Vic: Melbourne University Press. n.d. p. 119. Melbourne, 1997

«Gestern ist Heute – Lebensraum Rumänien (1996) III.» YouTube. hanshedrich, 2017. https://www.youtube.com/watch?v=vB_mo7GA2Oo.

"History of the Stone Soup Folktale from 1720 to Now, by William Rubel." Stone Soup, August 20, 2019. https://stonesoup.com/about-the-childrens-art-foundation-and-stone-soup-magazine/history-of-the-stone- soup-story-from-1720-to-now/.

"Horticulture (n.)." Index. https://www.etymonline.com/word/horticulture#etymonline_v_14473.

"Human Development Reports." The 2019 Global Multidimensional Poverty Index (MPI) | Human Development Reports. 2018. http://hdr.undp.org/en/2018-MPI.

«International year of soil conference, 06th of July 2015.» healthy soil for a healthy life. Food and Agriculture Organisation of the United Nations. http://www.fao.org/soils-2015/events/detail/en/c/338738/

"Only 60 Years of Farming Left If Soil Degradation Continues." Scientific American. Scientific American, December 5, 2014. https://www.scientificamerican.com/article/only-60-years-of-farming-left-if-soil-degradation-continues/

Petti, Alessandro, Sandi Hilal, and Eyal Weizman. _"Architecture after Revolution: Decolonizing Architecture Art Residency"._ Berlin: Sternberg Press, 2013.

"Pluriverse." Merriam-Webster. Merriam-Webster. https://www.merriam-webster.com/dictionary/pluriverse.

"Prasāda." Wikipedia. Wikimedia Foundation, December 14, 2019. https://en.wikipedia.org/wiki/Prasāda.

"Sumak Kawsay." Sumak Kawsay | Ancient Teachings of Indigenous Peoples | Pachamama Alliance. https:// www.pachamama.org/sumak-kawsay.

"Sumac Kawsay." Wikipedia. Wikimedia Foundation. https://en.wikipedia.org/wiki/Sumac_Kawsay.

"Text" Online Etymology Dictonairy. https://www.etymonline.com/search?q=text.

"Topsoil." Wikipedia. Wikimedia Foundation, September 25, 2019. https://en.wikipedia.org/wiki/Topsoil.

Jinyoung Park

Leafy Brackets

_INTRODUCTION

I am not quite a dancer, but I wanted to write about movement. I had a wish to translate the breath into text. If I ever could translate the foot pounding on the floor to count, a head nodding without much conviction, little balls of frayed threads on the elbow of one's beloved sweater. The perpetual transference that we are all in. The radiation of the rhythm that we inevitably perform. Since I observed and magnified the moving as such, the translation of it had to be a gentle whisper, a slow sigh. By formulating, as can be imagined, the motif[1] that I particularly attuned myself to was molded in the shape of a plant.

While writing this thesis, if I choose to call it so, the hand that holds wanted to be the same hand that gives. I was constantly frustrated and felt even a bit guilty for the fact that I do not have the language of the plant but am merely projecting my own consciousness on their way of being. If I was asked why it is moving, I could only answer by telling how it has moved. To answer to its intrinsic contradiction at least with an honesty, I decided to imagine this piece of text also as a plant. Not necessarily meaning that it would appear green, more that it uses the method of a plant's resolution — to grow in near-symmetrical balance and go around the conflict if there is any, but to come back to the knotted thoughts in an altered shape.[2]

The following contains the observed research and a certain amount of fascination regarding the botanical way of moving. It is, to a certain extent, an attempt to bring to light their muted and nuanced movement. I wish to speculate on the different ways in which we perceive time and how that contours moving, and the notion of memory as an endeavour to anchor our perspectives in the flow of time. The imagery of plants helped both as an explanatory device and a stimulus to connect different things. Simultaneously, I also want to move/write in a botanical way myself — researching how to seed and germinate thoughts, writing about the phenomenon of speculation, giving it enough time to be watered and beamed at. To keep the sentences in the right sphere, perhaps no bigger than the shadow that a tree casts.

/A GNARL

I go for a small stroll. It is raining, a thin drizzle of drops fall almost diagonally with robust wind. The panorama of two different sights — of the iris of my mind and my eyes — alternately overlap onto each other, and collide occasionally. I trill a word that comes up in my mind. Mouth waters. Words are generally flavourless but not when outspoken. I roll my tongue exaggeratedly, just as he did with the name Lolita.

The circuit of thoughts goes exactly at the pace that my feet keep. Thoughts are webbing themselves out sporadically but not evaporating. They move hither and thither in aerodynamics of raindrops. Far behind the web an airship flies by slowly towing a placard on the back, on which the things that I should have and should not have said are written. I loosely promise to myself to be different next time, but I already know that I am probably going to make similar mistakes.

When a word comes up from the flow, it arises with slight gravity. It is a dent on the smooth trunk with a certain pulling force, in which following thoughts stagnate like a puddle. They tangle, coagulate into an excrescence — this braid of that which is repulsive and that which is attractive hardens, protruding from the surface of the bark. The ideal carpentry for a hard gnarl is not to cut through it but to let it support other things.

Nouns and adjectives — sets of words to describe the word — raid in continuously like the infinite train. The words arriving in the first compartment coach of the train are mostly pragmatic and knowledgable. They are often dismissed as cliché but very

useful. The following group consist of more sophisticated, poetic and delicate nuances. I tend to welcome those more than the words closer to the front of the train, it is my personal preference. Rarely do they emerge from our mind immediately — it is just easy for us to overlook the first compartment since its presence is so obvious to us, however the two compartments are closely and precisely connected. It is a bit complicated to describe the next one, but to name it, they are words that make me always forget what they mean. They are words of mouth; slimy, slippery, coming from unknown sources, seemingly never seen in the written form. They give us very sharp and intuitive insight when we cling onto them, but their process is never easy. Now I am at the last compartment. I can possibly cry, get angry, or if I am lucky enough, I can also be joyful or comforted when encountering these words. It is certain that it is the last cabin of the train, but it is not a summary of the train's earlier compartments nor is it the reason the train exists. Witnessing the back of the train does not prove that the train was operated. One thing that catches the attention: the first and the last compartment (though the imposed meanings are completely different from each other) are constructed from almost exactly the same materials. I finally acknowledge how meaningful, truthful and clear the words that I saw before were. It is a fresh leap of the discourse of thoughts, rather than a late realisation. It is a moment of attaching a feather to an arrow of thought, discharged inwards to my mind, a moment that the arrow in the air is finally able to be controlled. I roll the word 'moment' in my mouth again. It tastes like ginger.

//IN THE WORLD OF BOTANICA, IT IS NORMAL TO GROW FOREVER

Concerning its slower pace and inconspicuous manner, it is hard to give a proper name to a plant's moving. Its moving is not labelled with a simple tag, for it is too complicated to contour it according to the rather swift flow that we are in as animated beings. We know that a climbing plant has grown up as its winding fingers grasp at different heights of the wall; that a cattail bush is ripe enough if its leaves rustle just so in the wind; and that parachute-shaped dandelion seeds want to be landed by blowing them. Botanical moving that we can perceive takes place with an indirect methodology. Willingly engaging with different agents who are able to perform or indicate it.

In addition to its anonymity — or a polygonal name it attains along with each agent — shifting and moving plants also denote that the matter of time is an important factor. We sense that they are moving with a quiet but broad effect in unexpected moments — the changes in a plant's appearance have become synonymous with the passing of time. Their motion, in most cases, happens in close connection to their own locations. But since they are quite bound in terms of where they grow from, it is crucial for plants to determine and control the duration[3] of time when they make moves. By having different kinds of sequences, lengths and rhythms, varying from annually revived tomato vines to lush evergreen, they reconcile with and react to surroundings and the other species' bodily motion.

bamboo

In the ecology of bamboos, while they are one of the fastest growing subfamilies of plants, it actually takes a good few years for its shoots to come through the soil. They languidly nudge their way underground, forming a mass of rhizomic roots in the process. Intertwined clumps enable them to form a cluster of shoots rather than fending for themselves as individuals. The rest of their long youth is a quantum leap compared to their sluggish pace before growing in earnest. Certain species of bamboos can grow around a metre a day, if subject to the right moisture and temperature levels.

---

1   motif: 1. a distinctive idea, especially a theme elaborated on in a piece of music, literature, etc 2. a recurring form or shape in a design or pattern (from Old French motif, from Late Latin mōtīvus (adj) moving, from Latin mōtus, past participle of movēre to move)

2   "Discontinuity is essential to the essay; its concern is always a conflict brought to a standstill." T. Adorno, The Essay as Form, p.16

3   "[Duration is] the form which the succession of our conscious states assumes when our ego lets itself live, when it refrains from separating its present state from its former state." H. Bergson, Time and Free Will, p. 100

According to large amounts of weekly documentations, bamboo's flowering cycles vary from 1 to 120 years. Bamboo has a peculiar characteristic, namely that the entire grove blooms all at the same time. This gregarious flowering may occur over small areas, but can also stretch across large swathes of land, such as different continents. It has been observed to begin in one area and requiring a fair amount of time to cover the entire budding forest. This mass flowering (as flowers mean the utmost maturity of the plant) is followed by the death of the grove — the entire forest can be gone within a week.[4] Though much research has been dedicated to it, a reason is yet to be agreed on, with too little examples to be generalised, simply because its duration does not fit in our schedule.[5]

crown shyness

Far less dramatic but probably more hopeful, in the deep forest, a phenomenon called crown shyness (also known as canopy disengagement, canopy shyness) is observed, for tree species such as Dryobalanops, lodgepole pine, and some of Eucalyptus. It looks a bit like a map of Amsterdam done with your eyes closed — with the inter-crown forming a canal along with neighbour trees. The exact physiological basis of the phenomenon is still mythical, yet some hypotheses suggest 'the inter-digitation of canopy branches leads to reciprocal pruning of adjacent trees'. Trees in windy areas suffer from physical damage and less chance of photosynthesis, as they collide with each other during winds. As a result of abrasions and collisions, there is an induced crown shyness response. Studies suggest that lateral branch growth goes largely uninfluenced by neighbours until disturbed by mechanical abrasion. If the crowns are artificially prevented from colliding in the winds, they gradually fill the canopy gaps.[6]

When moving, light particles always decide on the destination beforehand and proceed to take the most efficient route. People say that water always know its way. As the mediator of those two, the plant utilises their properties to meet its requirements to grow. In the case of crown shyness, the strategy of the tips comes as distancing. The sun and the compactness of the forest contour the spacing in the middle, the trees are stretching the reachability of the sun, and reaching only until they can still coexist with the neighbours. It is a fine tuned relationship in-between different flexibilities of mass.

The moment that we can consider as death, the end of a plant, is when they do not grow anymore. They do not show a clear-cut signal, such as heartbeats aligned on an x and y axis. Their wet vitality is not of the palpitating kind but of humming. We can discern whether the suspended humming has faded out, nearly into silence — with its brown, brittle, and mushy innards, less firm and pliable, when they lose the flexibility of revival. Perennial plants are still known to live almost forever, because they are able to prolong their span of life as long as there is no specific occasion. But what is the definition of infinity for them? Perhaps it is more rightful to make an end in the form of a question, instead of a statement.

///THE CROWN

Writing is obsessive. It continues obsessively, continues word by word, phrase by phrase, sentence by sentence. There is a secret wish for repetition underneath every sheet of white paper. If it was a drawing, some parts might have been shaded with the strokes of pencil overlapping. If it were music, the foot might have pounded the floor to keep the rhythm. If it were sleep, the chest might have risen and fallen slowly with breath.

If anything repeats while writing, it is rather akin to branching than to overlapping. Instead of filling, its natural property is more of spreading, directed in a radial manner. Thinking of branching brings certain botanical imagery to mind, not only because its name supposes a clear metaphor but also because a text has a tendency to embody its continuation in a similar way that a plant grows. Words constitute a kind of apical and intercalary meristematic tissue[7], with origins in the roots crawling outwards. Each extremity of the branches works as the newly sprung centre of yet another speculation. Little toes try to reach further, seeking for the air and soil, a potential sugary mass.

Language is often imagined to give certain shape to thoughts (this time it configures them in the botanical shape) and it is good not to forget that the shape is not yet fixed. Intuition folds the shape of thought diagonally and time irons the fold. While calling out the inner pool of abstract thoughts and transcribing them into words, the lexicon and subordinating logic gets *complicated*. Like a flickering time table hanging in the busiest train station. Their transcription hopefully *implicates* enough and at long last gives itself out generously and *explicitly*. The Latin word *Plicare*, introduced in those words, refers us to the act of folding, bending or flexing in and out. Following process conceives *claudere*, another Latin word suggesting to close and lock up. The moment of consciousness, is getting to be aware of the need to *exclude* what is barely touched by its own branches. Amounts of perplexity and hesitation are *included*. *Conclusion* is a morning glory, pursing its petals again into a bud every dusk.

What can be written is not as innocent as what can be thought, and does not necessarily grant the size of what can be told. It lies on the thin mark of the repeated folds. Following the outermost foliage of the crown, down to its timid tips.

////TREE THAT NEVER FORGETS

Trees are "full of a life that is never entirely visible"[8]. There is no such prototype to be projected upon the sculpture of trees. Trees are imagined, not expected. I once read how Flusser described in one of his essays, the tree that slips through before getting penetrated by our cognition: "there is a dense, multilayered mist between the one who contemplates and the tree. The mist reflects the light that comes from the lighthouse of contemplative intention; thus, contemplation surreptitiously transformed into reflection and the one who contemplates cannot interfere in this. There is something that surrounds trees, something that is mysterious because it is nebulous."[9]

The very presence of a plant is a record of the time it has been through. The nebulous and ethereal spectre that roams around every tree consists of the memories they always bear. Every moment that the plant existed is preserved in the form of an annual ring, humped gnarls, fragments of tissue hidden underground.[10] Like a lonely tree near the cliff grows almost horizontally, with hairs and limbs swept by the wind, each tree is an accumulated imagery of its constant moving. The minute, constant transformations pile onto what was before. Plants are slowly becoming other plants.

The plant's wish to move resembles the wish to remember. It cannot choose to ride upon time, as it is not possible to rewind time. But it is possible to gauge when to chase after the time, or how long we want to wait for the time. Slow gesturing of plants, the tacit becoming that we perceive only possibly in our own time, seems almost resistant to time flowing. Submerged in that largely unnoticeable, yet omnipresent flow, they wait until it almost squeezes them into a different state. Just as the flat fingerprint wrinkles into a landscape when soaked in water.

4   The prominent tendency to understand this phenomenon is as a defence mechanism. By putting so many seeds at once, bamboo plants overwhelm their predators with food. The rodents and other species of animals that devour seeds of bamboo are literally overfed, so that bamboos get more chance for safe propagation.

5   D. Farelly, The book of bamboo, p. 148-149

6   M.Q. Rovira, 'Crown Shyness: Trees That Don't Touch'

7   In the growth of plants, there are three different types of dividing tissue which take parts in. They are called meristematic tissue and are sorted based on the parts where it is found — roots or shoot tips, stem, and the limbs. Each type of cell makes the plant spread (apical), thicken (lateral), and separate itself into branches (intercalary).

8   J. Burger, 'The ideal palace', Selected essays p. 411

9   V. Flusser, 'The cedar in the park', Natural:mind, p.35

10   A number of 32,000 year old plant seeds and fruit were found buried. A group of scientists discovered prehistoric chambers of an arctic species of a ground squirrel. The forgotten seeds had been preserved in permanently frozen deposits and excavated from the fossil. The dominant was Silene stenophylla, a species of flowering plant commonly called narrow-leafed campion nowadays. The scientists were able to "grow ancient plants, from fragments of the placental tissue of three immature uninjured fruits." The seeds were newly revived to be the oldest plant. Russian Scientists Revive 32,000-Year-Old Flower, SCI News, 23 February 2012

Being slow might mean that one does not follow time timely.

We see the plant change as a consequence of its resistance. The movement comprises of tendencies; the tendencies are not solid but persistent enough. How do we know that the plant has moved? Why do we think that the plant moved? Because we remember how it was before. My climbing plant, which, as an ignorant caretaker I had put in the middle of my room, hovered around for a while, trying to find something to latch on to. I could not see in time its crawling nor its waving, but recognised what it had been looking for when it hooked itself on the little piece of crochet on my wall. Two months later, it is leaning towards the whole wall and has more or less a span taller. Movement of plants is in-vis-able and might not be experienced by our perception but traced by our memory. Memory becomes an evidence that allows us to believe in moving. Plant's movement resembles memory.

A plant, situated in front of the window facing the north, is reclining its own body to the long sunlight that is cast inside only during the dusk. It depicts the posture of a person running to escape, like a pictogram for an emergency exit. It is good to rotate the pot every now and then. Stalks and leaves will turn their orientation gradually to face the new direction of light. Plants are slowly becoming other plants. [11]

/////AN ENVELOPE

When I was once in despair — which I cannot recall now where it has rooted from — one of my friends kindly told me, it is going to be good in the end, and if it is not good, it is not the end. The confidence, engraved in her voice, was contagious and appeared a little naive to me. I will call it an end when it is good. And I start another thing after.

If one can decide which moment something ends by having their own reason for it, perhaps it is not fair any more to call it an end. Punctuation decides when and how the sentence is closed. But what about the inverted question mark — used in certain languages — at the beginning of interrogative sentences? In which direction is a couplet of parentheses arching their back, or mirroring themselves? Is the interferential energy of them growing from the inside, or is it a late appendix? Envelopes and other postal wraps are finally stamped but at the moment they reach their destination, they become the very first encounter to the one who reopens them. The end is conjured up with poetic rules to be an alternative start.

In Eastern poetry, a literary device which is called 首尾相關法 (su-mi-sang-gwan-beop) is frequently used. It can be literally translated into 'the head and the tail in relation'. A certain line is employed to be repeated both at the beginning and end of the stanza, sometimes throughout the entire poem. It functions as a marker and tool to guide the passage. Inclusio[12] is a corresponding example, as a typical term in biblical studies and Rabbinic literature which refers to a structural style based on a concentric principle. The term is used when an anecdote is written within a frame by placing similar material to start and end with. The repeated line or part, in both cases, will be read twice but interpreted anew by different senses and flow each time, as non-identical twin siblings. What can be considered as a type of refrain becomes the same entrance to different paths. A revolving door, that brings us back to the starting point.

```
Until peony blooms
I will be waiting for my spring
On the day it falls
I will finally lament over the loss

...

When it falls, it just falls with my whole year
Tears linger for the rest 350 days
Until peony blooms
I will be waiting for my spring,
the lustrous sorrow
```

Young-Rang Kim,
<Until the peony blooms>

I remember Emily Dickinson scribbling on the interior of the envelope, hand barely able to match the velocity of her thoughts. The scrapped manuscripts are handwritten inside the triangular flap of almost every letter that she sent. "Preserve the backs of old letters to write upon," wrote Lydia Maria Child in a book that Dickinson's father obtained for her mother. It opens: "The true economy of housekeeping is simply the art of gathering all the fragments, so that nothing is lost. I mean fragments of time as well as materials." Dickinson's envelope writing conveys a sense of thrift, but at the same time discloses the private spaces within that household. "we should respect | the seals of | others —" She inscribes next to the gummed seal of A 842 envelope.[13]

I imagine putting this text in an envelope, or folding it into an envelope. The same kind of material, but using internal surface divisions from all the angles. If a letter explains, an envelope decides. It rounds up what it can. It cannot be closed and open at the same time. An envelope embraces proximity, containing the miscellaneous branches of thoughts and loose ends of fragments. Maybe in an abstract way, or to be more precise, in an introspective way.

Not by chance, the literary device of inclusio is also known as bracketing or an envelope structure. The purpose of inclusio shares its function with that of an envelope; to start and make an end, to revolve us around what it holds inside. As the timid crown did with the neighbouring trees, the enveloping movement brings the idea of the boundary but in the form of a dotted line. A dotted line is, in itself, a repetition of shorter lines, an alternated series of utterance and silence. In the legend of any origami instruction, a dashed line softly invites us to fold, unlike straight and arrow-head lines which tell us to turn or cut. What is opposite to the enveloping movement is conquering.

An epistolary end convinces the structure of written sentences, where the subjective takes its place in front of anything else. It is naturally embedded with the impression of transmission from one to another, yet the line between the points can be drawn in different kinds of shapes. As a preservation of the monologue, it travels and arrives to become a dialogue. If taking into account the gap in between when the letter was written, when it traveled and when it was read, it might be wrong to say that the writer is not transmuted at all. A slight inclination can also be an effect, if not the swift enlightenment. The changes are never planned but somehow predicted.

I try to make an enclosure where I started — I trace back to the wet spring of thoughts, being worried and also consoled with that it has already happened before and had been posted in an envelope, to now. That all the nutritious drops had been transmitted through the fine net of veins of each leaf before they wilted and shedded. The temporal end always wants to be in between the pleats — in an envelope which is not yet sealed nor waxed. The envelope, a pair of brackets, lick their own lips.[14]

---

11 notes made while small gardening

12 For instance: the Book of Jeremiah can be found as having a similar question and imagery in the first and the last— that of almond rods and baskets of figs.

13 Jen Bervin, 'Studies in scale'. 'The Gorgeous Nothings' by Emily Dickinson, p.9-10

14 "…An exclamation point looks like an index finger raised in warning; a question mark looks like a flashing light or the blink of an eye. A colon, says Karl Kraus, opens its mouth wide: woe to the writer who does not fill it with something nourishing. Visually, the semicolon looks like a drooping moustache; I am even more aware of its gamey taste. With self-satisfied peasant cunning, German quotation marks («») lick their lips." T. Adorno, 'Punctuation marks', the antioch review, p.300, translated by Shierry Webber Nicholsen

BOOK

Theodor Adorno, The Essay as Form, Translated by Shierry Weber
Nicolesen, New York, Columbia University Press, 1991

Henry Bergson, Matter and Memory, Translated by Nancy Margaret
Paul and W. Scott Palmer, New York, The Macmillan Company, 1929

Henry Bergson, Time and Free Will, Translated by F. L. Pogson, New
York, The Macmillan Company, 1913

David Farelly, The Book of Bamboo, Sierra club books, 1984

John Burger, Selected Essays, New York, A Division of Random
House, 2001

Villem Flusser, Natural Minds, Translated by Rodrigo Maltez Novaes,
Univocal, 2013

Young-Rang Kim, Until The Peony Blooms, 3rd Edition 'Mun-Hak', 1934
(self translated)

Emily Dickinson, The Gorgeous Nothings, Edited by Jen Bervin,
Marta Werner, New directions, 2013

Han Kang, The Vegetarian, Changbi, 2007

Robert M. Pirsig, Zen and the Art of Motorcycle Maintenance: An
Inquiry into Values, William Morrow, 1974

Tine Melzer, Taxidermy of Language-animals, Rollo, 2015

Roland Barthes, The Pleasure of the Text, Éditions du Seuil, 1973

INTERNET

C. Zimmer, 'Bamboo Mathematician', The loom, 15 May 2015,
https://web.archive.org/web/20160330223041/http://phenomena.
nationalgeographic.com/2015/05/15/bamboo-mathematicians/ (accessed
in 8 December 2019)

M.Q. Rovira, 'crown shyness: tree that don't touch', All you need
is biology, https://allyouneedisbiology.wordpress.com/2018/12/09/
crown-shyness-trees/, 9 December 2018 (accessed in 15 August 2019)

'crown shyness' https://en.wikipedia.org/wiki/Crown_shyness
(accessed in 22 August 2019)

Russian Scientists Revive 32,000-Year-Old Flower, SCI News, 23
February 2012, http://www.sci-news.com/biology/article00194.html
(accessed in 12 July 2018)

'inclusio' https://en.wikipedia.org/wiki/Inclusio (accessed 18
December 2019)

Theodor Adorno's Philosophy of Punctuation, 24 July 2014, http://
www.openculture.com/2014/07/theodor-adornos-philosophy-of-
punctuation.html (ac-cessed in 3 December 2019)

Alice Peach

Still, Swaying and Backflipping

{The Lid Over the Steaming Pot

Through and within this text I am attempting to establish a balance between observations of structures meant to regulate and contain movement —and thoughts produced in a light state of wonder.

I search for an understanding of the world that is precise but simultaneously open for playful shifting. One that doesn't aim for determination and finitude and is not always based on fact or convention, but is rather coming from a desire to collect and connect sources of excitement.

Inspiration is often triggered by the partial view of something — mystery. If I accept the world is too great and wide for me to understand it in its wholeness — If I accept that it is an uncrackable code — or a code that can only be cracked through magic — then I can take pleasure in zooming in, lingering on and swaying from fragment to fragment in contemplation.

I see it more like an endless treasure hunt approach than a research — or a puzzle that can generate an infinite amount of outcomes.

My thinking and acting, often reflects an underlying aspiration for a child-like lightheartedness — one that isn't busy with the sometimes numbing struggle of owning up to the fugacity of meaning (the meaning of us, of nature and every other little and big fragment of it). Bruno Munari writes that adults are often fascinated by the imagination of children because of their ability to formulate thoughts that "transcend reality".

The world of a child is simple, charming and free of responsibility — and a world where every moment glows of the unwrapping of something new and enriching[1].

Children are unconditioned by dogmas, regulations of behaviour, bureaucracy and social structures — too young to even be aware of their relevance or function. Their sole occupations are discovery and play.

This is the aspect of "lightness" that is interesting to me — the one I'm looking to recover and perform, without encouraging ignorance, but rather proposing a way to deal with the awareness of our condition.

In other words, how to use practices of wonder in order to observe, understand and question our chaotic surrounding.

To learn, to see, to understand and to define — are all actions that imply a filtering of information, a clarification and a freezing of chaos. Chaos, however, doesn't applaud our attempts to frame it, it simply moves on and through, leaving us with nothing much but empty frames to aid our perception. Wondering is a practice of blurring and redrawing perimeters of these disposable frames, for the sake of perpetually generating new meanings, participating, and tuning into the motion of the world.

This text is a platform — much like a trampoline — where this generative game can be both explained and performed through the use language.

Language is a pencil with graphite on one end and an eraser on the other.

{Memory-foam and Rulers
[p, a, b, h, i, ï, ü, ū, x]

In the water the motionless body floats on the surface supported by salt — held and shaken by incoming waves — rocked and tossed from all sides — blinded and deafened. Deprived of the basic conditions that sustain life, a redefinition of balance, comfort, weight and rhythm occurs. The body tailors strategies to stay afloat and conscious. To be in the water means to open an enduring negotiation with it.

*

The city memory-foams itself around me, and my body is a soft shield making its way forward. Waves of sounds and movement diffract upon me, sliding up my sides and over my head while I trace my walking line in careful avoidance of the many other bodies streaming from all directions and intercepting one another. I am walking, counting, documenting, walking, thinking, writing, talking, walking, buying, eating, searching, hopping, always walking, noticing, noting, drinking. I could go on.

My walk adds movement to movement. {a}

Everything happens at once, everything happens in urgency — the city knows no concept of priority except when occasional overlapping of urgencies sets the sirens off, and a sudden contraction, to which an immediate reaction follows, splits the streets to make a way for rescue delivering vehicles. Signals, in bright colours and prominent characters, are placed everywhere, displaying safety measures or special procedures — they are tools for self and collective preservation, regulating behaviour in prevention of accidents — coordinating people — each on their own trajectory while sharing the same space at the same time. {h}

Being in the city means being unconsciously reminded, at all times, that each choice your body makes needs to be calibrated, moderated, shaped around all the other choices that other bodies around you may be simultaneously making.

*

Old telephone boxes and disused tram lines are discharge of progress — slowly disappearing from view and into the holes carved to raise new, bigger, shinier buildings. Change hits and morphs fashions of reality — distributing new rhythms and reconfiguring chaos. The inner and outer landscapes of bodies adjust to each other and to external disruptions bit by bit. Landscapes of dough, kneaded by transformations — expanding and making space for "the new" — the new folding over the old. {i}

*

Moved by my appreciation for the paintings of Agnes Martin, I bought myself a ruler. {i}

I chose my model from among four others because I thought it looked the prettiest. It's not particularly "fancy", but it does the job: It's 30cm long, 4cm wide, and it's made of see though plastic. The bottom side is lined with a stainless steel strip — the label calls it "stainless steel cutting edge" and I assumed it was meant to serve as a cutting facilitator, but it didn't work when I tried to use it. It does influence the object's appeal though, as it gives it a character of quality and finesse. Simple, black, legible numbers run along its tracing edge, a larger character size for each multiple of 5 (from 5 to 30). On the surface of the object, a 5mm square grid — supposedly meant to serve as extra guidance to line marking.

We design tools that are meant to compensate for our imprecision and laws of accuracy are studied and applied to our world. In the city everything is "ruler-designed"/"ruler-planned" and most things are a lot bigger than us. Humans are not precise in that way, in the way that straight lines are, I mean. Our precision lies elsewhere, perhaps in the way our bodies and mind function — the balance behind all the particles at work within us. That's pretty precise. But we can recognise accuracy — and use it to our advantage by creating tools that allow us to achieve it and exercise control over our chaotic

---

1   " […] the child eats, cries, sleeps, talks to his mother, poops, walks, sleeps — to the child who doesn't know the world, everything has the child's own qualities: The big ball, will be the mother of the small ball; if the ball is dirty it's because it has pooped itself; the ball will feel cold or warm when he does; and so on…"

nature (even when unnecessary or excessive). We conquer our limits in size, strength, precision through extensions of our frail, microscopical bodies. We are breadcrumbs when faced by our own creations.

Being surrounded by all this artificial order is confronting, and part of the confusion induced by cities comes from the presence of movement regulations, body restrictions and meticulously designed extra-large objects facing the individual. Maybe the overload of artificial order is the cause for the counter effect: backflipping {ü}

Uncontainable chaos is where nature takes over — and the city becomes a self-operating ecosystem, a modern kind of natural environment, to which the citizen is the natural inhabitant.

{When I look at gross city pigeons, rats, foxes, stray cats and dogs, squirrels and other animals that inhabit cities, I wonder if citizens are the gross-city-pigeon version of a human.}

{The Arm of the Tempest
[j, k, l, f, e, d, c, Ĵ, q]

{Ours, is a house with wide open windows and doors. Roaring air streams hitting and breaking on the walls and everywhere else. Air trapped in corners and cabinet drawers howling; boxes and jars and glasses and cups, rattling; flickering pages of open books on the floor or caught in mid air. Many noises.

Dust, voices, flavours, sometimes birds and other animals, are swept in and out of our gasping home — it's often hard to tell the inside form the outside.

Dust, voices, flavours, sometimes birds and other animals, are swept in and out of our gasping home — it's often hard to tell the inside form the outside. We don't hold hands through it all. We are no Paolos and Francescas[2] — we orbit the home and each other in a rhythmical and ever-changing motion — just as sweeping and flowing as every other fleeting visitor, except these open walls, to us, are a reoccurring station on our ways.}

*

We build our homes made of solid, steady, dependable walls to contain and protect us — in the same way that we construct our routines — based on regularity and repetition. Structures meant to navigate uncertainty. {j}, {k}, {l}.

Constellations of objects in space define our day to day orbits. Each object reverberating of the habits we perform through its use, and hinging us to a mode of existence we choose to identify with. These objects are gravitational points, "life-buoys" — material assets we regularly return to in order to give weight and significance to what we do and who we are. {e, d}

Through dissonance, contrast, differentiation we individuate and "thing" things.

So we can tell when the branch ends and the leaf begins — and we can situate and orientate ourselves in relation to the world. {Ĵ} In repetition we find coherence between them.

Repetition is a part of nature — we are, in each moment, directly involved in the repetitive, cyclical motion of the earth. The effects this cyclicality has on our environment sets the foundations upon which our entire lives are structured (day and night, the moon cycle, seasons, tides, and so on). So repetition is ingrained within us. {c}

Perhaps it's the reason why death can never fully make sense, the idea of this endless cycle to which we belong, coming to an end for us, seems inconceivable. Our cyclical minds can never escape the body they're contained in.

---

2   Paolo Malatesta and Francesca de Polenta are two historical figures that lived in the city of Gradara in Italy during medieval times. Their love story has since been the subject of many references in literature due to its tragic destiny.
    The two characters were murdered by Francesca's husband (also Paolo's brother), Gianciotto Malatesta, as they were caught indulging in a kiss after reading the story of Lancelot and Guinevere and being overcome by tenderness.
    During the infernal journey of the Divine Comedy, Dante encounters the two lovers in the second circle of hell — the one that hosts sinners of lust. Paolo and Francesca's doomed souls are holding hands, though trapped in the furious force of an an eternal hurricane.

Bodies bound to the incessant transformation and eventual collapse of the matter they are made of. Minds bound to the timeless force generating this transformation.

If humans are the convergence of these two opposing concepts, then it's easier to explain the many contradictions that constitute (and bother) our being. We are always torn between poles — oscillating from one extremity to the other in search of an unshifting truth — searching for steadiness and equilibrium, but simultaneously driven by a quest for discovery and novelty. Both needy of confinement and compelled to plunge into the borderless unknown. We do open the doors to noise, but often only if we have the means to analyse it, fragment it, categorise it, staple it to something we already know and shelf it. Only if in the chaos our motivation is a strong enough propeller and we hold on to a purpose that shines a bright enough light to orientate us along the way.

{Minion balloon serenade
[n, o, u, ü, p, q, r]

When my sister was three years old, my mother bought her a rather large helium balloon in the shape of a Minion. Over time the Minion began to deflate, but as my sister grew particularly attached to it, she periodically asked us to restore it to its fullness. Since we didn't own a helium machine, each time we operated on the balloon, the amount of oxygen would increase in relation to helium — making the Minion, fuller, but also heavier. There was a funny period of time in which it floated around the house at human height, bumping into us and all sorts of surfaces, sometimes making random appearances in the living room or the kitchen, carried by a draft of air from an open window or the movement of someone walking by. It moved across the house at a gentle, nonchalant pace that could either be contagious or extremely annoying.

*

On the one hand I want to teach myself to plunge in a wondrous state — to become a Minion balloon.

I want to inhabit the lifestyle of the "flaneur" — living through the movements occurring around me, following flows of thoughts = Helium inflation. {n} On the other hand I feel burdened by the inherited responsibility that comes from being part of a system that is way beyond me, but is still reliant on (and demanding) individual, systematical perpetrations = Oxygen inflation. {o} The intoxicating necessity of purpose and achievement is abused, nurtured and emphasised by our culture. The idea of success and "growth"and the idea that one must earn their fulfilment, resulting in the commodification of feelings and of the sense of self. This is gravity.

Making oneself useful is a way of connecting with others — it's part of our nature as social beings and it's the core of friendship, but trouble arises when the community is too large, too fast and too diverse, a community that is global. Then the responsibilities and the issues to address are too much of a burden. Conformism is the disillusioned acceptance and adherence to the configuration of the fragments of the world we inhabit — it is the renunciation of ones own weighty responsibility and its submission to circumstance and power. {p}

I know this as an easy observation to make from where I stand. This system, our grid, is simultaneously protective and submitting of me — but my place within it, is in a way the luckiest of all. I benefit from being right in the middle — not too wealthy or powerful, not too poor and struggling. In a way, I already am the Minion balloon in the global community — navigating the grid quietly, invisibly, hardly affected by most societal afflictions. But when I fall into the guilt-tripping trap that thrusts me to the ground I need to remind myself that this guilt is also a by-product of the submission to power, because the guilt triggered by awareness robs me of my agency, and it numbs me. That too, is gravity. And that too, with a spectacular backflip, might land upon conformist behaviour. {ü}

Lately I've been in conflict with the scholar in me that speaks in the tone of discipline and demand. {u}

I don't want to operate with a goal, I don't want to operate for the sake of productivity or success.

I'm reluctant to use punctuation, capital letters and to divide my thinking and acting in paragraphs. I'm disagreeing with language, structures, deadlines and pre established requirements. If I do not fit them it is because they don't fit me.

My urge to relentlessly express — be stained and stain back everything around me, unapologetically outruns formats of clarity. The education system that has nurtured me has not taught me how to listen and how to be patient. It has tried to make me disciplined — apt to efficiency and linear communication. Operative and useful. It has soldiered me into productivity.

Yes, It has also taught me loads of wonderful notions that I'm grateful to have learned — and I have immense admiration and respect for most of the teachers I've met — but I'm bitter. Because I was told school was the place where I would receive the tools to "grow" — tools that would make me the best possible version of myself — but instead, I have felt inappropriate for the past 18 years. Adults applauded the extra-ordinary and praised the brilliance of those who delivered revolutionary thoughts into the world, but they simultaneously expected order and used shame as a weapon against irregular behaviour. I was always too loud, too slow, too scattered, too hyperactive, too uncooperative. So I learned that being loud, slow, scattered, hyperactive and uncooperative were wrong, unfit character-traits to a person. Traits I had to work on. I was a disastrous student in my first few schooling years, then I became pretty mediocre, and held on sweatfully to the precarious "ok" position for most of my school career — until, ironically, I finally graduated from high school with top marks and a shit self-esteem. So now I have my self-esteem to work on. {ü}

Every moment is a moment in transition. And everything that constitutes the transitioning moment is transitioning with it. In this quiver lays the possibility of improvement. However obvious, this is a notion I easily forget.

Numbness, caused by an overload of gravity, can only be overcome through acts of participation to the centrifuge: re-actions to dis-comfort. The forwarding of utopian thoughts, the cutting and pasting of ideas that expand the limits of our understandings, the awakening of imagination. If every action is a response and a perpetration of a timeless chain reaction, any kind expression delivered into the world is bound to meet others and thus, leave a trace. {q} {r}

{A "pulling" that choreographs a motion

[j, ĵ, g, t, r]

Words demands to be arranged in a certain way in order to perform their purpose efficiently — in order to make sense — but in the struggle to translate experience, a lot of it collapses under the structure of logic. It goes unseen and forgotten like dust swept under the carpet — and whatever ends up being conceptualised and puppeteered into conversations, is nothing but an empty shell — a taxidermy of experience. {ĵ}

That's why I have so much admiration for writers who, through language, succeed in generating experiences that transcend it.

"Tender Buttons" is disguised as a book about elements of the everyday — about the mundane — but in fact it's an insight into Gertrude Stein's mind. It's an intimate portrait of a consciousness and a bold attempt at expressing through language, the tool of reason par-excellence, something as ephemeral and bodiless as the workings of our complex mind. The structure of the text provides a loose hinge for the writers stream of thought — by following an almost dictionary-like layout to explore the subjective significance of "objects", "food" and "rooms", she traces a trajectory which gives a suggestive form to the text — while her words flirtatiously pivot around

their meaning, never defining, never really giving it any weight. By not clarifying her intentions — whether the focus is on the objects, or the associations that are triggered by them — she's leaving readers in a suggestive haze. Hazy content and suggestive form, however, are in balance, allowing us to surrender peacefully to the rhythm of the of the text — cradled by and taking in the author's interpretations.

*

When one experiences a strong connection to another or to a particular situation, it feels like a washing away of the contours of things. The walls of the connected bodies dissolve and merge together into one being.

It's not even about connection anymore, because connection implies the notion of separate entities bound to each other by an in-between link. It's about a "pulling" that choreographs a motion — but not like synchronised swimming — there is too much control involved in being completely in synch — or in the imposition of procedural repetition. It's definitely more of a dance made of complementary responses. A kneading. I think this is the feeling Haytham El-Wardany describes as "disappearing"[3] — {t} which is maybe also the weightlessness I was mentioning before.

*

```
I have several times tried to think of an
apartment in which there would be a useless room,
absolutely and intentionally useless. It wouldn't
be a junkroom, it wouldn't be an extra bedroom,
or a corridor, or a cubby-hole, or a corner. It
would be a functionless space. It would serve for
nothing, relate to nothing. For all my efforts, I
found it impossible to follow this idea through
to the end. Language itself, seemingly, proved
unsuited to describing this nothing, this void,
as if we could only speak of what is full, useful
and functional.[4]
```

{This notion that when you're doing nothing you're being still is untrue. Routine, alienated, mechanical actions reek of stagnating water. }

*

In an interview[5] from 1974 Italo Calvino mentions the pleasure of travelling on the Parisian metró — running through the busy underground tunnels across the city and vanishing in the anonymity of large crowds of hustling citizens. {t} Imagination operates invisibly. Zooming in and out of the occurring. Quietly lingering in corners of rooms and travelling amid dust particles. Like dreaming and playing, it occurs in a dimension that is both immanent and parallel. I imagine it as a stream that is running alongside the cable network, stretching over our heads in the city. The first one feeding us ideas and the second one supplying our buildings with electricity.

Written worlds follow a different rhythm — a honey-spread-on-bread-like-time that runs undisturbed in this parallel dimension. The sticky coating slides over the mind of those who are looking for the perfect shine to the words — viscose building blocks .

```
"La fantasia é un posto dove ci piove dentro"
(Imagination is a place where it rains inside)[6]
```

3 Wardānī, Haytham, Jennifer Peterson, and Robin Moger. How to disappear. Cairo Berlin: Kayfa ta Sternberg Press, 2018. Print.
4 "The apartment" George Perec
5 https://www.youtube.com/watch?v=6jdiCztTLQw&t=542s
6 Italo Calvino

{The timid gap between the carrot and the table

[s, t, v, g, u, b, ü, i, ū]

I used to have a massive painting hanging on the wall over my childhood bed. It was a painting of a kid sitting on top of a rainbow, legs dangling off the side. The blue of the sky in the picture was so powerful it bounced out of the canvas and stained the walls of the room with a blue glow, especially when hit by the sun.

My room was the space between the two opposing windows — the one overlooking the fragment of a city sky in motion — and the one looking into a fantasy. Both oozing out of their frames and meeting in and out of me

I think of story telling as a tear in the fabric of the everyday life — an expansion of life in general — for it allows for one to slip into a gap in time and space and be a visitor in somebody else's depiction of the world. {s} {t} It satisfies both our need for adventure and our desire to connect with others through the sharing of experiences and perspectives. {v} It makes me think of that scene in "Yellow Submarine" where the Beatles end up in a field of black holes — and they bounce in and out of sight, from one hole to another, sometimes meeting and drifting together in the in-between. I've always been so hooked on this image. I would imagine the in-between to be way messier than white bearing black holes — but black and white are the colours of the undefined. A way of approximating what is non — intelligible. Every new interpretation, speculation, creative endeavour, is a scratching and sneaking out the walls and the birth of a new gateway into a black hole.

"The scratchers" are the ones who are floating in the weightless white space, riding drafts of magic. {g}

I realise now, I refer to "Chaos" and "Void" as two definitions of the same, ungraspable notion. Two extremities of a field so large, it encompasses "all", backflipping on itself. {ü} Both magnetically luring, pervasive and terrifying. Chaos is not necessarily loud — the void is not necessarily empty.

*

{A question asked and answered, a meeting for a coffee at 11am, an elevator-ride exchange, a smoke break with whoever lent me the lighter, my grandmother calling 4 times a week from Italy, a dinner that's been planned for months and countless times postponed, fast hallway greeting, broken-home-appliance-picture-correspondence with fixing company employee, the same lady with thick make up selling tickets at the cinema every Sunday night and the kind shop owner I buy my groceries from every week, receiving emails from websites I mindlessly subscribed to ages ago, feeling super close to a friend and recognising something very familiar in a stranger […]}

We won't drift away too far because some will eventually grab us by the end of our dangling string.

*

When I was in England over the summer I kept talking to people who had either moved away from London, or were thinking about it — smaller communities are becoming havens for city fleers. Along with this migration flock — as the ideal of the smaller, simpler, quieter life blows up, the smaller, simpler, quieter community begins its downfall. {ü}

*

The poetry in the "Pietà Rondanini" lies in its roughness, in the shyness of the lines, and in the tenderness of the trembling bodies of Mary and Jesus resting against and merging with each other. It is unclear how much further Michelangelo would have carried on shaping the piece before calling it finished, as he was still working on it when he died, but to leave a subtle unpolished quality with the work is also a tendency that rings true to his sculpting style. Giorgio Vasari called it the "Non-finito". The choice of not concluding gives life to the marble, a certain timelessness in the suggestion of potentiality, but it also makes the subjects of the representation a lot more human. The imperfection and evident vulnerability of both Mary and Jesus in this version f the Pietà triggers empathy. Here sculpture is no longer depicting an ideal meant to inspire perfection and divinity, like in the case of the "David" of 1504 or of the Pietà of 1499, but two individuals — flawed, struggling and therefore relatable.

A couple of months ago I bought a ruler because I was in distress and my fingers were bleeding from constant neurotic picking and biting. I thought, if straight lines worked for Agnes Martin, maybe they will work for me. There is undoubtedly a meditative aspect to the process of leaning and sliding the line across a surface and to repeat this many times at regular intervals, but I am too fond of spillages to fully embrace the order that results from it. I think It may have something to do with contact.

The space between the hand, the pencil and the paper is a microscopical slit, and yet it is the single opening that gives vitality to the line, by allowing it to receive pushes and pulls from all sides of the page and intrusions from the world that extends through that gap. This vitality, like the potentiality of Michelangelo's marble, is timeless — forever exposing the line to deviation and reinterpretation. The ruler acts as a clog to that world, like spray-foam for pipes and holes in the wall. It's used for technical drawing for this very reason. To be accurate means to exercise total control over the unsteadiness in and out of us, and to serve function. Just as Gertrude Stein clung to language — Martin stayed with the ruler and appropriated it — to create an order that fitted to her rather than using it to make herself fit to order. I think this is where the grace of Agnes Martin's paintings lies — in the tension between artificial rigour and implacable, hiccups. {ū}

{The Joining of Loose Extremities

[z, x, w, r, y]

Lingering and wondering in the in-between is not an act of evasion, rather an act of resistance. It is the insistence of searching for clues in our surrounding that restore excitement and inspiration — feelings that are targeted in a society that benefits from alienation and cynicism.

In a text called "planetary interlude" Kostas Axelos defines the essence of 'being' as a universal game — a "Game of the world", he calls it — in which man is always both "player and toy no matter what he does".

Within this infinite and rule-less Game, each individual finds and plays by his own accord — further mediated and restricted by collective regulations. Rules, like routines, are created in order to deal with the cheeky unpredictability of "the Game" and to attempt to seize and hold our own existence into our own hands. In a way, one could say our lives are a match played in the world between us and others and between us and the world itself. {z}

"Meaning" in the way we think of it as being a definable, linear unfolding of events and relations between elements, doesn't apply to the biggest picture. The Game of the world is always running ahead of us and right through the boundaries we fabricate to play along with it — but it doesn't do so out of spite, rather simply out of indifference. {x}

It shouldn't, therefore, want to be won (and ended) through understanding, but perhaps enjoyed — as it is like a rainbow. {w} Agamben talks about happiness and magic as things that can only be achieved when one is unaware of being in their possession[7] — it has to do with the profaning factor of language — and perhaps it's the reason why suggestions can sometimes be sharper and more permeating than statements. The contemplation of the illusory and the anticipation of the backflipping (which is also the expectation and the acceptance of failure) are the only practices of play that can't leave one feeling defeated. {r}

Perhaps the language of play is the most easy and natural for us to understand, if so, then it's no coincidence that children are brought up playing. Toys are miniatures of the world made to learn through simulation and the practice of imagination. By projecting their insights onto these objects, kids' personalities begin to develop outward.

7   Agamben, G., & Rueff, M. (2006). Profanations. Paris: Payot & Rivages.

The act of wandering, collecting and connecting observations, as a compulsion to hold on to the fleeting as I float — is a game that keeps me engaged with my surroundings. It reflects a will to treat the world itself like an extra-large toy. When I make the choice to call it a game — one with no beginning or end — and therefore one that cannot be lost — I am appropriating elements of a scenery with intention, but not for the sake of achievement, rather for the sake of play, illusion and participation.

In other words, I can wonder and float, without drifting too far — and I can observe, accumulate and analyse without growing stiff. I become the Minion balloon.

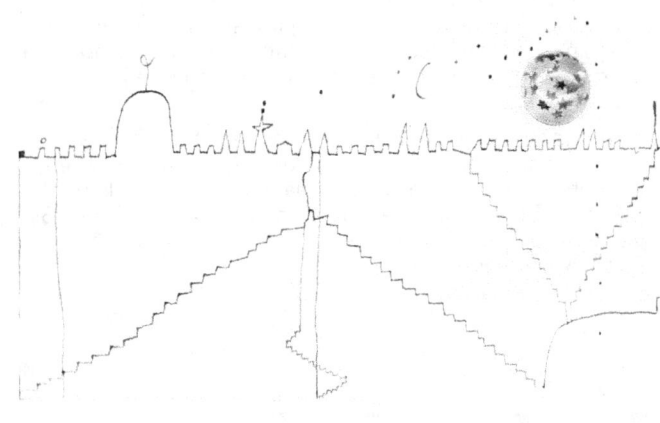

Dear,

A whole is not made of opposites.

A whole is like a rainbow: an unreachable illusion and a spectrum.

Also, something which visibility entirely depends on one's point of view.

Sometimes I think of the future as something so far away that it'll allows me to be 100 different people in my lifetime — so I often postpone big and small changes to an undefined "further on". Like when as a kid I wanted to have ice cream and my mother would say "later", but what she really meant was "never". I have learned that daydreams are very gratifying illusions — when one doesn't expect their realisation, they make a good release for unexpressed desires. I can still remember the taste of all the imaginary ice creams I had.

When we talk about utopias and imagination I'm reminded of "The life of Galileo" by Brecht — and the idea of looking far away in order to address issues that are close and pressing.

I also get the feeling of a very soft sofa and the smell of cedar trees — but I'll get back to the cedar trees later, or perhaps another time.

Anyway I have been daydreaming.

I'm daydreaming of a space that is simultaneously open and closed, inclusive and exclusive.

The space where you and I meet and blend.

Where visitors come to fade into whispers and borrowed ideas on "how to be"

Remember when we were children and I used to insist on us playing with polly-pocket, and you would frown, though you'd always end up enjoying it? We were architects without rulers or plans, animating a miniature world shaped around elements in my room — treating space like a ball of clay. I wonder if I'm still somehow fixated on playing the same game now, but on a larger scale — if perhaps my creative and, in general, daily endeavour is to see the world through the same eyes I wore back then.

I have become a bit frustrated with exhibiting formats, because I find it difficult to encounter or envision one that suits my idea of sharing. Inviting people to engage spontaneously in an exhibiting context is a delicate task because the common assumption when it comes to art is to engage as a spectator. It is especially difficult when the intention is not to choreograph a performance, but to simply suggest a lack of imposed distance and stiffness in the way one may wish to relate to a place. At the same time I wouldn't want to strip the daydream of it's magical elusiveness by encouraging its profanation — sometimes that can happen through touch. I guess that's why I'm looking back to the versatility of space when seen through the eyes of playing children. There are far less formulas of understanding in the mind of a child — reality meets the eye in a straight, piercing line and the relation between kid and surrounding is way more driven by impulse and "gut" rather than awareness, "decorum" and habit. But everything stays somewhat magical — and that kind of magic is contagious. It's the reason why you'd go from frowning to enjoying yourself when we used to play polly pocket.

Maybe I think of sharing as a contamination. Like a laugh that triggers a laugh, a gesture that stirs up emotion, or an insight gone from a maker to a making, that slips from its borders and permeates another.

I'm writing all this to you because you're my number one playing partner and if I think of a dimension where the space I keep mentioning exists, you exist with and in it. If you don't understand, good. If you think you understand I will deny that you have.

I don't want it to be over.

{The Hole on the Lid
Over The Steaming Pot
[r, z]}

There is an unresolved issue standing still and grinning at the heart of my reflections — a solitude of thought that is haunting, as well as deeply rooted in (my) wondering habits, and a necessary itch that fuels a further desire to share. {r} However it is perhaps simultaneously drawing me further and further away from "the other". One cannot scratch this itch alone.

It's important that we hold each other by our dangling strings, and that we do so with intention and awareness — and not just because we are coexisting and inevitably interacting, but because timeless games are generated by the communion of exchanging and moving perspectives. Mutual contaminations and perpetual inspirations.

I still haven't found the parameters of mutuality that I look for because this ink on this paper is a one way communication stream — a solitaire. It gives voice to a thought that completes itself with a backflip of 8000 words — one that begins and ends with me — and the feeling I get is that language brings me anywhere and nowhere. Stilling = Moving = Backflipping on an on and on. {z}

So perhaps I contradicted myself — because I treat wondering as a solitary practice, but I encourage and always search for ways of connecting with others through it — opening gaps and always hosting new and different voices in them. Mutually contaminating and perpetually inspiring each other.

This itch, which I could also call a wake-up caress or a nudge, is vital, for it causes a fundamental tension between agent, content and recipient — and we must never let it go, because if this tension goes loose then we are empty handed and quiet in the dark.

*

C'è un limite al dolore
in quel limite un caro conforto
un'improvvisa rinunzia al dolore
Il pianista cerca un fiore nel buio

e lo trova, un fiore che non si vede
e ne canta la certezza.
Il gioco è questo: cercare nel buio
qualcosa che non c'è, e trovarlo.

Ennio Flaiano

There is a limit to pain
in that limit a dear reassurance
a sudden waiver of pain
The pianist looks for a flower in the darkness

and he finds it, an invisible flower
and he sings of its certainty.
This is the game: to look in the darkness
for something that isn't there, and to find it.

Ennio Flaiano

BIBLIOGRAPHY

Munari, Bruno. Fantasia : invenzione, creatività e immaginazione nelle comunicazioni visive. Roma Bari: Laterza, 2007. Print.

Wardānī, Haytham, Jennifer Peterson, and Robin Moger. How to disappear. Cairo Berlin: Kayfa ta Sternberg Press, 2018. Print.

Condorelli Céline. (2009). Support structures. Berlin: Sternberg Press.

Burton, J., Cooke, L., McElheny, J., Albers, A., Ashford, D., Bachelard, G., … Zion, A. (2012). Interiors. Annandaleon-Hudson: Center for Curatorial Studies, Bard College.

Perec, Georges, and John Sturrock. Species of spaces and other pieces. London New York: Penguin Books, 2008. Print.

Ponge, Francis, and Beverley B. Brahic. Unfinished ode to mud : poems. London: CB Editions, 2008. Print.

Garcia, Tristan, and Vincent Normand. Theater, garden, bestiary : a materialist history of exhibitions. Lausanne Berlin: ECAL/University of Art and Design Lausanne Sternberg Press, 2019. Print.

Alighieri, Dante, Bianca Garavelli, and Lodovico Magugliani. La divina commedia. Milano: BUR Rizzoli, 2010. Print.

Borges, Jorge L., and Franco Lucentini. Finzioni : (1935-1944). Torino: Einaudi, 1985. Print.

Robins, Stephen. The importance of being idle : a little book of lazy inspiration. London: Prion, 2000. Print.

Calvino, Italo. Lezioni americane : sei proposte per il prossimo millennio. Milano: Mondadori, 1993. Print.

Agamben, G., & Rueff, M. (2006). Profanations. Paris: Payot & Rivages.

Ede, J. (1984). A way of life: Kettles Yard. Cambridge: Cambridge University Press.

Stein, G. (1989). Tender buttons: objects, food, rooms. Los Angeles: Sun and moon Press.

Brecht, B., Manheim, R., & Willett, J. (1972). Collected plays. New York: Vintage Books.

Axelos, K., & Hess, S. (1968). Planetary Interlude. Yale French Studies, (41), 6. doi: 10.2307/2929662

Ingold, T. (2009). The textility of making. Cambridge Journal of Economics, 34(1), 91–102. doi: 10.1093/cje/bep042

Wilde, O. (1891). The Decay of Lying: An Observation. Intentions: The Decay of Lying Pen Pencil and Poison The Critic as Artist The Truth of Masks.

Nero Magazine. (n.d.). Agnes Martin " THE UNTROUBLED MIND", 1972.

Retrieved from http://www.neromagazine.it/magazine/index.php?c=articolo&idart=1023&idnum=37&num=27&pics=0

Rea. (n.d.). Giacomo Leopardi – Dialogue between Nature and an Icelander. Retrieved from https://digilander.libero.it/il_leopardi/translate_english/leopardi_dialogue_between_nature_and_a_icelander.html

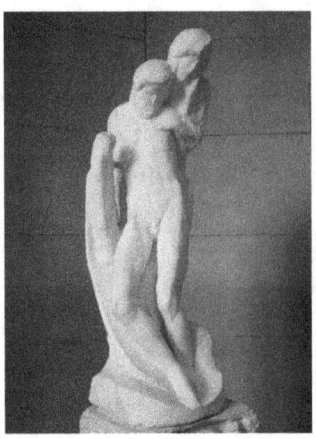

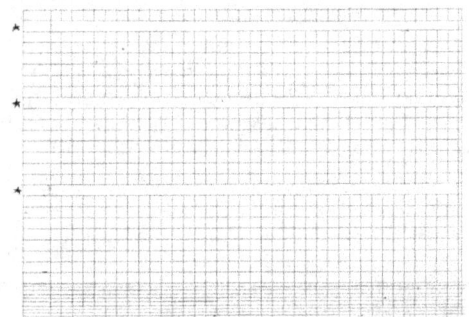

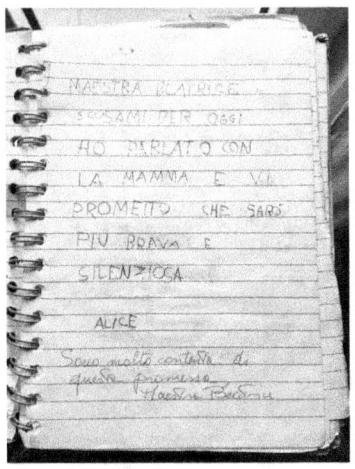

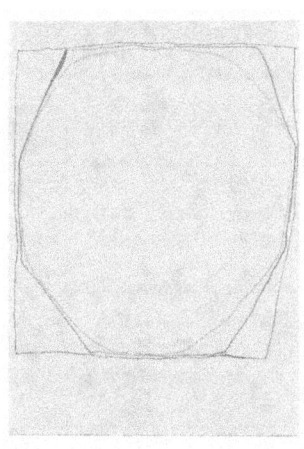

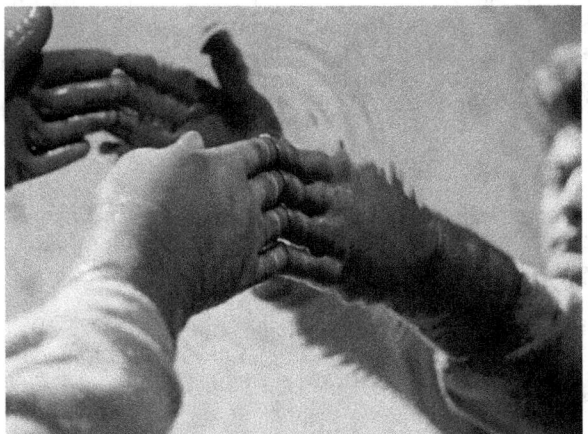

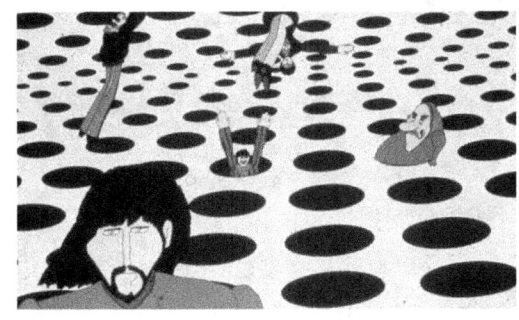

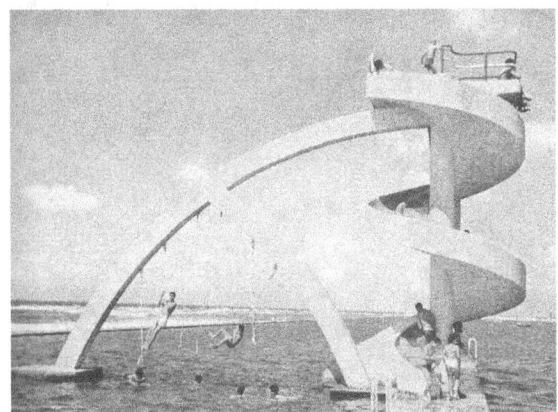

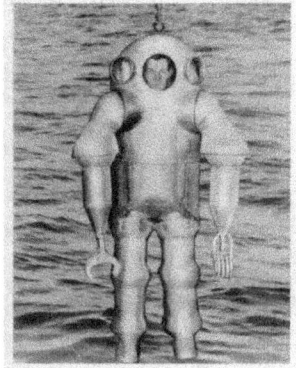

Metal Diving Suit Developed

FITTED with ball bearing knuckle joints, which provide mobility for the wearer, a new all-metal diving suit is said to enable a diver to descend to a depth of 1,200 feet. The suit eliminates the need for air lines, having a specially designed built-in air tank. Hand-operated grappling irons are a feature of the suit.

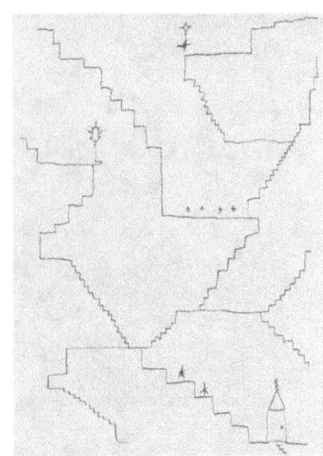

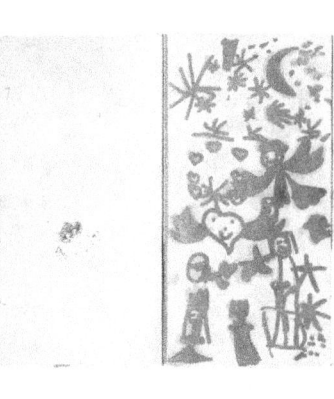

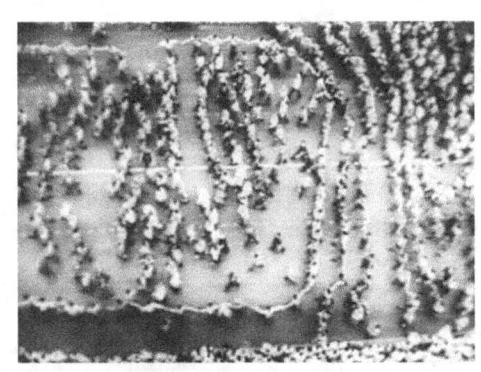

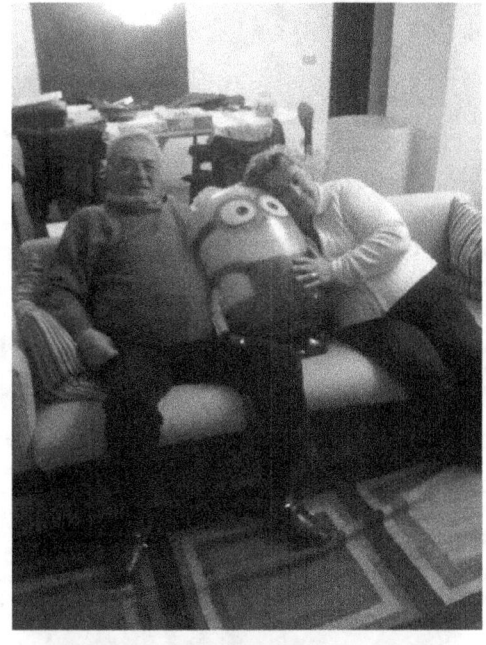

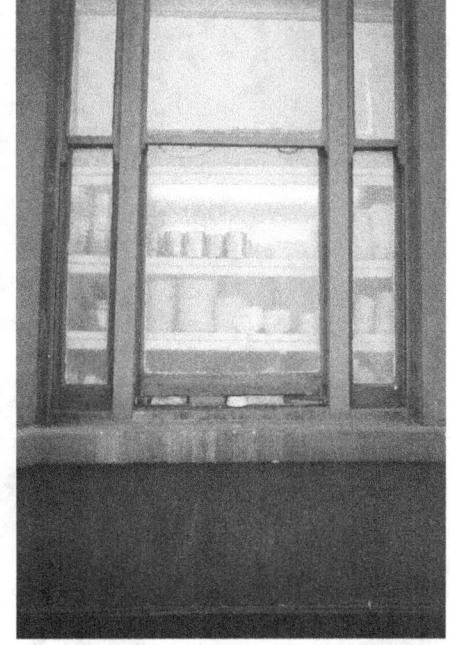

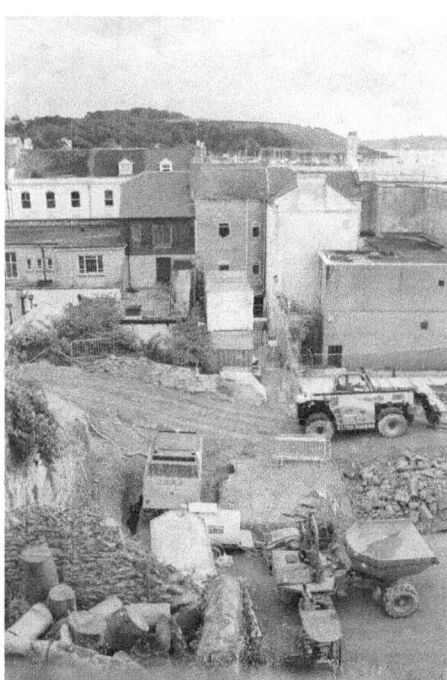

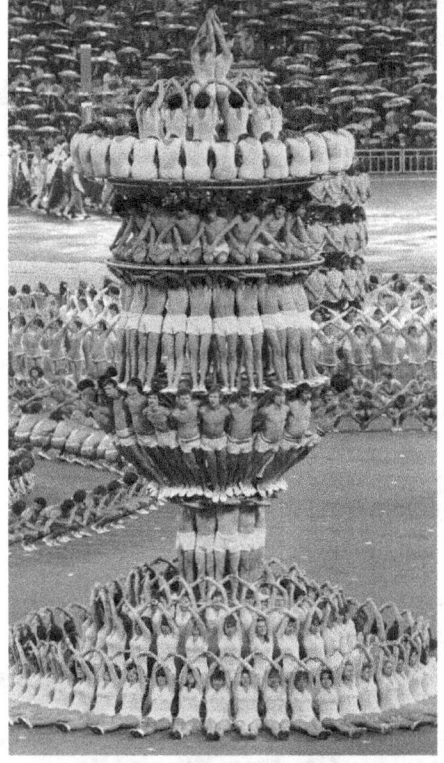

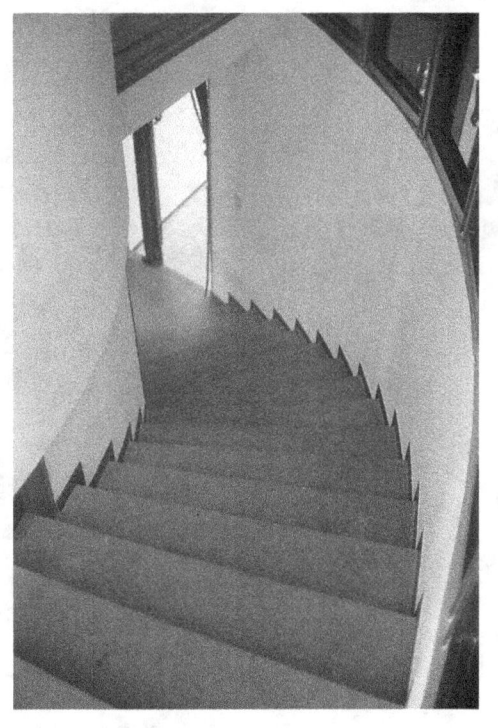

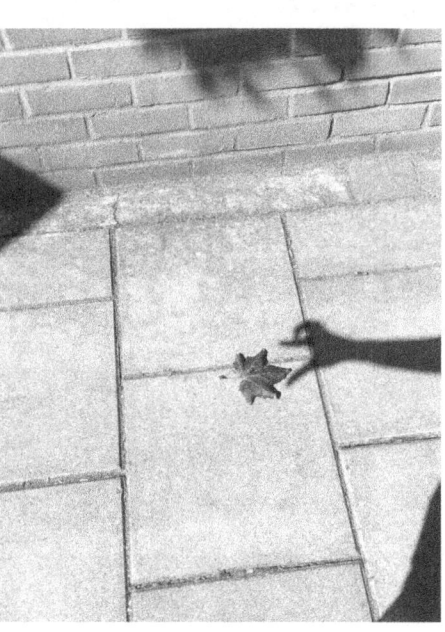

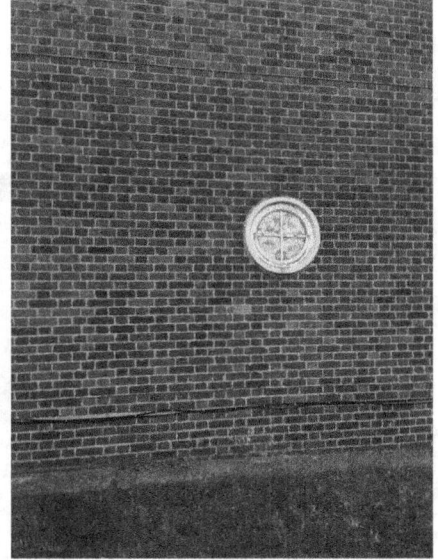

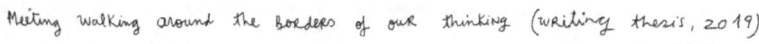

Meeting walking around the borders of our thinking (writing thesis, 2019)

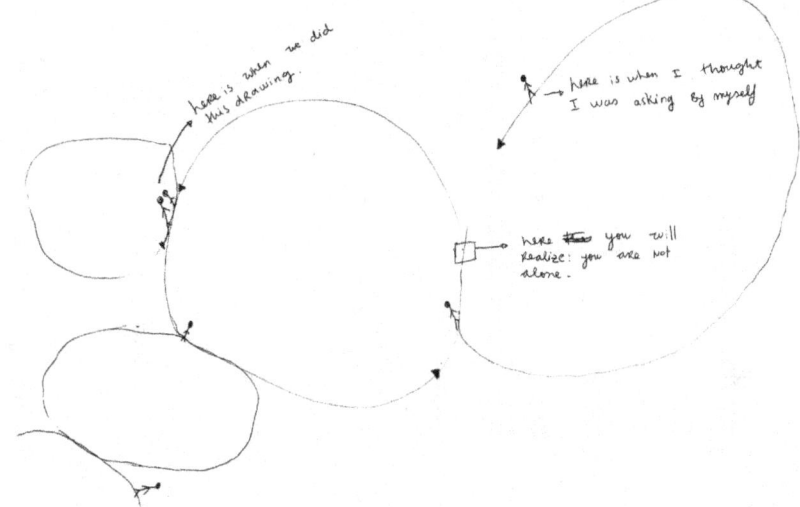

here is when we did this drawing.

here is when I thought I was asking by myself

here you will realize: you are not alone.

{a}

Wave : Shift and disturbance.
Everlasting, reverberation of energy, generated
by any movement of material and immaterial entities.

{a hand reaching for a cup; the utterance of a word;
dreaming a dream}

{similar: echo}

{b}

Chaos : The totality of waves simultaneously travelling,
propagating, intersecting around us — which become one
and indiscernible from one another.

[overload of movement = imperceptibility = stagnation]

{similar: noise, static}

{c}

Frequency : The regular rhythm of a wave travelling across noise.
Attribute by which movements are identified.

{Reading the world though rhythm and repetition. Intrinsically
bound to the body's pulse and the spinning of the earth.}

{d}

Gravitational points : Material and immaterial entities we
recognise, define, and keep coming back to.
Things and behaviours, we locate in the midst of the noise
and are repeatedly at-tracted toward, because perceived as
resonant to us.
Fragments of our identity.

{home(s);
the smell of a love;
a relevant object;
a personal ritual...}

{e}

Orbit : Reoccurring and occasionally mutating trajectories.
Patterns of thought and behaviour that define
the undertone to our lives.
Trajectories traced by the location of gravitational points.

{habits; conventions in language; iconography;
Traditions and customs in culture..}

"We are furnished by our manners and habits […]
Each gesture rhythmically completes itself with its object"
(Lisa Robertson in "interiors", ccs readers:
perspectives on art and culture, p. 39)

{f}

Generating Force: Ubiquitous and timeless energy inhabiting the
world, pushing across chaos, driv-ing the endurance of movement
and transformation of all material and immaterial entities (and
there-fore generating waves).

The playing act driving the game of the world.

{ Desire
       Wonder
           (Im)pulse
             ... }

{g}

Magic: Non-intelligible part of chaos
The unperceivable and deeply attractive side of
a partially visible whole
Everything that lies in-between the borders traced
by our understanding of the material world.
Movements we can sometimes perceive, but cannot name.

{similar: tangents, glitches}

{h}

Situation : Instantaneous and fleeting location of an entity
or a movement in time and space.

{Bodies like little google maps man, grabbed and dropped
onto a pinned point at a certain time.}

{i}

Ruler : Straight-line tracing facilitator = tool for accuracy
of measurement, drawing and modelling.
An individual or an apparatus exercising dominion over
another or a community.

{ï}

Inertia: The resistance met by change when it encounters
systems created to function and administer stability.

The assumptions that definitions provided by language
put a stop to (the endless) shifting of meaning.
The tendency of thinking patters and habits to perpetrate
themselves over time — even when their perpetration has
damaging repercussions for the future.

{The presence of broken telephone boxes and disused tram-lines
in cities; my grandpar-ents ignoring the importance of having
separate bins for recycling; periodically going over phone pictures to lighten the load — whatever I don't delete today, I might
delete next week, or the week after next; the past echoing in the
present...}

{j}

Walls: Perimeters, borders, frames of containing and understanding
— edges of knowledge, behav-iour and meaning, preventing spillages
and floods, tracing indelible and fixing lines, freezing the vi-
brancy (the life) in chaos, separating our bodies from all other
moving bodies around us, approximat-ing wholes.

{ĵ}

Language: Indispensable set of walls created in order
to navigate the world.
Instantaneous, fallacious and conventional freezing
of movements though words.

{The joined and sealed hand palms that meaning always slips away
from like a squirming fish; shells of once hid movements that have
since moved on.}

{k}

Windows: The eyes on our walls. Made to keep contact with the
other side of enclosed ecosystems so we won't go blind and get
lost in ourselves.

{l}

Doors: To walk in and out from — out into the noise, exposed to
multitudes — and back in, to the place where it can all sink in
undisturbed.

{m}

Gravity : Strategies, systems and tools provided to keep us from
getting harmed, lonely or lost in the undefined.
= The hand that grabs our "dangling balloon strings".

{Scheduling, communicating, co- and in-habiting…}

[see {d} {e} {u} — they are also grabbing us by
our dangling strings]

Societal configurations, and tools for the exercise of power that
may cause numbness and alienation.
Patterns of thought and attribution of value fed by and feeding
the above mentioned societal configurations.
= The dog chasing its tail.

{Bureaucracy; labour;
the emphasis on achievement, purpose, efficiency, wealth...}

{n}

Helium : The lightheartedness that fuels wonder (fuelled by
generative force).

{Excitement; delight; desire; adoration...}
{Ignorance; nonchalance; dissociation; tactlessness;
recklessness...}

{o}

Oxygen: The weight of gravity

{pressure, disillusionment, fear,
numbness, doubt, guilt, alienation}
{certainty, awareness, clarity, belief}

[The "lessness" in a word implies a lack
that causes an unbalance.]

Helium and Oxygen must always counterbalance each other in order
to sustain harmony

{p}

Conformism : A body shaping its form to fit
circumstance (con + form).

= caused by overdose of oxygen, the malleability
of human memory and value systems, and fear of loneliness.

{similar: laziness, apathy, inertia {ï}, withdrawal, languidness}

{q}

Success{according google}: /sək'sɛs/
noun

1. The accomplishment of an aim or purpose.
   The attainment of fame, wealth, or social status.
   A person or thing that achieves desired aims or
   attains fame, wealth, etc.
2. The good or bad outcome of an undertaking.

Success : Whatever comes after a success and
is followed by success.

The italian for "succedere" translates to "to happen"- offering
a reading of the word "success" that doesn't coincide with the
accomplishment of a final goal, but of one of many steps that
pan out in succession.
    Anyway, isn't there something super boring about achieving
(in the way we are taught achievement should be met as
a final destination)?
    "final destination".. And then what?
    Working from point A to point B, and then what?
    That's killing possibility, movement. That's operating
in favour of stillness, by putting an end to a game.
    In a way, it's operating in favour of death –
when systems are supposed to sustain life..

Success: Momentary "end" necessary
for the origination of new life.
    Procreation.
    The landing spot of a backflip – which coincides
with the lifting spot of subsequent one.

{A bit like the empty-blues-y feeling that washes over at
the end of a really good day and everything falls oddly silent.}

{r}

Failure : "This is not to give up the ambition of description or
conceptual Labour, but to do that in a particular way, that we
try and fail and try and fail again and try and fail better. I
take it as axiomatic that art is the experience of failure, and
that its vocabulary is the rhetoric of failure, but failure itself
becomes an imperative , an obligation: the courage to persist with
failure."

Simon Critchley,
from "the Mattering of Matter, Documents from the Archive of
the International Necronautical Society" by Tom McCarthy, Simon
Critchley, et al. (p. 157-158)

{s}

In-between : The undefined areas that extend
beyond and between enclosed systems.
    A place of elusive perimeters and definitions –
a place of magic, helium, noise, mystery and play

A dimension that drips.
The place where all things lost or forgotten go.

{The bedroom in the eyes of a playing child; the space between a
carrot and a table top; the intermittences in a grid-like system;
the dimension of forgotten notions, objects and memories..}

[similar: void, chaos, unknown, "abyss"]

{t}

Disappearing : The act of lingering in the in-between, erasing
one's own borders and merging with the motion of the world.

Some things want to be discovered, some want to stay concealed or
forgotten in order to namelessly exercise their influence over us.
They become indiscernible parts of us, refusing to be seen.
    When we practice disappearance, we meet the unknown and the
forgotten in their transparent and permeating formlessness}

[similar: drifting, wondering, contemplating]

{u}

Rupture : The popping of a swaying balloon.
    Bewilderment that follows of a sudden interruption.
    The telling of a story.
    The inevitable cut that the act of defining
makes to the generating force {Ĵ}.
    The glitch that gives away the act =
the crack in the credibility of a play.
    A sudden self-awareness = the mind folds over the body.
    The other hand that grabs our "dangling balloon strings"
{d}{e}{m}

{A sleep-talking person = the drooling of a dream; unexpectedly
catching a glimpse of oneself upon opening the camera app on the
phone; incidental encounter when caught in web of thought; a
phone ringing during a cinema screening...}

{ū}

Hiccups : A breaking out drawing power from an inside.
A propelling contraction.
    Visceral commotion.

{Tectonic shifts occurring beneath the crust of the earth; the
force lifting and thrusting my arms around a love; blooming...}

{ü}

Backflip : The folding over each other of two extremes.
    The convergence of opposites.
    The loss of significance resulting from redundancy.

{The end becoming the beginning; burning feeling of extreme cold;
being exhausted to the point of no longer feeling tired; when
something is so, so "ugly" that it becomes "beautiful"...}

{v}

to Dis-cover : The unwrapping of a previously concealed
"something" that causes a shift in per-spective.
    A convulsion expanding an unexplored frontier
    An achievement that for a split second feels like
the seizing of magic — when in fact, it's its profanation.

{(for) magic and happiness are a slippery fish, bolting out of
grip.}

{w}

Rainbow : The convergence of opposites gives birth
to a spectrum = metaphor for backflip {ü}
    A teasing illusion, a spectacular and unreachable vision.
    A bow with elusive extremities and irresistible charm.

{x}

Sublime: In romantic literature and art, the word sublime referred
to the overwhelming experience of the smallness of man when faced
by the magnificence of nature. It's the peak of terror coinciding
with the peak of ecstasy {ü}.
    Humans have an innate urge to pursuit pleasure, love and
discovery – always on the hunt for a better understanding of the
world while holding on to faith in transcendence.
    We think that if pleasure is what we are naturally drawn
toward, then Nature itself must be on our side.
    But here's the "cheekyness" of the Game of the world, and the
reason why it will always be ahead of us: in order to fight for
survival, we need to believe that Nature operates in the light of
reason and meaning – like us – when, in fact, it doesn't operate
in the light of anything at all.
    But it's not all bad – because if we owe our quest for survival
to illusion, then poetry and art are actual-ly very reasonable
occupations – and I write this knowing that I am contradicting
myself.

The heart-breaking indifference of Nature, comparable to
the rejection of an unloving mother, is the core of "cosmic
pessimism", the ideology of the Italian romantic poet and
philosopher Giacomo Leo-pardi, and it is beautifully narrated in
his "Dialogue between Nature and a Icelander" of 1824.

{y}

Play: Any action (or a set of actions) delivered with intention and
regulated by one or more pa-rameters = pretty much any action in
general.
    Spontaneous or moderated actions of relating subjects and
objects and/or others and/or spaces.

*"The great powers which comprehend thought […]
as well as the fundamental forces which unveil themselves in
saying and doing"* – Kostas Axelos – from essay "Planetary
interlude"(1968).

{Rituals (traditional or personal), collecting items comprising a
collection; work-ing a job...but in general, any action as simple
as sitting down, standing up, preparing a breakfast, going for a
walk, staying in bed all day…}

{z}

Matryoshka Configuration: Infinite possibility of further, deeper
discovery and exploration that each fragment of reality offers.
    A strategy of understanding that relates, thoughts, events and
people concentri-cally.

{A game in a game in a game in a game in The Game;

A letter, written by a friend, sitting at a desk, behind a locked
bedroom door, in an house, located in Milan, which is in Italy,
which is in Europe…;
    Me coming from my mom's womb,
my mom coming from my grandma's womb,
my grandma coming from my great grandma's womb... }

Celeste—Grace Perret

When the Bug Starts Breeding

An unstable introduction to patterns that are erected by systems in the realm of making.

WHAT CAN I BRING TO THE TABLE?

PREFACE

This essay intends to amplify my urges as a maker. I can not only immerse myself in the traditions of arts and crafts, but must explore further into what scientists, philosophers and politicians have to say, despite the fact that I am none of those. There is a part of me that likes to be carried away by sums, conversations, melodies and stitches that tell narratives of others. Here is where I tend to forget what my role is. What does it mean to be a maker? To me, a maker puts value into the process of the making, rather than the outcome. I believe that making and thinking are as inescapable for the maker as writing and reading are for the writer. That doesn't mean that a writer should not think, on the contrary, making and reading are quite alike.

How can I fabricate this into a vision? I do not remember the first time that my fascination for textures appeared, but I like to think of it as being part of my body, an unconscious desire. This text is not talking about textures, rather it will reveal an itch to unravel structures and a craving to shape systems. There are different ways of doing this – the approaches are endless – which makes it worth finding an approach to identify with. In other words: a way of making. The attempt at compiling a texture requires a lot of technicalities and raises many questions. In science, a phenomenon similar to textures is called *"the art of roughness"*[1]. Textures are quite an unspeakable phenomenon: when I attempt to describe a texture, it is not a texture anymore. Like poetry emerges through rhythms and form, meaning can lose its ambiguity when dissembled. When one describes a texture one might articulate upon what kinds of substance it contains, upon the tactile, the grain, endless irregularities, fractal universes or a resemblance of time. Textures can convey a resemblance of touching, the rhythm of words or the urgencies for mathematical equations.

Textures can be present at hand, either as the surface of a something, or a differentiation of another. A texture is not made out of one pattern but contains an entanglement of patterns. As for the aspect of making; what I do to unravel, to weave, to program or to think, comes from an urge to *entangle*[2].

INTRODUCTION

Maintenance of patterns can stand in the way of interdisciplinary thinking and making. That does not mean that traditional patterns cannot be present in our daily lives, on the contrary, patterns are part of the fundamentals of human perception and being. The patterns that we come across are a merging of those we ourselves shape with patterns that are erected by others. *How to identify these patterns?* In this essay I would like to break down what patterns are, how they stabilise, and, if possible, to tackle some that are deeply knotted in our nets, like *fishers*[3] who will not use the same knots for each net. I don't believe that patterns can be a solution to every situation, or that there should be a solution to every situation. Like fishers can fabricate different kinds of nets for different uses, I don't believe they are bound to use a net.

In this research I question the patterns that cause some of the passive behaviours towards our perceptions. "The regular row of dots, once defined and matched, merely repeats and brings nothing new. Only breaks or interruptions, in other words, disorder -- might provide something new".[4] *When the Bug Starts Breeding* gives a path to evoke and to poke, to pick on depictions and to picture new patterns.

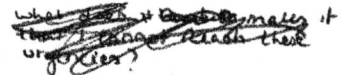

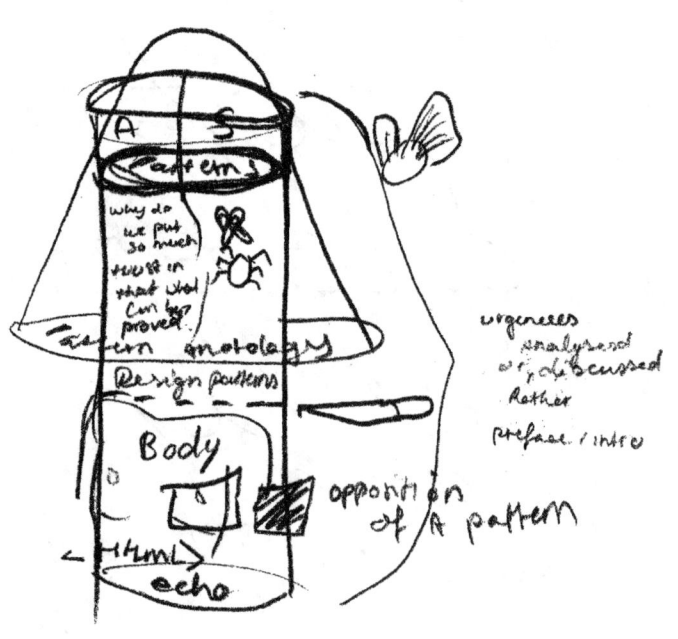

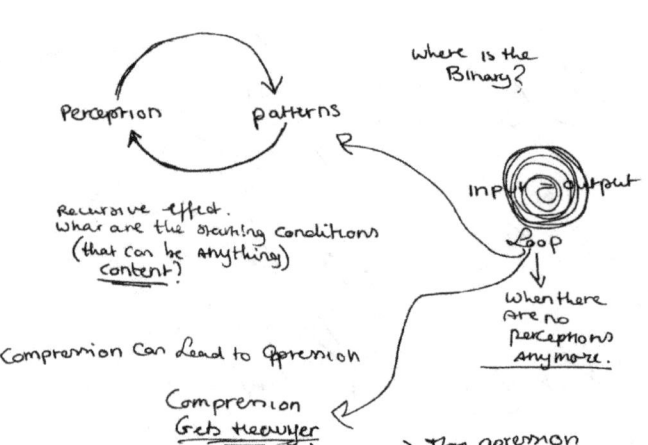

---

1   Mandelbrot created the first ever "theory of roughness" and he saw "roughness" in the shapes of mountains, coastlines and river basins; the structures of plants, blood vessels and lungs; the clustering of galaxies. His personal quest was to create a mathematical formula to measure the overall "roughness" of such objects in nature.

2   Entangle - to cause something to become caught in something such as a net or ropes.

3   'Fishermen' and the gender-neutral 'fishers' are the most common terms used in the English language to describe people who fish. While the gender-neutral term 'fisher' is more inclusive, it is far from universally accepted, particularly by women and men in the North American fishing industry.

4   *"the regular row of dots, once defined and matched, merely repeats and brings nothing new."* "Only breaks or interruptions in other words, disorder "– 'might provide something new, which is to say, specific information." - The Islands of Benoit Mandelbrot -- Fractals, Chaos, and the Materiality of Thinking p98 Seeing Order in Disorder by Margarte Pratchke.

Sensible & Analytical Patterns

What are patterns? Patterns are a regularity in the universe; in human-made design, or in abstract ideas.[5] As such, the elements of a pattern seem to repeat in a predictable manner. There are patterns observable by the senses: these are patterns that speak to the eye, ear, skin and taste and are perceived to be recurring. That which is considered a pattern by the senses can be speculated upon physically, and can be an impression of repetition. Sensible patterns can be a small resemblance of something relating to what the senses have sensed before, like memory or a feeling. However that same pattern might not be like others.

Patterns that do not speak to the senses can be identified through analysis. Analytical patterns are abstractions of a sensible pattern. These patterns that have originated from analysis can be proven by science, mathematics, economy and politics. Pattern analysis does have similarities to how patterns speak to senses. However, these patterns are only considered to be patterns when proven by analysis. The elements of the analytical patterns are taught rather than observed.

Fractal

Patterns, Perception, and an Interference with Nature

How is perception fuelled? It can occur that a sensible pattern is interacting with an analysed pattern. An example of analysing patterns interfering with sensible patterns are fractals. Fractals are born in the mathematical realm but 'existed' as a sensed pattern in nature. "*Fractal geometry has effected a paradigm shift in our concept of nature.*"[6] In other words, the senses project a depiction of a fractal[7] to 'real' nature. Some can be seen, for instance, in seashells and funguses[8]. Others less visible to the eye are cell structures and organs, like lungs. It is common to say that fractals appear in nature, though some of us don't know that this is a concept taken from science. Even less of us speak the language of science and cannot recall how the equations by Mandelbrot work. Nevertheless, we acknowledge natural fractals as part of nature and biology. We may never consider these depictions questionable, even though they take hold of our perceptions.

"*The dilemma of mathematicians is: what else is there to rely on, but formal systems? And the dilemma of Zen people is: what else is there to rely on, but words? Mumon states: "It cannot be expressed with words and it cannot be expressed without words.*"[9]

Why do we put so much trust in the things that can be 'proven'? The trust we have in analytics is not that different to the trust we have in what is sometimes described as irrational. When something is convincing enough, it can influence beliefs and change perceptions. To prove is to convince: science 'believes' that everything can be proven, and performs a language of persuasion. The system of this language acknowledges the fact that humans are unpredictable beings. Only by practicing and mastering that language can we understand the answers. Those who have mastered this language are few, nevertheless they don't necessarily grasp these patterns but still trust the

predictions that are made by those who do understand. *Does this trust stay between perceptions and depictions?* We don't only perceive depictions but also embody the products that are produced by science."In the beginning of the nineteenth century, scholars were no longer willing to accept the irregularity of mountains. Geographers and geologists searched for regular structures behind their disorder, which they took to be only superficial". This "profound scepticism regarding the world of our direct perception" is something encountered not only in science but also philosophy, art and religion. Here, science produces a scepticism around direct perception or sensible patterns and follows the line of philosophy in questioning reality. But science separates the 'self' from truth when the exchange of pattern depiction takes place. Science, which claims to be first of all empirical, pronounces its scepticism towards other realities as well.

The *Pattern* Ontology

It is hard to write about patterns and perception without referring to ontology, a recurring subject in philosophy. It addresses the entity of things or objects in relation to our way of living. It poses overarching questions around the nature of being and the relation between nature and being. The pattern ontology, however, is not present without life. An algorithm can recognise a pattern, but is scripted to do so by a human being. This pattern ontology is about the 'stabilisation' of a pattern, and can rather be distinguished as a set of *ontologies*[10].

This pattern *ontology*[11] is my way of unpacking methods to recognise a pattern. The terms I list below can lead to establish a perception, for something becomes a pattern rather than simply being one. Before it is a pattern, it is something that is not yet recognised by the senses or through analysis. Here follows the ontologies of the pattern *ontology*.

Content – content can be everything, for everything contains information and is constantly changing. Content itself is never stable.

Compression – a reduction of volume. "Content comes with compression. Compression can be layers of cultural life and or information, or it can be manifested, in experience, in the density of jungle habitat, volcanic eruptions, tsunami; yet like water, which is not compressible."[12]

Loop – a repeating engine, endless until interrupted by a different source. The loop can reveal that which has been recurring in the past.

Recursion – reconsidering an established position, feeding the input with the output, using parts of itself. Recursion is questioning the meaning of starting points in the past.[13]

A *reductionism*[14] of the ontologies of pattern. There is a field of lines, the lines are the content rushing and moving around constantly, in irregular motion, and tangling. This chaos makes it hard to define or to make sense of what the content is. To look closer at the content we separate a part, the separated part is still the content, only now moving in a smaller unit.

5   Wikis can be used as a great platform for understanding, with the spirit of multiple voices coming together. It is important to keep in mind, however, that Wikipedia has received some critique about its lack of diversity. https://en.wikipedia.org/wiki/Pattern

6   The Islands of Benoit Mandelbrot -- Fractals, Chaos, and the Materiality of Thinking   p116 'The Fractal View: Nature in Mandelbrot's Geometry''. Jan von Breveren

7   A fractal is an object that displays self-similarity; it contains parts that are similar to an object as a whole. This can often be accomplished by making use of recursion; repeatedly using the output of a function as its input.   – Arthur Boetes

8   References to picture A, a fungus-fractal-type growing. https://upload.wikimedia.org/wikipedia/commons/c/c8/Brefeldia_maxima_plasmodium_on_wood.jpg?download

9   "The dilemma of mathematicians is: what else is there to rely on, but formal systems? And the dilemma of Zen people is: what else is there to rely on, but words? Mumon states: "It cannot be expressed with words and it cannot be expressed without words."   Mum and Gödel chapter IX p 252 – Gödel, Escher, Bach: An eternal Golden braid. Published in 1979 by basic books inc.

10   *Ontologies* – Ontology is the ground and ontologies are forms. Forms cannot exist on their own, because forms didn't create themselves, so that it is rather the ground that carries forms. Ontogenesis: Ontologies versus Ontology p 34 Yuk Hui On the existence of a digital object.

11   Concerning existence, we can articulate two orders of magnitude: ontologies and Ontology. Ontology comes from the Greek words on and logos. On is the present participle of einai, meaning "to be." Logos comes from legein, meaning "to talk about,"or as Heidegger says, "to lay down in front of." Ontogenesis: Ontologies versus Ontology p 33 Yuk Hui On the existence of a digital object.

12   "Content comes with compression. Compression can be layers of cultural life and or information, or it can be manifested, in experience, in the density of jungle habitat, volcanic eruptions, tsunami; yet like water, which is not compressible." Variety of Subject (13) – Richard Tuttle Indonesian textiles, copyright 2004 Tai Gallery/Textile Arts

13   Referring to pictures of performance work – "Walking in Circles" https://celesteperret.com/walkinginircles.html

14   *Reductionism* is an approach to understanding the nature of complex things by reducing them to the interactions of their parts, or to simpler or more fundamental things. – https://www.philosophybasics.com/branch_reductionism.html

By compressing and decompressing the unit, the content is being shaped. The compression is airtight, which means that the process will switch from a chaos to a solid. In the state of being solid, the compressed content can be 'manipulated': this can be sliced into thin layers or break off into smaller units. Here, other information becomes visible. This is the part where the layers are categorised, the urge is to understand what their entity is. We loop through the content of the layers, scanning if there are resemblances, familiarities; a relatable paradigm. Here is where the two ways of observation take place; through senses or through analysis. The analysis likes to identify what the pieces possibly relate to, by going through the analytical tradition of observational methods. This can be by weighing, measuring and further experimenting until it is relating to something already in existence. The senses create relations with these pieces by giving an identification that relates directly or indirectly to oneself. With this identification, the senses might provoke a different approach to something existing and unfold new content.

Echo

In the paragraphs above I tried to untangle the elements of a pattern through perceptions; the analytical and the sensible. What makes this subject so hard to grasp is that there are so many different patterns that orbit around different central points, so what makes the centre worth orbiting around? Is it proof of fact? Or does it become of worth when stabilised and ready to be activated? *Activating* patterns can be laid out by a set of instructions, or as a plan. When made according to plan, the result has the expected outcome. Good design is understood by everyone, therefore, the use of patterns is necessary to maintain an expected quality of understanding.

A design pattern provides a reusable architectural outline. Design patterns are made to serve the senses, and are usually made through analysis. The traditional understanding of design patterns is that they're applicable solutions to recurring problems. My experience is that most patterns can be slightly changed in accordance with newly appearing problems. These problems appear by the fluctuation of content. The design pattern can dim this traffic of content by repeating in appearance over time. However, humans for whom design patterns are made can be unpredictable, and therefore a pattern needs an *update*.

The word *update* is often used in digital design where design patterns and premises rule the aesthetic of the *interface*.[15] The criteria for how the interface is built is carefully informed by logistics of user behaviour, according to *UI* and *UX*[16] designers. But why such user behaviour is taking place is rarely questioned; if the *burger button*[17] is not following the design guidelines, users get confused and are distracted from the content of the website. Phones and tablets are the death of interactive media, because it tends to loop through the same interaction behaviours. These devices use navigation systems through gigantic buttons and icons that often only reveal words and videos. Where does the actual interaction take place? In the comments or likes?

Christopher Alexander has a different take when it comes to design patterns. These patterns construct a system that does not need to be updated, but that contains enough space for the participants to anticipate, by interacting with the 'Pattern Language' manual.

The elements of this language are entities called patterns. Each pattern describes a problem which occurs over and over again in our environment, and then describes the core of the solution to that problem, in such a way that you can use this solution a million times over, without ever doing it the same way twice.[18]

What is important to note here is that the pattern language is not a loop applied to generate an expected UX outcome, but rather that it methodologically uses the unexpected outcome to its advantage. The pattern language is assembled through an analytical approach, but it does not overpower the senses.

An analytical approach in Alexander's Pattern Language relies on combinatorics and probability theory[19]. I will explain; the core solution is dependent on multiple environments and interpretations of the patterns. These environments can be almost anything and so we have many elements that can be combined. In architecture, every optional environment grows exponentially with respect to the amount of 'originated' environments. Thereby the chances are small, if not zero, that the same outcome is selected twice.

> ...We have called it "A Pattern Language", with the emphasis on the word "A," and… we imagine this pattern language might be related to the countless thousands of other languages we hope that people will make for themselves, in the future. The Timeless Way of Building says that every society which is alive and whole, will have its own unique and distinct pattern language; and further, that every individual in such a society will have a unique language, shared in part, but which as a totality is unique to the mind of the person who has it. In this sense, in a healthy society there will be as many pattern languages as there are people—even though these languages are shared and similar.[20]

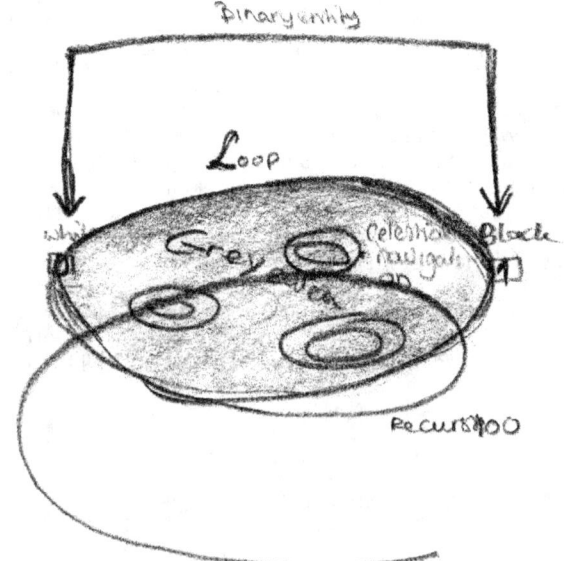

15　*Interface* – a connection between two pieces of electronic equipment, or between a person and a computer –https://dictionary.cambridge.org/dictionary/english/interface

16　*UI, UX* – abbreviation for User interface, User experience.

17　Referring to icon burger button – Timothy Miller – https://www.iconfinder.com/icons/134216/hamburger_lines_menu_icon

18　p4 A Pattern Language 1977 by Christopher Alexander Library of Congress Catalogue Card Number: 74-22874 ISBN-13 978-0-19-501919-3. Christopher Alexander, Sara Ishikawa, Murray Silverstein. "A Pattern Language." iBooks

19　These theories deal with combinations, specifically how many there are depending on what is combined and how much of what is combined there is, probability can be calculated by dividing the amount of possibilities of a certain configuration by the total amount of possible configurations – Arthur Boetes

20　p14 A pattern language 1977 by Christopher Alexander Library of Congress Catalogue Card Number: 74-22874 ISBN-13 978-0-19-501919-3. Christopher Alexander, Sara Ishikawa, Murray Silverstein. "A Pattern Language." iBooks

Body

An experiment I conducted at a workshop[21] can perhaps resonate with Alexander's pattern language. The participants were assembling patterns in an order within the exact same framework and yet all came up with different compositions. Afterwards, we calculated together what the chances were that two of the participants could have the same combination, and this was less than one percent.

My body is mine - what influence does the body have on the *metaphysical*[22] pattern? As a moth is attracted to light, we ourselves are attracted to rationality and predictions, but tend to forget that our perception is influenced by bodily interpretations and desires. Cells, hormones, genetics and body receptors conduct their own flows of information. Like the experiment mentioned above, we loop through faculties and rationalise why we did not fabricate the exact same combinations. Even though the result was laying in front of us, there is the tendency to desire proof. Why certain orders were chosen in the creation of these patterns [despite our similarities to one another] cannot be solved through calculations *alone*. I see the construction of the assignment as if feeding a compression with loads of content that is forced to decompress. The entity of the compression lives through the scattered variations of the new compressions. These compressions are not totally separate: they share similarities, but are not copies of one another.

The participants were able to generate a composition without the intention of a certain order, which means that without a plan they were still able to create. Intuitive creation does not always have to be rationalised, explained or understood. The mystification of unintentional creation can enhance new connections and questions, leading to ideas and other expressions of the body.

Judith Butler writes:

Every time I try to write about the body, the writing ends up being about language. This is not because I think that the body is reducible to language; it is not. Language emerges from the body, constituting an emission of sorts. The body is that upon which language falters, and the body carries its own signs, its own signifiers, in ways that remain largely unconscious.[23]

As a person you may think; "*My body is mine,*" or "*It is my body, I can do whatever I want.*" Did it ever occur to you that our bodies have that same influence over the I? For the body gives as many signs of awareness as the mind does. Our bodies play a grand part in our experiences and perceptions, but what is generated from the body is often not valued as proof, or evidence. When it comes to a work of art, we can all agree that it did not just appear, but that a creation took place. Performance art is an expression or choreography that exists in the moment of performing. The bodies that carry the memories – the audience and the performer – are essential to the performative work.

The Opposition to a Pattern

The opposition to a pattern is in favour of a proposition for unexpected discoveries or the interruption of what is seen as harmony. This is what I would like to call the anti-pattern. The anti-patterns are the breaks, the interruptions or, in other words, a *disorder*. Like a pattern, anti-patterns are present in our routines but are not as desirable because they can disturb the creation of regularities. Here, what the oppositions to patterns imply is the opposite of regularities in human-made design, or in abstract ideas. An anti-pattern appears through the frame or construction of a pattern.

On the website Wiki.c2 there is a definition of an anti-pattern. This definition, however, is merely summarising the position of anti-patterns in design and software engineering. "An AntiPattern is a pattern that tells how to go from a problem to a bad solution." ... "*According to Jim Coplien.*[24] "*An anti-pattern is something that looks like a good idea, but which backfires badly when applied. It's not fun documenting the things that most people agree won't work, but it is necessary because many people may not recognise the AntiPattern.*"[25]

This definition raises the same question as before, "*...who or what is it patterning for?*" Speaking from the perspective of design with this definition, the anti-pattern is an important factor in designing patterns. It teaches what the regularity in designs are, and can open possibilities to new designs and approaches. As for the documentation of Jim Copliens anti-patterns, that would work in the opposite direction. Maintaining the stigmas of these documented anti-patterns and using them as a manual to prevent design mistakes causes the effect of looping through the same design choices from a) to b) and over again. This does not allow the creation of deviation or innovation in design. What often happens is that deviant design is categorised as arts.

This same conflict seems to appear in arts and other disciplines. When a work is not crafted by certain tradition, it is swept under the carpet of 'undefined,'or in some way archived to be exhibited at a moment of relevance. The relatable paradigm of the arts, sciences, philosophy and design is that the consistency of each is questioned. It is as if they are watching each other from a high tower, waiting for someone to cross a border, while desiring to be that someone.

To entangle is to perform; it cannot be a stack of blocks. Spaghetti must be cooked in order mingle. It takes a pattern to anti-pattern.

When the Moth Meets the Bug

The moth, the bug, when do they appear? Is it because the light of the screen was on all night? Perhaps it was some lemonade spilled on the desk. How did it find its way into the closet, or into the lines of our code?

The moth's larvae crave natural fibres and, if tucked away in their favourite habitat, eat holes in the fabric. The favourite dish of the larvae is wool, since it contains keratin, but most fabric owners are not so happy with their knits being eaten. The holes are so small that they seem invisible in the beginning, but what happens if there is a tiny hole in a knit? Knits are made of interlacing loops, so the knit gets fragile when the structure is damaged. The tiny hole expands like a stain; every pull pushes the edge while the larvae feast. Washing by hand is an option to remove the larvae, but repairing the hole is crucial. Holes can be filled by darning or tiny weaves. It is a slow process completed by hand and can be captivating if the technique is good. There is always the option of throwing the fabric away, but why not maintain what you have kept for so long?

Getting into a flow of micro-processes, casting on can be the start of fabrication, though it is possible to intervene in an already existing creation. *The process of repair will build a relation*[26] with that which has been repaired and new thoughts and ends can arise.

Looking from the moth's perspective, the wooden sweater is the perfect circumstance to continue a production cycle. By removing the eggs we interrupt the life-cycle of the moth, while maintaining an artificial habitat for it.

---

21 https://hackersanddesigners.nl/s/Summer_Academy_2018/p/Weaving_ Anti-Patterns

22 *metaphysical* – "relating to the part of philosophy that is about understanding existence and knowledge" https:// dictionary.cambridge.org/dictionary/english/metaphysical

23 p 474, The End of Sexual Difference?, Judith Butler, Routledge, 2004. Excerpt from: Judith Butler, "Undoing gender".

24 https://wiki.c2.com/?JimCoplien – Last edit January 10, 2011, See github about remodeling. Last checked and read for this text on January 16, 2020

25 https://wiki.c2.com/?AntiPattern – Last edit November 21, 2012, See github about remodeling. Last checked and read for this text on January 16, 2020

26 Thoughts constructed during; Marjanne van Helvert's lecture talking about; "The parliament of things" at the Stedelijk Museum April 2019

"Constant Frustration and Bursts of Joy"[27] is the title of the third chapter in the book *Coders* by Clive Thompson. Here, Thompson emphasises that finding bugs is an inescapable aspect of programming. Big tech companies and IT departments are filled with programmers that are hunting for these bugs. How do they appear? Just like an anti-pattern, a bug is an interruption of a working system. There are unattended bugs that are bred from the mistakes of coders. Could those mistakes be an unconscious sabotage of a linear structure? This 'sabotage' acknowledges that the body is not entirely compatible with the *binary*[28] nature of the coding language. But there are also bugs that are not blinded by the pattern of the *syntax*,[29] and are bred with intention. In this case there is someone that interferes with code without explicit permission. With regards to permission, I could include a whole chapter dedicated to what or who should one ask for permission, but in this essay I will not elaborate too much on that.

Accessing a system using a bug is called hacking. 'Hack,' which in its formal definition implies a cut or a chop, resonates with the enactment of interruption that may cause the entanglement I am looking for. So, why would someone want to hack? The motivation for entering a system can vary greatly. The motive that is presented to us by the media, for example, is that hacking is a criminal act. This can be compared with entering private property without permission, however the internet was – in its original state – not a private space. That is until it became a platform where *data*[30] takes the commodity form. Hacking is an approach to doing and seeing things differently. That can be through an improvement of one thing or a dismantling of another.

> Syntax highlights blinding one's eye. The lines, the code, are compressed modules of patterns, making it hard for life not to enter.

There are scattered sources explaining where the terms 'bug' and 'debugging' derived from, though it is worth mentioning that in 1947 *a moth* interfered with an early *electromechanical computer*[31] and caused a malfunction. This intervention was logged and published with the heading: "*First actual case of bug being found*" – with the monstrous moth's image attached to it.

TRANS (–LATION)

Compilers

The researcher writing this log was Grace Hopper, who worked on the project Mark II – a computer at Harvard University – where the moth was found.[32] Educated in mathematics and physics, Hopper was familiar with symbolic languages and wanted to make them more accessible to larger audiences. She proposed the creation of a new programming language that would use English words instead of zeros and ones, which was received sceptically by the board who uttered that, "she couldn't do this because computers didn't understand English." Nonetheless, she worked with a team to create a compiler.

Compilers are a translation tool working to shift from a '*higher-level*'[33] programming language to a '*lower-level*'[34] language. In Hopper's time, all programming languages here 'lower-level' languages, whereas contemporarily our programming languages are specified based on the field in which they are used.

Hopper saw the potential of engaging other people into programming, other people that did not have scientific backgrounds, and thereby opening up the possibilities that other voices, other languages, have in products that derived from science. The computer would not maintain a compressed production, hidden in the realm of science where its functionality might loop through the same visions and goals, but rather would be opened up by the invitation of interaction and discussion with others. This would enable it to become not only a tool for scientists but also for philosophers, engineers, artists, makers, and ultimately for anyone that takes interest in learning programming languages.

Intertwined

In the early days of programming, lower-level languages [binary code] were manually punched in cards. Programming through punchcards can be seen as an earlier form of *compiling*. Weaving looms were one of the first mechanisms adopting this technique, and one among these is the Jacquard Loom. This machine became an inspiration for the Analytical Engine that Ada Lovelace and Charles Babbage were working on in the 1840s. Lovelace is considered as the pioneer of programming language and was only credited a century later, when the language ADA was named after her. Lovelace was one of the few women of her time with access to learn symbolic languages. When she was young she was tutored in mathematics by her mother Annabella.[35] Besides being a mathematician, Lovelace was also a translator and an admirer of poetry. She worked on the notes of the Analytical Engine and notated the potential of adding functions, storing combinations and executing algorithms, which was different from the calculating system. "We say most aptly that the Analytical Engine weaves algebraical patterns just as the Jacquard Loom

27   p 59 – Thompson, Clive. CODERS:; The making of a New Tribe and the Remaking of the World. 9780735220560, Penguin Press. 2019, United Sates of America

28   *Binary* – consisting of two – apposing – parts https://dictionary.cambridge.org/dictionary/english/binary Relating to the spirit of this text, such as; black and white, zero and one, male and female, punches or closed.

29   *syntax* – the structure of statements or elements in a computer language. https://dictionary.cambridge.org/dictionary/english/syntax

30   *Data* – collected information of users – information in an electronic form that can be stored and used by a computer. https://dictionary.cambridge.org/dictionary/english/data

31   *electromechanical computer* – electro-mechanical computer (plural electro-mechanical computers) (computer hardware) an early type of computer that used storage wheels, rotary switches, and electromagnetic relays and was programmed by punched paper tape. https://en.wiktionary.org/wiki/electro-mechanical_computer

32   While she was working on a Mark II Computer at Harvard University in 1947, her associates discovered a moth that was stuck in a relay; the moth impeded the operation of the relay. While neither Hopper nor her crew mentioned the phrase "debugging" in their logs, the case was held as an instance of literal "debugging." For many years, the term *bug* had been in use in engineering. The remains of the moth can be found in the group's log book at the Smithsonian Institution's National Museum of American History in Washington, D.C. – Anacdotes https://en.wikipedia.org/wiki/Grace_Hopper

33   *higher -level* – A type of programming language that uses mainly English words and mathematical concepts which makes it easier to read/understand, adjust, move, reuse, conceptualise and is more general than a low level(binary or machine based –) language. Now a days, a vast majority of programmers write in high level programming languages. – Arthur Boetes

34   *lower -level* – A programming language that is closer to a binary or machine based language. Low level languages are often platform/hardware specific, and are hard to read as they contain hardly any words and use a lots of hexa decimal or binary codes.- Arthur Boetes

35   Plant, Sadie. *Zeros and Ones*. 9781857026986. Doubleday,1997, Great Britain

weaves flowers and leaves."[36] Through the notes of Babbage she proposed that it was possible to manipulate the binary instead of merely adding or summing. Unfortunately, the Analytical Engine was never realised, however the ideas behind it run through the veins of our devices today.

Just as Lovelace never received acknowledgement for her contribution during her lifetime, many other people that have propelled technology are not considered part of the tradition of science. "The spindle and the wheel used in spinning yarn are the basis of all later axles, wheels, and rotations; the interlaced threads of the loom compose the most abstract process in fabrication. Textiles themselves are very literally the software linings of *all* technology."[37]

It is unfortunate that these roads have never been mapped. Would that have changed our perception towards the devices that we carry so closely on our bodies? These early technologies might not always have been invented in laboratories or by academics, but also in less credited circles of manual labour, like households or factories.

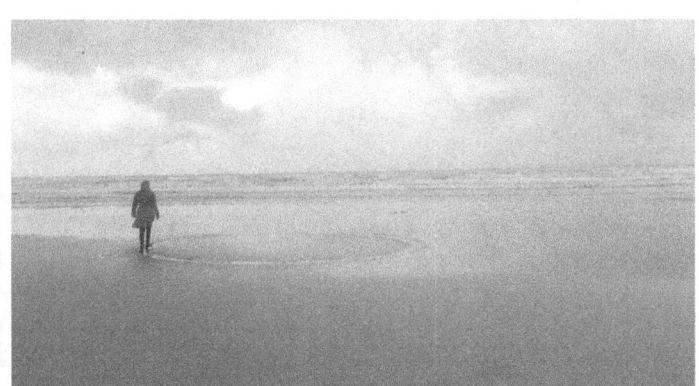

UNZIP

Normaal

Through my research I try to question which tools construct our patterns of reality. As previously mentioned, "*patterns are one of the fundamentals of human perception,*"[38] and that includes perceptions of the past, present, and the desire to foresee the future. Active patterns or designed patterns tell us that we can imagine patterns, communicate through patterns, or build constructions with patterns. Patterns are used as an *apparatus*[39] by perception. The apparatus can be rebuild and, just like perception, it can transform, which makes it difficult to separate the two. What seems to be different is that patterns can bring stability or a sense of foundation, lying in stark contrast to the fluidity of perception. Stability can provide a foundation: a solid form. In my definition of the pattern ontology I name this state a form of *compression*. From that foundation a 'normative' ideology tends to be built. But what exactly is normative? 'Normative' should not be confused with the word 'normativity' – they are different. 'Normative' relates to an assumed norm - part of the word 'normative.' 'Normativity' is a phenomenon that will be explained following the below paragraph.

'Normal' is actually different for everyone: as previously mentioned, perceptions in individuals are different. However 'normatively' is often assumed to be the norm for everyone. What the norm is remains a perception, but what we have discovered in an early passage of this text is that perception is fluid; it is not a brick, even when it seems to be a very convincing brick, perfectly crafted by someone. That brick is not absolute and can still be broken, built into something else. The trust we put into what manifests from patterns can be contradictory to what is meaningful or truthful to oneself.

Letter

In January 2017, the prime minister of The Netherlands wrote a letter on behalf of his political party (VVD), to citizens of the country. In this letter, he tried to elaborate on what he thinks is happening to national norms. Unfortunately there is no translation to English, so this is a compression and translation of the text by me.

The letter begins with the statement: "Sometimes it seems as if nobody is normal anymore." It remains slightly ambiguous as to what this *normaal*[40] means, however he does state what he does *not* consider as 'normal'. This includes violent acts, abuse of money provided by the state, female assault, gay[*homo*][41] harassment and excusing 'normal' Dutch people to be racist. *Niet normaal.*[42]

It then hints at what the causes might be, and states that he understands the feeling some citizens have about deporting those that are 'not normal'. It follows that the solution is not to "treat everything or anyone in the same way," but that the solution lies in the matter of mentality. The best thing we could do, he thinks, is "... to continue to make crystal clear what is normal and what is not normal in this country." He shares what he considers to be normal; no act of violence, working for money, to get the best out of your life, helping each other

---

36 "*We say most aptly that the Analytical Engine weaves algebraical patterns just as the Jacqard-loom weaves flowers and leaves*" – p. 696 ``Ada, The Enchantress of Numbers,'' by Betty Alexandra, Strawberry Press, Mill Valley, CA (proposed by Anita Burato)

37 p 67 Shuttle systems Plant, Sadie. *Zeros and Ones*. 9781857026986. Doubleday,1997, Great Britain

38 Refers to introduction of the text; "*That does not mean that traditional patterns cannot be present in our daily lives, on the contrary, patterns are part of the fundamentals of human perception and being.*"

39 *apparatus* – *a set of equipment or tools or a machine that is used for a particular purpose* – https://dictionary.cambridge.org/dictionary/english/apparatus

40 *Normaal*. Dutch word for normal Anecdote: "*Doe normaal dan doe je al gek genoeg*" – An adage in Dutch for "*To behave normal, is behaving crazy enough*".

41 *Homo* (homosexueel) In dutch often used as a synonym to address a romantic 'relationship' between men. – Thereby not taking other sexualities in consideration.

42 *Niet normaal* Dutch word for: *abnormal, not normal*.

and having a proactive attitude towards finding solutions. He ends with "...we can sustain everything we have achieved together."[43]

The arguments in this letter are divided into dualities: there is no grey area between the 'normal' and the 'abnormal'. The opposition of norms stated by an authority are not necessarily the norms for *everyone*, and it is here that the word 'normativity' comes into play. The letter illustrates the construction of a normativity, rather than questioning normativity itself. What if I do abuse money from the state to make sculptures, help refugees with integrating, transition into a *non-binary gender*[44] and call my Dutch neighbour a racist? According to the conditions this will not fit into the criteria of the norm, which can lead to questions such as: *Am I not considered Dutch or normal by the prime minister?* What about those that spend their time in the fields of the arts, those who research in the realm of science, work as volunteers, take care of domestic labour or create communities? Do they not fit the norm of this society either? The foundations of normativity are *compressed* patterns that come with a weight. This weight can lead to *oppression*. Oppression is not invisible, and has a physical and mental influence on perception.

Why is the normativity described by the prime minister important to this essay? Because it fuels the question: why is art not acknowledged by society? Counter-systems are not part of the norm. By becoming active in understanding the tools of perception, one can build counter-systems and anti-patterns. This can be liberating and open all kinds of doors for creation, questions, translations and conversations. Systems and counter-systems are what I tend to be mesmerised by, which can be described as a *will* for building. That is hard to consider as a form of art, because it is often invisible, without an identification. Nor can it be installed on a pedestal.

Being aware of the above begs me to question: what will happen if I want to establish myself as an artist? Am I not making art, if I would only build systems *without* a visual outcome? Should art not be a door to different realities, an interruption of systems, a remaking, a rethinking, a realisation of urges, a translation of thoughts and other forms of languages, without being necessarily rationalised by the traditions of art?

The white cubes of the fine art galleries and contemporary museums have been white for over fifty years. Those white walls have been the subject of many critiques among artists, but continue to be considered as the norm. There are artists that cannot even imagine a work outside of these walls. It is a reality and a beautiful metaphor for *isolation*. Art is similar to design, science and philosophy, which all create tools for society, either as perceptions or objects. But just like society, design and science, art needs new perceptions as well.

SUM

Zip

I don't want to change my passport
I don't want to market my weaves
I don't want to shut up on behalf of your beliefs

I maybe want to watch Netflix
I maybe want to start to rearrange
I maybe want to stay in bed because you think I am strange

I do want to ask you a question
I do want us to exchange
I do want to engage in society but some things need to change

In the preface, I proposed that my urge is to entangle, and in this attempt I followed different variations of threads that lead to knots of perception, language, patterns, interruptions, bodies, normativity, anti-patterns and bugs. The itch that drove me to dig into such research is one that wants to direct some of the norms and technologies that I am entangled with. Entanglements are present from the moment that you're a seed, and even before the existence of an I or a you, it is inescapable.

My intentions for this text are to open up this research through the form of publication. This will appear in different forms. One is through an open document online that invites conversations, participation and feedbacks from unpredictable sources. The webpage will host small editorial functions that provide possibilities for customised reading and adjustments. To complete the circuit, every now and then a physical publication will be made to press those inputs onto paper. Those booklets may in time grow into a catalogue of thoughts. Our contribution to these thoughts might not appear in *nature*[45], but perhaps will loosen some of the readers knots, making room for other thoughts to appear. Rethinking systems creates possibility to decompress, to loop through content, and to recurse into new threads of entanglement.

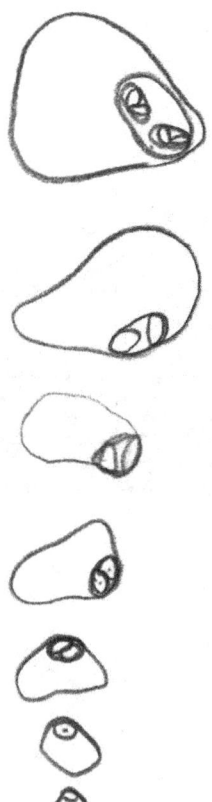

43 The letter of the prime minister of The Netherlands, Mark Rutte
   on behalf of his political party VVD. (only available in dutch)
   https://www.vvd.nl/nieuws/lees-hier-de-brief-van-mark/

44 non-binary gender - Aberration of the binary gender-
   construction: Female or Male.

45 Nature magazine.

BOOKS

Thompson, Clive. *CODERS:*; The making of a New Tribe and the Remaking of the World. 9780735220560, Penguin Press. 2019, United Sates of America

Plant, Sadie. *Zeros and Ones.* 9781857026986. Doubleday, 1997, Great Britain

Sandberg, Sheryl. *Lean In: For Graduates.* 9780385353670, Knopf Publishing Group, 2013, United Sates of America

Samuel, Nina et. al. *The Islands of Benoît Mandelbrot; Fractals, Chaos, and the Materiality of Thinking*, 9780300186437, Bard Graduate Center, United Sates of America

van Dijk, Tessa; Peeters, Norbert. *Darwins engelen.* 9789045037592, Atlas Contact, 2018, The Netherlands

Trichilo, Josh, translator. *100 Whites*. By Kenya Hara, 9783037785799, Lars Müller Publishers, Zwitserland

Marinucci, Mimi. *F.eminism is Queer.* 9781783606757, Zed Books, 2016, United Kingdom

Hofstadter, Douglas R. *Gödel, Escher, Bach: An Eternal Golden Braid*, 9780465026562, Basic Books

Hui, Yuki. *On the Existence of Digital Objects.* 9780816698912, Electronic Mediations, 2016, United states of America

Tuttle, Richard. *Indonesian Textiles*, 9781588860736, Tai Gallery / Textiles Arts, 2004, United States of America

Alexander, Chritoper; Ishikawa Sara; Murray Silverstein et. al. *A Pattern Language*, 9780195019193, Oxford University Press, 1977, United States of America

Albers, Anni. *On Weaving*, 0289370043, Studio Vista Publishers, 1974, United Kingdom

Smith, Shawn Michelle. *At the Edge of Sight*, 9780822354864, Duke University Press, 2013, United States of America

Dabiri, Emma. *Don't Touch My Hair.* 9780241308349, Penguin Books Ltd. 2019, United Kingdom

Monteiro, Stephen. *The Fabric of Interface: Mobile Media, Design, and Gender*, 9780262037006, Cambridge, MA : The MIT Pres, 2017, United states of America

Haraway, Donna J. *A Cyborg Manifesto: SCIENCE, TECHNOLOGY, AND SOCIALIST-FEMINISM IN THE LATE TWENTIETH CENTURY*, University of Minnesota Press, 2016. ProQuest Ebook Central, http://ebookcentral. proquest.com/lib/warw/detail.action?docID=4392065.

MAGAZINES/NEWSPAPERS/ARTICLES

Broeke, Asha ten. *"Hoe gaan we ooit de wereld ten volle begrijpen als wetenschappers vrouwen maar half zien?"*, de Volkskrant, 29-12-1018, The Netherlands

McLean, Alex ; Harlizius-Klück, Ellen; Jefferies, Janis *Introduction: Weaving Codes, Coding Weaves*, TEXTILE, 15:2, 2017, 118-123, DOI: 10.1080/14759756.2017.1298232

Gillberg, Minna, *"Liquid love, liquid sciety, free yourself from blockchain, the capitilasation of Tinder and how to fight capitalism from within."*, Girls Like Us, Jessica Gysel, 2018, The Netherlands

Bratich z. Jack and Brush M. Heidi. *"Fabricating Activism: Craft-work, Popular Culture, Gender"*, Utopian studies January 2011, DOI: 10.5325/utopianstudies.22.2.0233

PODCASTS

Blankesteijn, Herbert; Burg van der, Ben. "De Technoloog". BNR (NL)

West, Stephen. ''Philosophize This!" West, Stephen. (ENG)

Sautoy, Marcus du. "A Brief History of Mathematics". BBC Radio 4, (ENG)

Kyra Philippi

Da Capo al Fine

INTRODUCTION

When exactly does repetition lead to standardisation and when does it lead to diversification?

For this thesis I research the role of repetition and the appreciation of the space in between repetitions. I search for overlapping factors within the field of music practice, textile production and education.

For examples with a historical context, and where crafts and repetition are an integral part within a social setting, I focus on the invention of the first knitting machine by William Lee in 1589.

Most chapters are intertwined and I hope, by surveying a variety of examples and disciplines, to discover new insights on repetition between the fields that are touched:

The knitting machine of William Lee, the statements of Queen Elisabeth I, the citations of Hume, Deleuze, Sennett and Chomsky, the initiatives: The London Cloth Company and the Textile Research Center and my own experiences as a musician and textile student.

The title of this thesis is a musical reference: to start over again from the top (da capo) and proceed to the ending (al fine).

HISTORY

Repetition
Understanding a movement.

William Lee

William Lee, who, after more than 10 years of research, in 1589 invented the first knitting machine, grew up in Calverton, England, a village in an area famous for its wool production. At that time, wool processing and garment production was organised in guilds. Knitting guilds were further extended by a system of affiliated knitting schools, which offered the poor, the sick and children a source of income. The knitting guilds carefully checked whether these schools met required standards, and controlled that correct materials and models were applied. There was little room for innovation. Surprisingly, this particularly conformist setting became a source of inspiration for Lee, allowing him to make a keen analysis of all the parameters of the manual knitting process. This would lead to his mechanical simulation of the hand-knitting techniques he observed.

First of all, we have the visible factor dealing with knitting: needles, yarn and patterns and the interaction between these three elements. The second factor, less visible but of equal importance for the success of repeating the knitting stitches on a knitting machine, is the human extension. What exactly do I do with my arms and fingers? This can vary from knitter to knitter, but it is certain that all hand knitters become routined through the constant repetition of the same movement, and that, between repetition of the knitting stitches, knitters analyse and apply improvements iteratively starting from the very first stitch.

The concept of a knitting machine, the transfer of what happens with two arms, two hands, two knitting needles and 1 thread, to a device that produces the same knit with multiple needles, bears witness to a very inventive mind.

While studying the process undergone by Lee in his quest for perfect mechanical replication, for making the details work, through trial and error, the constant loop of repetition and analysis, I also reflect on my own work. What role does such a quest for perfection play in music practice?

The Frame-work Knitting Machine

Drawing of the first knitting machine: the amount of hooked needles (b) corresponds with the amount of stitches on the knit. A thread (h) is laid in front of the needles. By using one pedal (f) sinkers (d) between the needles make sure the tread is pushed down. The thread is pushed into the hooks by the presser (c) using the middle pedal (g). Release of the sinkers by pushing the other pedal (f). By pushing the frame handles (e) forward, the thread slides through the loops, and by setting the frame handles back again, a row of stitches is made.[1]

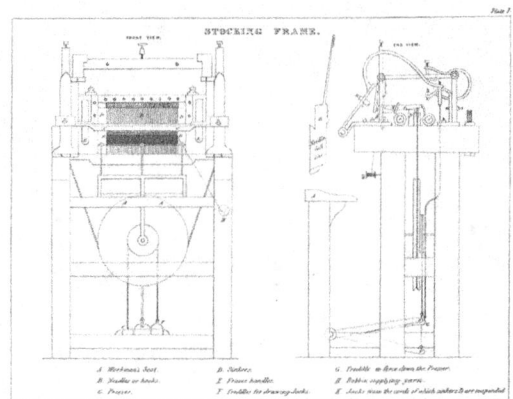

---

1   Felkin, W., & Chapman, S. D. (1967). History of the Machine-
    Wrought Hosiery and Lace Manufactures. New York, USA:
    Augustus M. Kelley, Publishing.

Viola I

I have just finished reading a fascinating book by Milton and Anna Grass about the life of William Lee. This book describes the social setting in which Lee operated and tells about his personal life, for as much that it is known.

In the period that I was reading the book I was asked to participate in a recording session, as the violist with a string quartet. Below a snippet from the rehearsal: "Let's play this passage again, taking the intonation a bit lower, especially with the F-sharp," the sound engineer is telling me through the speakers. With the headset on one ear, I put the second violin on my console a little louder and we play the same passage again. I estimate the placement of my second finger, the F-sharp, half a millimetre lower on the fingerboard of my viola.

All four of us in our quartet use a click-track, a metronome on the headset, but we are especially keen on keeping an eye of each other's fingers to play rhythmically together.

I realise that there are a lot of similarities between playing and knitting; the same efficient analysis and application of the ideas for improvement. Whereas with playing there also is the auditory factor. The knit is the performed or recorded music so to speak. With my viola I seem to manoeuvre between knitting needles and a knitting machine; however, the instrument, my viola, is a lot more complex than two knitting needles, but still the majority of the movements are manually done, just as is the case with hand knitting.

Practical implementation and conceptual thinking are complementary to each other, both in knitting and in music. Understanding a movement in music starts with step by step seeing and feeling the movement, the direction, the tension, the size of the movement, the pressure applied by the fingers and the use of gravity and speed. Understanding all these aspects is only possible by endlessly repeating the movement and each time focusing on a different detail. Zooming in. Then, and in between, merge elements and zoom out again to the result, thereby approaching the process from a different perspective and repeating it again. Repetition in this situation is made to establish parameters and standardise the output in regards to intonation, rhythm, tempo, dynamics and musical phrasing.

As much as this might seem like a solitary process, receiving feedback and adjusting one's goals play a major role as well. The learning path for a musician is not only based on one-on-one tutoring or solitary practice sessions, but also on group rehearsals and regular performances in front of an audience. Learning combines mental and physical efforts, listening, reading, reflecting and repeating.

Can we say that these repetitive processes are based on traditions? And at what point do we give them that distinction?

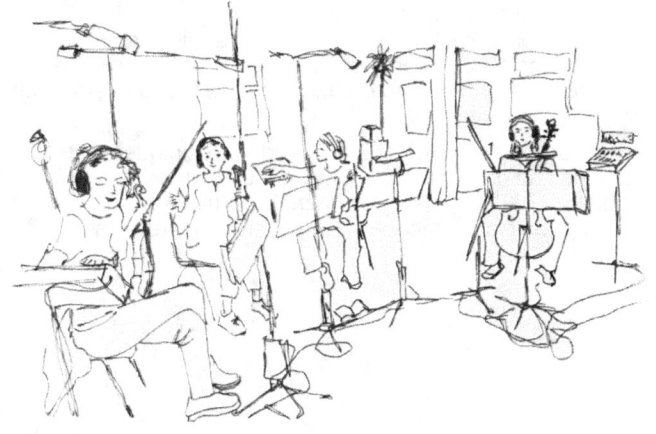

2

TRADITION

The Queen

Traditions are repetitions embedded in society. These repetitions appear to be extremely important, to such an extent that stepping away from them will disrupt life dramatically for the people within that society.

William Lee, an inventor focused on making his knitting machine a success, perhaps did not fully realise how large the socio-economic impact of his machine would be on the knitting industry in England. Queen Elisabeth I at that time, however, did:

> 'My Lord. I have too much love for my poor peoples, who obtain their bread by the employment of knitting to give my money to forward an invention which will tend to their ruin, by depriving them of employment and thus make them beggars.'[3]

Citation of Queen Elisabeth I, after William Lee in 1589 showed his knitting machine to her and asked her for a patent on it. With this plea, the knitting machine of William Lee is an early attempt at speeding up a textile production process with the use of a mechanical device. Its use would have replaced multiple individual manual actions of different knitters, their different hands and minds, by a machine that was, through a flow of repetitive movements by identical needles, quicker, more uniform in the output and probably more reliable.

There was a practical and financial reason for Lee to ask the Queen for a patent on his machine. By granting Lee a patent, the Queen would de facto have approved the invention and this would have opened doors to production. The knitting machine would have had the opportunity to gain access to one of the existing guilds (weaving or knitting) or to form its own guild, which then again would have enabled the renting of a workspace or shop and the selling of goods. However, Queen Elisabeth I denied the patent and therefore the British market was, at least for that time, deprived of Lee's invention and of machine knit products.

The application for a patent posed moral questions to Queen Elisabeth I regarding the value of efficient repetitions versus originality in the knit-work, quantity versus human quality of living. To her, there was also a concern regarding independence and control; if the knitting machine were to be a success, the knit production would be soaring and it would be more difficult to control the production process. With the existing traditions regarding the making and selling, things were tightly managed within the existing guilds.

The interesting matter here is that Lee, by repeating and deeply internalising the hand knitting process, came up with a new invention, his knitting machine. In terms of production techniques, it represented an alternative method, or diversification. The machine itself, a product of meticulous study, was a new thing that changed the process of knitting while at the same time standardising the outcome. The Queen and her advisers wanted to maintain the manner of knitting production that was already standardised by the guilds, preserving therefor the diversification in the output. So while William Lee was innovative, the knitting machine actually caused a more monotonous output. Here innovation caused standardisation (the knitting machine) while standardisation (in the form of tradition) caused the conservation of diversity (hand-knitted items).

2 Drawing: Studio Arnold Mühren, Volendam. With Emma Breedveld,
   Janneke van Prooijen, Kyra Philippi en Eva van de Poll, 2019

3 Grass, M. N., & Grass, A. (1969b). Stockings for a queen:
   The life of the Rev. William Lee, the Elizabethan inventor
   (First Edition/). London, England: A. S. Barnes.

Just as Queen Elisabeth I protected the traditional way of knitting, the classical music world is similarly hesitant to embrace innovation; where some instruments have gone through an evolution, from harpsichord to grand piano, for example, other instruments have virtually stayed the same over the past 350 years. On my viola, built in 1745, the only adaptation so far was a slight lift of the fingerboard and different quality strings. Contemporary violinmakers still consider the old Italian instruments exemplary and these makers are repeating the building codes of the old masters. I feel that repetition here contains a mix of fascinated mysticism of an alchemist kind, paired together with the practical notion that the old ways of building string instruments actually have technically been proven to produce the best sound.

There are contemporary examples of a choice made between live-music versus recorded music in theatre and ballet performances. The Musician's Union in the US for example has negotiated that on Broadway a minimum of three live players have to be added to all recorded scores, to protect the work for musicians.

Are there, in the field of textiles, contemporary examples of the preservation of traditional skills as well?

AWARENESS

The Textile Research Centre

The Textile Research Centre in Leiden reaches back to pre-industrial textile techniques, and connects in that way with the era of Lee and Queen Elisabeth I. Queen Elisabeth I's objective was to preserve the market of hand knitters, using repetition to protect standardisation. William Lee, at the same time, invented the knitting machine by close observation of hand knitting, and thus spawning innovation. The TRC again underlines the standardisation aspect of repetition. Not to protect the market, but to preserve the skills by creating awareness of manual textile production techniques that we were once, or still are, able to execute.

> 'The basic aim of the TRC is to give the study of textiles, clothing and accessories their proper place in the field of the humanities and social sciences. The TRC does so by providing courses and lectures, carrying out research and by the presentation of textiles and dress from all over the world. The two main focal points of the TRC are (a) dress and identity: what people wear in order to say who they are and (b) pre-industrial textile technology.'[4]

I spent my internship at the Textile research Centre in Leiden where I was primarily documenting garments and other textiles that were donated from all over the world. I learned about the production techniques and about the history and the usage of these garments and accessories. I was absolutely thrilled having all these textiles go through my hands, and loved learning about their fabrication and usage. It was there that I had the opportunity to read from their extensive library, which is where I found the aforementioned book of Milton and Anna Grass on William Lee.

In the depot of the TRC 25.000 pieces of garment and dress from all over the world are stored, ranging from ancient fragments of a Chinese tunic dating 2000 B.C., to a Yellow Vest, used last summer in the Paris demonstrations. From hundreds of different veils to hand-stitched shoes from a Himalayan farmer and a handkerchief embroidered in 1947 by women Nazi-collaborators held in a post-war detention center. The TRC makes sure that all textile techniques found in its collection are traceable. Specialists of the TRC give workshops to become skilled in these techniques and offer presentations and exhibitions on the history, usage and social settings of the garments.

I strongly feel that this awareness of manual skills, in the case of the TRC, textile techniques, is important. Manual skills are at the basis from which all machine and computer-related techniques stem. Manual textile techniques tell us about the history and social habits of societies. Besides this, working with these manual techniques can have a therapeutic effect on people's well-being.

The TRC focusses on pre-industrial textile techniques in its workshops and presentations. They are concerned with the kind of repetition that keeps existing manual textile production skills alive. They leave active innovations to other institutions.

---

4   https://www.trc-lei-den.nl/index.php?option=com_content&view=article&id=103&Itemid=118&lang=en. Director: Gillian Vogelsang-Eastwood

Tweeds

Whereas most businesses in textile production constantly seek cheaper and more efficient production methods, often through outsourcing, off-shoring, disregard for the environment, and modern mechanisation, at times there are new initiatives emerging that I would consider to be countertrends. Some initiatives preserve skills, similar to what the TRC does, by revisiting. Other initiatives are also actually employing manual textile production methods. They return production to its historical location, often closer to the customer. When this return occurs, the production returns with a different status. An article in the Financial Times about the start-up of David Harris illustrates one such case.

David Harris founded the London Cloth Company in 2011. He started with one old loom that he had found. He refurbished it returned it to working order. His fascination with the mechanism of the old loom led him to acquire more antique looms. He began weaving tweeds on them, both on commission and for his own production. Harris's stated aim, according to the article, is 'to reignite the manufacturing industry in Britain and to conserve diminishing skills and crafts'.[5]

Harris started his company out of curiosity for an old skill; weaving with a mechanical loom. His sense of ownership and aim for originality are his motors and add an innovative layer to the idea of re-ignition. I do feel connected to the fascination that Harris feels to figure out how these old looms function, and his intention to stretch their possibilities.

It is interesting that while in William Lee's time the knitting machine was seen as a mechanical device, in contrast with hand knitting, nowadays the weaving of Harris on his old looms, which are actually just as mechanical as Lee's knitting machine, is considered handwork, in contrast to the much bigger, computerised electrical looms. The definition of ' handwork' clearly depends on the time setting and the alternative techniques that are available.

Putting the effort of Harris in context with William Lee, I would say that, by totally understanding all aspect of hand knitting, Lee could develop his knitting machine which was very innovative at that time. Harris, by thorough understanding of the old loom, could go back to the old technique of weaving with a manual loom, which is, in modern context, also innovative!

History and reality are, to me, causing another interesting tension here: weaving on an old loom, in the case of Harris, is not a necessity but a choice. Locality, the fact that the shop is unique in London, brings additional value to the tweeds that the London Cloth Company produces.

The TRC and the London Cloth Company both apply repetition but in different ways:

The TRC institutionalises by collecting textiles to document the making and usage. This is reinforced by their teaching ancient techniques to future generations. They do not produce textiles themselves. David Harris is initially using repetition to perfect his weaving skills and then applying the repetition productively to create his own innovative myth, his tweeds, literally within the frame of the old loom.

Comparing this to the music scene that I am working in I see contemporary violinmakers follow the same procedure: using the old masters' methods to build their own instruments, trying to create originality, within the frame of the old school.

Production

One can distinguish three periods within textile production; the pre-industrial period when textile was exclusively manually made, the industrial era in which mechanical production replaced the manual production of goods, and the third period, which is the post-industrial era in which we, consumers and makers, find ourselves right now. This third era shows ever growing awareness of the negative effects of industrial production processes.

The moral questions regarding efficient repetitive mechanical production processes are massive. This is true of many industries, and is not less in the textile industry. Before the industrial revolution, textile was produced close to its users. Textile production provided a (modest) living, defined social structures and the products gave identity to both the makers and the users.

Now that nearly all production happens in foreign countries, far from our eyes, any connection between the maker and the user has all but disappeared. The maker is often badly underpaid and works in jurisdictions that provide few, if any, protections. He or she is complying with factory orders regardless of the quality of the products. The identity and situation of the maker is unknown to the end-user. This disconnect relieves the user from any social requirements to give respect or status to the maker. Such dynamics are often paired with a drop in quality that depreciates the value of textiles. This, in turn, is compensated for with overconsumption and overproduction.

The two previously mentioned institutions, The Textile Research Centre and the London Cloth Company, are examples of efforts to revive the interest in textile fabrication, where repetition in the shape of tradition and in the shape of innovation is taking place. In the case of the London Cloth Company, diversification, the personal touch in the textiles, is generating additional value.

But how does it exactly work, this emerging personal touch in repetitive processes; how does repetition allow diversification?

5   The Financial Times: 30 March 2013, Arts & Culture section
'Run of the Micro-Mill' by John Sunyer

MULTIPLICITY

Hume

If I want to be able to freely use skills creatively, to think out of the box, I would want to use repetitions in a more experimental way. To become a highly skilled weaver, knitter, or musician, repetition of technical patterns is expedient to understanding the link between cause and effect. The eighteenth century Scottish philosopher David Hume, about a century after the knitting machine of William Lee had finally been accepted and was functioning in its own guild, succinctly sums it up:

> 'All human knowledge is solely
> founded in experience (...)'[6]

In terms of building experience, repetition can be seen either as a way to establish the experience, or else as an intermediate step in inspiring new experiences. According to Hume, those new ideas emerge from impressions that are engrained in our minds through repetitions.

Hume continues:

> 'We must place the power of repetition
> within the enlargement of multiplicity.'[7]

So, by multiplicity of instances that seem to occur independently, awareness of a pattern or repetition occurs. The more repetitions, the clearer we see a pattern, and that is where new ideas arise. In other words: by expanding the multiplication, we are able to recognise the repetitions and can (re-)act upon them. An external example is the weather; with two dry and hot summers in a row we think this might be coincidence, whereas after eight dry and hot summers in a row we would consider this a pattern and can react accordingly.

A more personal example is when, while playing, I would notice that tones played with my first finger are consistently flat for intonation. I might question the correctness of my hand position, or consider changing something in my concept of how I am approaching placing my first finger.

Visualising Time

When I am knitting by hand, I am using two needles. The manual act of looping the thread around the needle, pulling the loop over and sliding it down, the stitch, is visually disappearing once it is completed. The time taken to knit is only recorded within the knit itself.

I realise that, from Hume's perspective, what Lee did with his knitting machine was to narrow down the imaginary space, making the imaginary space partially more concrete by adding as many needles as there are loops or stitches in the knit. In this way, the knitting machine establishes the maximum width of the knit. But there's more beauty in it: the knit itself has the ability to stretch out. So within the analog visualisation of time, one finds this hidden treasure. This hidden, subjective time, I consider the most attractive characteristic of a knitted textile.

Music

The same kind of visualisation of a repetition or narrowing down of the virtual space of a repetition, I feel, is present in the range of music practice; the more complex the mechanics of an instrument, the more visual its repetitive qualities are. In my instrument, the viola, we see four strings that are of different thickness. A logical conclusion therefore is that we are able produce four different notes or tones. All the other notes are hidden in the magic of the fingers of my left hand. Other instruments are highly developed in a mechanical way, similar to the knitting machine of William Lee or the looms of David Harris. For example a piano: fifty white keys and thirty-five black ones making eightyfive different tones! Or the pedal harp with forty-six strings of different length and therefore of different intonation. These possibilities are tangible, just as is the case with a knitting machine and a weaving loom. Using the shafts of a loom even visually reminds me of playing chords on a piano.

Both the piano and the harp are instruments of which the strings are tuned in half-tones.

The fingers are not at all concerned with defining the intonation, as they are on my viola. So, where the piano and harp have their intonation standardised, concrete and visible, the viola has an invisible, variable structure for intonation that reminds me of the hidden stretching potential of knitted textile.

All three musical instruments, piano, viola and harp, require constant repetitions of their players to get into this Hume power of recognising possibilities and obtaining new ideas.

Next to this aspect of repetition, musicians need repetition as well, to memorise and internalise and to expand on these new possibilities and ideas.

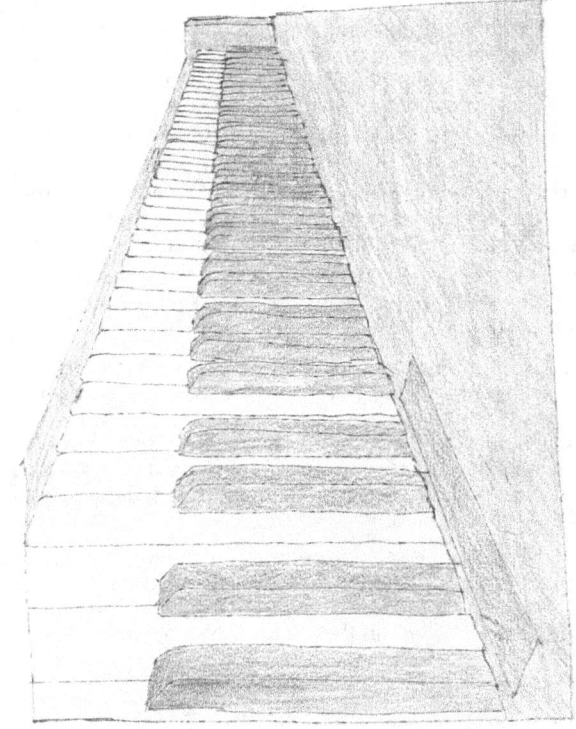

8

6 Hume, D. (1986). A Treatise of Human Nature (Herz. ed.). Geraadpleegd van https://www.gutenberg.org/files/4705/4705-h.htm

7 Hume, D. (1986). A Treatise of Human Nature (Herz. ed.). Geraadpleegd van https://www.gutenberg.org/files/4705/4705-h.htm

8 Drawing: Kyra Philippi, Rittmuller Grand Piano, own collection

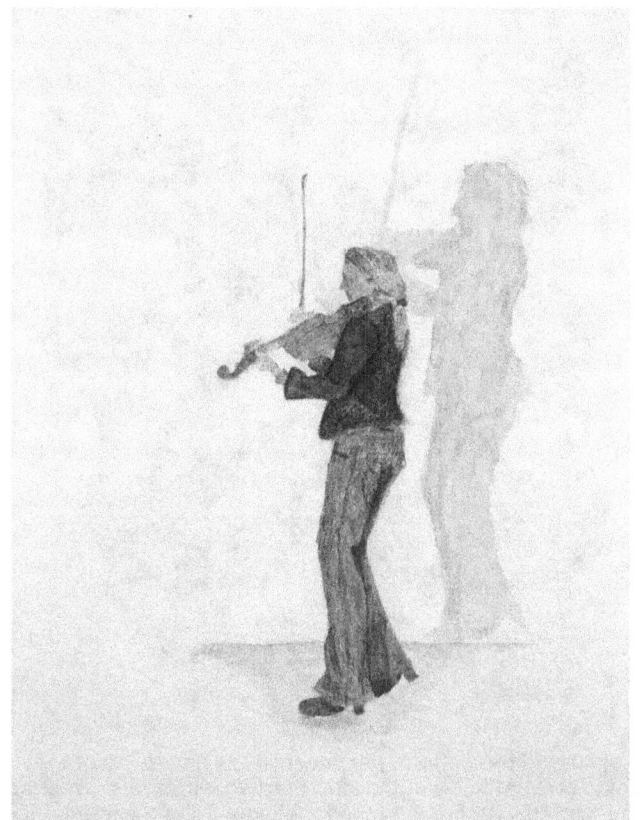

9

Viola II

Aware of repetition in music practice, I document the steps that it takes me to prepare a piece of music: In the practice room, while preparing a program, I first take an overview of the whole work. I isolate difficult passages, analyse them and repeat them using different strategies. With each repetition I focus on a different aspect, first intonation, then rhythm, bow use, pressure, coordination between left hand and right arm, placement of the bow on the string. I examine the musical aspects: what do I want to express in this passage, what is the mood and how do I want to use phrasing to express it? Having gone through this process, I put all he passages back in context. Usually, by then, I am able to play the passages from memory; I internalised the passages in all their detail. As a last step I visualise the actions in my mind and merge all layers into a multi-dimensional work of sound. The repetitions are not at all noticeable here anymore. The average listener has no way to hear or see how the preparation was built up. And in the end, what is the goal I want to reach with all these repetitions and ideas that emerge through multiplicity?

ORIGINALITY

Shifting parameters

When I am recording a CD, my parameters are differently geared than for a live concert situation. It is not acceptable to find errors of any sort on a CD. Recording techniques are highly advanced and only time is the limit. With technical perfection as base requirement, I should add free musicality and an original interpretation.

For a live performance situation the preparation is similar, but the parameters shift; in a concert I take more risk, prioritising interpretation to prevent the outcome from being boring or calculated. In a live performance I am communicating with the audience and reacting on circumstances like acoustics.

Comparing it with manual textile production nowadays; we do appreciate the variation in output and the fact that the maker is identifiable or at least traceable. While we expect machine-made products to be perfect, with manually produced textiles we do like to recognise the maker, even in the imperfections. There are still a lot of requirements in terms of quality but a piece's originality is what counts most. Be it a live performance or a locally-made textile, if there is a connection with the maker we will have a different appreciation for the product; it makes us clearly aware that the product is human-made. Sometimes this concept of identifiability is taken one step further, as in giving higher priority to the maker, or the idea or the concept. Repetitions then would become interpretations. Does the multiplicity of Hume lead to new ideas that in turn become new main parameters?

9   Drawing: Cecelia Palumbo 2019

TRANSLATION

Experiment

What is the difference between a repetition and a translation? I have been thinking about it, and I realise that there is a big difference between the two concepts. In a translation I feel I am stepping away from the urge to keep similarity as a primary requirement. The connection between a first and a second repetition is concrete and inspirational, yet looser than in a strict repetition meant to improve the original plan. So, while a repetition where one is zooming in on the previous is a motivation, as an introvert internalising focus, with a translation, I would say, the aim is a stretching out of the original concept, which is more of an extrovert action.

With this in mind I executed an experiment:

I used a pattern that I found on a traditional Turkish hand-knitted sock during my internship at the Textile Research Centre. I wanted to translate this pattern multiple times, searching for what it would give me and how long it would inspire me. The pattern in itself is mirrored, both horizontally and vertically.[10]

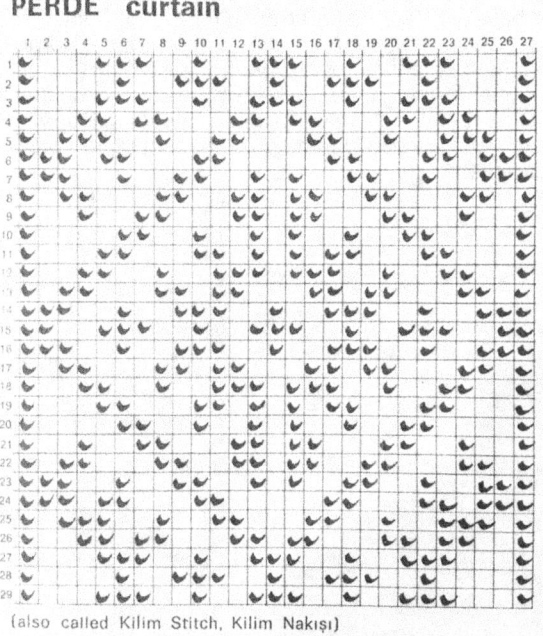

PERDE curtain

(also called Kilim Stitch, Kilim Nakışı)

11

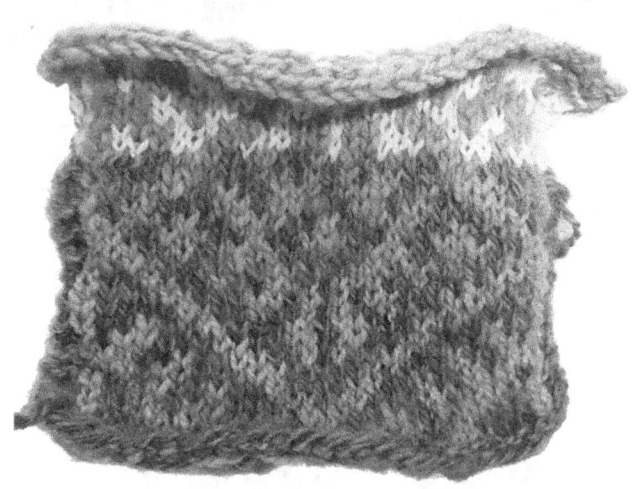

12

First I knitted the pattern. I experience the entwining of the wool to prevent holes in the knit. Starting with a bird-eye's view of the pattern, I zoom in to the repetition of the rows, then the stitches, the latching of the two threads, the tension. With each row I am unconsciously analysing and drawing conclusions on what could be done better, and what I would do differently the next time I knit this pattern, and also what I like this time around. I would choose wool that has been twined more evenly. I really do like the colour and I think the pattern would look beautiful in an actual sock.

Knitting has a rhythm, a quiet monotonous rhythm, only paused by finishing a row and reversing the work to knit the next row. As a musician I look at the pattern as if it were a score, here a change of field is emerging and the repetition is transforming into a translation. I imagine the empty boxes being rests, the filled in boxes being notes. But actually, this is not right since the empty boxes are not voids in the pattern, but the background colour. And the pattern involves continuous thread as well, and different stitches: knit & purl and the concepts of time and touch.

The pattern is transforming into a multi-layered sound work. For each row in knit I use the tonality of the major scales, for the purl I use the paired minor tonality. Which raises a dilemma; in textiles there is always a back and a front side. What would be the analogy in sound, what do I consider the back or front side of sound? Is indeed the minor tonality the back sided, shadow partner of the major scale? Repeatedly looking at the pattern and combining it with my experience in music practice is inspiring and leads me to new ideas, and reminds me of Hume's citations.

On the image you see the first version with only the rhythm. You can clearly see the pattern in the notes. The multi-layered pattern interpretation, YouTube link: https://youtu.be/ku9tlYtqrag

10 Harrell, B. (1981). Anatolian Knitting Designs. Istanbul: Redhouse Yayinevl

11 Harrell, B. (1984). Anatolian Knitting Designs: Sivas Stocking Patterns Collected in an Istanbul Shantytown. Istanbul, Turkey: Redhouse Publications.

12 Photo: Kyra Philippi, own collection

13

PROGRESSION

Viola III

As a musician I am interpreting music of which the output depends, in addition to the aspects of musicality and intuition, on my technical skills on the instrument. In order to bring the sound production closer to my expectation or imagination I have to make the physical movements as effective and efficient as possible. To achieve this goal, I am constantly repeating passages and, by making mental notes in between the repetitions, slowly approaching what I want to hear. More than making meters, it is about analysing and adjusting; an interplay between ears, mind and circumstances. No repetition is a real repetition, even if nothing changes in the circumstances, I still am in the same room, playing the same notes on the same instrument. I am reacting on the previous round and therefore no repetition is an isolated event. So to speak; every repetition is a new proposal waiting for an answer that then again is a proposal waiting for an answer.

> 'Does not the paradox of repetition lie in the fact that one can speak of repetition only by virtue of the change or difference that it introduces into the mind which contemplates it? By virtue of a difference that the mind draws from repetition?'[14]

Considering the above citation of Deleuze, which without a doubt is applicable within the field of music, I wonder how those knitters in the 16th century knitting schools were thinking about their work. Were they just knitting with their minds on a different planet, or were they thinking actively, with each stitch or with each stocking, challenging themselves to improve or embellish? Were circumstances such that there was room for inspiration? Deleuze states that change always happens between repetitions. Circumstances, nevertheless, do make a difference, in motivation and the risk one is willing to take when making changes.

I realise that both the space in between repetitions, the external sides, and the repetition in itself, the internal side, are changing.

I illustrate this with the following example.

Inspiration

I realise that, while knitting, one part of my brain is very concentrated, learning from the repetition and aware of what I want to change in the outcome, while another part of my brain is active and inspired, already conceiving totally new versions or translations; projecting options that urge you to reach beyond the obvious. Repetition in the context of changing fields is definitely leading to diversification. But what role does the space, time or place that lies between the repetitions play in the development of these so called repetitions?

13 Print: Kyra Philippi, using Noteflight, 2020

14 Deleuze, G., & Patton, P. (1994). Difference and Repetition. New York, USA: Columbia University Press.

Socks

Recently I did extensive research on the fabrication of socks. I studied their history and use and I also was designing, knitting, felting and folding various types of socks. Soon enough I was confronted with the intriguing yet blunt fact that with socks you need two. A mirrored pair. Until factory production took over, starting with the invention of the knitting machine of William Lee, and delayed by the denial of the patent that Lee requested with Queen Elisabeth I, socks were made by hand, and, as it is with handwork, two identical items never turned out quite the same. To me this has to do with a philosophical precept: humans and human development are always in flux. The moment you make a work, perform an action, you learn. Circumstances are changing and therefore the conditions and parameters are changing and with this, the concept is altered, however slightly. We see this also earlier in the thesis were I write about music practise and in the above citation of Deleuze.

The industrial revolution has created not only the option to mass-produce, but importantly, has made replication possible to a point of precision that had never been a possible before. With industrially produced textiles, many of the parameters that were flexible in hand-crafting have stabilised or become standardised; the machine hardly changes, tension and speed stay constant, intervals are shorter since production speed is higher, and one machine can do the work of multiple people.

Now that we are used to perfect industrial replication, are we conditioned to expect this level of stagnated creativity in handwork as well?

While experimenting with various techniques of making socks and foot wraps I found it quite frustrating to make a second, identically mirrored partner while my head was full of other ways to execute the job. I therefore decided to let go the idea of creating two identical socks one after the other, and instead focus on the development of thought and apply the new insights in the second item of each pair. This led to a collection of non-identical pairs of socks and foot wraps. Repetition became a window for diversity. Aside from the internal and external factors that influence repetition, can we optimise our use of repetition to extract more from it?

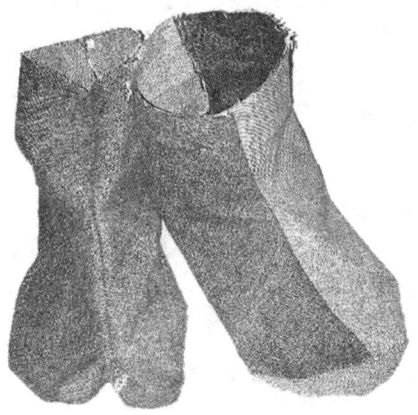

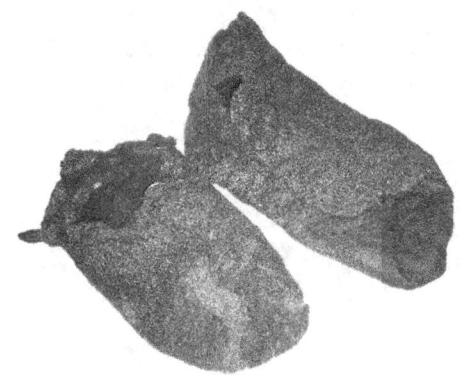

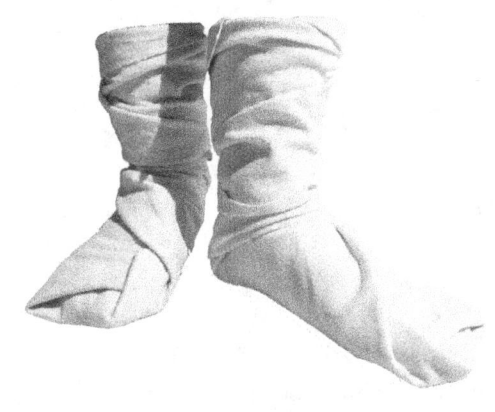

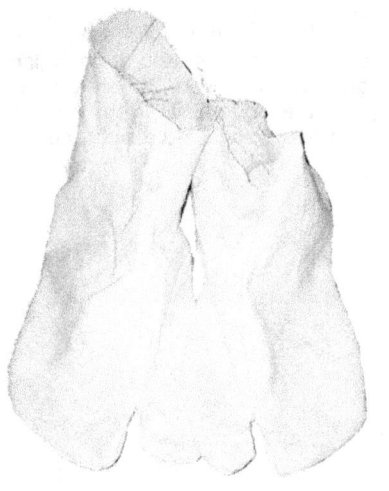

15

15   Images: Tabi socks with extra room for the toes, felted socks, Portyankis, traditional Tabi socks. Kyra Philippi design, 2019

Rhythm

In his work 'The Craftsman', Richard Sennet discusses repetition as itself an essential thing of v alue in the work process:

> 'Doing something over and over is stimulating when organised as looking ahead. The substance of the routine may change, metamorphose, improve, but the emotional payoff is one's experience of doing it again. There's nothing strange about this experience. We all know it; it is rhythm. Built into the contractions of the human heart, the skilled craftsman has extended rhythm to the hand and the eye.' [16]

Richard Sennett is referring here to the daily practice of a musician. But this idea could very well be applicable to sportsmen and dancers as well. And, moreover, almost everyone feels this kind of fulfilment in repetitive action itself, if it's done in a certain rhythm or natural flow.

When, in former days, a work routine needed stimulation for smooth repetition, songs were the perfect medium. Farmers, fishermen, and other workers have used songs to keep the rhythm going of their repetitive work. I am sure that, especially because of the human vocal factor, the environment was open to changes within the repetitions. Adjustments had to be made; if people were ageing, or younger hands came in, the season or the weather changed, tools broke or demands were altered. The singing added a personal mark to the repetition, people were appreciated for their good voice and even though each individual was clearly part of a team, they each 'had a voice' in the matter.

So while Sennett's citation counts for the musician in the practice room, it also applies well to many other situations and activities that do not immediately require sophisticated hand skills. Were the knitters in the 16th century singing while they worked? Did the singing comfort them and inspire their knitting? Was the ticking of the needles defining the tempo of their songs or vice versa? And was Lee humming in his beard while he assembled his second, more refined, knitting machine that had not 8 identical knitting needles per inch, but 20?!

Nowadays, most singing during production processes has been replaced by the rhythm of machinery and singing is reduced to entertainment, but we still find the power of it in education, for example, when children memorise the alphabet with a song, using melody, rhythm and repetition.

How do I use rhythm and repetition while teaching?

Celtic women singing while waulking the tweed.
https://youtu.be/ekO8W0zSZO8

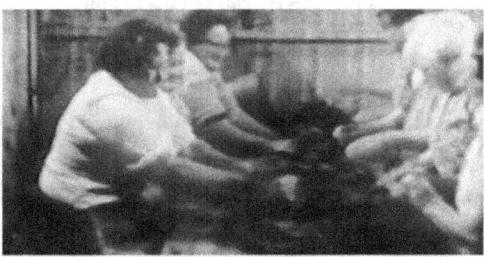
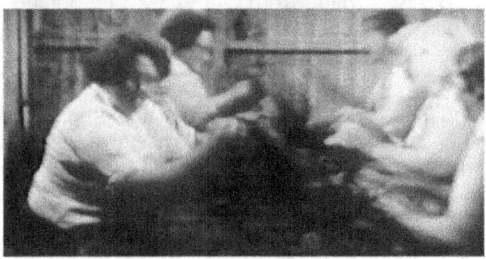
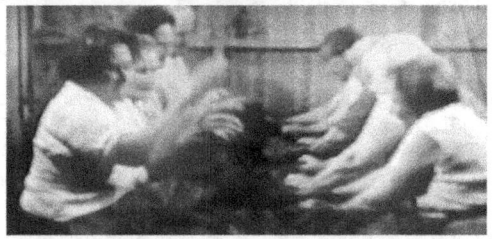
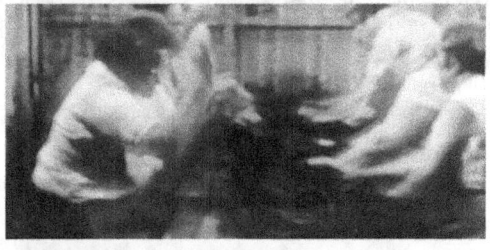
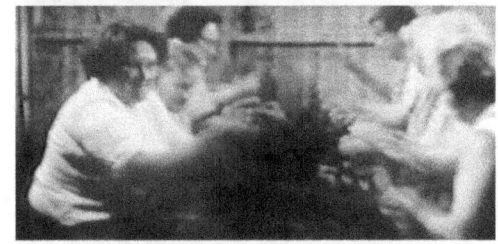
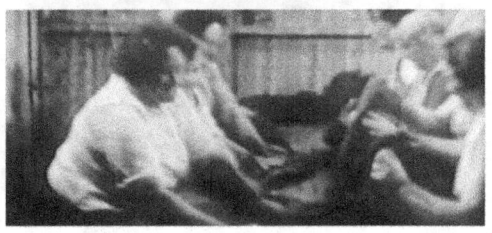

17

16 Sennett, R. (2008). The Craftsman. New Haven, USA: Yale University Press.

17 Kappers, r. (2006). YouTube. Geraadpleegd op 2019, van https://www.youtube.com/watch?v=ekO8W0zSZO8&feature=youtu.be

INTRINSIC MOTIVATION

Education

The role of rhythm in concentration, as explained by Sennett, is very useful for musicians and music students. Another theory, complementary to that of Sennet, is put forth by the linguist and philosopher Noam Chomsky. Chomsky explains in one of his talks that a learning process is only worthwhile when the student is finding knowledge by exploring. By having the feeling that the discovery is made from within. Repetition and giving the time to discover and learn are indispensable in a learning process. Spooning up facts and working for exams just to get good grades is not enough. Real interest should be triggered.[18]

When I teach violin, viola or chamber music I strive to activate this discovery process in students, no matter their level of playing or their age. If I do not do that, the teaching becomes impersonal and boring and knowledge will not stick. I literally see the happiness of students when they discover and truly understand how to tackle a tricky technique or passage. This is not because I told them to do certain things but because they were inspired to find the answers themselves.

Considering the idea of Sennet that the rhythm of repetition provides a reward in and of itself, and Chomsky's idea that experience can be derived from focused repetition, I would conclude that the combination of the two would deliver a "practice groove" in which there is very focused self-analysis as well as the capacity to look beyond the required task.

Knitting, weaving, practising, teaching, performing, recording, translating and inventing are all based on an active awareness of that what is and that what might be. Or, as my dear viola teacher at the Yale School of Music, Jesse Levine, had posted for years on the blackboard in his studio:

'Explore all possibilities'

CONCLUSION

In this thesis I researched the function of repetition within the fields of music, textile and education. I explored where repetition can lead to: standardisation, diversification, translation and innovation. I looked at the function that repetition can serve: as a tradition or as part of method. I discussed the concepts involved in greater detail, including what has been written about repetition over time and how I experienced repetition in my own work.

One of the discoveries I made while working on this thesis that every single thing we do is a repetition as soon as you identify it as such. Once a repetition is identified there is a choice to define it as standardisation or as a way to give room for innovation or diversification. Traditions and routines would fall into the definition of standardisation while translation, interpretation and innovation would be diversifications through repetition.

The Textile Research Centre and the London Cloth Company provided clear examples of repetition in the areas of textile conservation and fabrication. I included both my own professional work as a classical musician; the experience of playing concerts and recording sessions as well as teaching, and my activities as a textile student. As such, I conducted experiments to become more aware of the precise function repetition serves in connection with refinement of movement and motor skills.

To understand the evolution of repetitious processes in the field of textile production in a historical context, I reviewed the circumstances surrounding the invention of the first knitting machine in 1589. Here I discussed the economic and social implications of this mechanical introduction. Citations of, among others, Queen Elisabeth I, Hume and Sennett guided my timeline into modernity and provided additional perspectives on the role of repetition in learning. Within the thesis itself, I applied repetition as translation as well, through my drawings and through the composition 'When a violist, two knitting needles and lots of books meet'.

The journey of my thesis was a major effort which I thoroughly enjoyed. Standardisation and diversification through repetition are still every day exposing different insights to me and will keep me intrigued for the rest of my life!

---

18 Noam Chomsky: The purpose of education:
   https://youtu.be/DdNAUJWJNO8 Presented at the Learning Without
   Frontiers Conference – Jan 25th 2012– London (LWF 12)

APPENDIX 1: POEM

THE KNIT

I also have it.
The curves that knit,
The fingers that count,
The crossings that sustain.

I also have it.
I also have questions and that is why
I look into books for methods, for
stories – a glimpse of an instruction.

Rosa Mesquita

A poem written to me by a friend. Without knowing it from each other, we both were fascinated by the same picture, illustrating the 6 steps of knitting a row on William Lee's Frame work knitting machine.

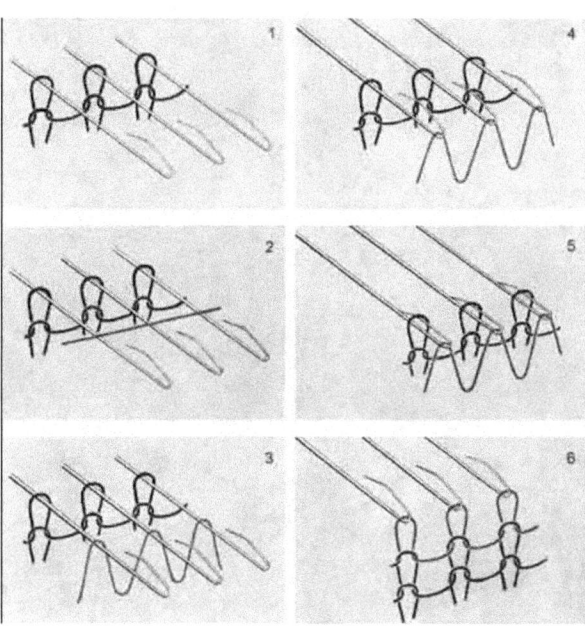

19

APPENDIX 2: COMPOSITION

WHEN A VIOLIST, TWO KNITTING NEEDLES AND LOTS OF BOOKS MEET

16th century, real old times, knitting was done by hand
In an area full of virgin wool, Elisabeth I reigned the land

One man just really had enough,
and made his brain spin round
Used repetition, motion exhibition, a detailed, analytic vision
The 'knitting machine taking over hand skills'
Is what he slowly thought out

The queen said no, it cannot be
A patent is not for you
Bad for business, no forgiveness
So it was France that Lee fled to

Long story short after 100 years, the patent was assigned
Innovation over conservation, replacing knitted variation
Industrialisation underlined

Entering modernity, my life and musicality
Here too repetitions apply
In concerts, shows and studio work
Sound is getting better, changes really matter
While you try, and try and try

In a studio, sound is set on disk, perfection is a must
We analyse, no compromise
Repeating and adjust

My internship shone yet another light to repetitions over time
Standardisation and preservation
As the Textile Research Center has in mind

Where they then stop
David Harris goes on
Giving old looms back their lives
Re-igniting local manufacturing,
his weaving workshop back in swing
With a modern touch, is what he clearly strives

Then Hume and multiplicity, and visualising time
To improve and/or to alter,
Changing actions, pace by pace
It gives an inner knowledge, applied where mental space

While practising my instrument, repetition's guiding me
To improve my tone, getting into the groove
Ideas are floating free

These free inspirations, give room to new creations
I would say: translations
A step further from repeat

Rhythm plays a major role, in work done with a group
In memorising, education, for tempo and good concentration
Read Sennett's The Craftsman, his excellent book

Repetition is tradition, where folks and places meet
The rhythm is a rhythm only when I do repeat

Chomsky also mentions: Exploring things is good
Owning by experiments are repetitions understood

Researching, Writing, Reading, Reflecting, Repeating

19 http://www.deutsches-strumpfmuse-um.de/
technik/04mechflachwirkstuhl/Bild_flachwirk_01.htm.
Erstes Deutsches Strumpf Museum, Gelenau.
Currently closed and website is down.

BOOKS

Deleuze, G., & Patton, P. (1994). Difference and Repetition.
New York, USA: Columbia University Press. (parts of it)

Dormer, P. (1994). The Art of the Maker.
London, UK: Thames and Hudson.

Grass, M. N., & Grass, A. (1969b). Stockings for a queen: The life
of the Rev. William Lee, the Elizabethan inventor (First Edition/).
London, England: A. S. Barnes.

Harrell, B. (1984). Anatolian Knitting Designs:
Sivas Stocking Patterns Collected in an Istanbul Shantytown.
Istanbul, Turkey: Redhouse Publications.

Hume, D. (1986). A Treatise of Human Nature (Herz. ed.).
Geraadpleegd van https://www.gutenberg.org/files/
4705/4705-h/4705-h.htm

Korn, P. (2015). Why We Make Things and Why It Matters
(1ste editie). Boston, USA: David R. Godine Publisher.

Schafer, R. M. (1993). The Soundscape: Our Sonic Environment
and the Tuning of the World. Rochester, Vermont, USA:
Inner Traditions/Bear.

Sennett, R. (2008). The Craftsman.
New Haven, USA: Yale University Press.

Yalom, I. D. (2014). Het raadsel Spinoza (12de editie).
Amsterdam, The Netherlands: Balans, Uitgeverij.

NEWS ARTICLES

The Financial Times: 30 March 2013, Arts & Culture section 'Run of
the Micro-Mill' by John Sunyer

IMAGES

Felkin, W., & Chapman, S. D. (1967). History of
the Machine-Wrought Hosiery and Lace Manufactures.
New York, USA: Augustus M. Kelley, Publishing.

http://www.deutsches-strumpfmuseum.de/technik/
04mechflachwirkstuhl/Bild_flachwirk_01.htm

WEBSITES

https://www.trc-leiden.nl/index.php?option=com_
content&view=article&id=103&Itemid=118&lang=en.
Director: Gillian Vogelsang-Eastwood

VIDEO

Noam Chomsky: The purpose of education:
https://youtu.be/DdNAUJWJN08 Presented at the Learning Without
Frontiers Conference - Jan 25th 2012- London (LWF 12)

Kappers, r. (2006). YouTube. Geraadpleegd op 2019,
van https://www.youtube.com/watch?v=ekO8W0zSZO8&feature=youtu.be

RECORDINGS

Challenge Records International. (2009). String Quartet no.
4 - String Quartet no. 1 - Lagos Ensemble. Geraadpleegd
op 11 december 2019, van https://www.challengerecords.com/
products/1252418248

Amanda Ramona

Slyly Sticky Stuff

Nearness, it seems, cannot be encountered directly. We succeed in reaching it rather by attending to what is near. Near to us are what we usually call things. But what is a thing?

Martin Heidegger, The Thing

Object: Within, within the cut and slender joint alone, with sudden equals and no more than three, two in the centre make two one side.

If the elbow is long and it is filled so then the best example is all together.

The kind of show is made by squeezing.

Gertrude Stein, Tender Buttons

INTRODUCTION

The experience of being alive haunts me. I am oh so gently bruised. While observing the behaviour of the stuff in the world, I experience how frustration and inspiration arises. It seems the consistency of my surrounding is constantly being reconstructed and morphed into new modes of existence. I hear someone talk about fluidity and formlessness, and a reorientation towards the things and beings in our environment[1]. I am not sure whether I understand what is meant and ask out loud: "WTF is matter and why does it matter?"

In front of me, on my desk, I have some popular theory books that address different branches of ontology.[2] They have the potential to answer the question. I feel intrigued when reading those books, but do not really understand how to get grip on the ideas presented. They somehow lack consistency. I am eager to do my own research. To find my own language.

This text therefore embodies my investigations into existence and agency, and performs through the observations I have gathered while having a very particular focus at a particular time (during the process of writing). Subsequently, I have come to realise that the method through which I proceed has affinity with phenomenology.[3] This means that my writing is extruded from the way I subjectively perceive the activity around me. I have had to write myself i-n-t-o this text and explore writing as a method in itself to articulate my observations and the bodily experiences those have facilitated. These experiences are important images of the many wonderings I am addressing in the text. They are there for you to stick with me throughout your reading.

I want to realise how I relate to my own bodily presence, in a complex constellation between me, the other and our shared surroundings. In order to realise what glues us all together, I will try to profoundly investigate an ungraspable blurb consisting of *stuff*[4] in all its stickiness. I hope to pull you closer to your surrounding at this very moment, and make you feel along this line of thoughts. I will drag you into my research through an overload of sensitivity and encounters with untamed behaviour—along wonderings about agency of objects which seem to become animated—further towards questioning the movement of affection between things and myself—where examples of embodiment (and abstractions) of language are used as cues to an indistinct conversation. Then we will look into material qualities, in an attempt to make the continuous wonderings more palpable, while touching upon emotions—for then to analyse the objectness and thingness of things, and thereby elaborate on the difference between empathy and sympathy. Finally, we will take a look at the whole and come to the non-realisation of essence, through a permeable rupture.

Although some of my readings and encounters with theory have frustrated me, they have thus increased my permeability in such a way; even words have started to feel thick and active. Words are now performing with a will of their own, and I have to keep the tongue in my mouth.

1   Especially when reading the essays in 'Realism Materialism Art', eds. Christoph Cox, Jenny Jaskey, Suhail Malik, (Sternberg Press: 2015)

2   The etymological description of 'ontology' is; "the metaphysical science or study of being and the essence of things", from etymonline.com

3   Phenomenology' is coined from phenomenon ("that which appears or is seen") + -logy ("a speaking, discourse, treatise, doctrine, theory, science"), from etymonline.com

4   Stuff: "sense extended to material for working with in various trades (c. 1400), then "matter of an unspecified kind" (1570s)", from etymonline.com

UNEQUALLY UNTAMED

We are sitting in the tram. I pay attention to my protruding limbs and facial expression. We make it difficult for ourselves, when wanting to escape this situation. You don't have to look up and around to perceive the presence of flesh and bone sitting way too intensely close. Neither do I. I can hear the scratching of that man's skin against his jeans. His leg hair sounds rough. I do not want to think about his leg hair. I feel the weight of a little person on my lap. It makes the blood concentrate its flux in the upper body. The little hand is fumbling with the button on my jacket, it makes a subtle sound that no one else seems to notice. I try to focus on this sound to see if I can recognise a pattern in the touch. My mind wants to find a little melody in the movement, and— by following that—flow away. They say this should be the perfect break.

You notice the rhythm. It seems that your thoughts made you absent for a while, but the textual melodies of other dressed bodies throw you back to us. It starts in your stomach. It gets warm and active, maybe boiling. Your chest and neck shivers, while it moves through to the vocal cord, and out of your mouth it burns; "eeeeiiighteeeen fffffffuucking yesssss". So unexpected. So untamed. Your tongue is still vibrating.

I finally look around, but the eye contact I did not want to have before is not even to be caught now. I hear you again; a roar. My little one is silent and I realise that she is not even with me today. Another roar and some swearing. The blood that was concentrated at my solar plexus explodes to all possible parts of my body. Burning finger tips. They are pulsing heavily. I look at you and try to trace the machinery. You look as if nothing has just happened. Everyone looks as if nothing just happened, out into the air.

I question myself. But there is no question. The heat has risen in here. Dense air—I can even see it. It is my turn, so I get up and push myself through towards the door and out. Wonder about the agreement I never agreed on; that human behaviour is unquestionable.

POROSITY

I often lose track of the borders of the skin. Bodily perception becomes muggy and the receptors hyper-alert. In fact, it goes both ways: I do not know what I feel, you feel, they feel, that feels, that says, they say, you say, I say. It gets misty in the midst of things.[5] I definitely draw a fat line between this feeling of permeability and the fact that I have experienced the growth of a small child, namely my own daughter. This experience has made me hypersensitive towards reading the needs of others— especially the ones that are nonverbally communicating. I enter a position of boundless openness towards all possible information I can harvest, from what I experience in my being amongst stuff. That being (especially in the case of this thesis) non-human bodies. The load of affection hitting my emotional experience is overwhelming. All gets animated—and important to note is: this animation carries anthropomorphic characteristics. Meaning, I trace humanlike activity in the way things operate around me. But does that mean I can only understand the agency of things through my limited human experience? Or can I stretch my boundaries? Can I stretch my language? I try to trace the language things might speak and wonder if they share a certain solidarity towards each other. Are things social? Do they need each other and do they even need me? Is there a way in which we can agree on things about things with things?

As things seem to become animated, I wonder if it is me who is applying this animation onto them or if they do actually act by themselves. What I have experienced is, when I become aware of the insisting existence of objects and look deep into their materiality and mobility, I realise that they are not only standing there standing: they are actually full of will. For though they stand still, their volume and density make them capable of doing things. They hit me with a certain feeling of dependency, or maybe mutuality, which leads to curiosity. They do really pull me towards them. Not because I need them in order to use

them, but because I wonder about why they are here. Why a particular thing ends up at a particular place at a particular time. Is coincidence the only answer? I think there is more to this choreography—because I feel it—and that amplifies the way I care about it, the thing. A quality like care is catalysed by a shared feeling. We have to feel in common in order to understand each other's needs. What are the words for this? Empathy? Sympathy? What is the difference between empathy and sympathy?

FUZZY AGREEMENT

From the view out of my window, I have been observing an old yet shiny football on the roof of the opposite building. I saw it—as if it was an intruder in the actual—and my mental—landscape, which somehow kept me alert, always re-thinking my ideas. I was reading about 'Labanotation' which is a notation system created by Rudolf Laban to notate and analyse human motion. In the book I was given in hand, they were creating a choreography based on a specific goal made in a specific football match.[6] Labanonatation has signs attached to the different body parts: head, neck, shoulder area, left upper arm, right ankle etc. When these signs are written into the system, they direct the movements. It thereby becomes a language as well.

The ball on the roof had been there for months. As if crystallised. Absolutely no motion. But then one day, when I was standing next to the opposite building, I saw a guy walking around on the roof. He was collecting leaves that had fallen from trees that are around. Without notifying me, he kicked the old shiny ball down to the ground and it rolled directly towards where I was standing. "I don't know how I feel about that" I said to myself, and went upstairs again. The day after, I stood at the same spot once again. I looked at the ball, still there. Still as still as before, but not exactly in the same place. Then, I took it in my arms and walked back to my studio. Now it is right here next to me. Intensely staring.

A few weeks later, I went to an open football field with my brother. We felt like moving around—shaking our bodies down into the ground. After walking around on the field with bare feet for a bit I tried to verbalise the tickling feeling the grass created. "It's exactly like having little fishhooks under the feet, it makes you hang on to the ground for a few seconds when taking a step," I told him. Feeling weightless on ground.

A few days later, I walked through a park full of trees. I remembered a Danish podcast I recently listened to, in which the subject 'tree hugging' was discussed. In the podcast, a woman was saying that you have to stop up and observe the trees around you, and then wait for a tree to call to you. That is how you are being picked by the right tree at the right moment.

When walking through the park I tried to do that. So I stopped and looked around for a sign. A heron flew from behind a thick birch. That would be my tree. I went to it and threw my arms around it. Just stood there for a few minutes. But nothing. Nothing happened and I felt a little disappointed. I released my grip and took a few steps away to look up. I could then see a gigantic nest at the very top of the branches. I hesitated for a moment, grasping for meaning. But no. Then I walked away, but as I walked I felt something weird under my shoe's sole. I stopped and had a look: a big rusty fish hook deeply penetrated into the rubber. I could only think of getting it out of there ASAP. But it was completely stuck. I tried for ten minutes to pry it out. Sweaty in the end. Then it plunged out. I took it in my hand and walked out of the park. Still did not understand the purpose of it.

I threw the hook into a trash can.

5   Diana Coole, "From Within the Midst of Things: New Sensibility, New Alchemy, and the Renewal of Critical Theory", Realism Materialism Art, eds. C. Cox, J. Jaskey, and S. Malik, (Center for Curatorial Studies, Bard College, 2015)

6   Alec Finlay, Labanotation: The Archie Gemmill Goal, (Polygon An imprint of Birlinn Limited, 2002)

INWARDS/OUTWARDS

In order to trace the movement of the activity between human and non-human bodies, I come to think of two kinds of behavioural characteristics: hoarding and Tourette syndrome. The act of hoarding is contextualised by Jane Bennett when she talks about "vibrant powerful things" and their "uncanny agency."[7] She does this in order to "put things in the foreground and people in the background."[8] We understand that hoarding has an inward direction that accumulates masses of things. Furthermore, the act of hoarding might have to do with an urge to fill up an emptiness felt on the inside.

Tourette syndrome, on the other hand, moves in the opposite direction. Tics in the muscles cause an uncontrollable urge to burst out—indistinct voicing. Elaborately, Tourette can also be traced in my own bare urge to express my experiences. Something floods the body and the body floods with something. Whilst hoarders accumulate things, Tourette seizures accumulate utterance. The two different behaviours are infiltrated with external influences, meaning that they are caused by events in the connecting environment. I will call these events pulling and pushing forces. In order to be aware of these forces we need to orient ourselves to the stuff around us. Thus, we also have to step into an increased sensible state or be overtaken by hyper-sensible activity. It requires a natural feeling of curiosity.

By coincidence, I have recently been in two different settings where I experienced a person in the crowd having Tourette seizures. It was intense; experiencing how they shaped a tension around them, making all other people in the room alert and ready to act upon the immense sequences of irregular, uncontrollable utterances—but also physical spasms. The weird part was that the way people acted alert was by paralysing themselves, seemingly ignoring the extreme behaviour, but undoubtedly raising an increasing, penetrating tension in the space.

THE LANGUAGE AND BODY OF STUFF

I ask myself how to find the right language through which I can try to verbalise the pushing and pulling forces that I experience between myself and the things operating around me. In the investigation towards finding a language of things[9] , I am sincerely blown away by an experience of materiality in words having a potential to verbalise physical experience.

Although it seems nonverbal—this push and pull—there is a certain resonance in certain verbs that are loaded with weight, temperature and texture.[10] Imagine if the words you formulate when speaking or writing were objects you could take and hold in your hand. Imagine this not only in order to project a voice onto the non-human object, but to try and feel the experience of what this object could potentially experience. Words can perform and choreograph the very movement of visceral affection experienced in certain word-work: when words are put together and placed next to each other in relation to syntax, or in order to deconstruct syntax.

When reading about Luce Irigaray's 'embodied syntax'[11] I am immediately sparked to investigate embodiment of language. As a notion, embodied syntax acts viscerally in its image construction. In doing so, it activates a bodily understanding of the production of language. What I want to extract from embodied syntax as an image is to refine the importance of keeping a tension in the constellation of concepts. Concepts that treat the dynamic forces of artistic practices in a way where they are articulated to a point of abstraction. What I mean by this is that the search for a correct language (verbal or visual) somehow goes through a process of deconstruction. You start working from what you know, but as I see it—when working within art—you pass a phase where things seem to have dissolved into a blurry perplexing mass. There is no way in which you can linguistically translate the state of your work. Abstraction, in this case, is therefore meant as the state where meaning has dissolved for a while. At this point, I try to embody what I have in front of me: the material itself. The dialogue becomes more of a dance. I reconstruct my understanding and integrate my new discoveries based on how it feels. A new vital meaning appears. That is why I love these words: e-m-b-o-d-i-e-d s-y-n-t-a-x.

I once randomly watched a documentary where scientists were investigating the phenomenon of 'speaking in tongues'.[12] They discovered that the part of the brain that is active when you construct a familiar language was not activated when the person being examined would speak in tongues. The language that occurs is nonsense. No linguistic traces. Yet the people performing tongue-speech claim that it is a divine language, one that puts sound to their contact with 'God'.

I come to think of Gertrude Stein who, in her poems, plays around with the definition of familiar objects. In her book 'Tender Buttons'[13] she experiments with language by juxtaposing grammar and the familiar constellation of words. She pushes us to create new meaning and by doing that, "Stein is able to displace everyday objects into new contexts, resulting in the reader's redefinition and reassessment of the reality of the mundane."[14] Her definition of 'object'[15] for example, is more depicting and active than specifying and elaborating.

Another approach is the work of artist Michael Dean who says; "I feel when you turn writing into an object, there's more a chance that the viewer can take possession or… they're implicated in the physical experience with the work."[16] Michael Dean is somehow working against the fact that we are hermeneutical, pursued in our interpretations. He is reducing writing to its bare bones and uses the production of books and sculpture as a way to facilitate a certain feeling of language, extracted from moments of writing. A method he often uses is to repeat words to the extent that there is no linguistic meaning present. Another trace I find in his gesticulation and speech is, interestingly enough, Tourettes.

A third visual cue to language production, which reaches a point of abstraction in its articulation, is 'asemic writing'. Asemic writing is a form of writing that dissolves any verbal meaning. Asemic writing strives to create a vacuum of meaning by merging text and image, so that space for interpretation is left open. It is therefore more likely a visualisation of the movement of syntax. As sort of visual soundwaves, perhaps. Related to asemic work is the idea that meaning evolves over time, and thus the reader becomes co-creator of the work. This approach is what I have envisioned for the writing of this thesis: a text that is dense to the extent where boundaries between the written and the read are cracked open.

7   Jane Bennett, "Artistry and Agency in a World of Vibrant Matter", Hosted by the Vera List Centre for Art and Politics, September 13, 2011, https://www.youtube.com/watch?v=q607Ni23QjA

8   Bennett, Ibid.

9   Hito Steyerl, "The Language of Things", Transversal Texts, European Institute for Progressive Cultural Policies: 2006, PDF from https://nowherelab.dreamhosters.com/thelangaugeofthings.pdf

10 Helen Marten, "A Cat Called Lettuce, A Conversation Between Helen Marten, Beatrix Ruf and Polly Staple at Kunsthalle Zürich, October 25, 2012", Helen Marten, ed. Tom Eccles (JRP Ringier, 2013)

11 Alyson Lieberman, "Accessing Women through Masculine Discourse: Lucy Irigaray's Embodied Syntax", Philosophy Senior Thesis, Haverford College, 2012

12 "Glossolalia, also called speaking in tongues, (from Greek glōssa, "tongue," and lalia, "talking"), utterances approximating words and speech, usually produced during states of intense religious experience. The vocal organs of the speaker are affected; the tongue moves, in many cases without the conscious control of the speaker; and generally unintelligible speech pours forth", from Encyclopædia Britannica

13 Gertrude Stein, Tender Buttons, (New York: Dover Publications Inc., 1998), originally published in 1914

14 https://en.wikipedia.org/wiki/Tender_Buttons_(book)

15 Object: Within, within the cut and slender joints alone, with sudden equals and no more than three, two in the centre make two one side. If the elbow is long and it is filled so then the best example is all together. The kind of show is made by squeezing.

16 Michael Dean, "The Roots and Shoots of Language: Artist Michael Dean", Presented October 22, 2016 at Nasher Sculpture Centre, https://www.youtube.com/watch?v=5qrq0WwLwuc

Dealing with the physicality of text is also to think of the written matter as a speaking body. The affectations within the text are supposed to treat the reader as part of this loaded, sticky, visceral experience of experiencing. In order to do so, I constantly read out loud the sentences I write and think of how they could potentially be shot into the organs of you, the reader. Because what I really want to do is to create an awareness of how we interact, behave and communicate while we slide past each other (the other) in our everyday lives. It seems that it is solely extreme experiences that cause us to stop and reflect on our position within our environment, and I wonder if I can somehow kick you to a pause.

Through a disruption between private and public, and inner and outer, I am exploring how the rhythm of collective stress can be shocked into a rhythm more indistinct from the familiar.[17] This disruption is something I experience with objects that makes me question their purpose. Over and over, I have been observing specific, strange objects that were hard to place mentally—to grasp functionally. This counts especially for toys. But also strange utility objects, which do not make sense when taken out of their context. I figured that most of the time I could only extract meaning from the function of certain objects when animating them. I came to the conclusion that the way I imagined them moving, if being alive, would load them with the meaning they did not have when just being (still). It would thus be the emotions I loaded them with, while touching them that would define them. Although, I still want to elaborate on the direction of the movement of this emotion: is this the very feeling that facilitates a conversation between things and us? Or is the language more textural?

STICKINESS

"Wax is a good material when working with anatomy," my friend said. I immediately felt resonance and biked directly to an art supplier. I found the biggest chunk in stock. Dark red, rusty nuances. Rust! I paid attention to the metal constructions on my way back. Especially the solutions on the bridges I crossed. Curvy metal sticks shaped into ornamental attachments. Not for support, but definitely for funky ornamentation. I felt intrigued and associated the quality of melted metal (warm, liquid, expanded three-dimensionally) with the quality of wax.

The wax felt the heat from my body already from the first touch. It was as if the material was eager for a massage. I went to my studio. The week before, I had ordered a paper roll dispenser (floor stand). It was waiting for me. It had been standing there, a bare skeleton. I realised that it was in need of a cover. Flesh and skin. The room was cold. I was surprised by how hard it was to pull a part of the wax from its solid base (suddenly very solid). I held it for a while and it woke up. It fitted perfectly, like a hand soap. I began to smear the wax onto the dispenser. In the beginning, it was still quite stiff and needed a lot of effort. I just accepted it. Tried to figure out what tempo, what direction was best for applying the material. I thought of the idea of 'meeting a body.' I thought of when I give a massage to a naked back: the skin cold and joints locked in the beginning. I can't force it. I need some kind of acceptance, a "hello". The wax started to adapt to my own temperature. The longer I kept it in my hand before applying it onto the dispenser, the warmer and more flexible it got. Easy, all of a sudden.

I entered the rhythm (something I could not have measured before), and the wax became generous as honey. I searched all corners of the dispenser with my hands, so the wax would cover all the metal it met. After hours of smearing, I started to sweat. Repetition of motion but difference in the state of the material. I realised that the wax had reached my own body temperature, 36.4 degrees maybe. What was happening? I felt the choreography had been interrupted. I looked at my hands and I saw that the wax had disappeared into my skin.

REFERENCE TO MEDICINES THAT HEAL WOUNDS WHEN APPLIED TO A CLOTH STAINED WITH BLOOD FROM THE WOUND

I often forget to breathe all the way down to the very deepest part of the lungs. But when I do, I feel more alive. How about you?

There is this thing about air: it has capacity. It is compact. It contains stuff that it carries with it. It brings along smell and temperature; take a fart, for example. On the other hand, even though air somehow memorises, it is also a crazy abstract substance —escapist, in a way. I cannot hold it between my hands, you cannot hold it between your hands, but it exists in the microscopic space between our palm and any surface we press against. Aside from that, we contain it every few seconds, when we breathe air into our lungs. Oxygen is carried from our lungs to our tissues via red blood cells. That is why blood is red: oxygen and iron react on each other when combined.

The same is what happens to porous, rusty surfaces of material that contains iron. Over time, when in contact with air and exposed to water, ferrous material creates the compound we call an oxide. Iron oxide.

Such a lovely name.

I am sitting next to some of it: looking at a table leg made out of rusty iron. I see how the oxide has weakened some of the more delicate parts of the structure. I can peel off a layer of its skin. There is a dredging in the centre of the object, where rain water has recently dried out. That part is intense orange— a foamy, dusty, bright orange. I get a little obsessed with the beauty of time and decay all of a sudden. My finger just painted orange on the touchpad of my computer. Swoosh. I remember to breathe again.

Do you know how far the lung reaches down in your body? Do you understand how far down your inhalation can reach? I know that lungs contain a few thousand kilometers of airways. That means they are not hollow shells, but a rather complex infrastructure of tissues and other masses. Try to think of the whole body as one big lung. One big respiratory machine (which it is of course, but think of it visually). When I breathe in, I imagine the air reaching all possible parts of the body: ears, fingertips, toenails. After some time, I turn orange. With every inhalation I feel how the air is strong and fierce when inside the body. It feels like thousands of little palms massaging me from the inside. A determined pressure, organising my organs.

---

17 Idea from Franco 'Bifo' Berardi, Breathing — Chaos and Poetry, (South Pasadena: Semiotext(e), 2018)

SLYLY STICKY STUFF

Phenomenologist Maurice Merleau-Ponty uses honey as an example in his reflection on 'Sensible Object', where he says:

"Honey is a slow-moving fluid; it definitely has some consistency. It lets itself be held, but then, slyly, it runs from one's fingers and comes back to itself. Not only does it come undone as soon as one shapes it, but still, reversing roles, it sticks to the hands of the one who wanted to seize it. The living hand—the explorer which believes it can master the object—finds itself attracted by it and stuck in an external being."[18]

This brilliant choreography, depicted by Merleau-Ponty, really touched me when reading it. It describes what I cannot describe, but what I feel—not only from direct contact with material, but also in the affection felt from a distance. Merleau-Ponty's words here relate to the way Sara Ahmed proposes how shared feelings surround us like thickness in the air—in the way they are not only accumulating tension, but are in tension. She writes: "It is through emotions, or how we respond to objects and others, that surfaces or boundaries are made: the 'I' and the 'we' are shaped by, and even take shape of, contact with others."[19] I wonder if the density of this certain tension is simultaneously materialising and performing. Does it create the boundaries and surfaces (in)between the experience of the things around me, and how I am experiencing that experience? Is it so, that the pushing and pulling forces are diffuse in their directions and eventually produce a tension field? A tension in which things and I get stuck? Is the stickiness what happens on surfaces of things, felt by touch? Or is it happening in the space between us? Or is it more inward, more emotional?

Besides being sticky as a characteristic in its materiality, a thing can be sticky without having an actual sticky feel to its surface. According to Sara Ahmed, it is important to stress the fact that emotions are moving, and she notes; the word 'emotion' comes from the Latin, emovere "to move, to move out."[20] She traces this movement by suggesting that, " Itis the objects of emotion that circulate, rather than emotion as such", and explores, "How emotions can move through the movement or circulation of objects."[21]

In the movie Kunskabens træ (The Three of Knowledge),[22] the teenagers depicted give the name 'Klister'–meaning 'Sticky' in Danish—to one of the girls in their class. The girl does not have a voice throughout the movie, but is somehow presented as the constant intruder in the rest of the group's self-image. I cannot remember exactly what happens, but at a certain point, Sticky's frustration is physically let out on one of the other girls. The other girl's reaction is to scream "Det klister! Jeg siger det KLISTER! SLIP MIG," meaning, "It's sticky! I say IT'S STICKY! LET ME GO."[23] What is interesting here is both the idea of something unwanted sticking on to you, and the expression of this unwanted touch as being the quality of the feeling, and not the action of the doing. The quality of the feel refers to the quality of a material surface. A materiality performing stickiness, without needing me to consciously expose my permeability in order to be shot by affection (or disgust).

Could emotions be the very substance that perform the stickiness, so that emotions stick on to us and thus carry the object with them? But then, does that mean the stickiness happens emotionally?

SHAPING THE EMOTION

If we, as humans, can reach a bodily understanding that we are made of materials, it might be understood through the study and recognition of lively materials such as iron, wood and marble, but also the formability of a surface, especially in relation to giving a material human form.[24] In her book 'A Heart in Everything', Amalie Smith calls this idea a "radical solidarity with the material."[25] A humble, sympathetic perception of things. Would this extent of recognition of the object catalyse a sympathetic experience of experiencing through the object? Do things consciously facilitate the empathetic or sympathetic feelings I have? They do ask for care in some kind of way. When we take care of an object— un-dust it, fix it, pass it on—we maintain it. Does the fact that we maintain things answer the question about whether the things around us need us? Could a thing be consciously sly?

Shit, how would the conceptions within the tradition of phenomenology answer these questions? It feels like trying to carve into the mother mold of an original positive, which is stuck and leaves me unable to see its form. I cannot grasp the perspective of the concealed object, I did not give shape to the original, and I therefore would not know how to handle it. On the other hand, when you are the one making the original positive of a mother mold out of plaster, for example, you carve in order to shape.

Is it up to each of us to carve through the space between things and ourselves in order to shape the emotional connection we feel towards certain objects or things?

I lose my orientation—my wonderings start to decompose my arguments—I ask, how to navigate?

EMPATHY & SYMPATHY
AND OBJECTNESS & THINGNESS

There is a muscle that needs attention. Like the verbal machinery of the tongue, in order to articulate the boundaries of the emotionality I experience in my encounter with objects or things, I have to elaborate on the meaning and definition of sympathy and empathy.

What is important to know is that the two terms originated at different times in history, sympathy being the first formulated notion. Etymologically, sympathy refers to "affinity between certain things,"[26] assimilated from syn- (together) and pathos (feeling). The term is said to be used in "reference to medicines that heal wounds when applied to a cloth stained with blood from the wound."[27] Sympathy is therefore understood as the ability to share a certain feeling felt by someone else, thereby also understood as a capability of embodying the feelings of another.

In addition to this notion, empathy as a term derived later on in history, from the field of psychology. Etymologically formed from en- (in) and pathos (feeling), and first coined as a term in the context of aesthetics, it explained appreciation in terms of the viewer's ability to project his personality onto the viewed object.[28] Empathy thus emphasises an emotional distance in terms of projection: you are aware of your separateness from what you observe. Accordingly, it means that you are partly removed from feeling the same feeling, but are capable of cognitively understanding the emotional state of someone else.

To be able to put the two notions into practice, I feel enticed to harvest more meaning. For though they are grammatically different, they carry a potential to define the agency of objects and how things in the world possess a certain power in themselves: a power that blurs boundaries between human and

18 Maurice Merleau-Ponty, "Exploration of the Perceived World: Sensible Objects", the third of Merleau-Ponty's 1948 radio lecture series", https://www.youtube.com/watch?v=iuqkIM0rm0Y. Note: Since I could not find a translation of this lecture, written down anywhere, I wrote the whole of it down from the video myself.

19 Sara Ahmed, The Cultural Politics of Emotion, (Routledge, 2004), p. 10

20 Sara Ahmed, The Cultural Politics of Emotion, (Routledge, 2004), p. 11

21 Ahmed, ibid.

22 A film by Nils Malmros, Denmark 1981

23 Det klister!!!, https://www.youtube.com/watch?v=I3fbZZpMqUo

24 Amalie Smith uses the example of the Greek myth about Pygmalion, who carves an image of a female body, out of marble, so lively that it actually is brought to life.

25 Amalie Smith, Et hjerte i alt, (Gyldendal: 2017, printed in Germany: 2017)

26 Online Etymology Dictionary, https://www.etymonline.com

27 Ibid. - see also chapter: Reference to Medicines that Heal Wounds…

28 Ibid.

nonhuman forces. In order to give a body to these forces, I will carve an image of how empathy and sympathy can perform, respectively, as object and thing.

In his text "The Thing"[29], Martin Heidegger stresses a possible perception of a specific thing, that being a handmade ceramic jug. He puts language to the understanding of what this thing is, and thus not only how it appears to us. What is important to realise here is that Heidegger's idea of 'thing' is complex and manifold. I can therefore not wrap my head around his 'thinging thingness' and run a thorough parallel thinking process. I know the 'thing' disappears when I try to explain it. Nevertheless, Heidegger talks about the objectness of an object and the thingness of a thing, and investigates the distinction between the two. According to him, a thing calls to us as a thing and not as an object. It thus asks us to take a step back from the way of thinking it represents. We are not asked to think things, but called to think. Oh fuck! It somehow speaks to a process of becoming, and I feel sparked to trace the movement.

The objectness of the object, says Heidegger, is the quality of it having a materiality in the process of its making. It has a function of self-support, which makes it capable of being placed and perceived. The object also has a form consisting of a base and supporting sides. Accordingly, Heidegger describes how the objectness is shown in its outward appearance, as an idea of its being as standing forth—opposite us who perceive it. The object is represented through this idea, and is present in the way it is available.

When the thing gathers itself as "the void that holds", that is where its thingness resides; "we become aware of the vessel's holding nature when we fill it."[30] He continues by saying that when filling the jug with a liquid, we fill the emptiness of the inside of the vessel between its sides and over its bottom. It is therefore the empty 'void' of the vessel that does the holding—and it is in this void that the thingness exists.

As Heidegger puts it the potter does not shape the clay—he shapes the void: "for it, in it, and out of it, he forms the clay into the form." Even though his hands are pressing and sliding against the clay, he "takes hold of the impalpable void and brings it forth as the container in the shape of a containing vessel."[31]

A choreography appears in the idea that the vessel's potential to contain a substance is realised when we fill it with a substance, and thus awareness of the nature of the vessel is being catalysed. The jug is a thing ready for stuff to be poured into. This tension of potentiality captures me, genuinely. The act of pouring needs human hands and its muscles as actors, and thereby something or someone to animate the compact element that contains the liquid.

When feeling empathetic, we are projecting ourselves onto and into an object (that being any robust form existing), while simultaneously being aware of ourselves as being separate from the object. We understand its existence, in the same way that we understand the objectness of the object; the idea shaped out of its outward appearance. The objectness is experienced as a representation of the object standing forth, and empathy, you could say, is likewise experienced as a sort of simulation of the feelings coming from the one observed.

On the other hand, the thingness is in the void that holds. It holds what it is filled with. Hence sympathy can be seen as a motion through which we fill ourselves with the feelings of another—we enter those feelings and our feelings are being contained by others. It has to do with capacity. Furthermore, it creates an image of proximity that seems more intense than the boundaries experienced with empathy.

MOLD CRACKS SMTHNG LEAKS

I choose to stick with thingness—sympathy, and look at this phrase again: "it is in the void, which holds, that the thingness exists... he doesn't shape the clay—he shapes the void." When reading this over and over again, I realise that I am not trying to find a certain essence. I realise that, to me, matter does not matter only because of its materiality, or because it can potentially encapsulate a mass (even as a term). It strikes me that answering the many questions I have is not done by an archaeological carv-ing-in-to phenomena. The phenomenon is much more shocking. It has tempo and it surprises me. As I said earlier: it seems that solely extreme experiences cause us to stop and reflect on our positions within our environments. Perhaps because they are rarely encountered. So, if I think of the feeling that resembled the idea of a mother mold, which conceals its original positive, it might be that the task of carving could be overtaken by the act of dropping the mold onto the floor. And it would crack. Crack open!

The experience of a shock kickstarts processes for me, for us, for matter. Maybe the shock provokes an experience and thereby the experience is lived as a shock. Maybe there is no actual direction. Maybe the push and pull move spontaneously and invisibly through to my nervous system, whereby it renders the experience I am experiencing. Caused by a shock of surprise which lingers in me. The spasm reoccurs. Irregularity, and that which is uncontrollable. I am merged with the experience, embodying the indescribable. Someone mentions resonance. I think of miscommunication. "Grrrr."

The question about agency seems to come back as well, but remains blurred, although things indeed need me or other living beings to animate them. Things become animated by how I perceive them, in relation to the particular moment in which the encounter happens. My expectations, my emotional state, my tempo and, most importantly, the words I use to describe the qualities of particular things, are altogether the actors directing the experience. I do indeed animate things with the words I use for them. And the total of each specific experience either expands or restricts my contemplation throughout each experience.

As Merleau-Ponty puts it in 'Sensory Objects': "The unity of the object does not lie behind its qualities, but is reaffirmed by each one of them: each quality of the whole,"[32] and he continues: "Our relationship with things is not a distant one: each speaks to our body and to the way we live. They are clothed in human characteristics (whether docile, soft, hostile or resistant) and conversely, they dwell within us as emblems of forms of life we either love or hate. Humanity is invested in the things of the world and these things are invested in it."[33] I see this as indicating, if the reaffirmation happens with each quality of the whole of an object, senses are important agents: they help me in navigating within the clash and merge with things in my surroundings. Hence, senses also help with digesting these experiences, as sensory perception massages the sometimes frustrating, yet very stimulating apprehension of why things happen as they do. Embedded in this acknowledgement is also the realisation that the communication coming from objects is translated into a language that depends on the way in which objects appear to me in the specific moment of encounter. That might have to do with their materiality, texture, number of surfaces, their shape. These physical characteristics affect me emotionally and re-animate their physical capabilities.

Sometimes the encounter is direct and loaded with sensory affection, and sometimes the encounter happens through an upscaled diffuse choreography of activity. An object is of limited size, but the interpretations are boundless and subjective. So (then, still, but), what about the times where 'shape' is not even a word that can be applied to the appearance of a material? When surfaces crack open as a permeable explosion? When substances seep out of their own materiality...

29 Martin Heidegger, "The Thing", originally delivered as a lecture to the Bayerischen Akademie der Schonen Kunste, 1950. Translated by Albert Hofstadter in Poetry Language Thought (New York: Harper and Row, 1971)

30 Heidegger, Ibid.

31 Heidegger, Ibid.

32 Maurice Merleau-Ponty, The World of Perception, translated by Oliver Davis, (Oxfordshire: Routledge, 2004), originally published in French in 1948, p. 62

33 Merleau-Ponty, Ibid, p. 63

LEAKAGE

I woke up the other day knowing that I would spend the morning with my daughter. I felt a pressure from inside. An urge to express and just get things done. It stressed me out, but I had to ignore it. So I filled the bathtub for her and she jumped in. I sat next to her in the shower and washed my hair. "I don't want my hair washed," she said, "I don't like it. I don't want it!" She looked at me with burning eyes. "But we haven't washed it for two weeks, it's really time now," I said, and I washed her hair. She screamed at me. We got out of the shower, walked naked to the living room. She began to cough. It intensified and the coughing got louder. Then she started screaming, and then it came. Vomit. Again and again it splashed down onto the floor. Tears ran from her eyes. I went to get a bucket with soap water, questioning myself which soap I should pour in. The all-round cleaner or the body soap? (I chose to care for the floor.)

I got dressed and started wiping. The room was humid. I couldn't recognise whether it was air that I breathed in. My phone started ringing. The doorbell rang. A plumber came to fix the water heater in the kitchen. The radiators didn't work. "Do you need something?" I asked him. He ignored me. My daughter started screaming again. "My diaper!" "Oh!" I couldn't recognise the substance. Brown pee? No, shit! While I was dealing with it, I could hear a body of water sliding through the pipes—a bulb that had been stuck, blocking the flow. It flowed through the outlying pipes and ended in the radiator. It might have imagined a journey of release. "Do you hear it?" I asked my daughter. "It's getting through."

I felt the heater with my hands. It was burning. "It's working!" I shouted to the man in the kitchen. He didn't respond. I stood up and hung the moist towels on the doors. "They're ghosts," she said. "Do you have an old towel for me?" asked the plumber from the kitchen. I ran around to find an old towel, but could only think of the ones I had as being newborn. But I found some kitchen cloths and went to the kitchen. The floor was full of puddles of water. "Yes, sorry," he said and packed his stuff, while I bent down to wipe up the stains. "It's working," I said. "Is it warm?" he asked, "Yes, it's burning." Then he left through the front door. I hung the cloths to dry and sat down for a few seconds. I couldn't feel any border. I was sweaty and my hair moist. The room was sweaty with moist towels hanging from the doors. I looked at my daughter. "Should we go out and get some fresh air?" We got dressed and went down the staircase. I looked up into the sky and took a deep breath. The sky opened and rain started pouring, violently.

Later that day I went to the library. I sat at one of the tables with a book and a notepad at hand. Opposite me was a guy who had just finished his reading. He collected his stuff and stood up to leave the table. He looked down and addressed the librarian, "Hey, there's a leakage here," he pointed at a stain of liquid on the table where he had just sat. The librarian came over and touched underneath the surface of the bookshelves positioned above the table. He took out a couple of books to feel the wall behind them. "Maybe it comes from the ceiling?" said the guy.

I looked at the ceiling. A sound-insulating material covered the whole surface. It looked very similar to moss. It even had the same green tones as moss. The librarian took a step up onto the chair, then one more onto the table. He reached for the ceiling and pushed his hands onto different spots. "I don't feel any moisture," he said. "Strange," said the guy. "It was probably there already, then." The guy went away and the librarian went back to his desk.

I looked up again and saw the ceiling smile. It was drooling.

CON-CLU(E)-SION

(The experience of being alive haunts me. I am oh so gently bruised).

Answering the questions raised in this text is a hardcore task. Questions continuously lead to new questions and I am still not aware, in depth, of what language to use.

While writing this text I was absorbed in its density to such an extent that I would catch myself drinking a glass of water while peeing. Liquids have felt thicker around my tongue and the urge to get drunk has increased. Something floods the body and the body floods with something. There is porosity in the syntax and meaning-making of verbal language, in the same way as there is porosity between the body and the material it encounters. The encounter with material substantiality and structures of activity becomes so meaningful that meaning gets disrupted. If it had not been for the circumstances around writing this thesis, and a feeling of unsaturated hunger for understanding more about my surroundings, I might not have been as alert and aware as I have for the last period of time. I have had an intense commitment to my investigations, from where all the material came that now constitutes this thesis.

The merging of human and material bodies, and languages, is the point where things articulate themselves while also being the point from where abstraction arises. The reading of this abstraction is a subjective one, and that is why I have only been able to write from my very own experiences. Although I have come to realise that the way we use language means a lot in relation to the way we can make an attempt at translating the communicative forces of things. Some words lead to certain interpretations and other words to other interpretations. Thus, when using certain verbs and joining them to things, I anthropomorphise them, for instance—and (re)animate them with my words.

As an overall acknowledgement, I can say that we live in a world of activity and we are thereby pushed and pulled in directions we could not have anticipated. There is therefore one thing I am even more certain about now: the visceral affect, that things around me shoot into my organs. My perception has entered, and stays in, a state of flux. Even when sitting here, on a burning chair, I feel the heat transmitting back and forth between the surface of the seat and myself, and I wonder who holds the most warmth.

I have definitely increased a sympathetic relationship towards everything in my surroundings, and since the amount of impressions are pressing an and itching me, they need to be digested further to be cultivated into practise—in order to work more profoundly from now on. In the aftermath of this writing, I have started to work in a bigger scale, and what is interesting is that I have knocked down the barrier I previously felt towards sculpture-making: it seems the concentration around objects now drags me into making objects, in a way I have not done before. I am deeply drawn to the juxtaposition of meaning-making, which indeed opens up for a much freer, but also more appropriate, way of working sensorially (and viscerally!) with raw materials. Appropriate in the sense that I do not have to question my choices as much as before.

Now positioning myself in the sympathetic holding void, I do not only feel squeezed by existence, but have expanded my absorptive capacity and learned to control the permeable buttonholes. We slide past each other in our everyday lives, yes, but, as a matter of fact, things have really stuck with me after this exploration. The particular focus on a particular thing at a particular time has nurtured, broadened and deepened my perception of and emotions towards others and our shared environment.

What I hope is that someday we will share a language through which we can speak, and operate into what cannot be expressed in forms that have a finite syntax. So far, it has mostly been the words around the void that have shaped a certain tension. I really want to hold on to this intensity of liveliness for a moment, since the wonderings are ongoing: they are volatile, flexible, sagacious, hyper, hitting, hooking, porous, leaking, sticking, kick-starting…

A multitude of ideas have been generated through reading into
the work of these different authors. I find it important to note
that I have worked freely in dialogue with the ideas presented
by these people, and therefore not engaged in the conclusions
made in these writings—in order to leave open ends for my own
research. I definitely recommend reading the following, as many of
these writings are interesting examples of (amongst other things)
a way of using language to construct meaning indistinct from the
hermeneutic circle—and thereby (as I have approached it) instead
play with the idea of a hermeneutic spiral. Besides that, I also
refer to the authors who have frustrated me, but thus kickstarted
the writing of this thesis:

Alyson Lieberman, "Accessing Women through Masculine Discourse:
Lucy Irigaray's Embodied Syntax", Philosophy Senior Thesis,
Haverford College, 2012

Amalie Smith, Et hjerte i alt, (Gyldendal, 2017, printed in
Germany: 2017)

Amalie Smith, Læsningens anatomi, (Copenhagen: emancipa(t/ss)
ionsfrugten, 2012)

Anna Zett, Artificial Gut Feeling, (Divided Publishing, 2019)

Ed Adkins, A Seer Reader, (London: Serpentine Sackler Gallery,
Koenig Books, 2014)

Franco 'Bifo' Berardi, Breathing – Chaos and Poetry, (South
Pasadena: Semiotext(e), 2018)

Gertrude Stein, Tender Buttons, (New York: Dover Publications Inc.,
1998), first published in 1914

Gloria E. Anzaldúa, "How to Tame a Wild Tongue", Borderland / La
Frontera: The New Mestiza, (Aunt Lute Books, 2012)

Helen Marten, "A Cat Called Lettuce, A Conversation Between Helen
Marten, Beatrix Ruf and Polly Staple at Kunsthalle Zürich, October
25, 2012", Helen Marten, ed. Tom Eccles (JRP Ringier, 2013)

Hito Steyerl, "The Language of Things", Transversal Texts,
European Institute for Progressive Cultural Policies: 2006, PDF
from https://nowherelab.dreamhosters.com/thelangaugeofthings.pdf,
accessed January 28, 2020

Jane Bennett, Vibrant Matter – A Political Ecology of Things, (Duke
University Press Books, 2010)

Jean-Paul Sartre, Nausea, translated by Lloyd Alexander, (U.S.: A
New Directions Paperbook, 1959), originally published in French in
1938

Martin Heidegger, "The Thing", originally delivered as a lecture to
the Bayerischen Akademie der Schonen Kunste, 1950. Translated by
Albert Hofstadter in Poetry Language Thought (New York: Harper and
Row, 1971)

Maurice Merleau-Ponty, The World of Perception, translated by
Oliver Davis, (Oxfordshire: Routledge, 2004), originally published
in French in 1948

Rae Johnson, Embodied Social Justice, (Oxon: Routledge, 2018)

Realism Materialism Art, eds. Christoph Cox, Jenny Jaskey, Suhail
Malik, (Center for Curatorial Studies, Bard College, Sternberg
Press, 2015)

Sara Ahmed, The Cultural Politics of Emotion, (Routledge, 2004)

Stacey Alaimo, "Thinking as the Stuff of the World", O-Zone Journal
of Object-Oriented Studies, Issue 1: Object/Ecology: 2014.

Timothy Morton, Realist Magic: Objects, Ontology, Causality (New
Metaphysics), (Open Humanities Press, 2013)

ONLINE SOURCES

Jane Bennett, "Artistry and Agency in a World of Vibrant Matter",
Hosted by the Vera List Center for Art and Politics, September
13, 2011, https://www.youtube.com/watch?v=q607Ni23QjA, accessed Oct
2019

Michael Dean, "The Roots and Shoots of Language: Artist Michael
Dean", Presented October 22, 2016 at Nasher Sculpture Center,
https://www.youtube.com/watch?v=5qrq0WwLwuc, accessed Dec 2019

Maurice Merleau-Ponty, "Exploration of the Perceived World:
Sensible Objects", the third of Merleau-Ponty's 1948 radio lecture
series", https://www.youtube.com/watch?v=iuqkIM0rm0Y accessed Nov
2019

Online Etymology Dictionary, https://www.etymonline.com

Cambridge Dictionary, https://dictionary.cambridge.org

Asemic Writing, https://en.wikipedia.org/wiki/Asemic_writing,
accessed Oct 2019

Labanotation, https://en.wikipedia.org/wiki/Labanotation, accessed
Oct 2019

Tourette syndrome, https://en.wikipedia.org/wiki/Tourette_syndrome,
accessed Dec 2019

Det klister!!!, https://www.youtube.com/watch?v=l3fbZZpMqUo,
accessed Nov 2019

Julius Cornelis Jacob Stahlie

Narcissus' First Love

Notes on the relation between idealization, desire and the imagery of the self within gay male culture

BEFORE READING

In this text I mention the term Queer several times. I am aware that this term can be offensive for some people. I come from a generation of LGBTQI+ individuals whose community reclaimed the term Queer for themselves and made it into an empowering word that is inclusive for everything non-heteronormative and thereby creates a communal queer-normative language.

This is also how I use the term Queer in this text. If anybody is offended by the term, I apologize.

Furthermore,I often refer to gay men instead of Queer men in this text. This is not because I think gay men cannot be Queer, because that is indeed possible. I use the term gay men in these cases because I refer to gay men as a specific group that sometimes is located within the Queer community, and sometimes not.

INTRODUCTION

A friend of mine told me that he, as a gay man, sometimes questions whether he is attracted to a man, or whether he wants to be like him. At the time I did not have an answer nor an idea as to how I related to this question. But I did know that, for me at least, there was not a strict line between the two. What actually was in between became the basis for this text.

A while after this conversation with my friend, I read an essay written by the American writer and academic Michael Bronski, titled *A Dream is a Wish Your Heart Makes: Notes on the Materialization of Sexual Fantasy*[1]. I recognized myself in the way he looked at imagery of himself, his search to be his own ideal man, and the way he placed this into (gay) sexuality and sexual desires. It was the first time I read something that put this search into words. The essay clarified parts of my own search for my ideal self as a man, my longing for the ideal man in a sexual context, and the overlap they could have. The way Bronski's writings clarified these things to me made it possible for me to construct my further research into these topics and to question how this was and is for me.

Bronski's text sprang from American culture at the end of the 20th century. My upbringing happened in Amsterdam in the early 21st century, and this is also where I place my work and practice. So apart form my research into how I relate to the connection between idealization, desire and the imagery of the self, I became very curious about how gay male culture (throughout wider history and also in Amsterdam between 2000-2020) places itself in this, and how clothing and aesthetics react to this.

I investigate this through reflecting upon Narcissus and the Pool, darkrooms, the Great Dark Man, the Gay Clone, the imitation of heteronormative aesthetics as an act of activism and how the Gay Clone can play a role within this.

ON NARCISSUS AND THE DARK

When Narcissus died, the pool of his pleasure changed from a cup of sweet waters into a cup of salt tears, and the Oreads came weeping through the woodland that they might sing to the pool and give it comfort.

And when they saw that the pool had changed from a cup of sweet water into a cup of salt tears, they loosened the green tresses of their hair and said, "We do not wonder that you should mourn in this manner for Narcissus, so beautiful was he."

"But was Narcissus beautiful?" said the pool.

"Who should know better than you?" asked the Oreads. "Us did he ever pass by, but you sought he for, and would lie on your banks and look down at you, and in the mirror of your waters he would mirror his own beauty."

And the pool answered, "But I loved Narcissus because, as he lay on my banks and looked down at me, in the mirror of his eyes I saw ever my own beauty mirrored."

Oscar Wilde[2]

According to the myth, Narcissus would live as long as he did not know himself. He needed the pool in which to be able to look at himself, and therefore be able to know himself, to know the looks of himself, the imagery of himself. In Wilde's version of the story, it was not only Narcissus who loved the image of himself, it was also the pool who was taken by it. They needed one another to be able to look at themselves. It raises the question whether it is possible to know oneself without the reflection one gets from others. And furthermore, is it possible to be a self, without the reflection of others?

Narcissus' first love was himself. And like many first loves, it is one a person hardly forgets, one that possibly defines other loves one might have and might receive. Narcissus lived, as long as he did not know himself, yet when he did see the image of himself, it was all he chased, longed for, without realizing it was him all along, and therefore he already had it. We desire and idealize that which we think we cannot be, but want to be, while it is sometimes simply a reflection of our self. Portrayed by others in order to see it, it is ourself we see, ourself we get to know, while being reflected by others. By being in the Dark, we try to see what this imagery of self is without a visual reflection, by being allowed to solely focus on our self. In what ways can this Dark and the Other teach us more about ourselves? In what ways can the Dark, the Other and the Self answer all our longings? And in what ways can we embody those three?

1   Bronski, M. A Dream is a Wish Your Heart Makes: Notes on the Materialization of Sexual Fantasy: Thompson, M. (2001). Leatherfolk: Radical Sex, People, Politics, and Practice. Los Angeles: Alyson Books.

2   Wilde, O. (1894). The Disciple, in: Poems in Prose. Great Britain: The Fortnightly Review.

ON THE EFFECT OF DARKROOMS AND THE IMAGERY OF THE SELF

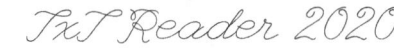

"It is a place where you can redefine cruising"

Julius Stahlie

"Totally, but it is also a place
where cruising can redefine you"

Taka Taka

It was completely dark around him, and he could only hear two things: the music that had faded away, and the soft moaning of the men around him. Adrenaline flooded through his body, this was his moment of letting go of control. Since his ears were not very good, he saw a lot of what happened around him. In this room, sound was very limited, and seeing was almost impossible. You were feeling, that is what you did there. He was aware of the sling that should be almost in front of him, but still he bumped into it and broke the soft sounds with the harsh ringing of the chains. He walked through the room, slowly; he became the master of his own actions there, while letting go of any judgment over those actions.

"Without the possibility of becoming reality, a fantasy is of no use whatsoever. Fantasy draws its potential from the fact that it can, might, become real. It is precisely at this moment – the crossover when fantasy becomes reality – that we experience the power we can have over our own lives."

Michael Bronski[3]

I do not entirely agree with Bronski's statement that a fantasy is only of use when there is the possibility of it becoming real. For some fantasies it is impossible to become reality due to the fantasy being placed in a world that does not exist, for example. Still they can be entertaining, relaxing or they can broaden your imagination around your own life and self – a self often placed and reflected by this life.

I do not think it is necessary for a fantasy to have the possibility of becoming reality, but I do think that fantasies that have the possibility of becoming real are the most interesting and valuable ones. Those fantasies are ways of positioning ourselves without knowing yet whether that position is one we would like to take. Those fantasies are ways to test ourselves, to test what kind of self we would like to be. Is the self we are now enough, too much, too not-us? Those fantasies are ways of testing our ideal self. If we do not like the self in the fantasy, we just stop dreaming, imagining, and then we can test a new one. Safe as it is.

A darkroom is more than a space where people can have sex, because it is about more than sex. Clearly this is a big motivation for people to go into such a space, and eventually it is the physical outcome, or goal. But where it differs from any other form of sexual interaction for me is the darkness and the clarity of the purpose of the room. You could argue that the darkness is a way of creating anonymity, an urge coming from times were gay men where not allowed to have sex, and where this act was made difficult by society and state. For cruising as a way to fulfil desires that are not accepted by a society, anonymity is a very important factor. But in the Amsterdam of 2020, it is allowed to have male on male sex. So is the act of cruising, with darkrooms as one of its outcomes, a leftover of past times? Did it slip into gay culture as some sort of tradition? And how does this anonymity serve us nowadays? Could a darkroom be seen as a fetish? And how can a darkroom function as a tool to research the Self?

In the Dark this visual self is not visible, and therefore the inner-self has more freedom to be defined. To be in a darkroom is an extremely tactile experience. All of your senses are made irrelevant, except feeling (and tasting, but this sense is not experienced differently in the Dark). Apart from all your senses to be experienced different or not being experienced at all, the mental notion of not being recognizable, nor the other people in the room being so, is creating an experience that is unknown, or new to us, since being unrecognizable is hard to achieve. It can allow you to feel more free in the acts that you might carry out, and it challenges your self-image, since in this space it is very little about who you are and who the other is. That raises the question: who do you want to be? This is a question that one might ask themselves more often than only in a darkroom, but in a darkroom simply no-one has an idea of who you are, which gives the opportunity to redefine this self.

Because of this, a darkroom can function as a way of experimenting with the image you have of yourself. It is a reflection of the self, purely for the self. It is solely about the self, because it is impossible to see the image of others. They can't see you, nor can you see yourself.

Their reaction to you is never a reflection of your image, because for that moment it is invisible and unimportant, and thus can be reformed, be invented, be anything it maybe never was or always wanted to be. The Other and the Dark give the individual the space to communicate to this self.

Of course one always has an idea of the self, but this idea is always reflected upon a visual self, and even upon the idea of the inner-self, simply because one is always visible.

Other dark spaces, such as a club, your own room with the lights off, the cinema, the night, also have this strength. Those spaces contain a perfect balance between a calmness and sharpness. Calm because of the muted visual senses disguised by the darkness, and sharpness created by the will and need to be able to function: due to the muted visual position one is placed in, one's other senses must be sharp in order to still be able to act. One must both surrender to the Dark and criticize it. Surrender to the Dark, because it is suppressive, suppressive to your visual image.

The Dark places all the focus on your other senses, yet the absence of imagery and the illusion of anonymity creates the freedom to form an image of self, because that is what one is left with. You are alone with all that is in a dark space, then to interact with all that is in this space gives again a reflection to look at the self. To criticize the Dark, because there one can totally focus on criticizing the imagery of the self, therefore the Dark needs to be able to fulfil this function.

---

3 Thompson, M. (2001). Leatherfolk: Radical Sex, People, Politics, and Practice. Los Angeles: Alyson Books, p.63.

ON THE GREAT DARK MAN

He woke up, on this cold winter morning. He threw the blankets off his warm body and went to the bathroom. The freezing air embodied him. While he rested his arms on the sink he watched himself in the mirror, stared deep into his eyes. His face represented the maybe too-long sleep he had had. He opened the water crane and formed a small bowl with his hands. While he slowly let his face sink into the little pool, the cold ice cold pool of water, he thought of the last time he gave a blowjob and if so if there was a possibility of doing it again and if so if he could do it again tonight or did he have other plans? He stepped under the shower that felt like fire steaming his body that had been frozen for too long. When he stepped back out of the shower, minutes later, it was him who was steaming and started freezing again when he entered the bedroom, his scars turning from healthy red to questionable blue. He always loved cold winter mornings. He always had loved them more than warm summer mornings when you wake up sweating like crazy not knowing whether it is your sweat or not. You are not in doubt of the origin of the sweat because you wake up next to that boy but because the whole city is sweating gushing bumping into each other. No he wants this cold winter morning and he wants it long and he wants it tonight and he wants to sweat for the right reasons and he wants to blow off steam with you or with him or actually yes with you, but first he has to check if he has other plans for tonight.

As stated before, both Narcissus and the Pool needed one another to see themselves, and therefore to define that self. Yet Narcissus was not aware of the fact he was looking at himself. What ways and metaphors do we have nowadays to see, research and define our Self? And in those ways and metaphors are we aware that we are looking at ourselves or not?

In his book *The Naked Civil Servant* (1968), Quentin Crisp[4] mentions the Great Dark Man (GDM). He states that he was in search of this GDM, a man who was the man he himself could never be. The reason why Crisp, or any homosexual man in that time – the early 20th century till the 1970s – for that matter, was unable to be this GDM, lays in the way society looked at gay men back then. The dominant idea was that gay men were not 'real men'. This caused a strange paradox for gay men, since their sexual identity rested upon the fact that they were men who were sexually or romantically attracted to other men. Did the idea that they were not 'real men' then have the consequence that they were actually not gay? I wonder. This GDM was a 'real man' which, I can imagine, was an appealing ideal figure to lust after as a gay man in a society where the identities of gay men were put into paradox. The GDM would give one the opportunity to desire something that society would support and that one still was attracted to. But the only problem with the GDM was that once a man would interact with a GDM in a sexual or romantic way, the GDM was attracted to men him-self and therefore not a 'real man,' let alone a GDM. Crisp thereby stated that, in fact, there was no such thing as a GDM.

Michael Bronski stated in his essay *A Dream is a Wish Your Heart Makes: Notes on the Materialization of Sexual Fantasy*, that "*Gay liberation had given gay men power over their own lives,*" providing that "*in a very real way, Quentin Crisp is wrong: we have become our own Great Dark Men, our own obscure and not-so-obscure objects of desire.*"[5]

The gay liberation he refers to takes place around 1960s and 1970s and is mostly referred to as 'post-Stonewall' (taking Stonewall as the leading, starting event of this liberation).[6] I believe that the theory of the GDM is not only relevant for gay men, but could be a metaphor for much more than masculinity alone. I believe, in continuation of Bronski's interpretation of Crisp's GDM, that the GDM is in fact the aftermath of the thought that one cannot be a certain person. It is a parallel self, one that functions as a notion for the more conscious self. It is a metaphor for the person one thinks he can never be. Why somebody has the belief he cannot be this person can be caused by many things, such as society, the person, reactions of others, good or bad experiences etc. Maybe the person is just not ready yet to be this self. The GDM is the ideal man, the person one looks up to, thinks about when in doubt or insecure, one desires – maybe even sexually or romantically.

Some will become their GDM. Maybe you look into the mirror and see him, your ideal man. It is only after a few seconds you realize it is you, the GDM is you and it was you all along. Maybe you are in a club and realize that everything you have done that night is exactly what the GDM would have done. But these moments of balance between the Self and the other Self will also fade away, come back, and fade away again. Maybe we will always be in search of our GDM.

4   Crisp, Q. (1997). The Naked Civil Servant. New York, N.Y.: Penguin Books.

5   Thompson, M. (2001). Leatherfolk: Radical Sex, People, Politics, and Practice. Los Angeles: Alyson Books, p.62.

6   The Stonewall Riots were a series of riots in 1969 as a reaction to the police raids on the Stonewall Inn and other police raids and police violence against members of the LGBTQI++ community.

There is another phenomenon of a certain type of gay masculinity, coming from and existing mainly in the 1970s and 1980s: the Gay Clone, or Castro Clone. This was a type of gay man who took the aesthetics of the blue-collar male of that time and made it their own.

> "The clone was, in many ways, the manliest of men. He had a gym-defined body; after hours of rigorous body building, his physique rippled with bulging muscles, looking more like competitive body builders than hairdressers or florists. He wore blue-collar garb – flannel shirts over muscle-T-shirts, Levi 501s over work boots, bomber jackets over hooded sweatshirts. He kept his hair short and had a thick mustache or closely cropped beard. There was nothing New Age or hippie about this reformed gay liberationist. And the clone lived the fast life. He "partied hard," taking recreational drugs, dancing in discos till down, having hot sex with strangers."

Martin P. Levine, edited by Michael S. Kimmel[7].

This quote from Martin P. Levine is almost a manifesto on how to be a Gay Clone in the 1970s and 1980s, otherwise called the Castro Clone. It describes the way these Gay Clones dressed themselves, cut their hair, trained the physicality of their bodies and even the social lifestyles they had.

Gay Clones were changing society's view on gay men as not being 'real men' by embodying the social ideal of the male in that time. It is a type of man, and generation of gay men, that is quite related to the act of cruising, to redefining (gay) sexuality and, mostly, the rules and standards that are created for sex and sexuality (rules and standards created, of course, by the heteronormative society). Through the gay liberation movement, gay men freed themselves from society's ideas of what gay men were 'like', and through the Castro Clone they created a new type of gay masculinity.

In fact, it could be said that the Castro Clone is the Great Dark Man that Quentin Crisp referred to. The Castro Clone embodied the type of masculinity of that time that gay men were never considered to be able to become, just as the GDM was a type of man that gay men never were considered to be able to become, yet they both became this type of masculinity, just as Michael Bronski stated that "*in a very real way, Quentin Crisp is wrong: We have become our own Great Dark Men, our own obscure and not-so-obscure objects of desire.*"

This seems especially likely considering that the book was written in 1968 and the most prominent time of the Castro Clones was roughly the mid-sixties to the mid-eighties.Yet, if this is true, it can also be stated that the Castro Clone was only one of the GDMs. Officially it could be the first embodiment of the GDM, since the term was raised in 1968, but across all times there can be found a GDM and, thereby following, a Clone. The aesthetics of the GDM and the Clone differs with time, place, sometimes per gay scene and even per a city. Yet, there are some similarities to be found.

Take for instance the 'Sports Clone.' Millennials, Generation Z (and those who are born in 1996, 1997 and 1998 because it can be stated they belong to both) grew up with a certain kind of macho masculinity, to be portrayed by men and boys in sportswear. This sportswear has evolved from the early 2000s with its loose-falling tracksuits, to the tight, bodyshape-hugging sportswear that has been produced since the late 2010s until now. There are the types of macho boy, adolescent male and adult male who wear this sport clothing. They often walk with their shoulders going back and forth and with a serious and tough face. They embody one of the ultra-masculinities of the two decades between 2000 and 2020, and sportswear is their trademark. Therefore, they can function as the GDM of Millennials and Generation Z; their aesthetics can be imitated as a parody to criticize the heteronormative aesthetics and culture they represent.

ON THE IMITATION OF HETERONORMATIVE AESTHETICS AS AN ACT OF ACTIVISM

Last winter, he was walking to the supermarket in the evening. It was dark and cold. He had only left his house to buy dinner for himself, so he wore a tracksuit with a big hoodie. A woman was walking ten meters ahead of him. After a while he noticed that she started walking faster and faster, to get away from him. It was the same was as he used to walk away from guys in tracksuits with big hoodies at night. He was shocked that someone could see him like the men he had always feared, but at the same time it was flattering. It felt like he had finally made it to a certain level of manhood, one that had disgusted and fascinated him his whole life, but also one that seemed impossible for him to obtain.

This level of manhood should not be mistaken for scaring women, or other people for that matter.

It is about something completely different. The line between idealization and desire is related to that which one does not want to be. Most of the time when someone does not want to be something, they will not explore this further. But it is also possible that someone has the idea that he simply cannot be something, and therefore he creates the idea that he does not want to be it. So, then, there is no need for researching the possibilities of becoming it. This presents an interesting friction. Where is the line between not wanting to be something, and not exploring the Self?

To create the illusion for the outside world that you have become the matter you once feared is a way of taking revenge on the thing that caused the fear in the first place. It is a way of dealing with it and protecting yourself from it. I do not think it is a way of protecting your present self from those fears, but it is about protecting your younger self from it.You take power over this fear in a way you could not when you were younger; you wear it like a uniform and visually become the thing you feared, and were seemingly unable to become in your life.

> "But it is not their size that casts fear into her neoconservative soul but the fact that they are no longer willing to be victims, that they took their lives into their own hands and became strong."

Michael Bronski[8]

It is not fear of those men, but it is fear of a society that does not place you into its heteronormative views. To dress as the men and boys that are given a place in society – because that society can understand them – can make one feel safe. They will most of the time mistake you for something they know, that feels familiar, that is like them. Yet you are not them, so you probably will not totally dress like those people. To aesthetically find a resemblance between them and you, can give one not only safety but most of all the power to be the man you want to be, because you make it your choice and yours only.

This fear I am describing, and those men and boys visualizing themselves in a heteronormative society, are exactly what results in the longing for the GDM and the becoming of a Clone.

> "Some might be more sexually explicit than others – and not all may be understood by the straight world viewing them – but to consciously present oneself as a (homo)sexual being is to grapple with and grab power for oneself."

Michael Bronski[9]

In order to be part of heteronormative society, one has to follow certain 'rules'. These are the norms and values of this heteronormative culture. Queer individuals do not follow these 'rules' from the very basics, and are therefore being excluded from a large part of society. This dominant hetero-normative culture exposes its norms and values constantly, and as a result Queer individuals are also influenced by it. At the same time

7   Levine, M. and Kimmel, M. (1998). Gay Macho: The Life and Death of the Homosexual Clone. New York: New York University Press, p.7 and 8.

8   Thompson, M. (2001). Leatherfolk: Radical Sex, People, Politics, and Practice. Los Angeles: Alyson Books, p.62.

9   Thompson, M. (2001). Leatherfolk: Radical Sex, People, Politics, and Practice. Los Angeles: Alyson Books, p.64

there are expectations, from both the heteronormative and Queer sections of society, of how heteronormative and Queer individuals ought to behave.

The expectations of Queer culture on how Queer individuals behave are mainly formed or adjusted by Queer culture. But heteronormative culture is quite often suppressive towards Queer individuals, imposing their expectations and 'rules' on Queer individuals.

This forced enculturation within heteronormative culture can unbalance how all Queer individuals experience themselves, especially in relation to what they are being told by others. However as they grow older, Queer people often find more possibilities to choose their own norms and values and will most likely meet other Queer people sharing the same understandings.

To imitate aesthetics of groups that belong to heteronormative culture is an act of activism for a Queer individual. It can be used to parody the forced enculturation that most Queer individuals endure, and thereby to criticize this process in a way that stretches the ideas about how a Queer person looks or ought to look. It claims power for the Queer individual and Queer culture.

To behave in a way that the suppressor does not expect, and to redefine its aesthetics – making it your own and making it Queer – is a way of claiming ownership over these 'rules' and expectations. To play with the expectations of others over your behavior, in order to make your behavior yours again, to turn around these expectations and to exaggerate them even further, is a very strong way of getting to know yourself and to present yourself. It also frees you from the eyes of others, because it is exactly their looks that you mirror.

> "Drag identity comes forward by empowerment and playing with expectations, appropriating characteristics of known symbols and pushing forward a dramatic sense of the ideal self."

Eva van der Moer (curator)

This quote talks about precisely that, but locates it in Drag culture and performance. Drag is prominent in Queer culture and, mainly, in Queer nightlife. It is a form of entertainment, a very strong and playful tool for activism, for stretching boundaries, self-expression, and reclaiming society's rules over our lives for ourselves once again.

What happens when all these things that Drag can do are used in daily Queer life?

I do think that it would also be an act of activism if one would dress in a way that heteronormative society would view as 'Queer' or 'gay'. To dress and behave in a way that the dominant culture of society expects a person to can be a powerful tool, when aware of it. It can create a friction of expectations when used against the ideas of behavior the dominant culture has. To be almost undercover in one's expectations is a way to educate others about their possibly limited view, and this can be by both dressing in the way that heteronormative society views as heteronormative, or by dressing as Queer. But to dress in the way this heteronormative society views as Queer-normative would be adhering to the stereotype it casts on all of us, whereas to imitate heteronormative aesthetics criticize these very aesthetics, making it Queer. Yet both ways of dressing are a big 'fuck you' to give as a Queer person to heteronormative norms and values.

The Sports Clone can be a way to criticize this heteronormative culture, and the Sports Clone can also criticize and parody 'Masc4Masc' gay men.

Masc4Masc is a term used in the gay male scene to address men who look very (heteronormatively) masculine who are only interested in sexual and romantic interaction with other very (heteronormatively) masculine-looking gay men. They often look on upon gay men who are not as masculine as them, sympathizing with the idea that ruled society before the 1970s but clearly still exists, namely that gay men are not 'real men.' It could be stated that Masc4Masc men are another type of GDM and Gay Clone. But since Masc4Masc is quite a general term, which is not so much applied to one type of (gay) aesthetic, it can rather be understood as an umbrella term of Gay Clone lifestyle (taking Gay Clones who do not parody or criticize the

heteronormative aesthetics they imitate). Masc4Masc as a term is also more related to the use of internet slang and the rise of social media, instead of aesthetic styles relating to historical archetypes and movements.

But one can also be a Sports Clone in a Masc4Masc way, and that is also what is happening in general with Gay Clones. Gay Clones are often not being used by gay men to parody the heteronormative society and are also not being used to criticize it. Gay Clones often imitate heteronormative aesthetics in a very serious way, without any critical intention. Rather they wear it in order to portray a masculinity to be understood by heteronormative society. But even though Gay Clones almost try to blend in with heteronormative society, Gay Clones show very much gay male or Queer aesthetics, due to the people who do wear those aesthetics being in a very closed societal scene (the gay male / Queer scene). Therefore their translation of these heteronormative aesthetics, even though not meant to differ from the heteronormative aesthetics imitated, are linked to these closed scenes. Therefore their translation of these heteronormative aesthetics are being linked to the gay male / Queer scene embodying them.

> "But there's the World where one adapts and stretches the boundaries of the Other World through keys of the imagination. But then again, the imagination is encoded with the invented information of the Other World"

David Wojnarowicz [10]

This 'Other World' Wojnarowicz discusses could be interpreted as the heteronormative world, and the 'World' as the Queer world. It can be a metaphor for more things, but here it will be used as the above. The GDM is a way of portraying the Other World in the World. It is a way of idealizing and desiring aspects of the Other World, but it is also a way of criticizing the Other World, by its own means, for instance when using the Gay Clone to parody and criticize heteronormative society. What codes of the heteronormative world can be used for this redefining of expectations, and what codes can be used from the Queer world in order for the aesthetics to be clearly playful and activistic? What new ways can be found and created by Queer people in order to adapt and stretch the boundaries of the heteronormative world? From the existing codes forced upon Queer individuals, and therefore upon Queer culture, we can create a new reality. One that refers to our ideal selves. An ideal self not pre-invented by how society can understand it. No, an ideal self constructed by how we feel and see it. Our GDM as the man we were taught we could never be, combined with the man we always envisioned for ourselves, the way we want and see it for ourselves and our community.

Returning to the quote from Michael Bronski on fantasy, can this ideal self, and maybe even this ideal Queer culture in which there is no influence from heteronormativity, be named a fantasy?

In general, when a fantasy becomes reality, it is extremely powerful, right before it loses its power and influence. It loses its power and influence because it has served its function. It has been lived, executed. It is at this point that a new fantasy arises. A new ideal self occurs. This new self will not be extremely different from the old one, since in the very basics it is the same self. The ideal self has been redefined in order to learn and to grow. The fantasy has become reality, and therefore is going to become boring with time, because in time you will get to know it, you will get used to it, you will not be challenged by it anymore. Yet, when a new fantasy arises, it is the exact same self that one has been chasing.

10 Wojnarowicz, D. (2017). Close to the Knives.: Great Britain: Canongate Books, p. 96.

ON THE SPORTS CLONE
AS THE NEW MOVEMENT

My practice is one of a platform creator. I choose platforms as my medium, because they can take many forms. For me, a platform can be a party, a magazine, a drag house, documentation of a group of people, a manifesto, a clothing style, etc.

I use platforms to combine entertainment, education, health, friends, clothing, sex and performance, in order to create, use and build community. I place my practice in the Queer scene of Amsterdam.

To place myself in a very local and relatively small community, makes it possible to have an impact on this Queer scene and to take care of it, together with other people from the scene. It is important for me to work together with other people from the Queer scene of Amsterdam, because by doing that, we actively contribute positively to the scene. To use platforms as a medium creates the need to work together with other people from the scene, because a platform is never something you do on your own.

The Sports Clone can function as one of these platforms. It can be a visual protest against the societal suppression of Queer people. This visual protest can be documented, written about, be a (walking) manifesto, a performance, a magazine, it can educate, etc.

As stated before, the very basic core of the Gay Clone is not used as a parody of heteronormative society and its view on masculinity, and it is not used to criticize this society and its views. But, Gay Clones have everything that is needed to be used as a medium to do this. First of all, clothing and therefore style have always been used as a medium for activism, protest and as a megaphone for opinions of an individual and of groups. As explained before, to imitate the aesthetics of heteronormative society by a Queer individual or group, as a parody of this heteronormative society, is, in the first place, a way of breaking its enculturation of Queer people, by Queer people. When this is done, Queer people can criticize this enculturation. They can criticize it by playing with the mix-up of the aesthetics of heteronormative society and the aesthetics of Queer culture, or by simply being a Queer person following exactly the heteronormative aesthetics, as a way of criticizing it.

Sportswear is a sign of ultra-masculinity in this Western-European society. Therefore embodying these heteronormative sports-aesthetics as Queer people, and the follow-up of altering them to their own aesthetics, is the ultimate parody and tool of criticizing this suppression of heteronormative society, its views, its norms and its values. Not only their rules on relationships, sexuality, sexual habits and promiscuity, but also their rules on masculinity resulting in toxic masculinity, can be criticized by the means of imitating ultra-masculine sportswear aesthetics and, next up, altering it, executed by Queer people.

In order to collectively and individually do this as a Queer community and as Queer individuals, I hereby declare the Queer Movement of the Sports Clone. Within this movement, Queer individuals parody and criticize the suppressive enculturation that heteronormative society throws upon them. They are free to alter the aesthetics to the extent of their wishes and to make it Queer, make it their own. We become a collective, walking protest in which we make our lives ours again, our bodies ours again, our relationships ours again, our sex and our sex lives ours again.

We take the power over our lives,
like we have had to do so many times before.

We take the power.

BIBLIOGRAPHY

Bronski, M. A Dream is a Wish Your Heart Makes: Notes on the Materialization of Sexual Fantasy: Thompson, M. (2001). Leatherfolk: Radical Sex, People, Politics, and Practice. Los Angeles: Alyson Books.

Crisp, Q. (1997). The Naked Civil Servant. New York, N.Y.: Penguin Books.

Levine, M. and Kimmel, M. (1998). Gay Macho: The Life and Death of the Homosexual Clone. New York: New York University Press.

Thompson, M. (2001). Leatherfolk: Radical Sex, People, Politics, and Practice. Los Angeles: Alyson Books.

Wilde, O. (1894). The Disciple, in: Poems in Prose. Great Britain: The Fortnightly Review.

Wojnarowicz, D. (2017). Close to the Knives: A Memoir of Disintegration. Great Britain: Canongate Books.

Nikki Swarts

Bloemwezen

HOE HOUDT EEN DRUPPEL WATER ZICHZELF BIJ ELKAAR?

In het zwembad. Het rook er altijd naar chloor, maar nooit helemaal schoon. In het zwembad, waar de muren van glas bij elkaar werden gehouden door zware metalen balken. Een beslagen afscheiding tussen binnen en buiten. Waar de tegeltjes op de grond de kleur van vanillevla hadden en gestructureerd waren met ribbels zodat haar voeten niet weg gleden over het natte oppervlak.

In het midden van de ruimte stond een grote, metalen bal die functioneerde als fontein. De bal was geel met rode strepen en in haar belevingswereld meters hoger dan zij was. Hij stond gebalanceerd op het muurtje dat het grote bad van het kleine bad onderscheidde. Zij stond in het kleine bad. Het metaal van de fontein was de ondergrond waar ze naar op zoek was. Maar als de fontein 'bezet' was, deden de metalen trapjes het werk ook. Als ze met haar hand wat water over het metalen oppervlak heen goot, even wachtte, en daarna haar hoofd dicht naar het oppervlak bracht, kon ze zien dat er kleine groepjes druppels op het metaal waren achtergebleven. Kleine, opbollende pareltjes die zichzelf bij elkaar hielden. Ze categoriseerde de druppels in haar hoofd op formaat. Als ze heel lichtjes met haar vingertop een grotere druppel aantikte, verplaatste het bolletje zich naar haar vinger. Nu was de druppel verbonden met zowel het metaal als met haar vingertop. Als ze haar vinger naar de kleinste druppel toe bewoog, volgde de druppel haar langs het metaal, tot de druppel zich samenvoegde met de kleine druppel. Ze had een grotere druppel gecreëerd. Nog een druppel, nog een druppel, en nog een druppel. Tot ze zichzelf niet meer bij elkaar konden houden en de zwaartekracht hen langs de metalen bol naar beneden liet vallen.

DRUPPELS DIE DOOR JOU EN MIJ HEEN VLOEIEN

Een gemeenschappelijke tuin

Hoe houdt een druppel water zichzelf bij elkaar? Ik begon deze opsomming, deze stroom van gedachten, wat tevens geleid heeft tot dit onderzoek, door een interesse die ik als kind had voor druppels water. Hoe houden zij zichzelf bij elkaar en wanneer kunnen ze zichzelf niet meer vasthouden? Een vraag die ik tot op heden onbeantwoord heb gelaten, maar nu ik het antwoord weet, kan ik zeggen dat het voor mij een bevredigend antwoord is. De druppels houden zichzelf bij elkaar, omdat dezelfde soort moleculen in het water elkaar aantrekken. Water trekt zichzelf aan. Het samenhangen van dezelfde soort moleculen heet cohesie (latijnse; com = samen en haerere = blijven steken)[1] . Zij rangschikken zich zo dicht mogelijk op elkaar, en daaruit ontstaat de vorm van een bol. Kleine pareltjes van water. De druppel is belangrijk. Maar waar staat zij symbool voor en waarom is de cohesie (innerlijke samenhang, onderlinge samenhang) belangrijk in mijn (textiel) werk en de manier waarop ik naar de wereld om mij heen kijk? In deze tekst wil ik een aantal punten uit het *Radical Tenderness* manifest gebruiken om hierachter te komen. Onder de punten van het manifest zal ik een metafoor van een tuin gebruiken. Ik kom later terug op zowel de tuin als het manifest. Ik wil deze twee met elkaar in verband brengen om te zien of ik een antwoord kan geven op de vraag wat het betekent om tederheid te ervaren en uit te dragen, en om deze fluïde concepten in te zetten om te schrijven over fragiliteit, gender, dromen, mijn rol in de maatschappij en (zelf)acceptatie. De cohesie, een actie van een geheel vormen, vond ik terug in het concept *hydrofeminisme*[2]: het idee dat we allemaal verantwoording dragen voor lichamen van water.

Van een druppel naar de zee

In haar boek 'Sex in The Sea' legt zeebiologe Marah J. Hardt uit dat het belangrijk is om te begrijpen hoe zeedieren zich voortplanten zodat we deze kennis kunnen inzetten om de oceaan te beschermen. Een simpel voorbeeld: als er duizenden vissen bij elkaar komen in een groep om zich voort te planten, moeten we die plekken dan niet beschermen in plaats van ze leeg te vissen voor voedsel. Niet alleen mensen hebben invloed op het ecosysteem dat leeft onder het oppervlak van water, ook de opwarming van de aarde zorgt ervoor dat er grote verschuivingen plaatsvinden. Denk aan het stervende koraalrif door de verandering in temperatuur van het water. Volgens Marah J. Hardt is het nodig om op een andere manier over het leven, en daarmee seksualiteit, van levende wezens in de oceaan na te denken. Ik vond in Hardt's boek 'Sex in The Sea' vooral de ontelbare fluïde voorbeelden van gender en seksualiteit van onderwaterwezens interessant. Het boek schetst een beeld dat te herkennen is in ons leven op het land, maar tegelijkertijd ook compleet anders is.

> "That's the thing about sex in the sea, it is at once utterly foreign, yet there are hints of the familiar - but only just. For the most part sex beneath the waves looks nothing like we think of as intercourse. That is what happens after several hundred million years of intense battles over who can reproduce the most - evolution gets a little funky.''

Zo zijn er minuscule vrouwelijke wormen die op de oceaanbodem leven van de botresten van grotere vissen. Zij dragen duizenden malen kleinere mannetjes in hun baarmoeder die daar puur leven om ze te bevruchten. Bij de inktvis zijn er prachtige, lichtgevende en kleurrijke mannetjes die zich voordoen als vrouwtjes (ze trekken hun tentakels in en veranderen van felle kleuren naar grijs en bruintinten) om zo bescherming te krijgen van andere mannetjes en hierdoor

---

1   druppel: wikipedia https://nl.wikipedia.org/wiki/druppel

2   Astrida Neimanis, Hydrofeminist: Or, On Becoming a Body of Water

dichterbij de vrouwtjes te komen. Veel vissen hebben geen gender tot het moment van baren, hun lichaam past zich aan de hoeveelheden mannetjes of vrouwtjes om ze heen aan. Clownvissen bijvoorbeeld zijn, net als veel zeewezens, hermafrodiet. Ze gaan twee keer door de 'pubertijd' heen in hun leven en veranderen van mannelijk naar vrouwelijk op het moment dat het dominante vrouwtje in hun omgeving overleden is.[3]

Het leven onder het oppervlak van de zee is, behalve mooi en mysterieus in al haar kronkelende en groeiende vormen, allesbehalve binair. Als ik dit idee van evolutie in het water toepas op mensen, die veel minder lang rondlopen op deze aarde, vraag ik me af wat dit zal betekenen voor onze genderidentiteit en seksualiteit. Ook vraag ik me af waarom het zo belangrijk is om ons bewust te zijn van wat ons onbewust beïnvloedt.

In de laatste jaren zijn we al meer gaan praten over het spectrum van gender en seksualiteit. Het idee van een 'mannelijk of vrouwelijk' bestaan bestaat voornamelijk uit regels over hoe je je behoort te gedragen om te functioneren binnen onze maatschappij. Ik zie het genderspectrum niet zozeer als een lijn, een gradiënt van roze naar blauw - waar je ook in het paars gekleurde midden kan zitten - maar eerder als een cirkel zoals we ook het spectrum van kleur weergeven. De menselijke biologie illustreert dit en vertelt ons dat er niet iets bestaat als mannelijke of vrouwelijke hersenen - geen roze of blauw, maar dat we allemaal andere gebieden ontwikkelen in onze hersenen die we uiteindelijk zouden kunnen indelen als 'mannelijke en vrouwelijke' eigenschappen. Interesses die we individueel hebben ontwikkeld. Menselijke eigenschappen dus, die beïnvloed worden door de manier waarop onze hersenen dingen opslaan en leren via invloeden van buitenaf. En ons 'buitenaf', onze maatschappij, is enorm verdeeld in twee genders. Leefregels die diepgeworteld zijn, die opeens onderuit zijn gehaald door wetenschap. Door deze externe invloeden, ons 'cultureel aangeleerd' gedrag zouden we dus op een hersenscan kunnen zien of iemand zich heeft ontwikkeld als man of vrouw, maar kunnen we er niet van uitgaan dat 'mannelijke' en 'vrouwelijke' hersenen zich op een bepaalde vastgestelde manier hebben ontwikkeld. Er zijn dus geen twee verschillende soorten hersenen.

Ook met betrekking tot hormonale en fysieke ontwikkeling zit er veel meer tussen het uiterste van een 'man' en een 'vrouw'. Tot voor kort zijn wetenschappelijke onderzoeken voornamelijk gericht geweest op mannen en in het belang van mannen. Gebaseerd op culturele vooroordelen. Naast mensen die met mannelijke of vrouwelijke geslachtsorganen geboren worden zijn er ook mensen die, net zoals de clownvissen, worden geboren met beiden. Helaas wordt er binnen onze maatschappij vaak bij de geboorte al beslist met welk geslacht deze persoon door het leven moet gaan, zodat dit duidelijk past binnen het idee dat we hebben over mannen en vrouwen. Zelfs als iemand hier de rest van zijn leven hormonen voor moet slikken.[4]

Als we onze statische genderopvattingen zouden inruilen voor het idee van de onderwaterwereld, waar geen sociale leefregels over geslacht vaststaan, en daarmee al die sociale structuren overboord zouden gooien, dan zouden wij ons veel vrijer kunnen uiten binnen onze identiteit.

Er is nu al een grote groep mensen die zich niet meer kunnen vinden in het binaire systeem van gender en die zich identificeren als *non-binair, genderqueer, demi-gender, pan-gender* etc. Mensen die zich in mijn ogen revolutionair inzetten om met het binaire systeem te breken. Ik geloof dat deze verandering de toekomst van gender is.

De tuin

Seksuologe Emily Nagoski gebruikt een metafoor van een tuin om te praten over de manier waarop we naar ons eigen lichaam en naar cultureel aangeleerd gedrag kunnen kijken. Ze zegt dat we allemaal geboren worden met een lapje grond. Een vruchtbaar lapje grond waar de cultuur waarin je geboren bent, je omgeving en je familie meteen van alles in planten, om vervolgens de tuin voor je te onderhouden en te verzorgen. Dit doen ze totdat je oud genoeg bent om er zelf voor te zorgen. Ze planten ideeën over liefde, over de maatschappij, over je toekomst, over je lichaam, over normen en waarden en over seksualiteit. Normen en waarden die je aanneemt als die van jou. Wanneer je oud genoeg bent om opnieuw naar je tuin te kijken zie je misschien planten die je helemaal niet bij jouw lichaam vindt passen. Planten die giftig zijn of planten die niet thuishoren in jouw perfecte tuin.[5] Misschien wil je liever violen dan distels. Kleine, zachte viooltjes die van zwart naar paars kleuren en suède-achtig aanvoelen tussen je vingertoppen. Die hun kopje naar de zon toe draaien. En liever een kleine aardbeienplant vol met vruchten dan een appelboom (want soms valt de appel wel ver van de boom). Het is dan aan ons om onze handen diep in de aarde te graven, de wortels te omsluiten met onze vingers en de complete plant met al onze kracht uit de grond te trekken, zodat er een gat overblijft in de grond vol met losse aarde. Op deze plek kunnen we nieuwe plantjes planten, en de grond stevig aandrukken zodat de gezonde planten sterk in de grond staan. Het kost wat tijd en er zal aarde onder onze nagels komen te zitten, maar op deze manier kun je je tuin zo inrichten totdat zij het beste bij jou past. En daarna zal het makkelijker zijn om energie en liefde te steken in jouw tuin.

3 Mary J. Hardt, Sex In The Sea, Palgrave Macmillan Ltd, 2016
4 Dordelia Fine, Testosteronerex: Het Einde Van De Gender Mythe, uitgeverij TerraLannoo, 2017

5 Emily Nagoski, Come as you are, Simon & Schuster, 2015

HET RADICAL TENDERNESS MANIFEST

Een tijdje geleden ontmoette ik een vrouw die indruk op me maakte. Ik heb haar maar een half uur gesproken en daarna ben ik haar nog een keer tegen gekomen, kort, voor misschien tien minuten. Beide keren dat ik haar sprak waren aangename en enthousiaste ontmoetingen. Ze was positief, maar kritisch, trots, nam ruimte in en voelde, ondanks haar aanwezige stem ongelofelijk zacht aan. Niet dat er iets mis is met aanwezige mensen, maar soms raak ik geïntimideerd door luide stemmen en durf ik het gesprek niet meer aan te gaan. Ergens in onze korte gesprekken noemde zij de term *radical tenderness*, een term die sinds dat moment niet meer uit mijn hoofd is verdwenen. Een term waar ik mijn eigen betekenis meteen aan heb gegeven omdat ze me zo erg raakte: Wat betekent het om teder te zijn, om de wereld om je heen te verkennen met zachtheid en zorg? Wat betekent het om fragiel te durven zijn, om te zijn en te praten zonder verwachtingen en oordelen. Om jezelf niet continu duidelijk te hoeven verwoorden, of misschien wel zonder te praten. Voor mij voelde deze term als een opluchting, want misschien maakte dit concept ruimte voor een andere vorm van communicatie. Een zachtere vorm, een stillere vorm. De term *radical tenderness* voelde als iets dat kon slaan op de sensuele beleving.

Wat voel ik, wat ruik ik, wat proef ik, wat hoor ik. Subtiele aanrakingen die wij misschien anders maar misschien ook wel hetzelfde ervaren.

Toen ik op het internet begon te zoeken had ik niet verwacht dit manifest tegen te komen: deze regels geschreven door Dani D'Emilia en Daniel B.Chavez, twee kunstenaars die onderdeel zijn van performance collective *La Pocha Nostra*. Het manifest is ontstaan tijdens een online jamsessie, en handelt over de vraag of tederheid ook radicaal kan zijn. Geschreven in ons digitale tijdperk, vanuit twee bedden, allebei aan de andere kant van de wereld.

1.
Radical tenderness
is to embrace fragility

Fragiel zijn omarmen als positieve act. Maar wat is fragiliteit? Ik denk aan breekbaar, broos, niet sterk, teer, zwak, vergankelijk. Woorden waarmee we vaak een negatieve connotatie hebben, maar belichamen we niet al deze woorden als mens? Een mens is breekbaar. We breken botten en als we vallen scheurt onze huid kapot. Waarom mogen we niet zwak zijn als deze zwakte de waarheid is? Mensen worden ziek, overlijden en zakken weg in depressies. We zijn vergankelijk. Zowel fysiek als mentaal. En hoewel we ze minder graag ervaren, komen we ook over deze emoties en ziektes heen. Dit maakt ons bewust van de fysieke en mentale gezondheid waar we ons wél comfortabel bij voelen. Door de vergankelijkheid en breekbaarheid te ervaren, weten we beter wat we nodig hebben om goed voor onszelf te zorgen.

Een tijdje geleden heb ik een Hydra gekocht. Een klimop. Mijn plafond is meer dan drie meter hoog en ik heb haar aan een haak aan het plafond gehangen. De eerste twee weken heb ik haar water gegeven, maar de weken daarop heb ik haar compleet verwaarloosd. Het gebrek aan tijd heeft mijn aandacht voor haar doen ontglippen en ik was verdrietig. Ik zag met de dag het vocht uit haar wegtrekken. Haar bladeren werden droog en donkergrijs. Diezelfde bladeren begonnen een knisperend geluid te maken wanneer ze tegen elkaar aan bewogen. Ik vergat voor haar te zorgen, zij, als wezen waar ik verantwoordelijk voor was. Maar ik wilde haar niet langer langzaam zien doodgaan. Door te observeren wat ze nodig had, kon ik beter voor haar zorgen. In haar bescheidenheid vroeg ze immers niet veel van me, maar slechts water, voeding en zon. Ik heb haar toen helemaal kortgeknipt en in een andere pot gezet. En nu ben ik aan het wachten op kleine, krullende, frisse en lichtgroene blaadjes.

Hoe kun je fragiliteit omarmen? Ik denk dat fragiliteit 'omarmen' betekent om niet te kritisch te zijn naar alles wat je voelt. Want alles wat je voelt is er, mag er zijn en er bestaat geen goed of slecht. Geen gevoelens die er wel mogen zijn en geen gevoelens die er niet mogen zijn. Woede, angst, schaamte, verdriet, walging en jaloezie, ook deze emoties mogen ervaren en gedeeld worden.

Je hebt de complete vrijheid om je emoties al dan niet of wel te delen. Je bent vrij om te willen wat je wilt. Emotionele ontwikkeling is een voortdurend proces. Woede, angst, verdriet, schaamte, walging en jaloezie hebben een functie, net als positieve emoties zoals blijdschap en liefde. De emoties die we als negatief beschouwen hebben de functie van bescherming. We voelen ze omdat onze hersenen een situatie herkennen en willen aangeven dat die situatie zorg of aandacht nodig heeft (Ik heb ooit gelezen dat jaloezie de problemen belicht waar we binnen onszelf aan moeten werken). Gelukkig lijkt er steeds meer aandacht te zijn voor mentale gezondheid en het delen van onze gevoelens. Hoe meer wij onze gevoelens delen, en niet te kritisch zijn naar alles wat we voelen, des te meer zullen wij in staat zijn om onze fragiliteit te omarmen.

Ik lees op het moment graag feministische zines. Kleinschalige zines zoals Polyester[6], gemaakt door jonge, activistische vrouwen en queers die onderwerpen bespreken zoals mentale gezondheid, body image en goed zorgen voor elkaar en onszelf. Deze zines worden gemaakt met een anarchistische insteek. Het is druk- werk dat niet gesponsord wordt en lokaal wordt uitgegeven en gratis te downloaden is op speciaal daarvoor bedoelde websites. Een zine loopt door analoog uitgegeven of geprinte clickbait en zij houdt haar modellen/auteurs privé.

Populaire hedendaagse media zoals televisieomroepen, magazines en social media sporen niet aan om fragiliteit te omarmen. In plaats daarvan stimuleren zij om het 'perfecte' plaatje te zijn en te leven. Ze creëren ongezonde aannames die niet alleen hun wortels hebben in content en context gemaakt door mannen en voor mannen (male gaze), maar ze sponsoren ook grote miljoenenbedrijven die helemaal geen waarde hechten aan jouw ontwikkeling, privacy en mentale gezondheid als individu, maar slechts enkel als consument. Dit is het tegenovergestelde van fragiliteit. Kies voor zachtere media input die bedoeld is voor jouw (emotionele) groei, die motiveert om fragiliteit te omarmen en er zorg en aandacht aan te schenken.

2.
Radical tenderness is to not insist
on being the centre of attention

Kamille is een kruid waar je geen tuin voor aanlegt, maar ze is wel heel fijn om te hebben. Naast het feit dat de thee van dit kleine bloemetje verfijnd en zacht smaakt, is zij goed voor rust, voor je darmen en maag en werkt ze ontstekingsremmend. Voor je tuin werkt het goed om haar naast andere planten te planten. Bijvoorbeeld fruitbomen of kool. Hoewel een appelboom haar compleet zal overschaduwen, zal de kamille ervoor zorgen dat er geen schimmelvorming in de wortels van de boom zal vormen. En door de ondersteuning van kamille zal de smaak van deze groente en vruchten verbeteren. Kamille groeit op veel plekken in Nederland in het wild. Zij wordt gezien als onkruid, als een plant waarvan subjectief is besloten dat zij ongewenst is. Grote bossen van kleine bloemetjes zijn te vinden langs de weg en langs weilanden. Je kan haar plukken, ondersteboven vastbinden en laten drogen op een donkere plek.

Maria Theresa Alves[7] is een Braziliaanse kunstenares die onze koloniale geschiedenis leest in onkruid. In haar werk 'Seeds of Change' verzamelt en groeit ze planten op locatie die via de route van slaven en handelsschepen terecht zijn gekomen op andere continenten en eilanden. Op het ene stuk land werden zakken gevuld met aarde om met dit gewicht het schip in balans te houden, en op het andere stuk land werd de grond

---

6   Polyester: To have faith in your own bad taste, Ione Gamble en Gina Tonic. Polyester is een eigen-uitgegeven, intersectioneel feministisch fashion en culturele publicatie die de kloof tussen URL cyberfeminisme en the IRL wereld probeert te overbruggen.

7   Institute for Figuring. https://www.theiff.org. Een altijd ontwikkelende natuur-culturele hybride, het Crochet Coral Reef bestaat in het gebied van kunst, wetenschap, mathemetics, environmentalisme en communitie.

vervangen door nieuwe aarde en zand. Op deze manier groeien er planten uit zowel Afrika als Europa op Amerikaanse grond, en is er een botanische route te volgen van de (geforceerde/ onderdrukkende) beweging van de mens. Alves gebruikt haar kunst om een verhaal te vertellen van een onderdrukt verleden en heden.

Ik denk dat ''to not insist on being the centre of attention'' op heel veel aspecten van het leven van toepassing is, maar als witte vrouw uit de middenklasse pas ik het toe op de gedachte dat we in een tijd leven waarin we bewust zijn geworden van het feit dat alles wat we te zien krijgen, vanuit een 'wit' standpunt is geweest. En met 'we' bedoel ik in dit geval witte mensen, die hun eigen geschiedenis en cultuur als de enige beschouwd hebben. Mijn tuin, de tuin waarin ik ben opgegroeid, is wit, en bovendien heteroseksueel, ondanks dat ik dat niet ben. Ik vind het belangrijk om te weten dat het systeem waarin ik leef systematisch minderheden onderdrukt. Dat ik hierdoor ben opgegroeid met systematisch racisme zonder dat ik mij daar bewust van was. Dat de geschiedenis, cultuur en de verhalen van de witte, heteroseksuele cisman uit de middenklasse een verhaal is dat in de Westerse wereld (en op plekken daarbuiten) is opgelegd als een universeel verhaal. En dat het nu (en eigenlijk altijd al) tijd is om te luisteren naar elk ander verhaal. Het is tijd om onze ogen en oren te openen voor verhalen van mensen en vrouwen van kleur. Verhalen van mensen die niet hetero-normatief leven of zijn en verhalen van mensen die met een beperking leven. Het is tijd om ruimte te maken voor nieuwe planten in onze gemeenschappelijke tuin, en die even goed te behandelen als de planten die er ooit stonden.

3.
To believe in what not can be seen

Ik kan niet verder kijken dan mijn tuin groot is. Maar als ik mij toch wil inleven in andere mensen, en samen wil functioneren met andere levende wezens, moet ik toch proberen te begrijpen hoe hun tuin is gegroeid en wat voor zorg zij nodig hebben voor het onderhoud.

Als ik heel dicht om me heen kijk dan weet ik dat ik bewust moet zijn van het feit dat als ik met jou praat en als ik over jou oordeel, ik dit doe vanuit mijn positie en mijn gedachtes. Ik kan niet weten waar jij doorheen gaat, wat jij hebt meegemaakt of wat jij voelt en ervaart. Ik kan niet objectief over jou oordelen. Ik geloof in verdriet en woede dat ik niet kan zien maar ook in vertrouwen en liefde die ik niet kan waarnemen.

Op een iets grotere afstand van mij, probeer ik te begrijpen dat mensen een goede intentie hebben, dat mensen dromen over dingen die hen dicht bij hun hart staan. Ook als ik deze dromen niet begrijp, dien ik te erkennen dat zij bestaan. Dat mensen religieus zijn, spiritueel zijn, dat mensen geloven. En dat er vele vormen van de waarheid zijn die allemaal de waarheid zijn, en waar ik allemaal in geloof.

Als ik nog verder af mag dwalen, ik geloof in verhalen die ik nooit zal leren kennen, in de verhalen van mensen die duizenden jaren geleden over deze aarde liepen. In verhalen die zich aan de andere kant van de wereld afspelen. Ik geloof in leven op andere planeten, en ruimtes en structuren die ik nooit met mijn blote handen aan zal raken. Ik geloof in verschillende versies van de toekomst en het verleden, in de andere werelden die parallel lopen aan die van ons. Ik geloof in systemen van micro-organismes en in sociale structuren diep in de zee.

Ik kom even terug op de druppel die de zee werd. Daar benoem ik een probleem dat we niet kunnen zien, maar wat wel te lezen valt als problematisch symptoom van een groter probleem waar zorg en aandacht naartoe moet. Het afstervende koraalrif. Een ondiepte in de oceaan die bewoond wordt door koraalpoliepen, levende wezens die we bloemdieren (bloemwezens) noemen.

Het *Institute for Figuring* (IFF), opgericht door Margaret en Christine Wertheim, werkt aan een maatschappelijk en wetenschappelijk doorlopend kunstproject: *Crochet Coral Reef*[8]. Een project dat in 2018 te zien was in het Van Abbemuseum. Het project reist over de hele wereld en vraagt publiek om mee te haken aan een textiel koraalrif. Haken is een textieltechniek waar je met een gekromde naald één lange draad met lussen aan elkaar verbindt waardoor je vrije vormen kan maken, die

lijken op een breiwerk, maar makkelijker spontaan te vormen zijn. Een felgekleurd, groot, indrukwekkend textiel koraal dat zich ondertussen over de hele wereld verspreidt. Dit doet het IFF om aandacht te vragen voor het probleem van stervend koraal en klimaat, en daarnaast symboliseren ze (door zowel haken als samenwerkingen van de mens en water) hoe wij, allemaal gevormd door de natuur en gevuld met water, met elkaar verbonden zijn. Geloven in wat je niet kan zien en daar aandacht aan schenken: dat is *Radical Tenderness*.

4.
Radical tenderness is to share dreams, wildness

Je openstellen is niet alleen je gevoelens en gedachtes delen, maar ook de dromen die daarbij komen kijken. De dromen die je in jouw denkbeeldige wereld beleeft. Ik denk dat we als kind bijna allemaal droomden over andere werelden en onzichtbare vrienden, en fantaseerde over alles behalve de realiteit. Als we de route volgen van educatie, in dienst gaan voor een ander, en beïnvloedt worden door media, krijgen we een andere realiteit aangeleerd dan die waar we over fantaseerden. De andere werelden vervagen, de onzichtbare vrienden worden vergeten en de magie van fantaseren verdwijnt. Ik haal graag inspiratie uit science-fiction boeken omdat juist deze schrijvers ervoor kiezen om via deze alternatieve 'denkbeeldige' realiteit kritisch te kijken naar onze wereld.

```
"Write what you know," I was regularly told this
as a beginner. I think it's a very good rule and
have always obeyed it. I write about imaginary
countries, alien societies on other planets,
dragons, wizards, the Napa Valley in 22002.
I know these things. I know them better than
anybody else possibly could, so it's my duty to
testify about them."
```

Ursula Le Guin is een feministische schrijfster van science-fiction boeken. De thema's die zij veel gebruikte in haar werk waren feministisch, psychologisch, sociologisch en anarchistisch. Ursula La Guin ziet science fiction schrijven als een 'denk-experiment'. Als je fictief aan het schrijven bent, heb je de vrijheid om te zeggen 'maar wat als..'. Dit experiment in denken en schrijven geeft de vrijheid om vragen te stellen zoals: 'Wat als de mens maar één gender had'[9] of 'Wat gebeurd er als we mensen kweken en we ze in bedwang houden met drugs en een klassensysteem'[10] . 'Wat als de overheid complete sociale en economische controle heeft'[11] . Sciencefiction geeft de vrijheid om te dromen over een wereld die niet of juist wel dealt met de sociale en economische problemen die spelen in onze wereld. Door rollen om te draaien, door problemen te vergroten of te verkleinen of door ze te verplaatsen naar een andere tijd of plek. Ik vraag me af of het lezen van science fiction iemand stimuleert empathischer te denken. Dit genre vraagt je immers om in te leven in een realiteit die niet hedendaags is. Om rondjes te lopen in een fantasie zonder een oplossing te hebben voor bepaalde problematiek of de verantwoordelijkheid te dragen voor de realiteit.

Ik zal je leiden door één van mijn fantasiewerelden. We leven in een wereld die gevormd is door het afval dat onze verloren maatschappij gevormd heeft, door alle destructieve vormen van leven die we hadden. Een landschap dat is ontstaan door jaren vervuiling en verwaarlozing. Waar mensen leven in kleine gemeenschappen, en waar echt menselijk leven vrij zeldzaam is. Het landschap is gevuld met grote, diepe kraters. Leven is niet mogelijk rondom deze zwart uitgeslagen kraters. Ze zijn ontstaan door bommen gemaakt van het kernafval uit een ver verleden. Een verleden van oorlogen over olie, water en land. Een systeem dat alles verwoestend was.

8 Een altijd ontwikkelende natuur-culturele hybride, The Crochet Coral Reef bestaat in het gebied van kunst, wetenschap, mathemetics, environmentalisme en communiteit.

9 The Left Hand of Darkness, Ursula Le Guin, 1969

10 A Brave New World, Aldous Huxley, 1931

11 1884, George Orwell, 1949

Alles in deze wereld is gemaakt van synthetische materialen. Materialen die niet meer terug kunnen naar de basis waaruit ze ooit zijn ontstaan. Materialen die niet zo zijn gegroeid, maar gemaakt zijn door mensen uit aardolie en aardgas. Nu hebben zij een plekje in de wereld ingenomen zonder dat zij ooit nog kunnen verdwijnen. Een grote klomp plastic. Een gesmolten gebergte van felle kleuren en een glad oppervlak. Bergen die kilometers langer zijn dan jij. Je zou ze kunnen beklimmen als je wilt, maar je voeten zouden wegglijden door het gladde oppervlak dat door de jaren heen is gevormd. Zoals de gesteende bergen waar mensen vroeger over wandelden nu uitgesleten zijn door massagebruik en leeg zijn gehakt voor marmer. Als het je toch lukt om deze berg te beklimmen, zal je tijdens je reis af en toe langs een meer lopen. Warme bronnen die bubbelen en borrelen en waar een dieppaars gekleurde damp vanaf komt. Sommige bronnen hebben de doorsnede van een meter, en sommigen liggen in een vallei en zijn kilometers breed. Ik zou niet naar deze bronnen toe lopen als ik jou was. Ze zijn ongelofelijk giftig en zoals je op afstand al zal merken, slaan je longen dicht als je probeert te ademen. De kleine deeltjes plastic zullen je poriën verstoppen en een laag op je huid vormen die hard aanvoelt en moeilijk te verwijderen is.

De natuur uit een verleden die nog waar te nemen is, is geometrisch en hard, maar in het door mensen geproduceerde plastic kun je alle soorten paars vinden. Hard plastic, zacht plastic en plastic dat strakgespannen is over luchtbubbels. Plastic in vloeiende en groeiende vormen op de grond die de patchworks van teer

en asfalt vervangen. Je hoort geritsel. In het paars zit de kleur van een heftige bloeduitstorting maar ook de kleur van de opkomende zon. Je ziet vormen die je vaag herkent, maar ze lijken anders te groeien. Ze geven de suggestie onder water te kunnen ademen, in de zoute oceaan waar de lijken van ooit levend koraal de zeebodem sieren. Ze zijn gedecoreerd met felgekleurde synthetische linten en zwarte bellen van teer. Alles dat je aanraakt zal je vingertoppen zachtjes terug strelen, en je zult niet weten of je dit ervaart in de realiteit of dat je bent vergeten uit te loggen. Het ruikt hier zoet, in tegenstelling tot bij de bron, naar iets dat refereert naar sinaasappel.

Als je gestrest wordt van de hoeveelheid prikkels en van de aantrekkingskracht is dat oké, ook als je je afgestoten voelt. Ik raad je aan om daar even te gaan liggen, om te gaan rusten op het met synthetisch mos begroeide bed. Om je lichaam weg te laten zakken, je ogen dicht te doen, je te laten omhelzen en misschien even in slaap te vallen.

Laten we dromen met elkaar delen. Laat mij een stukje van mijn innerlijke tuin delen met jou, en laat jij die van jou delen met mij. Dan zou dit de grond kunnen zijn van gedeelde creativiteit en inspiratie.

5.
Is to activate sensorial memory

Sinds ik textiel studeer ben ik gefascineerd door synthetisch materiaal. Een simulatie van de waarheid. De oorsprong van synthetisch materiaal is iets waar we vaak zelf achter moeten komen. Het is niet iets dat we in ons educatiesysteem leren als basiskennis, en de meeste mensen zullen niet in elk glad, dubbelgevouwen label achter in hun nek duiken om achter de oorsprong van hun kleding te komen. We weten wel dat synthetisch materiaal in brand kan vliegen, en kan smelten in druppels van gloeiend, brandend plastic. Maar waar komt het vandaan? De grondstoffen van synthetisch textiel zijn aardgas en aardolie. In fabrieken wordt het materiaal met hitte of met stoom door een spindop geperst. Lange oneindige plastic filamenten moeten daarna afgekoeld worden in een koud bad. Als een draad geacht wordt natuurlijker te ogen, wordt zij in kleinere vezels geknipt, zodat indien er een textiel van wordt geweven of gebreid je net als bij natuurlijke textiel kleine vezels uit ziet steken wanneer je langs de stof kijkt. Neem bijvoorbeeld een pluizige, wollen trui of een theedoek. Bij synthetische stoffen zijn de draden oneindig glad. Dunne, kilometerslange buisjes, waardoor je de stof aan haar glans kan herkennen.

Deze synthetische plastic draden zijn overal. We dragen ze als warme, niet kriebelende wol om ons lichaam. We dragen elastische kleding die geen vocht opneemt tijdens het sporten en verwerken ze in producten zoals kwasten, tandenborstels en je rugzak.

Ik kan mij nog precies herinneren hoe de (synthetische) make-up kwast van mijn moeder rook. Ik rook er vaak aan als kind omdat ze zacht aanvoelde tegen mijn gezicht en ik me geen andere geur kon voorstellen dan deze geur. Mijn make-up kwasten ruiken nu hetzelfde. Make-up ruikt vergankelijk, poederig en dof, maar ook heel persoonlijk, na een tijdje een product te gebruiken. Een meisje met wie ik een tijdje samen was, vertelde mij dat ze de geur van mijn gezicht, mijn make-up, niet fijn vond. Ik vind de geur van make-up prettig en vraag me af of zij minder prettige herinneringen heeft aan de geur van make-up.

De vloer bij mijn opa en oma thuis was bedekt met (synthetisch) hoogpolig, donkerblauw tapijt. Diep donkerblauw, lichter donkerblauw als ik het de andere kant op kamde met mijn vingers. De golvende blauwe structuur leek oneindig. Het uiteinde van elk draadje 'wol' was iets pluiziger en zachter dan het gespinde lichaam. De zachte ondergrond bood mij een veilige speelruimte aan, sterk contrasterend met het hoekige marmer waarvan andere meubels gemaakt waren.

In het fysieke werk dat ik maak, wil ik diezelfde zachtheid, veiligheid en oneindigheid ervaren. Materialen die uitnodigen om erop te gaan liggen en daar misschien even te blijven. Fijne kleuren en een synthetisch nestje van hoogpolige bedekking. Het synthetische materiaal waar ik mee werk is gerecycled. Ik ontrafel gebruikte truien die gemaakt zijn van gemixt materiaal.[12] Materiaal dat niet meer hergebruikt kan worden in de fabriek. Op deze manier heeft het toch een plek in de wereld waar zij gebruikt kan worden als zachte bekleding tegen de muren van de buitenwereld.

6.
Is to sustain ourselves from distinct places though not every of them is beautiful

Ik wil het punt gebruiken om over de term 'safe space' te praten. Iets wat ik zeker wil dat mijn tuin bevat of uitdraagt. Binnen de LGBTQI+ gemeenschap wordt er het symbool gebruikt van een roze driehoek omringt door een groene cirkel om aan te geven dat een ruimte bedoeld is om vrij te zijn van homofobie, misogynie, transfobie, xenofobie, racisme en bigotry. Een ruimte die niet is ingericht naar de meerderheid maar voor de minderheid. Eentje die veilig voelt, waar je altijd jezelf kunt zijn zonder je zorgen te maken over vooroordelen. Een ruimte waar je jezelf en de mensen om je heen viert.

Als jong persoon in de Westerse wereld groei je vaak op met televisie, literatuur, drukwerk en film. Media die je een idee geven van de wereld om je heen en hoe jij je tot die wereld verhoudt. Als ik nu naar de media kijk, die ik heb bekeken als jong persoon, vind ik deze 'culturele scholing' via media bijna obscuur. *Obscuur = donker, dubieus, geheimzinnig, glibberig, onbekend.* Mainstream media laten maar een klein stukje zien van zo een groot en divers geheel. Een klein, specifiek stukje. Ik kwam in mijn puberjaren tot de ontdekking, dat alles waar ik naar keek en wat ik las heteroseksueel/normatief was. De media plantten op deze manier heteroseksuele/normatieve planten in mijn tuin. Heteroseksuele cultuur, rolmodellen en gewoontes. Verkering, naar het bal gaan, trouwen en op zoek gaan naar mijn prins (of als ik Disney moet geloven, gevonden worden door mijn prins). Ik had behoefte aan andere planten, de zachte viooltjes vooral. Viooltjes werden vroeger gedragen en gegeven als symbool van een lesbische geaardheid en

---

12 Met dank aan alle mensen op Youtube die mij hebben uitgelegd hoe ik truien moet ontrafelen.

herkenning[13]. Ik moest door deze hetero normatieve media, net zoals veel queer jongeren, op zoek naar personages die misschien niet heteroseksueel waren en waar ik mezelf mee kon identificeren. Het is zo belangrijk voor jonge mensen om positieve rolmodellen te hebben die ervoor zorgen dat we weten dat we gerepresenteerd zijn in de maatschappij en die ons leren over onze cultuur.

"All the Reading I was given to do in school was always heterosexual, every movie I saw was heterosexual. And I had to do this translation. I had to translate it to my life rather than seeing my life. Which is why if people say to me "Your work is not really gay work, it's universal" I say "Up yours. It's gay. And that you can take it and translate it to your own life is very nice, but at least, I don't have to do the translating"

(Harvey Fierstein, The celluloid closet, 1995)

The celluloid closet[14] is een belangrijke documentaire voor mij, omdat deze mij liet inzien dat de meeste verhalen waarin homoseksualiteit een rol speelt, homoseksualiteit ook meteen het onderwerp van het verhaal is. Vaak gaat het om de gebeurtenis van uit de kast komen, met daaraan voorafgaand een tragisch leven voorafgaand. Hoe kun je functioneren in een heteroseksuele wereld als je weet dat je deze waarheid niet leeft en ondertussen weet dat jouw eigen waarheid nog altijd als taboe wordt gezien.

Sinds het begin van film werden queer stereotypes gebruikt als slechteriken, mentaal onstabiele mensen of compleet aseksueel. Tussen de jaren 30 en de jaren 70 was in Amerika de *Hays Code* van toepassing. *De Hays Code* was een lijst met regels waar films in theaters aan moesten voldoen en één van deze regels was dat homoseksualiteit gecensureerd werd. Als je dan toch een queer personage tegenkwam in de film zei dat dus meer over hoe pervers jij zelf was. In Populaire Hollywood films zoals bijvoorbeeld Alfred Hitchcock's *Spycho* (1960), Micheal Canes *Dressed to Kill* (1980) en Jonathan Demme's *Silence of the lambs* (1991) werden queer personages als de slechterikken gebruikt. Er is hier veel kritiek op geweest. Deze populaire films bevestigen het vooroordeel dat transgenders geesteszick, onstabiel en pervers zijn, terwijl in de realiteit transvrouwen door de geschiedenis heen voornamelijk en onophoudelijk slachtoffer zijn geweest van (seksueel) geweld. *Silence of the lambs* is een afstotelijk voorbeeld van transfobie. De motieven achter de moorden die Buffalo Bill, de psychotische seriemoordenaar, heeft gepleegd in de film zijn bijna volledig gebaseerd op het feit dat zij een transvrouw is, die de huid van andere vrouwen nodig heeft om het lichaam te creëren dat zij wenst te hebben. Dit is een uiting van angst voor mensen die zich niet aan gender conformeren en die angst is diepgeworteld in de maatschappij.

De representatie in Hollywood films heeft mensen, die zich identificeren als queer, geleerd hoe anderen naar ze (moeten) kijken, maar ook hoe zij geacht worden zichzelf te zien. Dit stond en staat duidelijk in een slecht daglicht. Om dit te veranderen is het belangrijk om andere verhalen te horen en te vertellen, dan het verhaal afkomstig uit de witte, hetero normatieve middenklasse. Deze andere verhalen worden verteld door personen die dit leven vanuit een andere realiteit beschouwen. Verhalen die niet persé over de tragedie gaan, maar ook gewoon over het 'zijn'. Ik denk dat in Harvey Fierstein's quote 'universeel' gelijk staat aan 'heteroseksueel' en dat Fierstein aan wil geven dat dat voor hem niet van toepassing is en dat zijn werk dus ook niet universeel zal zijn. Iets waar ik mij in kan verplaatsen. Queer filmmakers zoals Cheryl Dunye (director en hoofdrolspeelster uit *The watermelon woman* (1996): eerste feature film van een lesbische vrouw van kleur) roepen jonge mensen op om deze verhalen te verfilmen in een tijd waar we films kunnen maken met onze mobiele telefoon (Sean S. Baker's *Tangerine* uit 2015, compleet gefilmd met een iPhone).

Al het werk dat ik maak beschouw ik als niet hetero normatief. En dit terwijl ik maar één werk heb gemaakt dat dit ook als onderwerp droeg. Een synthetische, lichtroze quilt waar ik elke scene van de lesbische cultfilm *But I'm a cheerleader* (1991) van Jamie Babbit op heb geschilderd en geborduurd. Dit werk was belangrijk voor me omdat het het eerste textielwerk is dat ik gemaakt heb. Een glanzende, roze lappenwerk dat bestaat uit vierkantjes die aan elkaar genaaid zijn. Het is doorgestikt met dikke borduursels op de deken waar ik als klein kind onder sliep. Een structuur die het verhaal draagt van een christelijke cheerleader die naar een heroriëntatiekamp wordt gestuurd door haar ouders en daar verliefd wordt op een vrouw. Een film die van aardtinten naar roze en blauw kleurt door de film heen net zoals de inktvis die zich vermomt, en van natuurlijke materialen naar materialen van plastic groeit.

"To sustain ourselves from distinct places though not every of them is beautiful" betekent plekken opzoeken die gezond voor je zijn. De tuin die een LGBTQI+ safe space is waar alle hetero normatieve planten zijn vervangen door een palet aan diversiteit van planten.

7.
To allow yourself fysical contact

Ik heb me tot nu toe op het emotionele proces van het uitoefenen van radical tenderness gefocust. Op de manier waarop ik gegroeid ben en op hoe de wereld om mij heen verwacht van mij, om te groeien. Maar naast het mentale aspect zie ik ook het fysieke aspect. We leren vanaf een jonge leeftijd aan welke aanrakingen wel oké zijn en welke niet. En wie je wel aan mag raken, en wie niet. We gebruiken objecten met gebruiksaanwijzingen en leren hoe fysiek we met deze objecten mogen zijn. En niet anders. Met dit punt wil ik radical tenderness in haar letterlijke vorm benaderen. Hoe voelt een materiaal aan onder je vingertoppen en wat voor invloed heeft de zwaarte op je gemoedstoestand. In mijn werk ben ik altijd bezig met aanraking. Ik gebruik textieltechnieken om structuren en objecten te creëren die je wilt aanraken, ook als ze je afstoten. Met dit punt wil ik schrijven over de vraag: welke aanraking is gezond voor je lichaam en geest?

Er bestaat een knuffel machine die bestaat uit drie roterende, ronde kussens waar je je doorheen kan persen als mens. Zij is ontworpen door een autistische vrouw[15] die zag hoe goed koeien reageerde op fysiek contact, geknuffeld en gekamd worden. Een knuffelmachine bestaat uit een metalen frame met twee kussens onder en een kussen boven die je kunt verstellen op verschillende hoogtes zodat je 'knuffel' steviger word. De kussens zijn van PVC zodat ze makkelijk zijn schoon te maken. Een glad, maar tegelijkertijd stroef oppervlak. Je kunt je lichaam door de kussens heen drukken. Hoofd eerst, armen schouders, torso en benen. De druk die dit uitoefent op je spieren en elke centimeter van je lichaam zorgt voor een aangename 'hele' ervaring.

Toch lijkt deze ervaring bijna exclusief te bestaan voor kinderen of mensen met een beperking. En ik vraag me af waarom. Ik was laatst met mijn kleine neefje in een overdekte speeltuin met tunnels, geheime gangen, ballenbakken, luchtkussens en ...knuffelmachines! Waarom staan die soort machines nooit in ruimtes bedoelt voor volwassenen? Er bestaan wel vergelijkbare voorbeelden voor het opzoek zijn naar 'druk op je lichaam voelen', maar deze voorbeelden zijn vaak direct gelinkt aan fetisjisme (bijvoorbeeld de druk van ballonnen), *bondage* (een lichaam in een bepaalde houding vastknopen) of aan *kinks* (bijvoorbeeld een veel zwaarder iemand op je laten zitten voor hetzelfde effect als de knuffelmachine). Op de seksuele context ligt een cultureel taboe. Ik vraag me af waarom ik in mijn volwassen leven nog niet in een ruimte ben geweest

---

13 Nu opgezocht op wikipedia, ooit elders gelezen.'Biseksuele en lesbische vrouwen gaven viooltjes aan minnaressen, als een symbool voor hun "saffische" liefde. De Griekse dichteres Sappho beschrijft in een gedicht hoe zij en haar minnares een hanger van viooltjes dragen. Het geven van viooltjes was populair in de periode 1910 tot 1950.

14 The Celloloid Closet, regie: Rob Epstein, Jeffrey Friedman, 1995. In 1981 was het boek The celluloid closet: homosexuality in the movies een openbaring. Vito Russo beschreef hoe de filmindustrie mannen en vrouwen met homoseksuele gevoelens tot dan toe in beeld had gebracht: als lachwekkend, pathetisch of griezelig. Als ze überhaupt in beeld kwamen, want 'seksuele perversie' was in Hollywood jarenlang taboe. Filmakers wisten de censuur soms handig te omzeilen. Rob Epstein en Jeffrey Friedman namen 'The celluloid closet' als uitgangspunt voor hun gelijknamige documentaire, die in tal van film-fragmenten onvermoede signalen laat zien. Filmklassiekers krijgen hierdoor opeens een extra dimensie.

15 Temple Grandin is een Amerikaanse zoöloog, en hoogleraar. Ze heeft o.a 'Het autistische brein' geschreven, de knuffelmachine is ontworpen gebaseerd op haar onderzoeken. https://www.senso-care.nl/squeeze-machine.

waar spelen en voelen samen worden gebracht zoals in
een speeltuin – zonder dat ik dit hoef te linken aan wat er binnen
in onze maatschappij word gezien als seksueel. Ik zou het
eerder linken aan therapie. Ik zou deze plek of objecten graag
willen maken.

Want druk op ons lichaam uitoefenen (knuffelen, knijpen, aaien
en vasthouden) heeft een positief effect op ons lichaam een
geest. Er komt endorfine en dopamine vrij in onze hersenen,
onze bloeddruk verlaagd en door deze combinatie gaan we ons
rustiger en minder angstig voelen. Zou dit een remedie tegen
huidige maatschappelijke problemen kunnen zijn?

Voor mensen met een angstoornis, een depressie, ADHD
of autisme bestaan er verzwaarde dekens. Eigenlijk is een
verzwaarde deken[16] een quilt waar gelijkmatig verzwaringen
in zijn genaaid. Deze dekens zijn ontwikkeld om een druk op
het lichaam uit te oefenen om te profiteren van de positieve
gevolgen van 'druk'. Voor mij nodigt dit punt uit om op een
andere manier fysiek te zijn met objecten, of met andere
mensen. Op een manier die niet cultureel of structureel vast
staat, maar op een manier die therapeutisch werkt. Om te
luisteren wat er gezond is voor ons lichaam. Het nodig me uit
om een 'speel-tuin' te maken.

Water verbindt ons. Water stroomt door de aarde, via mijn kraan
in mijn lichaam, en verder de wereld in. Zij stroomt door jouw
lichaam heen, terug in de zee, doorvloeiend naar een ander
lichaam van water. Onze lichamen. We bestaan grotendeels
uit water (80%). Net zoals dieren en planten. Zelfs de droogste
plantsoorten bestaan voor 50% uit water.

Astrida Neimanis is een professor die gespecialiseerd is in
culturele en gender studies. Zij roept in haar boek *Hydrofeminist:
Or, On Becoming a Body of Water* de vraag op wat het
betekent om 'waterig te denken'. 'Thinking through water'.
Hydrofeminisme is solidariteit met lichamen van water. De fluïde
tegenhanger van het hokjes denken en individualisme. Ze biedt
ons een nieuwe manier aan om ethische vragen te stellen over
alles wat ons met elkaar verbindt of we dit nou willen of niet.
Het is nodig. Met elkaar verbonden zijn geeft een gevoel van
verantwoording naar elkaar. Voor zowel onszelf, de ander, en
de planeet. Deze verantwoording dragen, en hierop reageren
is feministisch. Wij, als mensen, denken vanaf het land; vanaf
de grond boven het water, in de structuren die wij gecreëerd
hebben. Dit doen we in een wereld die grotendeels uit water
bestaat, een wereld waar wij grotendeels niet kunnen leven.
Toch dragen wij de verantwoording voor wat wij niet kunnen
zien. Om te zorgen, en aandacht te geven aan andere lichamen
van water. We dragen de verantwoording voor de fragiliteit en
de kracht van de natuur, voor het leven van een ander, voor
de dingen die we niet kunnen zien, maar waar we wel mee
verbonden zijn, voor een nieuwe manier van kijken en delen en
om veilige plekken creëren.

Voor mij gaf het *Radical Tenderness Manifest* een structuur om
deze fluide manier van denken te manifesteren. Het water als de
voeding en basis van Emily Nagoski's tuin metafoor. Ik hoop dat
mijn scriptie uitnodigt om teder te zijn voor elkaar en onszelf, om
open te zijn en om vooral verbonden te zijn.

---

16 Een quilt is een doorgestikt textiel dat bestaat uit twee lagen
   textiel met een vulling ertussen.

Rosa Dilaça Mesquita

The Swallowers

PREFACE

Lack of company will soon lead a man into a brown study[1] — they said and I didn't listen, as a stubborn cat fixated on my ball of yarn. What does it mean to be engulfed by a colour? To let it take you, by closing your eyes in the style of a guided meditation, imagining the intense coloured light around you and even slowly entering your body; or to enclose oneself in a room where all the walls are painted with the ink from the same bucket.[2] In any case, its affinity with light and the senses means that you need to open up to it and to let it affect you.

It is a longing and a desire at the same time. Something in between fascination and intrigue. I took brown as I could have taken something else, but brown had all the qualities and nuances I was looking for. It spoke of mixture, of solidity, of immersion, of togetherness, of shadows, of practicality, of unimportance, of certainty, of silence, of real things, of expansion and restriction, I could go on. It seemed full of contradictions — *Therefore I trusted*. And I rolled the ball of yarn in my hands while trying to display some of its facets that lured me from the beginning. And the ball rolled and rolled, confusing me and escaping into my text making it become a bit brown itself, at times muddy and ambiguous, with the wish to escape confinements.

The perspective I write from is that of a collector of objects, images and fascinations, someone born in a small village in the countryside, a retired amateur painter, one who wishes more or less for calm and clarity. I don't want to define it, even less am I a dissector of meanings. The brown I roll with is my brown, the puzzling brown of certain intensities. It is not enough to say it is my favourite colour because maybe it is not yours. That hundreds of odes and meditations on colours have already been written throughout the years by thinkers and poets and other humans is just a matter of fact. Oh well, I guess it is my turn.

A bit embarrassed, I try to tie the thread around my paw: it is also what I do not want to forget.

UNDER THIS UMBRELLA

This text wanted to start with brown.
Brown, the colour that ate all the other colours and couldn't move anymore, the colour that by being the absolute opposite of blue and distance, is the colour of such proximity that you are inside. I wanted to start with Brown. A brown wish I may call it. Of dressing all in brown, a brown suit and mixing with another landscape. Dark brown, the colour of no infinities. Colour of furs and skins, of the ground, chicory and carob. All the other colours are there but hidden in its grain, perhaps it is where all the colours go to die, or live forever. *Couldn't it be grey?* But I wanted something with more chewiness. Brown has no distance, brown has deepness.

What is this ground you — Fall into,
If brown is also a colour of Moderation?
A colour with a tail, with hair, that walks on a shadow,
that carries a bit of obscurity.
I do like brown. I really like brown and brown things. Brown.

What are these brown things, what do they share, *is this a family or is it a village?* What are the limits of a colour, what are the limits of this colour that is by definition so wide and encompassing? If each colour is a family, brown is a very large one. The limits of brown truly depend on the generosity of the one who sees it. How far into the red can you go? How far into the grey, into the yellow, into the pink? Can golden belong to brown? Some say that brown is any mixture of the three primary colours, others say, instead, it is spoiled red. A muted colour. Several directions. Brown asks you for patience. Brown waits.

rown is a but, a not yet, an almost. Brown is this almost, the almost touching. Brown is the during. There is no centre to brown, brown stretches into the direction of multiple colours, yet brown never arrives. Brown never shows its face, always under a shadow, always following, mysterious and tinted beauty. Brown is warm. Brown was focused on something else so it didn't notice that you arrived. Brown smiled but didn't answer.

It is timely, it is *November*. The ground has brown leaves, the sky greyish tones. Amanda just arrived and shared dark bread with tahini, some cocoa nibs on top. Bitter and concentrated, we drink coffee, some of it spills.
I write down my wish: still looking, for a *brown flower*.

Let me try again to explain,
to reach you with my urge, my need.

Why a colour? Because maybe
there was *no* shape to talk about.

If illusion has a shape, disappointment has not,
disappointment disin-te-grates.

Why brown? Because there was not
so much but there was some acceptance.

Brown was always there. I was just unable to see it.

1　From *Dice-Play*, a book from the 16th century, where the expression *brown study* first appeared, as in gloomy (brown) reverie (study). Interpretations: "gloomy meditation or melancholy","absorbed in one's own thoughts", or even "To be in a *study* was bad already; a *brown study* really served to emphasise the gloom".

2　"In order to experience these influences (of one colour) completely, the eye should be entirely surrounded with one colour; we should be in a room of one colour, or look through a coloured glass. We are then identified with the hue, it attunes the eye and mind in mere unison with itself.", Goethe, Johann Wolfgang von. *Theory of Colours*. Cambridge, MA: Massachusetts Institute of Technology, 1970.

UNDER, THERE IS A LAND OF ROOTS

To say to the body: enter, To say to the body: surrender. To say to the body: is the mend on your feet? And on the way it embraces the soil? A vessel for what? I am, we are, the humans of lava pots, the volcanoes that have gone cold, the streets connecting the deserts and the plaza.

To go under,
as a mole
To explore the subterraneous, to trust the subterraneous, to adjust the vision to the dusky shadow. To find the masses and the threads, to try to find the connections that are only imaginable from the visible layer, to be stubborn.

That is the work of the *dispositor*, worker of superficialities: to trust the first impression, not to trust the second one, and to be able to trust, now transformed, the 351st, when the complexity has already gotten peaceful.

Do you know where your matter has come from? We almost know, from history and imagination, the explosions that are behind the conformity of the daily-body. Before the daily body there was another body and another body and another body, a matter of scale, a matter of digging. Scaling down, suggesting a distance, in truth, always means a digging. Scale it down as you dig, scale it down as you dig, become very small, let it go, become very small, let it go. Yet digging knows of no measures and composes a danger: you need to become very precise and even then. Adjust your small trunk to the hole, learn to move on that hole and find the movement that is the exactitude of the ins and outs of the knot.

Psychology is on the body, fills the body. A family is always under the same spell and its members repeat the same words, compulsively and unprepared. Genealogy looks for homeostasis through its limbs, trying to solve its problems through new sproutings, through the open mouth of the newborn child. The process has already begun and you just arrived.
To smell: a strategy to go around and then beyond, curving and essing the obstacles of the vision. To follow a smell is to try to find its origin.

All which moves is an extremity. It started because you already have a specific shape, the shape of an extremity. Reaching into other extremities with the hand, reaching the cosmic with the yell.

COMMON GROUND

That the word extremity comes to this text — be it in the figure of a hand or through the opening of the mouth — has the taste of a mistake. The extreme is what brown is not. Everything but an extremity, more easily the trunk than the flower, more easily a murmur than a yell.

Trying to draw a form out of the shade, to find a clear association of what brown seems to be I come across an adult figure. That which dresses in uniformed clothes, goes on the clock to the repetition of one's day, dulling himself into a routine, becoming a member of something, inscribed in social roles, obeying time and restriction. The child, thinking of infinities and playing in the backyard in between the cabbages, looks and doesn't fully understand. The child still doesn't know that its house is built by other people, that the walls are kept upright by the effort of days of work, and that the marble that shines and rolls in its hands didn't magically appear there. That the child one day grows its fingers to the size of its dad's or mother's and learns to look at its parents in a horizontal line — carrying on its back a bit of the same strength — is part of the same brown archetype.[3]

The routine hides the bright colour:
Because what you see repeatedly you cannot see as vivid. But it's the habit what makes the form, the shadow what holds the figure straight. And the sullen skies press down with a certain seriousness, announcing the limits of a day.

Seemingly dull and worn-out, brown echoes, repeats, becomes sepia, walks in circles. And with the stubbornness of a shadow, it keeps coming without being invited. The floor of the balcony with the accumulation of little dusts, the fruit rotting unattended, some coffee stains. A little bit everywhere, sometimes very mundane, other times possessing a strange profundity. In a moment I see my table of oak wood, terracotta vases, the shells of devoured chestnuts. Outside, some forms of nature compete for the dullest shade.

It seems to have given desire away, to have renounced from the pleasures of the senses, from the intrigue of the cosmetic. And sometimes it is found in a less commonplace, on the edges of a village, the ascetic figure. Once I was told — the context of which I cannot trace back — that the hermit is the one that is visited by all in secret, in moments of need, but invited by no one to the dinner table.

A little tremor,
the oddity of a situation: also the mad poets one reads alone in the night, some truth that seems to evaporate in the light of a midday conversation.

But brown seems to continue to walk in circles, around the word common. Around the beans and the cockroaches.[4] Around my sins and my dinner table. Sometimes he runs so fast, I think he wants to become hazy and dissolve in a cloud of dust. Then, and because he is tired, he slows his movements. I see a bit of his face, defeated. With him I share a primordial wish to dissolve in the sea-foam of some wave, learning the creaks of the rocks and the spits of the ocean. It's a wish to give away the grip of a name with which till now I sign my efforts. He asks me what it is that we really share, from which ground could we talk. And I don't know it anymore.

Or I never knew it. But I must have the answer, somewhere in my bones. Somewhere under those nails that once scrapped the glimpse of a truth.

Sometimes, I am still a child but my cabbages grow on the richest humus, full of impulses and excrement. Sometimes I look into some other's eyes and ask — how was your day?

My day was repeated, my day was a sea of nothings.
If only I could..

One day.
In stretching steps, brown becomes liquid, shape-shifts, finds other ways. It escapes the solitary cave of the hermit and reunites in the monastery, where monks tone down their colours to be able to live together within a certain devotion. Then it spreads. It spreads to the soils of the middle ages, walks between the mountains of Umbria, in the image of the Franciscan friars[5] that stay in our memory praising the lark and living the gospel. It is a similar renunciation, their habits had the roughness of the peasant vests of the time and lacked the excitement of colouration. Without possessing, they begged.

But why would they give away their clothes if they didn't find in the vests of sackcloth a more truthful dress, and in begging the true shape of a belief? Because a wish for dissolution is also a wish for authenticity. As if, to fully be, one needs to be less and to ask. *And empty handed they prayed, an empty handed prayer.*

To beg and to continue begging.[6]
Which is also what is left, to continue.
The firm lesson of the ground, it somehow continues.
At the dust of the days, when it fades,
certain things only matter so much.

*

---

3   the Saturnian archetype, Saturn being the brown planet

4   An extra image, a gift from one poet, for beauty on the right tonality:"*the roaches, brown, their egg purses dark, the newborns, translucent amber. Color something we'd have to earn (…)*" Seuss, Diane. *Four-Legged Girl: Poems*. Minneapolis, MN: Graywolf Press, 2015.

5   An interesting etymological distinction: monk from the Latin monachus = solitude, friar from fraire = brother

6   "Satisfaction, contentment of being, as the mendicant which finally received what he begs for, but which will only manage to conserve it if he continues on begging.", Zambrano, María. *O Homem e o Divino*. Lisboa: Antropos, 1995.

In this table that we share there is still space for a bit of silence. My mum passes me the pot, I anticipate a wooden trivet. I bring my words a bit higher so she can hear me better, I try to make myself comprehensible in a soft tone as I share the contours of one more day. However, just as often, we don't say anything, we eat. I decipher the little gestures of her face, the velocity of her movements. Hoping for a conjoined smile of understanding.

CONCENTRATION

*

A soup, an infantile mesh — play dough — the triturating mouth, the triturating machine of life, that compresses, miles and dulls, silencing the spaces. The shadow of a mill on a body of water.
A one-pot meal: what is sophistication?
A meal of 15 little plates: what is the centre?

*

As I pass by the corridors of school in an attempt to get some water for the kettle I come upon a brown image, the washing sink, filled to the brim with the dirty water that takes on the babblings of all the paintbrushes from the floor. Its surface is opaque, no way to see the bottom, just the mystery of the traces of all those painters and coffee drinkers, no, no traces, just the silence of brown water. I think, and I get taken by it. On the surface, glimmering and oily reflections move around and stick to your fingers when you decide to playfully touch it. And it is from this bowl, from this indistinct glaze of an image that I pick and stretch my words, one by one, the colours of the text.

I remember that
Kafka wrote in his notebooks[7],

     Evil is whatever distracts,

Distraction..
Concentration, *its centre and its opposite*, is a concentration of matter. An alignment of the gazes, we can say. Isn't it there, in the idea of concentration, a resemblance or a glimpse of similar qualities to that which we faintly call the experience of fate? Absorbing and shapeless:
the elastic mud that makes the legs accept their inevitability.
Centred: The body falling on the right grave.
Time keeps passing.

An absorbing ground, the suction of molasses,
A colour that asks for the patience of the eye
To find its tridimensionality,

A *substance*. Was it dissolving or was it elastic?
Why did I walk towards it as if there was a charm pulling me? As if there was a soft string connecting me and future, not pulling but hissing the right direction. Eyes wide open, blinded by *certainty*.

I try to be careful with the words, to invite the right ones. And I maintain *elastic* and I *absorbing*. Because it gives it an affinity with an inwards and with embrace. It tells what it is, concentration: an experience without gap or tears, something unmediated, say, a friendship between stillness and time.

*

It was last summer, after wanting and wishing for a long time. Sam had given me a drop spindle and
I was learning how to spin.
(As of now, in the peripheries of writing this text,
my hands are still busy with these lumps of wool.)

There was a little statue of a spinning lady in the holiday room of my parents, facing east, sitting on a chair and fitting her fingers to the job. It was an old lady with white hair combed into a bun and I remember being young, pre-school age, and I couldn't wait to become her. I grew my hair long and as I learned to keep it contained, I waited for my white tresses.

With time I forgot my longing and I cut it short because of practicalities but some white hairs started to appear as my teens became twenties. Little did I know that I would find my way into her task, many years later.

When Sam taught me how to spin, Sam didn't tell me so many rules: to spin you need to spin, to get acquainted with the task, to get a sensibility for the fibres and the way they stretch.

*

The disconcerting thing about distraction and concentration is that they like to play around and dress as each other. It is a mad game, a game of directions. And destiny sometimes joins and plays as the stray dog, unwanted and wet, barking for kisses, that I try to forbid into my kitchen afraid of ruining the floors.

But appalled by these motions, in truth we always walk towards some sort of end: that is the certainty of the movement.

*

Certainty, Flusser says, is akin to faith, a state of mind before the doubt. "The naivety and innocence of the spirit dissolve in the corrosive acid of doubt. Attempts to regain authenticity/ original faith are attempts to regain paradise."[8] To take the leap is to trust, in animal steps, the bliss of a home to come, of a return to a centre. And where to find this centre that soothes, the direction that beats slow and soft. A question mark seems to look for foreign lands with its demanding hook but instead the notion of a primordial image brings me to the idea of a fireplace.

Then the history of words also twines *focus* and fire. It tells that the word focus came into his current use of *attention* when Johannes Kepler,[9] busy working up the mechanics of the telescope, found the burning point of the lens, the point where the light converges and makes fire. From analogy, the convergent point became *focus*, as its origin in Latin meant the hearth of the house, the fireplace. The place where all the eyes are fixed, absorbed into the scintillations of the flame, while stories are told.

*

I breathe in, hoping I have an excuse to write fire while I wanted to write brown and absorption. Maybe I need the red to write brown, or maybe I am guilty.[10]

*

But it is simple things, rather
banalities that have their own weight.
To spin you need Time and Fibre. And the grease and trust of your fingers. You cannot hold too tight, you cannot hold too loose. You start with a cloud of material, you stretch it, then you twist and compress, you create resistance. The thread, continuous. The spindle goes down, along its centre, the spindle goes down, agglomerating, concentrating, making the fluff matter, making the matter existent.

Simple, but difficult to find the right motion of things. Practise to forget, practise to be able to have without holding. An eternal work of forgetting, an eternal work of entering. Then you can walk while spinning, and this is the spinning song.

*

7   Kafka, Franz, and Max Brod. *The Blue Octavo Notebooks*. Cambridge, MA: Exact Change, 1991.

8   Flusser, Vilém, Rodrigo Maltez. Novaes, Rainer Guldin, and Siegfried Zielinski. *On Doubt*. Minneapolis, MN: Univocal Publ, 2014.

9   German astronomer, sec XVI

10   Older scholars traced *brown* to the root of *burn* (Old Engl. *brinnan ~ birnan*, Gothic *brinnan*, and so forth). Allegedly, that is why brown can refer to both dark and bright shades.

Some will also continue and say that evil is whatever separates, but I prefer to offer my lips to silence than to talk about the sadness of separation. What I know is that when the ball beats the wall it finds its own mass. Two forces at the same time: the wound wants to be touched and the wound wants to be closed. But one should rather go softly.

I take brown gently, compose my gaze into the sangue bruno of Dante[11], the clotting blood that is suited to mend the gap. To close the tear. To jump from now to then rather seamlessly.

*

A SINKING MOTION

When I think of imagination I see myself making a distinction of two different kinds, defined by the latitude and density of their movements. One is *to-the-top*, the other *to-the-bottom*. Both of them fit what I know of imagination even though you could call one of them a strange way of *remembering*.

The first one is productive and infinite. It has no ties nor knows of commitments. It is a spiral of oxygen, a wild child, a game of freedom. It goes out of the house and sees the world as a possibility. It is airy, unrestrained, *unthreaded*. It shares with laughter the idea of flying, and its colours are ridiculous and varied.

The second one is more like crawling. It is usually slower and distinguishes right from wrong. I could say it is faithful to a certain secret order of things, feeds on silence and takes muddy steps around the house. This one is brown, certainly brown.

EARTHLY CONTOURS

There, without fear or intent, but possessed by a natural hunger, a cow gives her tongue to the rock. Or the rock gives its salt to the tongue. Everyone knows that a cow needs her salt, to enrich the milk with minerals. With flies on her ass, in a fastidious activity, she needs. From that need, the salt-rock starts to take the shapes of the licking, the organic movement that becomes articulated through repetition.

The tongue, extra-sensible, sees everything big, enlarged and equally important.[12] And the warm tongue eats the meaning away, creating concavities on the block. Its movement describes the curved lines of desire with which nature draws its landscapes. (img3)

*

In a different village, across some other meadows and grounds, Ferdinand Cheval also started with a rock. A rock of specific contours that he found on a walk and which ignited the memory of an old dream. From this dream and the hunger to fulfil it, he carved stones. He built a house of stones, an exquisite palace. He gave his hands to the stones and he carved how he could and with what he had, the hands and the imagination.

Everyone was invited into his imagination. A flourishing cocoon, of gnomes and enchanted gardens, animals and small-scaled architectures, as multiple as the 33 years he took to construct this braided labyrinth of images. (img4)

It is a *crowded* place. From far, the delirious texture of protuberances growing on the skin of the earth. The sediments of a dream. The eye tries to find a line to follow and the eye is lost but follows through. Finding on the concavity of a moment the curve to the next one.

The one who carves, carves out of hunger. Other constructors may have different reasons to tend to their shapes, to develop their forms. The one who carves, carves because he needs.

What he needs he casts away from the stone, the indentations and creeks of an intermediary ground, that is neither empty nor full.

What he does need is tridimensionality.
And this tridimensionality that I talk about refuses to lay flat in the clearness of a forced conclusion, it doesn't simplify, not yet. Not yet yellow, nor black, nor white, it belongs to that which is possible, to that which is real. Even further, it does belong to the language of the textural, favoured by the imprecisions of the craft and the grain of the mineral.

Texture, as a wide term, is that which brings shadow to the shape, that which goes against it, and in doing so, reinforces it. It brings enough contradiction for it to be something other than an invention[13]: it is the little tremor of a body, the truth of the stalactite, a language of small surface hesitations. The vivid surface of the real hesitates, that's why it is so vivid. Perhaps even the fire doubts.

The carvings of Cheval, as well as the sculptures of salt-rock, are not there to be read, they are not there to be named.[14] They are there to be immersed in, to be travelled and touched by the eye. That's why they are so tender. That's why my eyes desire it to exist.

And if you look and you listen, each of them reveals its secret, curved and singular,

I'm a stranger, written by hand.
One stone at a time.

CLOSE, CLOSING, CLOSER (OR CONCLUSION)

Each moon confesses,
and you pretend you don't understand.[15]

This sentence hasn't left my mind since I encountered it some weeks ago. Every moon confesses, showing itself white and round. Every moon confesses and hides itself again, very fast.

The proximity of a confession, the certainty of a midnight. The repentance of a midnight. Or the repetition. The corners of Chevals architecture, disorienting and hiding secrets. Carved into a silence.

It is true that *November* starts with a no, a very certain no, and a little cat confined to its little ball of yarn. At times the trajectory resembled more of a lament, other times a questioning, stretching into possibilities. Now, approaching the end, I hope to have not lost the brown where I put my trust some months ago. And if I did, I hope it transforms into a new image, as a new something-else that I am able to trust in entering again without knowing, giddy on my steps.

Of what is written, one can follow the order as it comes but ultimately the texts are to be read as one pleases and if something resonates in any exquisite manner I would be happy. They come together as a whole but if a line is what is worth, take the line, skip the rest. Hopefully there are more days and different choreographies.

---

13 "There is no contradiction in what is imaginary. Contradiction is the test of necessity.", "Contradiction is the criterion. We cannot by suggestion obtain things which are incompatible. Only grace can do that.", Weil, Simone. Gravity and Grace. With an introd. by Gustave Thibon. London: Routledge and K. Paul, 1972

14 Or even: "You do not look at it any more than you look at a forest. You either enter it or you pass it by", in *The Ideal Palace*, Berger, John. *Keeping a Rendezvous*. London: Granta books, 1993.

15 Elýtîs Odysséas, Jeffrey Carson, and Nikos Sarris. *The Collected Poems of Odysseus Elytis*.

11 Translated: brown blood. Dante's "brown (that is, clotted) blood" is about the blood that lost its glow and no longer looked red, clotted blood.

12 Who hasn't found such evidence when breaking a small piece of a tooth or having a little protuberance on the inside of their cheek and imagined the incident several times bigger than what the eye saw?

(…)

And then he found himself inside, not seeing but living on a world of textures, reflections and shine, under the caresses of a rock, palpating the worms and finding treasures. After he was done and more settled, he started massaging the old map carried on his pocket, there was a slight fear on his heart and a slight anxiety on his thumbs but he continued till the colours became an even layer with the attributes of a pillow. Then, and finally, he slept on his pillow and the pillow changed shape according to the weight of his head. From this sculpture he created the other, less radical, sculptures.

Those who live from inside face themselves with different questions: questions of direction, question of weight, questions of placement and balance. As when one is learning to walk and takes it step by step knowing that too much comprehension would pull them out of the place of encounter. *'Not to understand is to be on the inside. To understand is to be on the outside.'*[16] Learning to walk is also learning to become a stranger to oneself.

How sweet not to have a beginning
because it was forgotten.

16 *Zhuangzi*, The complete works of Chuang Tzu, translated by Burton Watson

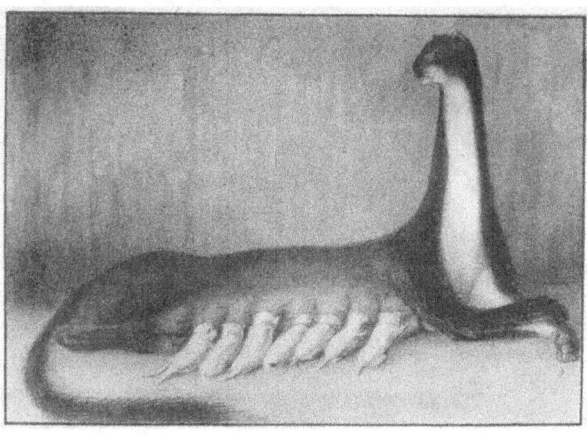

Img1
Alfred Kubin, The Brood : Cat and Kittens, Circa 1902

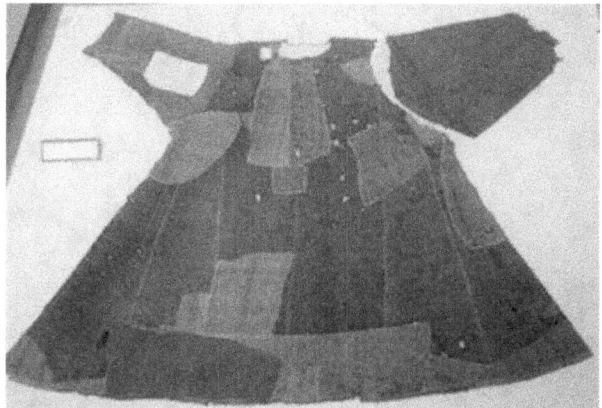

Img2
Habit of St.Francis. Repeatedly torn and repeatedly mended.

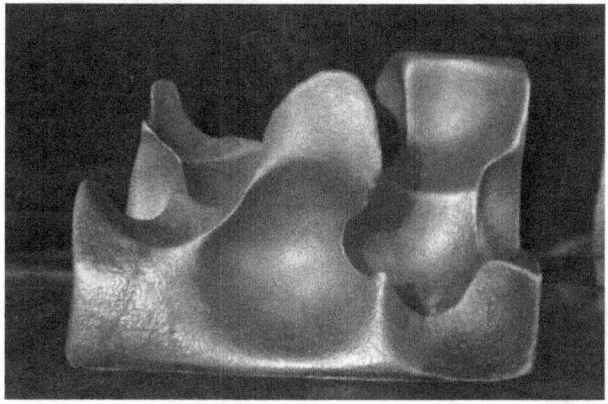

Img3
One sculpture resulting from the licking of a cow
into a salt rock. From an annual event — The Great Salt Lick —
where animal-licked salt blocks are displayed
and auctioned off as sculptures.

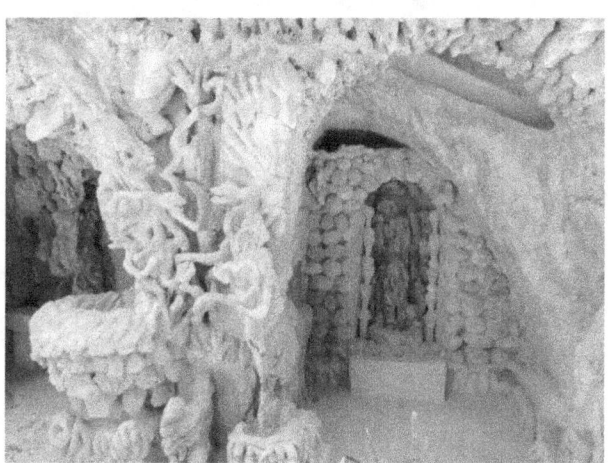

Img4
Ideal Palace, Ferdinand Cheval

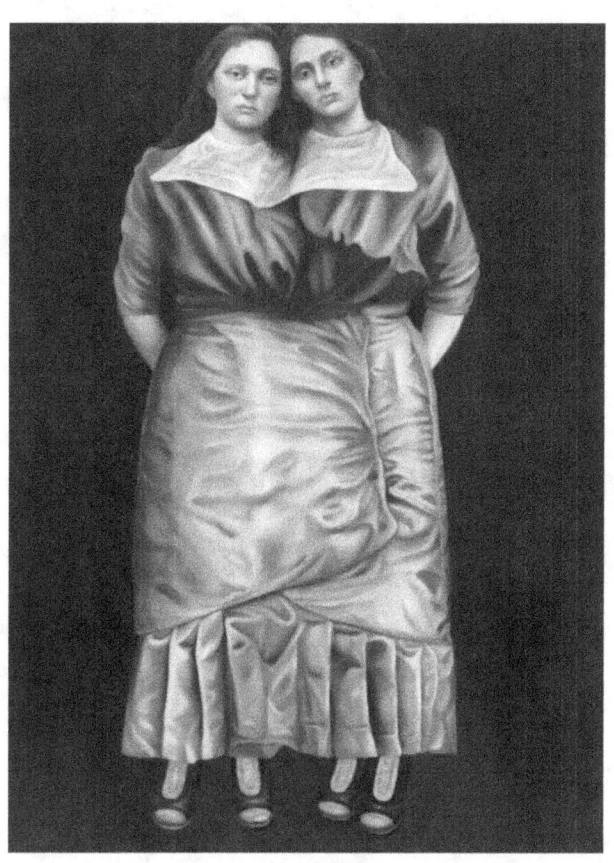

Img5
Sophie Kuijken, I.A.M., 2015

SOME OF THE BOOKS ON THE TABLE:

Barthes, Roland, and Thomas Clerc. *The Neutral*.
New York: Columbia University Press, 2007.

Batchelor, David. *Chromophobia*. London, England: Reaktion, 2013.

Berger, John. *Keeping a Rendezvous*. London: Granta books, 1993.

CIXOUS, Helene. *Coming to Writing and Other Essays*.
Cambridge, MA, London: Harvard Univ. Press, 1991.

Elýtis Odysséas, Jeffrey Carson, and Nikos Sarris. *The Collected Poems of Odysseus Elytis*. Baltimore (Md.): John Hopkins University Press, 2004.

Goethe, Johann Wolfgang von. *Theory of Colours*. Cambridge, MA: Massachusetts Institute of Technology, 1970.

Linderman, Deborah, Julia Kristeva, and Leon S. Roudiez. "Powers of Horror: An Essay on Abjection." *SubStance* 13, no. 3/4 (1984): 140.

Nelson, Maggie. *Bluets*. Wave Books, 2019.

Seuss, Diane. *Four-Legged Girl: Poems*.
Minneapolis, MN: Graywolf Press, 2015.

Weil, Simone. *Gravity and Grace. With an Introd. by Gustave Thibon*.
London: Routledge and K. Paul, 1972.

Zambrano María. O *Homem e o Divino*. Lisboa: Antropos, 1995.

Zhuangzi, and Burton Watson. *The Complete Works of Chuang Tzu*.
New York: Columbia University Press, 2002.

9781716829802

www.ingramcontent.com/pod-product-compliance
Lightning Source LLC
Chambersburg PA
CBHW081810220526

45467CB00006B/2159